American Civilization

The hugely successful *American Civilization* provides students of American Studies with the perfect background and introductory information on contemporary American life, examining the central dimensions of American society from geography and the environment, government and politics, to religion, education, sports, media and the arts. Fully updated throughout, the seventh edition:

- covers recent events including the 2016 US election and 2017 presidential inauguration
- contains new commentary on key themes such as terrorist incidents and their effects on the national mood regarding immigration, rapidly changing energy politics, police racial profiling and the Black Lives Matter movement, and progress in legislation protecting the rights of the LGBT community
- covers all core American Studies topics at an introductory level and contains essential historical background for American Studies students in the twenty-first century
- analyzes issues of gender, class, race, and minorities in America's cosmopolitan population
- is accompanied by a fully updated and integrated companion website (www.routledge.com/cw/mauk) featuring an interactive timeline, quiz questions, extensive references for further reading, links to key primary sources and advice for students on how to approach essay questions.

 Containing questions and terms for discussion, bibliographical references and websites at the end of each chapter and a new selection of color illustrations and case studies, this textbook is an essential resource for all students of American civilization, culture and society.

David Mauk is Professor Emeritus of North American Area Studies at the University of Oslo, Norway and is the author of *The Colony that Rose from the Sea: Norwegian Maritime Migration and Community in Brooklyn* (1997) and many articles on American politics, immigration and ethnicity, including chapters in *E Pluribus Unum or E Pluribus Plura? Unity and Diversity in American Culture* (2011), *Norwegian American Women* (2011), and *Norwegian-American Essays* (2014, 2015).

John Oakland is the author of *British Civilization* (2015, now in its eighth edition), *Irish Civilization* (2012, with Arthur Aughey), *Contemporary Britain* (2001) and *British Civilization: A Student's Dictionary* (2003, second edition). He is a former Associate Professor in English at the Norwegian University of Science and Technology.

American Civilization
An Introduction

Seventh edition

David Mauk and John Oakland

Routledge
Taylor & Francis Group

LONDON AND NEW YORK

Seventh edition published 2018
by Routledge
2 Park Square, Milton Park, Abingdon, Oxon, OX14 4RN

and by Routledge
711 Third Avenue, New York, NY 10017

Routledge is an imprint of the Taylor & Francis Group, an informa business

First edition published by Routledge 1995
Sixth edition published by Routledge 2014

British Library Cataloguing-in-Publication Data
A catalogue record for this book is available from the British Library

Library of Congress Cataloging-in-Publication Data
Names: Mauk, David, 1945– author. | Oakland, John, co-author.
Title: American civilization : an introduction / David Mauk and John Oakland.
Description: Seventh edition. | Milton Park, Abingdon, Oxon ; New York, NY :
    Routledge, 2017. | Includes bibliographical references and index.
Identifiers: LCCN 2017028322 | ISBN 9781138631717 (hardback : alkaline paper) |
    ISBN 9781138631724 (paperback : alkaline paper) | ISBN 9781315107158 (ebook)
Subjects: LCSH: United States—Civilization. | United States—Civilization—Study and
    teaching—Foreign countries.
Classification: LCC E169.1 .M45 2017 | DDC 973—dc23
LC record available at https://lccn.loc.gov/2017028322

ISBN: 978-1-138-63171-7 (hbk)
ISBN: 978-1-138-63172-4 (pbk)
ISBN: 978-1-315-10715-8 (ebk)

Typeset in Berling
by Apex CoVantage, LLC

Visit the companion website: www.routledge.com/cw/mauk

Contents

Plates

Figures

Tables

Preface and acknowledgments

This book examines central cultural structures of American (US) civilization, such as politics and government, the law, the economy, social services, the media, education, religion and the arts. Chapters on the country and the people also emphasize the geographical and human diversity of the US. Each chapter uses opinion polls to indicate the different attitudes that Americans have about the society in which they live and operate.

The book combines descriptive and analytical approaches within a historical context and examines recent debates and developments in the US. The format of the book is intended to encourage students and teachers to decide their own study needs, to assess personal responses to American society and to engage in critical discussion. Exercises in each chapter can be approached from material in the text. Additional information may be found in relevant websites, 'Further reading' sections in each chapter, and two reference dictionaries [Alicia Duchak (1999) *A–Z of Modern America*, London: Routledge and Jonathan Crowther (2005) *Oxford Guide to British and American Culture*, Oxford: OUP].

A book of this type is indebted for many of its ideas, opinions, facts and statistics to a range of reference sources, to which a general acknowledgment is made (see also 'Further reading'). Particular thanks are due to opinion polls and media, such as Gallup, Harris, Polling Report, Pew Research Center, the Roper Center, *The Economist*, YouGov, CNN, *USA Today*, *Fox News*, CBS, NBC, ABC, PRRI (Public Religion Research Institute), *Time*, *The New York Times*, *Los Angeles Times* and *The Washington Post*.

The term billion in this book follows the internationally approved standard, that is, 1,000,000,000.

Chronology of significant dates in American history

20,000–12,000 BC	Asian and Mediterranean peoples migrated to the Americas.	
c. 3000–2600	Mayan civilization flourished in Central America.	
c. 350–1250 AD	Anasazi built pueblo "apartment" complexes in the American Southwest.	
1001	Vikings established "Vineland" settlement in Newfoundland.	
1050–1250	Mississippian culture dominated the Midwestern and Southeastern United States.	
1300s	Aztec civilization rose in Mexico.	
1492	Columbus came ashore in the Bahama Islands.	
1492–1542	European explorers visited and mapped parts of the Americas.	
1497	Europeans began fishing in the Great Banks off the east coast of North America.	
1519–21	Hernán Cortéz invaded and conquered Mexico.	
1518–1620	Smallpox and other European diseases decimated Native Americans.	
1607	Jamestown, Virginia settlement established.	
1619	The first African workers arrived in Virginia, not as slaves.	
1622	Native Americans and Virginians waged war.	
1620–30	Pilgrims and then Puritans founded New England colonies.	
1637	Native Americans and Puritans waged war.	
1624–81	New Amsterdam (New York), Maryland, New Sweden, Carolina, New Jersey and Pennsylvania were founded.	
1636, 1647	Harvard College and then public schools started in Massachusetts.	
1680–1776	First Wave of non-English immigrants arrived in the North American colonies.	
1732	Georgia, the last of the 13 English colonies, was founded.	
1730s–1740s	Religious ferment reached a peak during the First Great Awakening.	
1757	New Yorkers rioted against British policies.	

1770	British troops fired on Boston protesters.
1775, 1776	American Revolution began; Declaration of Independence was published.
1783	The Treaty of Paris recognized the independence of the United States and granted it the territory south of Canada to the Mississippi river.
1787	Strong federal government under the US Constitution replaced the loose league of states under the Articles of Confederation.
1789	George Washington took office as President; Federalists and Anti-Federalists competed in Congress.
1792	New York Stock Exchange opened.
1803	Louisiana Purchase from France added a huge slice of the continent's mid-section to the US; US Supreme Court claimed the power to declare laws unconstitutional.
1808	Congress outlawed the import of African slaves.
1810	New York passed Philadelphia in population at third US census.
1808–13	Shawnee leaders, Tecumseh and the Prophet, organized the eastern tribes to resist US expansion beyond the Appalachians.
1812–15	The US won no major battle in the War of 1812 with Britain on American soil.
1815–25	Industrialization started in the New England and Mid-Atlantic states.
1820s–40s	Religious revival swept across the frontier in the Second Great Awakening; social and utopian reform movements spread.
1820s–80s	About 16 million Europeans and smaller numbers of Asians and Latinos immigrated in the Second Wave.
1825	Opening the Erie Canal secured the economic power of the East.
1831–38	Native Americans removed from the South along the Trail of Tears to Indian Territory in Oklahoma.
1830s	Democratic Party emerged and competed with the Whigs.
1845–48	Conflict and war with Mexico; annexation of Texas, California and the Southwest.
1848	First women's rights convention at Seneca Falls, New York.
1850s	Anti-foreign "nativist," abolitionist, and pro-slavery movements dominated US politics; Republican Party emerged.
1861–5	Civil War raged over slavery and states' rights.
1862	Homestead Act granted land to people who live on and farm it for five years, spurring massive settlement of the inland West.
1865–75	Constitutional amendments and a civil rights act were passed to secure the citizenship and rights of former slaves.
1877	Reconstruction of the South ended; Southern race laws progressively denied Blacks rights in the 1880s and 1890s.
1869, 1882–83	Transcontinental railroads completed.

1890	"Battle" of Wounded Knee ended centuries of open warfare against Native Americans; US census bureau announced the "closing of the frontier."
1890–1930	About 23 million "third-wave" immigrants arrived, mostly from south and east Europe but also from Asia, Canada, and Latin America.
1898	Anti-imperialist debate in Congress; Spanish-American-Cuban Filipino War.
1890–1920	Progressive Era reformed in social institutions, politics and government.
1917–18	America fought with the Allies in the First World War.
1919	First tabloid newspaper, the New York *Daily News*, appeared.
1919–33	Prohibition of alcoholic beverages became the law under the Eighteenth Amendment to the Constitution (repealed by the twenty-first Amendment).
1920	Women won the right to vote through the Nineteenth Amendment.
1921	Red Scare and general restriction of immigration started.
1929	Wall Street Stock-market Crash signaled the start of the Great Depression; Size of the House of Representatives set at 435.
1920s–40s	Hollywood's classic period of film production.
1920s–70s	Progressively more of the Bill of Rights applied to state law and cases.
1932	Franklin Roosevelt elected president and implemented the New Deal to bring the US out of the Great Depression.
1937	Supreme Court accepted New Deal powers of federal government.
1939	Commercial television introduced at the World's Fair in New York.
1941	On December 7, Japan bombed the Pearl Harbor naval base in Hawaii, and the US entered the Second World War.
1946	Post-war baby boom began.
1947	National Security Act transformed American government for the Cold War; Truman Doctrine set path of US foreign policy.
1950–53	McCarthy era "Red scare" and Korean War.
1954	Racial desegregation began with the *Brown v. the Board of Education* US Supreme Court decision.
1955	American Federation of Labor (AFL) and the Congress of Industrial Organizations (CIO) combined in a union of US unions.
1958	National Defense Education Act funded scientific competition with the USSR.
1953–74	US involvement and war in Vietnam, massive protests at home and abroad against the war in the 1960s; African Americans, Native Americans, Chicanos, Women, and gay Americans fought for civil rights.
1963	President John F. Kennedy assassinated; Lyndon B. Johnson assumed the presidency.

1960s	Great Society and War on Poverty social reforms; high point of youth "counter culture" and religious ecumenism in the US.
1964	Civil Rights Act outlawed discrimination in housing and jobs.
1965	Voting Rights Act protected voter registration, especially in the South: Elementary and Secondary Education Act provided massive funding for education reform.
1968	Martin Luther King, Jr. and Robert Kennedy assassinated; 168 cities erupted in race riots.
1969	Stonewall Riots, when gay men for the first fought back after repeated police raids.
1966–2012	Continuing fourth wave of immigration, when over 38.5 million people arrived, most from Latin America and Asia, but also from the former USSR, Africa, and the Middle East.
1970	More Americans lived in suburbs than in cities or rural areas.
1972	Nixon's "new federalism" began the return of power to the states.
1973	*Roe v. Wade* decision legalized limited abortion rights for women.
1974	President Nixon resigned because of the Watergate scandal.
1981	AIDS first identified in the US.
1970s–80s	Rise of Christian fundamentalism and conservative religious political activity.
1986–88	Mikhail Gorbachev and Ronald Reagan cooperated to bring the end of the Cold War; Iran–Contras scandal cast a shadow over the second Reagan administration; George H. W. Bush won the presidency.
1991	US led the Persian Gulf War to drive Iraq out of Kuwait.
1993–2001	President Clinton presided over the longest economic boom in US History.
1996	Devolution of policymaking power to the states occurred through the Welfare Reform Act.
1999	Congress impeached, but did not convict, President Clinton.
2000	George W. Bush won the presidential election after a 5–4 divided decision of the US Supreme Court stopped Florida vote recounts and called for uniform vote counting procedures.
2001	No Child Left Behind Act set in action the most far-reaching national educational reform since the 1960s. Terrorists destroyed the World Trade Center and attacked the Pentagon. US initiated a global war on terrorism in Afghanistan.
2002	Help America Vote Act was passed to standardize voting procedures within states; the USA Patriot Act and the authorization of the Department of Homeland Security transformed American government for the War on Terror.
2003	US-led "coalition of the willing" invaded and occupied Iraq; Supreme Court decision *Lawrence v. Texas* ended the criminalization of homosexual relations between consenting adults.

2004   No weapons of mass destruction found in Iraq; George W. Bush won a second term and Republicans secured larger majorities in Congress.

2006–13   Legal immigration to the US capped at 675,000 immigrant visas a year.

2006–08   In the longest and most expensive presidential election in US history, ten or more men and women announced their candidacy for each major party's nomination. John McCain emerged as the presumptive Republican candidate. The Democrats nominated the first seriously competitive woman, former First Lady and current New York Senator Hillary Clinton, who fought a close contest with Illinois Senator Barack Obama, the first immigrant, mixed race African American to run for president. Obama won the nomination, and in November, he won the presidency with unprecedented use of social media. In *District of Columbia v. Heller*, the Supreme Court decided that the ban on the private possession of handguns in Washington DC was an infringement of the Second Amendment. The worsening economic crisis, called the Great Recession, became the worst financial breakdown since the 1930s.

2009–10   Obama administration's financial policies rescued Wall Street firms and the Detroit automobile industry, extended unemployment insurance and initiated a jobs and economic stimulus package.

2010   In *Citizens United v. the FEC*, the Supreme Court ruled that corporations have the same right to freedom of expression as individuals, also regarding campaign contributions. Patient Protection and Affordable Health Care Act (PPACA) passed with no support from Republican members of Congress. The Act was upheld by the Supreme Court in 2012. In the mid-term congressional elections, Democrats lost the majority in the House of Representatives and with it, legislative support for Obama's legislative agenda.

2012   In the next presidential election cycle, a dozen Republicans competed for the party's nomination. Mitt Romney won and faced incumbent Obama in the general election. Obama won an electoral college and popular vote victory. In congressional elections, Democrats improved their majority in the Senate, but Republicans kept a majority in the House. SMS declined and gave way to smartphones and social networking sites, such as Facebook and Twitter.

2013   Another school mass killing occurred at Newtown, Connecticut, when 20 young children and six teachers were killed. Two Chechen immigrant brothers exploded bombs at the Boston Marathon, killing three people and injuring hundreds. The Black Lives Matter movement against racism in the US justice system began on social media, after the acquittal of a neighborhood watchman for the murder of black teenager Trayvon Martin in Florida.

2014   In a mid-term election landslide, Republicans gained control of the Senate and increased their majority in the House of Representatives. A policeman in Ferguson, Missouri, shot and killed Michael

Brown, an unarmed black teenager, leading to riots in the St. Louis suburb. Riots started again and spread across the nation when a court decided not to indict the policeman. Support for Black Lives Matter grew. Fracking to extract shale oil, said to cause thousands of earthquakes, in Oklahoma and across the US.

2015   Supreme Court ruled that same-sex marriage is constitutional. Anger and protest against police brutality erupted in Baltimore and again in Ferguson, Missouri. A white nationalist killed black worshippers in Charleston, South Carolina. Bipartisan majorities in Congress and President Obama enacted a new federal education law, the Every Student Succeeds Act (ESSA). For the major party nominations, 17 Republicans and six Democrats competed, and the Libertarian and Green Parties also chose candidates.

2016   US signed the Trans Pacific Partnership (TPP) with 11 other Pacific-rim countries, but the trade treaty was not yet in force. US ratified the Paris Agreement on Climate Change, which took effect November 4. The further participation of the US was doubtful following the formation of the Trump administration in 2017. The Standing Rock Sioux reservation with a coalition of Native American activists successfully protested the building of the Dakota Access pipeline near its water supply and sacred sites. After the most contentious campaign in memory, intelligence reports surfaced, accusing Russia of interfering in the election in Donald Trump's favor, and allegations by the FBI and candidate Trump were voiced regarding Hillary Clinton's use of a private e-mail server. Republican Trump surprised pollsters and commentators, winning an Electoral College victory, even though Clinton won the popular vote by 3 million.

2017   President Trump withdrew the US from the TPP. New administration and Republican-controlled Congress reevaluated the Patient Protection and Affordable Health Care Act (PPACA), 2012, meant to extend health insurance to 50 million Americans by 2014. Some remained uninsured; insurance costs rose. By executive order President Trump reallocated funds to begin building a wall to prevent undocumented immigrants from crossing the Mexican border. President Trump reversed the decision to reroute the Dakota Access Pipeline to protect the Standing Rock Sioux's sites and water supply.

The American context

This chapter examines foreign and domestic attitudes to the US and places the country within historical contexts. It describes six cultures (social building blocks or structures defined by beliefs, ideas and behavior) that have created an American civilization over time and continue to influence debates about national identity, values and institutional change.

The term "American civilization" describes an advanced society, which occupies a specific geographical space (the US) and has been settled historically by many different peoples. Its contributory cultures illustrate a distinctive, but complex, way of life. Although previously associated with notions of superiority and imperialism, "civilization" generally now has a neutral and inclusive meaning.

Central features have conditioned US history, such as:

- pre-Columbian (1492) migrations of peoples to the Americas from worldwide origins; colonial and military occupation by Europeans from the late fifteenth century; and the establishment of social values, religious faiths and institutional structures;
- the treatment of Native Americans and other minority ethnic groups (particularly African Americans);
- the War for Independence from Britain (1775–83);
- the westward, southern and northern expansion of the new nation;
- principles of dignity and rights to freedom, justice and opportunity in the Declaration of Independence (1776), the Constitution (1787) and the Bill of Rights (1791);
- ideologies of egalitarianism, individualism and utopianism;
- large-scale immigration into the country in the nineteenth and twentieth centuries;
- nineteenth-century industrial growth;
- the Civil War to end slavery and southern-state secession from the Union (1861–65);
- the development of capitalism with its corporate management and business models;
- increasing government regulation and bureaucracies;
- US isolationist and interventionist attitudes toward other countries during two world wars (1914–18 and 1939–45), the 1945–89 Cold War and early twenty-first century growth of the US as a dominant economic, military and cultural force since the nineteenth century;

■ the influence of contemporary globalization (worldwide interdependent economic, political and cultural forces) on both the US and other nations;

■ the current international status of the US as it responds to external and internal pressures and considers a more protectionist identity.

These (and other) historical events have created six major cultures in the US, which may conflict with each other and operate on different levels of idealism, pragmatism and rhetoric. The first is a diverse (and often divisive) ethnic culture founded on Native American civilizations, European colonial settlement, African American slavery and later waves of immigration. The second is a multi-faith (pluralist) religious culture, which reflects the beliefs of early inhabitants and remains prominent today. The third is a political-legal culture based on individualism, constitutionalism and respect for the law. It tries to unite the people under ideal versions of "Americanism," such as patriotism, egalitarianism and morality, which should be practically reflected in political and legal institutions. The fourth is an economic and consumer culture of corporate and individual competition and production, which encourages profit and the

PLATE 1.1 British forces surrender to American and French armies, Yorktown, Virginia, 1781, in this painting by John Turnbull. American General Lincoln on a white horse extends his hand toward the sword carried by the British General O'Hara, on foot. The American War for Independence (1775–83) was effectively decided by this victory, resulting in the loss of 13 British colonies.
© FineArt/Alamy

consumption of goods and services based on principles of supply and demand. The fifth consists of media cultures (information, communication and entertainment), which became diverse and technologically complex in the twentieth and twenty-first centuries. The sixth represents cultural expression in the arts, sports and leisure, which reflects the inventiveness of US life.

US society has been conditioned by these cultures. But, although their presence may be generally acknowledged, considerable numbers of people – such as political activists, the youth, the disadvantaged and minorities – may be alienated from them. Conflicts about assumed national values and unity have occurred throughout US history. Topics such as racism, religious and political polarization, gender roles, inequality between rich and poor, international policies, military intervention, abortion, same-sex marriage, immigration, national identity, ethnicity, social change and the roles of federal and state governments are sources of contemporary debate.

Nevertheless, the major cultures have, since the Declaration of Independence in 1776, collectively created what is seen as a national identity in the US

PLATE 1.2 Slave quarters at George Washington estate, Mount Vernon, Virginia. Washington was the victorious army commander of the American independence campaign and the first President of the US. Like other large landowners, he owned black slaves to harvest and sustain his fields. As here, they lived in barrack-type buildings on the estate.
© *Jordan Oakland*

for the majority of its inhabitants. The difficulty lies in determining what this may consist of in practice and how much cultural dissent from perceived norms may actually exist.

People inside and outside the US have very varied and conflicting views about the country and its inhabitants. Some opinions are based on quantifiable facts. Others are formed by ideology, hatred, prejudice, or envy. Many American self-images often stress the nation's supposed "exceptionalism" (its alleged unique mission in the world, idealism, aspirations and sense of destiny). But there are also internal disagreements about the country's values, institutions, policies and national identity and whether its vaunted ideals equate with American reality. US society is divided politically, religiously, socially, economically and ethnically, although efforts are made to reconcile differences and to unify the people under common beliefs and structures.

Opinion polls report that, under the impetus of national and international events, Americans alternate between feelings of positivism and dissatisfaction about their country. Periods of doubt and conflict, such as the Revolutionary War for Independence (1775–83), the Civil War (1861–5), world wars (1914–18 and 1939–45), the 1930s Great Depression, the 1945–89 Cold War, the 1950s–60s civil rights campaigns, the 1960s–75 Vietnam War, the 2003–4 Iraq

PLATE 1.3 Lee's Surrender at Appomattox Court House by Tom Lovell, depicting the Confederate Civil War General Lee signing surrender documents before Union General Grant in the parlor of the McLean house (Appomattox Court House) on April 9, 1865, effectively ending the American Civil War.

© *National Geographic Creative/Bridgeman Images*

War with its chaotic aftermath, the Afghanistan conflict (2001–15) and current struggles against terrorism have often resulted in adaptation and renewal.

The US is still conditioned by the September 11, 2001 terrorist attacks on New York and Washington, DC (9/11). In response, the Administration protected its domestic and global interests, declared opposition to terrorism and initiated coalition military action in Iraq and Afghanistan. Resulting strained relations between the US and other nations and groups continue. American respondents to a Pew Research Center/*USA Today* poll in August 2014 identified the following as major threats to world stability and US interests: Islamist groups such as al Qaeda (71 percent) and ISIS (67 percent), Iran's nuclear program (59 percent), North Korea's nuclear capacity (57 percent), tension between Russia and its neighbors (53 percent), China as a world power (48 percent), and the Israeli–Palestinian conflict (48 percent). A Pew poll in 2013 also reported that 9 percent of US respondents said that the US itself represented a danger to the United States and world peace. Other threats have been identified, such as cyber warfare from state and individual sources.

The 2014 Pew poll suggested changing opinions among US respondents about the US role in solving global problems. A large majority (65 percent) accepted that the world was now a more dangerous place. But while 39 percent thought that the US did too much to help to solve world problems, 31 percent said that the US does too little. Although 54 percent of respondents approved of airstrikes against Islamist militants in Iraq, Syria and elsewhere (31 percent disapproved), 48 percent said that the US was now a less important and powerful world leader, and 54 percent considered that its foreign policies toward Russia, Ukraine, Iraq, Iran, Syria and Israel were not tough enough. In terms of the Middle East, 63 percent of respondents expected militant forms of Islamist activity to grow in influence.

US foreign policy is frequently attacked by its enemies, allies and domestic critics. Polls suggest that many people believe that the US acts unilaterally in world affairs. But a majority of Americans believe that their country does take the interests of other nations into account when making decisions about foreign actions. In terms of America's standing in the world, a Pew Research Center poll in Spring 2014 reported a globally positive 65 percent rating for the US. This showed a stabilization of approval since 2004, when there was opposition to the US involvement in the Iraq war. The regional approval figures were 74 percent for Africa, 66 percent for Europe, 66 percent for Asia and 65 percent for Latin America, but only 30 percent for the Middle East. In Europe, the most favorable opinions were in Italy, France and Poland. However, globally young people aged between 18 and 29 were, perhaps surprisingly, more positive to the US, compared with older people.

PLATE 1.4 The twin towers of the World Trade Center, New York City were destroyed by plane attacks on September 11, 2001. They have been replaced by a Memorial Plaza, fountains, museums and a Freedom Tower sited on One World Trade Center, NYC, 2014. Similar memorials commemorate attacks on the Pentagon.

© *John Kellerman/Alamy*

Ethnic culture (see Chapters 2, 3 and 4)

US ethnic culture reflects the diverse origins of the population. After earlier Native American and Viking immigration, Christopher Columbus's arrival in 1492 in the Caribbean encouraged Spanish soldiers, missionaries, adventurers and traders to begin a European settlement of South-Central North America, such as the founding of St. Augustine in 1565 on the Florida coast, and Santa Fe (1609) and Albuquerque (1706) in New Mexico. Colonial settlement after 1607 was largely composed of British arrivals, who shared North America with Native-American communities, the Spanish and the French. Until 1776, over half of the population came from the British Isles and contributed to a white, mainly Anglo-American, Protestant culture. They promoted many of the new nation's political, social, constitutional and religious institutions. Their political principles were based on democracy, independence of the people and skepticism about government. Their values were conditioned by a belief in individualism; a Protestant work ethic (working hard in this life to be rewarded here and in the next); and the rule of law (legal rules applicable to all persons and institutions). Other European settlers, such as Germans, Swedes and the Dutch slowly contributed to this ethnic mix as a mainstream American identity gradually evolved.

After the colonial period and American independence from Britain (1776), northwestern Europe supplied over two-thirds of US immigration for most of the nineteenth century. There were also many Asian immigrants (particularly Chinese) during this time. At the end of the century, there was a shift toward newcomers from southern and eastern Europe. Much of this immigration was neither Anglo by descent nor Protestant in religion, and it altered the demographic composition of the country. Despite immigration restrictions, the twentieth century saw a variety of other nationalities from worldwide origins immigrating to the US, and some 60 million immigrants entered the US between 1820 and 2000. In the 1980s–1990s and early twenty-first century, immigrants came from Asia, South and Central America and the Caribbean, with the biggest groups being Latinos and Asians.

Immigrants to the US were often analyzed in terms of "ancestral groups." An American Community Survey (ACS), 2008, reported that more Americans traced their roots to Europe than to anywhere else in the world. But non-European ancestries were also self-identified in 2008, such as African American, American, Mexican, West Indian, French Canadian and Native American. Although ancestral claims could be vague, subjective or demographically weak and individuals might claim more than one identity, agencies (but not the US Census Bureau) continue to construct "ancestry" lists (see Table 1.1).

The effects of colonial settlement, importation of African slaves (from 1641) and later immigration on US culture have been substantial. This background

TABLE 1.1 Largest "ancestries" in the United States, 2014

"Ancestries"	Number
Total US population	318,857,056
German	46,047,113
Irish	33,147,639
English	24,382,182
American	22,097,012
Italian	17,220,604
Polish	9,249,392
French	8,153,515
Scottish	5,365,154
Norwegian	4,444,566
Dutch	4,243,067
Sub-Saharan Africa	3,223,885
Swedish	3,887,273
European	3,679,468
Scotch-Irish	2,978,827
West Indian	2,865,446
Welsh	1,757,657

Source: American Community Service (ACS), 2014, 1-year estimates

(inclusive of Native Americans) is different from that of most other nations; arguably defines American history as special; and provides the US with a distinct and ethnically-based identity.

The US Census Bureau Report estimated in June 2015 that the nation's population of 318.9 million in June 2014 consisted of six groupings: Latino (55.4 million); African American (45.7 million); Asian (20.3 million); American Indian and Alaska Natives (6.5 million); Native Hawaiians and Other Pacific Islanders (1.5 million); and White (197.9 million). Millennials (those born between 1982 and 2000) numbered 83.1 million of the country's population, exceeding that of the earlier 75.4 million baby boomers.

A US Census Bureau report in 2012 estimated that Whites would be a decreasing 61.8 percent of the total population by 2015 (from 63.7 percent in 2010) and Latinos would increase to 28 percent of the population. By 2050, non-Whites and Latinos together will account for 54 percent of the population, and Whites will be 46.3 percent (dropping to 43 percent by 2060). African Americans will form 14.4 percent of the population by 2050, and Asian Americans will be 7.7 percent. In 2014, the population was becoming more racially and ethnically mixed, at a time when Whites were becoming a minority ethnic group for the first time in US history. These changes result from immigration, higher birth rates among some ethnic minorities, intermingling of ethnic groups and an aging white population with lower birth rates. They will increasingly influence US social, economic and political life.

Immigrants and imported black African slaves have considerably affected public life at different times in US history. But they have also experienced difficulties of integration into the host society. There have been conflicts and racial tensions between settled groups, Native Americans, African Americans and immigrants, which have sometimes erupted into violence. These factors have revealed nativism (discrimination toward others by the existing population) and racism in many areas of American life, often in institutionalized form.

Ethnic diversity has brought advantages and disadvantages over time. It has also gradually reduced the dominance of the original Anglo-American Protestant culture, which had to take account of a growing social pluralism. It is argued that the US has historically managed to integrate its immigrants successfully into the existing society at varying levels, and newcomers have generally adapted to American life. However, despite significant structural and cultural improvement from the 1950s, racial and ethnic divisions still continue to affect American society in both covert (indirect) and overt (direct) forms; attitudes to immigration remain volatile; opinions about the existence of racism in the US vary considerably between Blacks and Whites; minorities in polls admit to being racially prejudiced; and Blacks and Whites arguably still largely live in separate worlds.

A *Washington Post–ABC News* poll in December 2014 asked whether Blacks and minorities receive equal treatment as Whites in the criminal justice system. While 54 percent of all respondents said "no," the individual figures were 89 percent for African Americans, 60 percent for Latinos and 44 percent for Whites. The poll suggests that the US is divided on racial issues between Blacks/Latinos and Whites, and between white Democrats and Republicans over race and justice. For example, a Pew Research Center Poll in 2013 reported that 49 percent of all American Whites saw no racism around them and felt that there was no unfair treatment of Blacks in many social sectors, such as the police, employers, doctors, stores/restaurants, voting in elections, healthcare and local public schools.

However, controversial police involvement in the shooting of black men in American cities in recent years has been widely reported, and a *Gallup* poll in 2014 found that white Americans say they are now more aware of the discrimination that non-Whites experience and that Blacks are treated less fairly by the police and in stores and shopping malls. It is debatable whether these opinions will be translated into action to remove racist views and systems and whether they will be permanent. A *Washington Post* poll in August 2015 found that 37 percent of respondents felt that the country had made changes needed to give Blacks equal rights with Whites, but 60 percent said that more improvements are still required. The number of Americans who see racism in the US as a big problem grew significantly in 2015 to half the total population (up from 17 percent in 2010), consisting of 40 percent Whites, 73 percent of Blacks, 58 percent of Latinos and 41 percent of Republicans.

Conflicts concerning the nature of racism and ethnicity in the US show that a majority of respondents to polls believe that legal immigration should be reduced and only a minority thought that it should be increased, while most want illegal immigration stopped. Many respondents feel that immigrants are a threat to traditional American values and customs; that immigrants take jobs away from American workers; and that skilled and unskilled US workers and consumers are harmed by immigration.

Critics argue that there is still a nativist or xenophobic current in American culture. Diverse ethnic groups have had to both coexist and struggle for individual expression in the US. Today, they must live together in spite of inequalities and tensions between them. Immigration can have a potential for political and social instability with either rejection of immigrants by settled Americans, or rejection of Americanization (adaptation to mainstream American culture) by immigrants. However, these conflicts (arising out of social pluralism) and the problems of assimilation and integration by new groups are not distinctively American; they occur in other nations that have diverse populations.

Religious culture (see Chapter 5)

American religious culture has its roots in ancient Native American beliefs, the faiths that colonists, slaves and immigrants brought to the US over the centuries and new American religions, such as the Mormons and Jehovah's Witnesses that were later established in the country. Some early settlers escaped religious persecution in their homelands and hoped to establish communities based on nonconformist beliefs, which reacted to and sought separation from, or purification of, national religions. Others brought established denominations with them. The religious faiths of initial arrivals, particularly those with a Protestant identification, provided institutional and moral bases for the new nation, although conflicts between the different religious faiths were common. Many immigrants in later centuries strongly identified with their home faiths, which they preserved in the new country.

However, not all settlers were religiously inspired, although many might have maintained a nominal adherence to a particular faith. Some traveled for adventure, freedom, new experiences, material gain, land acquisition, and to escape from European social and political habits. Religious observance fluctuated in later centuries. The US had periods when religiosity was very low and periodic Great Awakenings, and continuous missionary activity were needed to restore the faiths. Generally, strong religious belief, substantial observance at ceremonies and church services, and a diversity of faiths became defining features of American society, when compared with other countries.

Although US religion is a private, personal matter and separated from the state by the Constitution, it informs and may condition social, economic and political life in communities and at national levels beyond the purely denominational. The precise influence of religion (and its limits) on many areas of American life, such as education, politics and ethics, continues to be hotly debated. Despite a desire to keep religion out of politics by legislative and constitutional means, some critics question whether it is realistic or necessary to deny religion a full, active and legally decisive part in public life.

Political-legal culture (see Chapters 6, 7, 8 and 9)

The elements of the American political-legal culture have been largely shaped by:

■   the central place of law and the Constitution in American life;
■   the restrictions that the Constitution places upon politics;
■   the fact that many Americans believe in minimal government, especially at the federal level, which has historically required a balancing state and local apparatus;
■   the perceived need to produce consensual (widely agreed) national policies so that the system can operate.

The Constitution is central to this structure, but it has to be interpreted by the judiciary branch (particularly the US Supreme Court in Washington, DC) to determine through judicial review whether actions of government and other bodies are constitutional or not. The political system has institutional checks and balances at state and federal levels, which may result in stalemate. However, these features do help to solidify the society and move it toward consensus or centrist policies. Idealized versions of "America" constructed through its federal and state political organs and a general respect for the law can potentially minimize conflict.

The need in the political-legal culture for balance and compromise illustrates the degree of abstraction that is involved in defining "the US" and "Americanness." The notion of what constitutes "America" has had to be revised or reinvented over time and reflects the tension between a materialistic practical reality, with its restrictions, and an idealistic, abstract and rhetorical image of the nation. Words such as "hope," "democracy," "traditional values" and "independence" are part of election campaigns and the wider US conversation. Ethnic differences, immigration and social diversity have been barriers to national unity and are still problematic. Consequently, it is often argued that the American political-legal system consists of both hard-nosed manipulation of group and ideological interests and a constitutional legalism that might promote common resolutions. Americans are also aware of potential corruption, fraud, incompetence and imperfection in the political and legal systems and that claims to "liberty" and "freedom" are not always respected in reality.

Responses to pluralism have often resulted in consensus politics based on political and judicial compromise in an attempt (not always achieved) to avoid stalemate. US politics are not usually considered to be as oppositional as in other nations, and historically there has been a variable 60 percent support for the center-left "liberal" Democratic Party and 40 percent for the "conservative" Republican Party. However, in recent years, party politics has become more confrontational. A Gallup poll in May 2014 reported that 37 percent of Americans described their politics as conservative, 35 percent as moderate and 25 percent as liberal. Conservatives and liberals often describe themselves as closer to the political center than to the extremes. In the 2016 presidential election, on a low voter turnout of 55.3 percent, the Democrat candidate (Clinton) gained 48.2 percent of the popular vote (65.8 million votes), while the Republican candidate (Trump) gained 46.1 percent (62.9 million votes). But Trump won the election with 306 electoral college votes and while Clinton obtained 232.

Differences between party policies on ethnic minorities, the economy, education, employment, religion and social issues have increasingly played a divisive and polarizing role in US society and at bitterly fought elections with their fierce media electioneering. Voters may also register support and opposition across party lines on many single issues such as abortion, same-sex marriage, the death penalty, education, taxation and gun control. American politics, reflecting the federal nature of US government, tends to be more influenced by special or state interests than national matters. Politicians in the febrile atmosphere of Washington, DC and state capitals promote their own legislation as a response to local and regional pressures. These mixed concerns often persuade Americans to vote in election lists for political representatives from different political parties who support specific issues, and result in fiercely fought political battles.

Such struggles characterize American political/legal history, but critics maintain that the central political value is compromise. They argue that the Constitution is a document of concessions (balances) between competing interests; the legal rights of the accused judged against the power of prosecutors; the authority of judges placed against the elected Congress and president; and the power of the people against the strength of government.

Critics debate whether or not there has been increased apathy and low political participation among US voters in recent decades, even when crucial matters are at stake. Some 70 percent of the eligible population register to vote, others do not register and there can be a low turnout of registered voters (at a 54 percent average) in elections. Low turnout suggests alienation from the political process, a feeling that power is in the hands of a political elite at state and Washington levels and that politicians ignore concerns of the voters (see Table 1.3 on alienation in the US, 2009–16).

Economic culture (see Chapter 10)

The economic framework has a central cultural importance, and it is both idealistic/abstract and materialistic/practical. Americans generally have a belief in individualism and a free enterprise system, which is supposed to supply goods and services demanded by the consumer market. People historically have had to fight for their economic and social survival, but the process can result in exploitation of others and a Darwinian "survival of the fittest" mentality. The competitive nature of US life leads to great disparities of wealth, social inequalities and varying life opportunities. In 2014, for example, 46.5 million Americans were dependent upon the Supplemental Nutrition Assistance Program (SNAP), formerly known as government food stamps, with an average value of $125.35

PLATE 1.5 The Time Warner Center at Columbus Circle, Manhattan, NYC is an American mall, seen as typical of American social and economic life, where people gather to shop, meet friends, eat in restaurants, visit entertainment venues, live and work. However, the US mall's image as a place to buy and spend has been significantly weakened in recent years by the growth of the online sales industry, and some retail outlets have been forced to close.
© Björn Söderqvist

for each person per month in food assistance. Recent economic research suggests that the gap between rich and poor has grown but also that the middle class has been squeezed and its numbers reduced.

Although free enterprise and corporate domination of US economic life may claim to deliver what the market requires, the system can also produce inferior products, bad service, corruption and a lack of variety, quality or real choice for consumers. Many Americans have historically claimed to be skeptical of "Big Business" and tend to support the principle of small businesses. However, debates about the capitalist model often ignore significant economic cooperation, charitable organizations, volunteerism and a substantial public sector in the national economy.

Both private and public economic sectors are subject to considerable fluctuations, whether due to market and global influences, speculation or human error. For example, the US economy has been considerably influenced since 2007–08 by a worldwide financial crisis, which resulted in a recession in 2010, a large budget deficit, job losses and unemployment, corporate closures, bank collapses and individual suffering. Federal Reserve data suggests that the typical US household remains poorer following the 2010 recession, despite low inflation and some economic growth. The net worth (the difference between assets and liabilities) of the median family fell by some 40 percent from $126,400 in 2007 to $77,300 in 2010, driven partly by the collapse of the housing market and unemployment. Blame for this situation was placed on the banks and financial institutions for lending too much money in dubious subprime transactions, but individuals also often borrowed beyond their capacity to repay loans and mortgages.

Although the economy has slowly recovered to some extent since 2010, a *Gallup* poll in 2014 showed that on economic issues, 42 percent of Americans said that they were conservative, 34 percent were moderate and 21 percent were liberal in their views. The gap between conservative and liberal was 21 percent and was the smallest that *Gallup* had measured in 14 years. It suggested that the historical US conservative advantage and identity in economic terms over liberal had been narrowing in recent years.

Media culture (see Chapter 13)

Media culture has historically grown from simple methods of production and communication to complex modern technologies, online Internet services, a very diverse audience and market, and a change from analog to digital means of production and transmission. These developments have been tied to political and social concerns, concentrated ownership of media, class identification, mass literacy, a dominant communication and social role and the expansion of entertainment. The written word was succeeded by broadcasting; television followed the cinema and radio; mass cultures developed more outlets and markets for the media; and the Internet and social media (such as Facebook and Twitter) have increased further technological possibilities, communication and leisure opportunities.

The media have provided quality services, instant news, public participation and widened knowledge. But they have also sometimes allegedly abused their position, appealed to the lowest denominator of taste, encouraged a "celebrity culture" and arguably reflected a "dumbing down" of social and educational values and products. However, they have protection and freedom under the First Amendment of the Constitution, which states that Congress shall not legislate to abridge the freedom of speech or of the press. The apparent absolute nature of the amendment is still debated and some critics argue that it has been progressively restricted by judicial decisions.

Arts, sports and leisure cultures (see Chapter 14)

Arts, sports and leisure activities have historically been very diverse and often influential in the US and have reflected class, national and economic conditions. They have consequently been described in terms of elite or popular culture or divided into high, middlebrow and lowbrow cultures. These divisions have expanded and changed over time, but some of the traditional defining limits (and social exclusions) still remain.

The arts have been characterized partly by output from theaters, opera companies, orchestras, film studios and ballet and dance companies, which today can provide both classical and more popular offerings. A wide range of music, from classical to urban and street music, pop, jazz and rock is available, as are a range of dramatic plays and musicals at both amateur and professional levels. Museums and art galleries have also become increasingly popular and appealed to more sectors of society, although they are subject to economic downturn and fluctuating financial support. Cinema is generally considered to be a distinctive American art form that has influenced a global film culture. Many artistic activities are still carried out by individual participants themselves through different recreational, media and online outlets, as well as by the larger public and commercial organizations.

Sports and leisure activities are also marked by a large diversity of types, participation and attendance, although some of the historical distinctions between high and low culture still remain. These illustrate not only the class, economic and cost determinants of participation, but also the complex composition of the population and its varied cultural interests.

National identity

US cultures interact among themselves and in other parts of US life. They condition debates about what it means to be American, what constitutes a national identity and whether these searches should be restricted to formal civil guidelines (such as those contained in the Constitution and the Bill of Rights) or should also include informal American values.

A historical dilemma for the US has been how to balance a need for civic unity against the reality of ethnic diversity and to avoid the dangers of fragmentation and conflict. Emphasis was initially placed on "Americanization," or the assimilation of different ethnic groups into a shared, Anglo-American-based identity or "melting pot." But this aim was seen as pressurizing immigrants to move into an Americanized dominant culture, with a possible resulting loss of their ethnic identity. "Assimilation" implies absolute national unity, whereas

PLATE 1.6 The Fourth of July (Independence Day) is an official US holiday. It commemorates the day in 1776 when the Continental Congress in Philadelphia gave its approval to the Declaration of Independence from Britain. Now celebrated with processions, speeches, flags and fireworks, as seen here on Independence Eve at the Denver City and County Building, Denver, Colorado.
© *Efrain Padro/Alamy*

pragmatic "integration" occurs at more gradual levels of partial blending or mixing.

Debates on national identity have centered on questions of unity (Americanization) as opposed to diversity (ethnic pluralism or multiculturalism). In the 1950s, ethnic differences and issues seemed to be losing their urgency, but they were revived in the 1990s and early 2000s, particularly with the growth of Latino and Asian ethnic groups.

The debates have stressed either "American values" (often presented by consolidationist conservatives) or ethnic- or minority-group interests (supported by reform liberals). The assimilationist American ideal of *e pluribus unum* (out of many one) was supposed to reconcile the two views under a civic umbrella. This ideal is seen by some as an abstract concept, which does not reflect reality. On the other hand, emphases on ethnicity and difference arguably weaken the possibility of achieving formal civic norms that could represent a distinctive "American Way of Life." Some critics feel that American society is at risk because of competing cultures and interest groups, the conflicts about which have weakened the sense and possibility of an overarching American identity and resulted in a divided society.

From the late 1970s into the 2000s, there was a conservative reaction against liberal policies and affirmative-action programs for minority groups, which allegedly discriminate in the latter's favor in areas such as education and employment. Many conservatives are opposed to liberal policies on abortion, gun control, same-sex marriage, religion, the death penalty and immigration. The debates have increased anxieties about national identity and the direction of the country, which have been reflected in many polls.

Divisions of opinion have led critics to argue that the US should more realistically be regarded ethnically, culturally and ideologically as an integrationist "mosaic," "salad bowl," "pizza" or "stew mix," rather than a "melting pot." While the latter model of America has been rejected in some quarters, the metaphors of salads and stews nevertheless imply that variety and difference should be incorporated into a larger "American" whole. The difficulty lies in defining what the core identity and binding civic structure might or should be.

The reality of cultural and ethnic pluralism (difference) in US society continues, as do arguments in support of homogenization (sameness). It is argued that degrees of separateness and integration vary between ethnic groups and that absolute social assimilation is both undesirable and impossible. But this can lead to hybrid or "multicultural" identities on the one hand and the breakdown of strong national links or bonds on the other.

While there are extremes of opinion, unfairness, diversity and vested interests in US society, it is felt that underlying commitments to formal civil rights of freedom, justice, tolerance and equality under the law can succeed in limiting divisions and promote unity, homogeneity and stability. However, these ideals may not always be achieved in the complex real world, and the US has to

PLATE 1.7 The Abraham Lincoln Address Memorial, Gettysburg, Pennsylvania was erected in 1912 near the site of the Battle of Gettysburg, July 13, 1863, where Union success led to victory over the Confederates in the American Civil War. Here President Lincoln dedicated the Soldiers' National Cemetery, in Gettysburg National Park on November 19, 1863 and also gave his Gettysburg Address. The address is short (272 words), but it has become a fundamental American document, drawing together the ideal features of the nation at a significant turning-point in its history. Lincoln spoke of the principle of human equality in the Declaration of Independence, the Civil War as a new birth of freedom, and sacrifice to ensure the survival of America's representative democracy. His words are carved on the right side of the memorial.
© *Jordan Oakland*

live resiliently with conflicts and anxieties. Economic, political, religious, ethnic, class and populist conflicts have become more evident in recent years.

Arguably, the tension in the struggle to achieve national identity is between pluralism, where the interests of separate ethnic groups or minorities are equally valid on the one hand, and an acceptance of diversity under an umbrella of American identity on the other. The latter solution has to be achieved within defined civic structures, which acknowledge ethnic identity and roots. Levels of integration (such as citizenship for immigrants, education, homeownership, language acquisition, intermarriage, economic opportunities and upward mobility) are then achievable, while differences are seen as valid. However, although recent US censuses have indicated that natural forces of integration had grown and that a sense of civic commonality or a distinctive American nationalism had developed, increased immigration, the growth of ethnic groups, relations with the police and interracial violence have again caused problems for society and national identity. Liberals maintain that a multicultural society should be the ultimate national goal but demographers argue that terms such as "White" or "Latino" are increasingly being defined as multiracial or mixed race.

Such developments may cause problems for national identity and representative civic institutions or lead to more fragmentation and separatism. It is alleged that some immigrants to the US since the 1980s have rejected integration and bilingualism, and a supposed reluctance to reject old national identities suggests for some critics a contemporary model composed of one nation with at least two contrasting cultures.

But many immigrants have historically integrated on various levels into American society. Irish, Jewish, Chinese and Italian groups, among many others, have initially lived separate lives and been subjected to suspicion and hostility before achieving degrees of integration. The fear of a decline in national unity may seem exaggerated and overlook the US ability to Americanize immigrants or to overcome lingering ethnic divides. But attitudes to immigration (both legal and illegal) have become increasingly negative in recent years. Early immigrants tried to construct a sense of American national identity and institutional unity by connecting the ethnically diverse population to central images and documents of the US, such as the national flag (the Stars and Stripes, Old Glory or the Star-Spangled Banner), the pledge of allegiance to the flag, the Declaration of Independence, the Liberty Bell, Abraham Lincoln's Emancipation Proclamation and Gettysburg Address, the "Star-Spangled Banner" (the US national anthem), the Constitution and the Bill of Rights. These are meant to provide cultural signs that promote loyalty to notions of what American citizenship and America might be. They are tied to institutions, appeal to progress and try to avoid divisive elements of economic, social, class or ethnic differences.

Certain values are also perceived to be particularly American and have been ingrained in Americans' history, such as freedom, equality, democracy, and support against oppression and tyranny. Other values have been adopted over the centuries, such as self-reliance, optimism, progress, destiny, achievement, individualism, independence, utopianism, liberty, freedom, opportunity, anti-statism (suspicion of government), populism (grassroots activism), a sense of destiny and respect for the law. Some of these stem from the ideas of Puritan/Protestant religion and the European Enlightenment, which influenced the framers of the Declaration of Independence and the US Constitution. They constitute layers of idealism and abstraction in American life that coexist, and may often clash, with reality. This situation echoes the experience of other countries, particularly those that are unions, federations or collections of different peoples with contrasting roots and traditions, that need to erect new national identities while preserving some aspects of their origins.

PLATE 1.8 The Allegiance Ceremony marks a rite of passage for foreign immigrants who claim US citizenship. Here President Barack Obama listens to Secretary of Homeland Security Janet Napolitano administering the oath of citizenship during a naturalization ceremony for military personnel in the East Room of the White House, July 4, 2012, Washington DC.
© *White House Photo/Alamy*

The degree to which such values are propagated in US society is significant, irrespective of whether they are individually or nationally achieved. They are valid for many people, and a key feature of American life is how individuals manage to combine ideals of the nation with ethnic awareness and the actual tensions and realities of society.

Other critics have tried to explain the US, its people and its national identity by "American traits." Features like restlessness, escape from restraints, change, action, mobility, quests for new experiences, self-improvement and a belief in potential supposedly constitute typical American behavior. They are often attributed to immigrant and frontier experiences and a belief in progress for the individual and society. Americans allegedly refuse to accept a fixed fate or settled location but seek new jobs, new horizons and new beginnings in a hunt for self-fulfillment and self-definition.

On the other hand, many Americans seek roots and stability in their lives, their institutions and a national identity. While the alleged informality of American life is supposedly founded on individualism, egalitarianism and a historical rejection of European habits, some Americans respect and desire formalities, hierarchy, order and conformity.

Americans may stress their individualism, distrust of Big Business and Big Government and their desire to be free. But communalism, voluntary activities, charitable organizations and group endeavors are also a feature of US life. Individuals have to cope with corporate, political, social, economic and employment bureaucracies with their associated power bases, which reflect the tension between ideal aspirations and everyday facts of life.

Arguably, one cannot define a single set of traits or values that are shared by all Americans. Diversity, individual differences and departures from consensual norms limit possibilities and can result in contradictions or tensions rather than unified beliefs. Such traits and values are also universal characteristics, which are present in other societies and are neither exceptional in themselves nor distinctively American.

Nevertheless, the major US cultures have produced distinctive images or identities, which are recognized internationally and have influenced a globalized culture, whether simplistically and stereotypically or in more sophisticated forms. They are expressed through Hollywood films, television and radio, music and art, newspapers and magazines, sports, consumption, chain stores and brand names, corporate and financial institutions, business and management philosophies, political activity, ethnic concerns, religion and popular culture.

But the recent changes to categories (mixed or multiracial) of the population in US censuses suggest a continuing sense of differentiation and that people may primarily identify themselves in terms of a complex ethnic/ancestral background. It is an open question whether human division will grow under the influence of increasing immigration and changes in ethnic demography or whether the forces of integration over time will promote an increased sense of commonality, patriotism and American identity, without incurring a denial of roots.

Some critics argue that the meaning and definition of a more unified national and civic US identity remain elusive. They maintain that a candid debate about the essence of American identity is needed in the current fluid and polarized situation. Opposed positions between unifiers and pluralists/multiculturalists still operate. Many Americans may generally appear to believe in the inherent validity of American values and Americanism, but they continue to question what is meant by these signs, how consensual they are and, consequently, what it means to be American.

Social and institutional change

The major US cultures are not static. They may influence each other and other countries, just as foreign pressures can modify the American cultures. But although the latter are conditioned by increasingly globalized forces, they must also remain responsive to specific US political, minority, ethical and consumer demands. A national mass culture and economic system is an important integrationist force as it caters for and defines American society.

US social institutions have been a work-in-progress since independence in 1776 and reflect a variety of values and practices. Some are particular to the US and others are similar to those of other nations. All have developed to cope with, and adapt to, an increasingly complex, diverse and dynamic society. They take many different forms and sizes, operate on federal, state and local levels, and they may be public or private in character.

The larger elements, such as federal and state governments, are involved with public business, but there is also a diverse range of smaller social and cultural activities (both public and private) tied to sports, communities, neighborhoods, religion, the theater and ethnic identity. These may take on more individualistic forms than the larger institutions.

For some critics, it is the localized life and behavior of people in small-town America that typically define their society, rather than centralized federal institutions, regions and the big cities. However, the larger frameworks do serve as cement that holds local activities and people together. They also contribute to an umbrella sense of American identity and "Americanness." The US, like other countries, gains its identity from a mixture of the local and the national, which inform and influence, as well as conflict with, each other.

The American "way of life" is defined by how citizens function within and respond to local and national institutions and cultures, whether positively or negatively. The large number and variety of such institutions, subcultures and social groups means that there are many different "ways of life" and values, and all contribute to the diversity and particular characteristics of American society.

The following chapters stress the historical context of US growth and suggest that the contemporary owes much to the past. Social structures are adaptable and provide frameworks for new situations, and their present roles may be different from their original functions. They have evolved over time as they have been influenced by elite and government policies as well as grassroots impulses and reactions. This process of change and adaptation continues and reflects current anxieties and concerns in American life. Social structures contribute to a culture of varied and often conflicting habits and ideals, as well as being practical organizations for realizing them. They may also allow an attempt to describe what may, or may not, be regarded as distinctively American.

American attitudes to US society

Social structures and national policies affect individuals directly in their daily lives. Despite their diversity of origins and beliefs, Americans do have many common concerns. They identify the major issues facing the country in opinion polls. Items such as the economy, politics, government, crime, ethnicity, religion, morality, healthcare, racism and immigration have regularly appeared in lists of problems. Despite some recent skepticism about the accuracy of polls, they are still generally regarded as indicators of how respondents are sensitive to changing conditions and priorities over time. Poll results can be compared and contrasted and may be used as interpretative tools.

Polls in recent years have shown declines in approval ratings for the condition of the country and the performance of US administrations. A Gallup poll in January 2010 found that 75 percent of respondents could trust the Washington government to do what is right for "only some of the time" and 6 percent said "never." Prior to the 2012 presidential election campaign, a Rasmussen Report found that 30 percent of respondents thought that the country was heading in the right direction, while 64 percent said that it was on the wrong track.

In recent years, polls have shown that the economy (taxes, inflation, the budget deficit, unemployment, low wages, the gap between rich and poor, high cost of living, jobs and foreign competition) was a primary concern for people. However, the campaign against terrorism, homeland security and foreign policy have become increasingly important. Concerns about healthcare, Medicare (medical program for people over 65 years of age,) Medicaid (medical care for low-income people under 65), the cost of prescription drugs, social security (federal payments to people who are unemployed, poor, old or disabled), abortion and same-sex marriage were also prominent. Worries about corporate corruption, immigration, gun control, drugs, the death penalty and crime have risen in poll ratings. There was populist dissatisfaction with the Democrats, suggesting that they had not dealt adequately with the financial crisis, the 2010 recession, healthcare and other issues. Grassroots disquiet arguably contributed to the election of a "populist" Republican administration in 2016.

Respondents to an October 7–11, 2015 Gallup poll also mentioned the economy as a primary concern, exemplified by unemployment/jobs, the federal budget deficit/debt, the gap between rich and poor (inequality), wages, poverty, lack of money, corporate corruption, high cost of living/inflation, and taxes. These responses reflected the challenging conditions facing the US and its people. They suggested that the US continued to be affected by the budget and credit crisis and recession of 2007–10 and that the economy, in general, remained central to people's worries about everyday experiences and the future of the US.

Non-economic issues in the Gallup 2015 survey included problems that had appeared regularly in polls over the previous 20 years, although the priority given to some items fluctuated. The main issues were a dissatisfaction with government performance, immigration, illegal aliens, guns/gun control, healthcare, ethical/moral/religious decline, crime/violence, race relations/racism, education/public school weakness, terrorism, poverty/hunger/homelessness, foreign policy/foreign aid, lack of respect for each other, lack of military defense, war/fear of war, elderly care/Medicare and the environment. Forty-two percent thought that the Republican Party would do a better job in handling national problems than the Democratic Party (37 percent,) while 23 percent had the "Same/Other/No opinion." These concerns and attitudes were also evident in results for a Gallup poll prior to the 2016 presidential election (see Table 1.2).

Given the avowed optimism of Americans, their faith in their society and belief in an individual ability to achieve the American Dream, it is instructive to consider the results of polls that reported on alienation in US society (see Table 1.3) between 2008 and 2016. The responses indicated increasing alienation over the years. They suggest a degree of individual powerlessness felt by ordinary Americans in the face of political, economic, bureaucratic, corporate and institutional forces, and dissatisfaction with established elites. This poll was taken during contentious presidential primary campaigning in 2016.

TABLE 1.2 The main problems facing the US, 2016

Problem	Percent
Economy in general	17
Dissatisfaction with government	12
Race relations/racism	10
Immigration/illegal aliens	7
Elections/election reform	7
National security	7
Unemployment/jobs	6
Terrorism	5
Federal budget deficit/federal debt	4
Poor healthcare/high cost of healthcare	4
Ethics/Moral/religious decline	3
Crime/violence	3
Environment/pollution	3

Source: adapted from Gallup poll, October 5–9, 2016. Figures do not total 100%.

TABLE 1.3 Alienation in the US, May–June 2016

Americans tend to feel that. . .	%	2008	2009	2010	2011	2014	2016
. . . the rich get richer and the poor get poorer		71	66	68	73	81	78
. . . what you think doesn't count for very much anymore		57	56	52	66	68	68
. . . most people with power try to take advantage of people like yourself		59	57	53	63	71	70
. . . the people running the country don't really care what happens to you		62	53	50	73	85	82
. . . you're left out of things going on around you		41	35	37	41	42	42

Source: adapted from Harris Alienation Index, the Harris Poll, May–June, 2016

A further statement was included in earlier Harris polls, but not in the Alienation Index. Eighty-nine percent of respondents agreed in 2014 that "The people in Washington are out of touch with the rest of the country." Nevertheless, a Gallup poll in September 7–11, 2016 found that 42 percent of respondents thought that the Republican Party would do a better job in handling national problems than the Democratic Party (38 percent), while 20 percent had the "Same/Other/No opinion."

Exercises

Explain and examine the significance of the following names and terms:

the Civil War	alienation	integration	Native Americans
utopianism	the Enlightenment	rule of law	Latino
slavery	individualism	values	Constitution
populism	ethnic	anti-statism	exceptionalism
diversity	consensus	corporate	the Cold War
Big Business	Big Government	federation	"melting pot"
grass roots	culture(s)	consumerism	civil rights
work ethic	frontier	"salad bowl"	9/11
traits	pluralism	assimilation	the Vietnam War
nativist	egalitarianism	Americanization	Washington DC
ideology	brand names	multiculturalism	Vikings
globalization	regulation	Old Glory	racism
elites	zenophobic	rhetoric	Awakenings
recession	ancestral	airstrikes	turnout

Write short essays on the following questions:

1. What are some of the characteristics that you would associate with the American people and their society? Why?

2. Why are questions of "national identity" important in the US?

3. Do you find that the public opinion poll findings in this chapter give a valid picture of the US? Give your reasons after carefully examining the poll results.

4. Critically examine the views on American values from posts in the websites listed at the end of this chapter.

5. With reference to Plate 1.7, examine the central role that Abraham Lincoln has played in US public life. Reference his *Gettysburg Address* and *Emancipation Proclamation*.

Further reading

Addington, L. (2000) *America's War in Vietnam: A Short Narrative History*, Bloomington, IN: University of Indiana Press.

Alba, R. and Nee, V. (2003) *Remaking the American Mainstream: Assimilation and Contemporary Immigration*, Cambridge, Harvard: Harvard University Press.

Bloom, A. (1988) *The Closing of the American Mind*, New York: Touchstone.

Breen, L.A. (2011) *Converging Worlds: Communities and Cultures in Colonial America*, London: Routledge.

Campbell, N. and Kean, A. (2006) *American Cultural Studies: An Introduction to American Culture*, London: Routledge.

Campbell, N., Davies, J. and McKay, G. (2004) *Issues in Americanization and Culture*, Edinburgh: Edinburgh University Press.

Cullen, J. (2003) *The American Dream: A Short History of an Idea That Shaped a Nation*, New York: Oxford University Press.

Datesman, M.K., Kearny, L. and Keyerleber, J. (2005) *American Ways: An Introduction to American Culture*, White Plains, NY: Pearson Education.

Dubois, L. and Scott, J.S. (2009) (ed.) *Origins of the Black Atlantic*, London: Routledge.

Ferguson, N. (2004) *The Rise and Fall of the American Empire*, London: Allen Lane.

Hacker, A. (2003) *Two Nations: Black and White, Separate, Hostile, Unequal*, New York: Scribner.

Hall, J. A. and Lindholm, C. (1999) *Is America Breaking Apart?* Princeton, NJ: Princeton University Press.

Huntington, S. P. (2004) *Who Are We? America's Great Debate*, New York: Simon & Schuster.

Leach, E. E. (2004) *Interpreting the American Dream*, London: Palgrave/Macmillan.

Mancall, P.C. and Merrell, J. (2006) *American Encounters: Natives and Newcomers from European Contact to Indian Removal, 1500–1850*, London: Routledge.

Micklethwait, J. and Wooldridge, A. (2004) *The Right Nation: Why America Is Different*, London: Allen Lane.

Moen, P. D., Dempster-McClain and Walker, H.A. (eds.) (1999) *A Nation Divided: Diversity, Inequality and Community in American Society*, Ithaca, NY: Cornell University Press.

Morehouse, M.M. and Trodd, Z. (2012) *Civil War America: A Social and Cultural History with Primary Sources*, London: Routledge.

Pankaj M. (2017) *Age of Anger: A History of the Present*, London: Allen Lane.

Pope, D. (ed.) (2001) *American Radicalism*, Oxford: Blackwell.

Sandel, M. J. (1996) *Democracy's Discontent: America in Search of a Public Philosophy*, Cambridge, Mass: Belknap Press of Harvard University Press.

Sargent, L. T. (ed.) (1995) *Extremism in America*, New York: New York University Press.

Schrag, P. (2011) *Not Fit for Our Society: Immigration and Nativism in America*, Berkeley, CA: University of California Press.

Zinn, H. (2003) *A People's History of the United States: From 1492 to Present*, London: Longman/Pearson.

Websites

ABC News: www.ABCNews.com

American Community Survey (ACS): www.census.gov

American exceptionalism (Stephen M. Walt): http://foreign policy.com/2011/10/11/the-myth-of-american-exceptionalism

American Fact Finder: factfinder.census.gov

American values: www.commondreams.org/views 05/0420–20 html

American Values today: https://www.theatlantic.com/national/archive/2012/06/21-charts-that-explain-american-values-today/258990/

American Values: www.andrews.edu/~tidwell/bsad560/USValues.html

CNN: www.cnn.com/

Economist/Yougov polls: www.economist.com/yougov

Economist: www.economist.com

Gallup opinion polls: www.gallup.com

Harris polls: www.harrispollonline.com

Harris: www.harrisinteractive.com

New York Times: www.nytimes.com

Newsweek polls: www.newsweek.com

Pew Research Center: www.pewresearch.org

Rasmussen Polling Reports: www.rasmussenreports.com

US ancestries: www.businessinsider.com/largest-ethnic-groups-in america-2013.8

US Census Bureau: www.census.gov

usinfo.state.gov/usa/infousa/

usinfo.state.gov/journals/journala.htm

usinfo.state.gov

Washington Post: www.washingtonpost.com

www.firstgov.gov

www.georgetown.edu/crossroads/index.html

www.lib.duke.edu/reference/polls.htm

www.ropercenter.uconn.edu

www.pollingreport.com/prioriti.htm

YouGov polls: www.YouGov USA

Chapter 2

The country

- Political ecology
- Natural resources, economic development and environmental concerns
- Climate
- The regions: cultural geography
- Native American cultural regions
- Cultural regions in the contemporary US: political geography
- Changing public attitudes: where do we go from here?
- *Exercises*
- *Further reading*
- *Websites*

Political ecology

The most pronounced physical feature of the United States is its variety. Its natural environment varies from the arctic to the tropical, from rainforest to desert, from vast plains to rugged mountains. Exploiting its natural resources, however, has depleted reserves, caused extensive pollution and shown a wastefulness that has led to dependence on resources from other nations. The country's natural riches remain a main support of its economic life. Recently, a coalition of groups, including economists, politicians and national security advisors, helped the nation achieve the goal of energy independence. Environmentalist movements and public concern since the mid-1800s have successfully lobbied for a huge national system of nature preserves and the monitoring and regulation of the exploitation of resources. The use of natural resources has become a matter of balancing priorities among overlapping environmental, economic and cultural interest groups. The chapter therefore often focuses on political ecology – on attempts to understand the complex distributional issues involved in Americans' many-sided involvement with the environment.

Natural resources, economic development and environmental concerns

With an area of 3,615,122 square miles (9,363,123 square kilometers), the United States is exceeded in size only by Russia, Canada and China. Of the 50 states, 48 lie between the Atlantic and Pacific Oceans and between Canada and Mexico, while two, Alaska and Hawaii, lie in the northwest corner of the continent and the Pacific Ocean, respectively. Island possessions in the Caribbean and the Pacific add another 11,000 square miles (28,500 square kilometers) to American territory.

Approached from the Atlantic Ocean or the Gulf of Mexico, the country's first land formation is the Atlantic Plain, a coastal lowland stretching from New England to the middle of Texas. A narrow coastal strip in the North, the Plain gradually widens to include large parts of the southern states. As the coastal area where the first European settlers arrived in the early 1600s', the Plain today holds the country's largest interconnected metropolitan areas, sometimes called "Bos-Wash" and 100's of sprawling suburban areas. Its soil is mostly poor, but it includes a fertile citrus-growing region and the Cotton Belt in the South, which commercial farming has intensively developed.

The Plain's most important natural wealth, found along and in the Gulf of Mexico, is much of the nation's crude oil and natural gas reserves. Since the early 2000's, a new extraction process called "fracking" has greatly expanded the territory affected by the fossil fuel industry. Water pollution from industrial development in the North and commercial fertilizers and oil-drilling in the South have posed the most serious environmental threats to the Plain.

The Gulf's wetland wildlife and rich fisheries suffered greatly during the disaster on the BP Deepwater Horizon rig that poured enormous amounts of raw oil into that ecosystem for months in 2010. Drilling for petroleum further north, off the Atlantic coast, has become a more serious alternative, despite environmentalists' protests. As the nation strives to maintain energy independence, politicians have considered exploiting an "all of the above" approach and distributing the environmental costs across the country.

Inland from the Atlantic Plain, the land rises to the Piedmont, a gently rolling fertile plateau. Along the eastern edge of the Piedmont is the fall line, where rivers running down to the Atlantic form waterfalls. When waterpower provided energy for lumber, grain and textile mills, America's first industrial cities grew up along the northern fall line near the coast. The Piedmont rises to the Appalachians, much-eroded mountains from Canada to Alabama that separate the eastern seaboard from the interior. These mountains, the Appalachian Plateau, and the rugged ridge and valley country to the west delayed European invasion and settlement (see Figure 2.2). Although the Appalachians and the upland sub-regions contain minerals, only iron, building stone and coal deposits exist in large quantities. The coal deposits in Pennsylvania and West Virginia, in the area called Appalachia, are among the world's largest, and they once provided fuel for developing industry in the Northeast and the Great Lakes regions, as well as for heating homes across the nation. Today, in spite of the environmentally disastrous blasting away of mountaintops to uncover new coal veins, Appalachia remains one of the nation's most depressed areas. "Cleaner" gas, oil and atomic energy have partially replaced coal. Producing and using these newer energy sources, moreover, is one of the main sources of air pollution and acid rain. "Clean" wind and solar energy are among the environmentally friendly technologies the Obama administration supported.

West of the Appalachian highlands lies the Central Lowland, a vast area stretching from New York state to central Texas and north to Canada. The Lowland resembles a huge, irregular bowl rimmed by the Great Lakes and highlands. The iron ore in one of these, the Mesabi Range at the western edge of the Lakes, transported inexpensively over the Great Lakes to the coal of Appalachia, made the development of America's industrial core possible. This industrial ecology was the backbone of the nation's economic expansion, and it claimed priority over environmental concerns until many of its "smokestack" factories proved unable to compete on the global market in the 1970s. Industrial jobs disappeared to low-cost labor areas around the globe. The fracking of oil across the Lowland and Obama's rescue of the automobile industry have revived the region's economy.

The Central Lowland is not entirely flat. The glacial moraine, an area of rocky territory with many lakes, runs along a line just north of the Ohio and Missouri rivers. On both sides of the moraine, the lowland has a table-like flatness, except near rivers that have dug gorges. The lowland also varies in rainfall and temperature. Rainfall decreases toward the west, resulting first in a change from forests mixed with fields to the prairies, where trees are rare. Farther west, the high prairie grass changes to short grass at the 20-inch (50-centimeters) annual rainfall line where the Great Plains begin (see Figure 2.2). From north to south, the long winters of the Upper Midwest change to the snow-less winters of the Gulf states. The discovery of great amounts of oil-bearing shale, extractable with new technology, and the prospect of energy carried south from Canada through a pipeline across the Dakotas has altered the economy of the Great Plains.

The natural resources of the Central Lowland, often called the nation's breadbasket, are its soil and fossil fuels. The fields of oil and gas in Texas, Oklahoma and Kansas were the nation's most important domestic supply until the nation tapped reserves in the Gulf and Alaska. Today fracking's oil wells have sprouted up in farming areas and housing districts throughout the region as local residents try to supply their own energy from small deposits. Environmental experts say efforts to dispose of fracking and drilling byproducts and wastewater by injecting them into deep wells causes earthquakes. In 2014, Oklahoma alone experienced 5,415 quakes, of which 585 were of a seismic magnitude of three or greater.

Across the Lowland, the increase in large-scale agribusinesses in recent years has produced intense efforts to deal with unwanted side effects. These include polluted water supplies from plant fertilizers and insecticides and the leakage of concentrated animal feed and sewage from industrial pig, chicken and freshwater fish farming.

The Great Plains is a band of semi-arid territory almost 500 miles (800 kilometers) wide between Canada and Mexico. The plains rise so gradually toward the west that large parts of the region appear to be utterly flat. Most of the plains, however, are broadly rolling, and parts of the northern plains break up into spectacular gorge and ridge country called "badlands." The buffalo grass of the plains makes them excellent for ranching, but some areas, watered by automated artesian wells or irrigation, are now high-yield farm country. The Plains' mineral wealth declined in economic viability as the world price for oil and soft coal fell. Nonetheless, shale oil deposits in western Colorado have proven profitable to extract and helped make the United States an energy exporter.

From the western edge of the Great Plains to the Pacific Coast, a third of the continental United States consists of the Cordillera mountain chains (the Rockies and the Pacific ranges) and the basins and plateaus between them. Near the southern Rockies' western slopes is the Colorado Plateau, a maze of canyons and mesas, the most famous of which is the Grand Canyon. Surrounding the Plateau is the desert Southwest. Valleys and plains rather than mountains occupy much of the middle Rockies. The Wyoming Basin has provided a route through the mountains, from the Oregon Trail that pioneers followed to the interstate

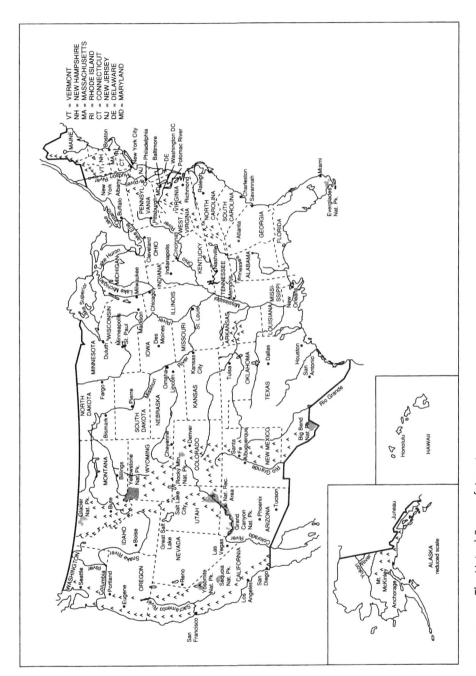

FIGURE 2.1 The United States of America.

PLATE 2.1 Smoggy morning in downtown Los Angeles, where topography, climate, massive traffic flows and population density make air pollution a problem.

Source: © Izzy Schwartz/Getty

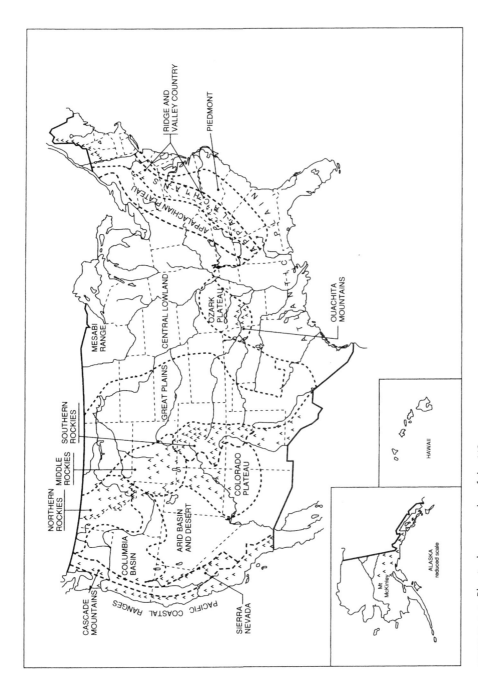

FIGURE 2.2 Physical geography of the US.

PLATE 2.2 Crop spraying in Idaho, improving harvests, but at what environmental cost?
Source: © Sipa Press/REX/Shutterstock

highways of today. In the northern Rockies are vast wilderness areas and the Columbia Basin that the Snake and Columbia rivers etch with deep canyons.

The western arm of the Cordillera consists of two lines of mountains with a series of valleys between them. In from the coast are the highest peaks, including active volcanoes. The inland valleys contain much of the West Coast's population and economic activity, from Washington's Puget Sound to the Willamette Valley of Oregon and California's Central Valley. Rich soils bless all these valleys, and the more southerly have been relatively easy to irrigate. Since the invention of refrigeration, these valleys have supplied the nation with fruit and vegetables. The mountains between the valleys and the coast include major earthquake zones, such as the San Andreas Fault, which caused the 1906 quake that leveled San Francisco. Distributing limited water resources fairly, however, rather than earthquakes, seems to be the most serious environmental challenge to a majority of Westerners today.

In Alaska, the Cordillera divide into three parts that include North America's highest peak, Mount McKinley at 20,320 feet (6,194 meters). Largely fragile tundra, Alaska's interior is comprised of mountains, broken plateaus and flat valleys with a cold inland climate. Much of coastal and island Alaska has a temperate climate because of warm ocean currents. The building of the trans-Alaska pipeline, coastal oil spills and, as recently as the 2012 presidential election campaign, the debate over plans to open the Arctic National Wildlife Refuge to oil exploration have tested the nation's will to protect Alaska's nature.

Republican Vice-Presidential Candidate Sarah Palin, the governor of the state in 2008, joined her party and a large majority of Alaskan voters in supporting the opening of the ANWR to commercial-industrial development.

The American Cordillera are world famous for veins of precious metals, such as the gold of the Sierra Nevadas and Yukon Territory and the Comstock lode of silver in Nevada. More recently, firms have focused on mining industrial metals such as copper and lead. Large occurrences of oil and gas exist in California and Wyoming, and the Colorado Plateau contains not only coal shale but also uranium and soft coal. To extract the oil and coal, mining companies say that open pit and strip-mining are necessary. Conservationists, on the other hand, argue that this mining devastates parts of the plateau as thoroughly as it destroyed areas of the Great Plains and Appalachia.

The natural riches of Hawaii are vegetable rather than mineral. The state contains almost a million acres (405,000 hectares) of commercial forest and twice as much land suitable for tropical farming. Trade winds give the islands a temperate climate. The volcanic mountains catch significant rain on the windward side of the islands so that the leeward side has only moderate rainfall.

Coastlines and river systems

Among the most important physical features and resources of the country are its coastlines, harbors, ocean currents and network of lakes and rivers. The shallow

PLATE 2.3 On January 23, 2016 a winter storm ravaged the East Coast, flooding neighborhoods of Long Neck Road, Millsboro, Delaware. High winds drove floodwaters inland, inundating homes, vacation camps, and businesses. Residents of low-lying areas near the Atlantic coast have found in recent years that climate change made roads impassable and produced repeated damage to private property.
© W.D. Auer/Alamy

waters of the continental shelf off the North Atlantic coast, known as the Great Banks, contain many kinds of fish and attracted fishermen from Europe even before European settlers established their first colonies in the New World. By the 1990s, the famous cod stocks had collapsed from international over-fishing, however, and made the need to manage these maritime riches clear to the US and Canada. The East Coast has a warmer climate because of the Florida Current. Fine harbors and estuaries made the sites of New York City, Philadelphia and Baltimore excellent locations for trade. In recent years, tidal flooding has become a nearly constant problem in low-lying districts along the East Coast due to rising sea levels.

The great eastern water systems are those that drain the Central Lowland: the Mississippi with its major tributaries and the Great Lakes–St. Lawrence system. One of the world's great inland water networks, the Mississippi system carries freight from New Orleans north to Minneapolis and east to Pittsburgh. Western tributaries of the Mississippi are mostly unfit for navigation, but since the 1950s, the Missouri has carried heavy barge traffic because of dams, locks and dredging. Because canals connect it to the Mississippi, the Great Lakes–St. Lawrence system functions as the second half of one vast network of inland waterways. The biggest group of freshwater lakes in the world, the Great Lakes carry more shipping than any other inland lake group. The fertile farmland surrounding the lakes and the iron, lumber and fossil fuels near their shores supported the rapid urbanization and industrialization of the Midwest in the 1800s. The opening of the St. Lawrence Seaway in 1959 made the lake cities international seaports by bypassing the obstacles to ocean-going freighters in the St. Lawrence with huge locks.

On the West Coast, limited rainfall and scant mountain run-off dry up all but three river systems – the Columbia, the Colorado and the San Joaquin–Sacramento – before they reach the sea. They do not support shipping, but the West's largest rivers have brought prosperity by providing hydroelectric power and irrigation. The Columbia, once a wild white river, now runs down through dams and calm lakes, turning the arid plateaus of Washington state into vegetable gardens and supplying electrical power and drinking water to several states and Native American properties. The Colorado serves the same purposes on a smaller scale. Proposals for its further development have met with opposition, because more dams would destroy the beauty of the Grand Canyon and other canyon lands.

Conservation, recreational areas and environmental protection

Although the country's population is now over 325 million, most of these people live in relatively small areas. Some parts of the country are not suitable for urbanization because of climate or difficult topography. Others have been set aside as recreation areas or wildlife preserves. Conservation of natural beauty and resources through national parks gained acceptance in the US in the late 1800s, with vocal support from President Theodore Roosevelt, among others. Congress created Yellowstone National Park as the first nature preserve and put it under federal control in 1872. Congress established the National Park Service

(NPS) in 1916 and gave it the double duty of making the areas entrusted to it accessible for industry and public enjoyment and preserving them for future generations. The NPS now administers more than 400 different sites, a combined territory of over 131,250 square miles (339,936 square kilometers), including national monuments, historical sites, seashores, lakeshores, and scores of huge wilderness areas in all parts of the US, the largest and most famous between the Rockies and the Pacific.

Government protection of the parks means controlled development. The federal Department of the Interior and its Land Management Bureau have long granted licenses or leases allowing private economic interests to use the parks' resources at low cost. According to federal law, the government must balance the interests of developers, holidaymakers, environmentalists and Native Americans. Some say this ideal of "multiple use" may have worked when the West was underpopulated but that today it satisfies no one and could lead to the loss of irreplaceable resources. In 2015 over 307 million people visited NPS sites.

In the 1960s and 1970s, a remarkable period of protest and reform in the US, conservationist and environmentalist organizations grew in strength in response to exposés of pollution, such as Rachel Carson's best-selling book *Silent Spring*. A series of environmental disasters, including a gigantic oil spill off the California coast and the chemical explosion and burning of the Cuyahoga River in downtown Cleveland, Ohio, also drew much attention. The high level of public concern became obvious in 1970, when 20 million people took part in the first Earth Day, a nationwide "teach-in," focused on the dangers of pollution.

Concerted lobbying of Congress by grassroots groups and highly organized environmental organizations, such as the Sierra Club and National Audubon Society, soon resulted in a series of landmark federal laws. In the same year an independent regulatory body, the Environmental Protection Agency (EPA), took on the national government's responsibility for monitoring and protecting America's natural environment, and the Clean Air Act gave the EPA the duty of identifying and reducing airborne pollutants. By 1980, the Clean Water Act, the Safe Drinking Water Act, the Endangered Species Act, the Toxic Substances Control Act, and the Superfund statute, which provides emergency federal funding for eliminating the health hazards of toxic-waste sites across the nation were in effect. Congress has reauthorized these laws in the decades since their enactment due to the environmental damage caused largely by sprawling urban development, new and outmoded industrial sites, and innovative commercial forms of farming and food processing.

Federal laws enacted from the 1980s to the 2000s have sought to protect rivers, beaches and estuaries from toxic dumping and the public from nuclear wastes and poisonous sprays and residues on foods and cosmetic products. After decades of largely ineffective attempts to limit these dangers, congress reformed the Toxic Substances Control Act in 2016 with bipartisan support. That achievement, the first update of an environmental statute in 40 years, provided authority and funding for removing asbestos and many other dangerous substances from the American market.

Climate

Arctic and tropical climates are limited to high mountaintops, inland Alaska, Hawaii and the southern tip of Florida. The middle latitudes, however, show wide variations in temperature and rainfall, and the great size of North America reinforces these differences. In general, the more distant a place is from an ocean, the more it has temperature extremes in the summer and winter. Near the inland center of the continent in North Dakota, temperatures have varied from a summer high of 121°F (49°C) to a winter low of –60°F (–51°C). Most climates in America are "inland" in this sense because, with the general eastward movement of air across the country, the Cordillera mountain system limits the moderating influence of the Pacific to a narrow strip along the West Coast. Thus, San Francisco experiences a small differential between winter and summer temperatures, but the same wide range of seasonal differences extends from the Rockies to the East Coast. The easterly movement of weather systems across the country also means the Atlantic Ocean has only a weak moderating influence.

Rainfall

Confined to the coastal strip by the Cordillera, rainfall from the Pacific Ocean so seldom reaches the areas between the mountains and the Great Plains that they are arid or semi-arid. Farther east, rainfall increases because warm, moist air

PLATE 2.4 The skyline of downtown Seattle with its famous "space needle" tower.
© F1 Online/REX/Shutterstock

moves up over the nation's middle from the Gulf of Mexico, producing rainfall. This rain often comes in cloudbursts, hailstorms, tornadoes and blizzards, with rapid temperature changes as cold Canadian air collides with warm, humid air from the Gulf of Mexico.

The seasons

In winter, dry frigid Canadian air moves south, spreading cold weather to the plains and lowlands and causing storms at its southern edge. In summer, that stormy edge moves north as gulf air brings hot weather that eliminates much of the temperature difference between the North and South.

Along the Pacific, seasonal changes follow another pattern. Winter in the Pacific Northwest is overcast and drizzly because of warm, moist air from the Alaskan coast. Southern California is a climatic refuge in winter because of its mild temperatures and long periods of sunny weather. In summer, the Pacific Northwest has mild air from the Pacific, and, except in the mountains, is nearly rainless. Farther south, summer means dry, hot air and high temperatures. Mild days, frosty nights and crystal clear skies mark autumn in the Northeast and Upper Midwest. Spring here brings temperate weather, but autumn and spring are also the seasons when the gulf and Canadian air masses lurch most violently together, spawning hurricanes along the gulf and Atlantic coasts in the fall and tornadoes in the Mississippi valley in the spring.

The regions: cultural geography

The definitions and boundaries of American regions vary according to the uses people put them to in local decision-making. Recent developments in the study of geography emphasize how political the subject is because mapping the physical world divides it in ways that decide where people belong and how resources are managed and distributed. More than one meaningful division of the country into regions is possible, and cultural regions defined as groups of states give only approximate borders because cultural boundaries rarely coincide with political units. Individual Native American cultures, geographic areas and states, moreover, often show a unique mixture of traits that makes their inclusion in regional cultures inaccurate at best.

Native American cultural regions

Many distinctive Native American cultures existed when Europeans arrived in the mid-1500s. An estimated 10 million Native Americans then lived in cultures with several hundred mutually incomprehensible languages and widely varying social structures. Any survey of cultural regions in such a diversity of groups must focus on broad similarities (see Figure 2.3).

PLATE 2.5 Waits River, Vermont, with autumn foliage.
© *Andre Jenny/Stock Connection/REX/Shutterstock*

In the woodland eastern half of the country were areas now known as the northeastern and southeastern maize regions, a variety of native cultures depended on hunting, fishing, farming and gathering. Anthropologists speak of these as "maize cultures," because maize (corn as it is called in the US) was the most important staple of these peoples' diet. The longer growing season in the southeastern maize region resulted in more extensive and highly developed agriculture. In the East as a whole, most people constructed housing of wood, bark and thatch. Women and children usually farmed and gathered wild foods while men hunted and fished. Well-known groups here were Iroquois, Huron, Mohican, Delaware and Shawnee in the north, and Powhatan, Creek, Cherokee, Seminole and Natchez in the south.

Anthropologists call the Native American cultural area in the prairies and Great Plains the plains or bison region. For thousands of years the population of this area was sparse compared with other parts of the continent. People lived along waterways and depended on riverbank farming, small game hunting and gathering. Lacking any other means of transportation, they went on a communal buffalo (bison) hunt once a year on foot. Then, between 1700 and 1750, they discovered how to use the horses that reached them from Spanish-controlled areas to the south, and plains cultures transformed themselves. The population grew because the food supply increased dramatically when people hunted bison on horseback. Learning of this, some tribes, such as the Dakota, migrated from nearby woodlands to the open steppes farther west. Plains peoples exchanged their settled farming customs for the nomadic culture of year-round buffalo hunters, discarding sod lodges for the portable *tipi* and evolving a society dominated by a warrior hunting class. The groups transformed by the arrival of the horse (the Blackfoot, Crow, Cheyenne and Dakota) are among the best known of Native Americans, largely because of their fierce resistance to white settlement on their hunting grounds.

The Native American cultural region called the Southwest once encompassed a diversity of native cultures, nomadic hunters and gatherers as well as farmers, but most of its people relied on advanced forms of irrigated agriculture. Hopi, Zuni and Acoma people, among others, lived in the two- to three-floor adobe, or stone buildings called pueblos, and farmed nearby land. These cultures all traced ancestry through the female line, and men did the farming while women owned the fields. The Navajo and Apache were latecomers to the region, hunters and gatherers who migrated south from the Canadian plains between 1000 and 1500 AD and who adopted farming from the pueblo-dwelling peoples. The Navajo later learned sheep raising, peach growing and silver working from the Spanish, while some Apache groups took up aspects of nomadic plains cultures, such as the *tipi* and hunting buffalo on horseback, and copied cattle raising from Spaniards and Americans.

The California-intermountain cultural area included the barren territory around the Colorado plateau and most of California. The nomadic hunters and gatherers that lived here were likely materially the poorest of the continent's native cultures. On the other hand, their loosely organized family bands win praise for their democratic political traditions and peaceful way of life.

The plentiful nature available to the coastal cultures from northern California to southern Alaska made them a stark contrast to highland cultures of the nearby inland areas. Among the most advanced groups of related cultures north of Mexico, the Northwest peoples lived in coastal villages similar to independent city-states. Well supplied with wild plants and game, the Chinook, Tsimshian, Kwakiutl, Haida and Tlingit did not need to farm. Fishing for salmon represented their primary economic activity, but saltwater fishing and whaling were also important. They made long seagoing canoes and massive wooden lodges, decorating these, as well as household items and totem poles, with symbolic carvings. These peoples of plenty traditionally practiced the *potlatch*, several days of feasting during which a leading family gave its guests extravagant gifts. The family demonstrated its wealth through the richness of its generosity, and the guests' degree of satisfaction determined their hosts' prestige in the community. The Northwest coastal peoples were among the few non-agricultural societies to practice slavery, which was common in Native American farming cultures.

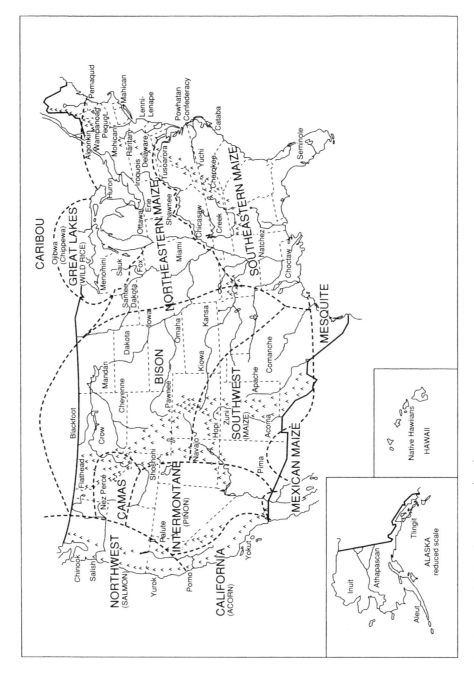

FIGURE 2.3 Native American cultural regions.

PLATE 2.6 In late 2016, Native American tribal members marched to celebrate the easement denial of the Dakota Access Pipeline in Canon Ball, North Dakota. The US Army Corps of Engineers decided not to grant a necessary permit to allow the pipeline to cross under the Missouri river just outside of the Lakota Sioux reservation of Standing Rock, North Dakota. Over two hundred tribes, joined by environmental activists and hundreds of United States military veterans, camped and demonstrated against the route for the pipeline. The gathering was the largest meeting of Native Americans since the Little Bighorn camp in 1876. Their victory was short lived, however. Within weeks of taking office, President Donald J. Trump reversed the decision of the Corps of Engineers, allowing the pipeline construction near the reservation to continue.
© *Anadolu Agency/Getty*

The various Inuit groups (including the Aleuts) are the native peoples of Alaska and the Aleutian Islands. The coastal peoples are skilled sea-hunters, while the inland cultures base their livelihood on hunting big game. The stereotype of the "Eskimo" as a nomadic sea-hunter living in an igloo comes from the Inuit culture of far north Canada. The Inuit of Alaska are settled villagers who build underground sod-walled houses. Fast and efficient dog sledges and kayaks made it possible for them to live in one place and supply themselves with food.

Indigenous Hawaiians gathered food from the tropical forests and terraced mountainsides and irrigated their fields to grow crops. Expert open-sea fishers from outrigger canoes, they also built semicircular fish ponds along the seashore. The priesthood, aristocracy and royal family owned most of the land, which was divided into strips that extended from a mountaintop to a distance under coastal waters to meet all the owners' needs. The common people lived in small areas where they had limited rights to fish, water, wood, wild foods and farming.

Cultural regions in the contemporary US

Political geography

Today's cultural regions result from varying mixtures of increasingly global antecedents, with Native American elements, at their most noticeable, representing one of several ingredients. The main American regions are much-used concepts for understanding subdivisions of American culture and society. Still, US regions tend to be less distinct than those in older, more demographically stable countries. The high mobility of the American population adds to the homogenizing effects of popular mass culture, modern transportation, urbanization, the centralization of the economy and government, and the rapid spread of information through mass and social media.

The Northeast

The Northeast often seems to be one unit when viewed from other sections of the country. Stretching from Maine, south through Maryland and west to the border of Ohio, the whole region is known as densely populated, highly urban and suffering from becoming post-industrial (changing from older heavy industry to a high-tech service economy). In fact, the Northeast is arguably still the nation's economic and cultural center, and is made of two regions (New England and the Mid-Atlantic) rather than one.

New England has two distinct parts. Southern New England (Massachusetts, Connecticut and Rhode Island) has long had a cultural importance out of proportion to its size, natural resources and population. Massachusetts received a very large number of early colonists from Britain and rapidly developed stable institutions, cohesive communities and an expanding population that strongly influenced the rest of New England and the northern half of the country during the eighteenth and nineteenth centuries.

Americans trace several aspects of the nation's traditional core culture to southern New England. Over time, the original settlers' goal of founding a model religious community became a generalized concept of "American exceptionalism," a belief that the nation has a special mission and ability to set an example for the rest of the world. The region supposedly also bequeathed the country a belief in the so-called Puritan work ethic, the faith that hard work and good morals bring rewards in this world and the next. In the mid-nineteenth century, New England authors such as Ralph Waldo Emerson expressed central values taught for more than a century in US schools as the foundation of the entire nation's culture. In the schools' popularized version, the American creed was an optimistic individualism expressed in introspective self-reliance and self-improvement, thrift, hard work and a belief in progress.

In the 1800s, New England Yankees became famous for their economic ingenuity as traveling peddlers, clipper-ship captains and mill owners. The fall line near the coast, by providing cheap waterpower close to trade routes, made the region the cradle of American industry. When industry converted to steam and electricity, the region lost manufacturing jobs to other parts of the country. One of New England's greatest strengths in its economic competition with other regions today is its concentration of quality institutions of higher education and research. New England is now a leader in innovative business methods, publishing and high-technology industries. The region's tourist industry flourishes because of its scenic qualities and status as a repository of the nation's history.

Northern New England (Maine, Vermont and most of New Hampshire) has long had a distinctive socioeconomic character. Less densely populated land industrialized, it won admiration for beautiful woodland mountain areas and abundant wildlife. Extensive logging and lumber industries have not changed that. Maine's fishing and seafood business has risen to global prominence. Recently, New England's north has developed a lucrative industry providing summer cottages and second homes for people who want to escape East Coast cities. Immigration of French Canadians has given some areas a unique population profile and strong bonds to Quebec. Politically, these three states have a strong tradition of support for independent candidates, such as Bernie Sanders, and political reforms, such as Maine's implementation of proportional representation in the choice of delegates to the Electoral College in presidential elections.

With a larger, more varied population, better soil and a greater share of natural resources, the Mid-Atlantic region surpassed New England in trade and manufacturing during the 1700s. During the next century, these advantages helped the Mid-Atlantic region grow into the nation's commercial-industrial hub. Its harbors became the country's premier port cities, and here too the fall line provided cheap waterpower. The Mid-Atlantic also has passages through the Appalachian Mountains. First roads, then canals and later railroads followed these east–west routes as they opened western New York, Pennsylvania and the Great Lakes states to settlement and carried farm products to the coastal cities of the Mid-Atlantic. The Erie Canal, joining Lake Erie with New York City, made the cost of shipping a ton of freight from the lake to the city nearly 24 times cheaper, and thus the pattern of transportation down the inland rivers to New Orleans rapidly shifted toward New York, which became the nation's largest and wealthiest city.

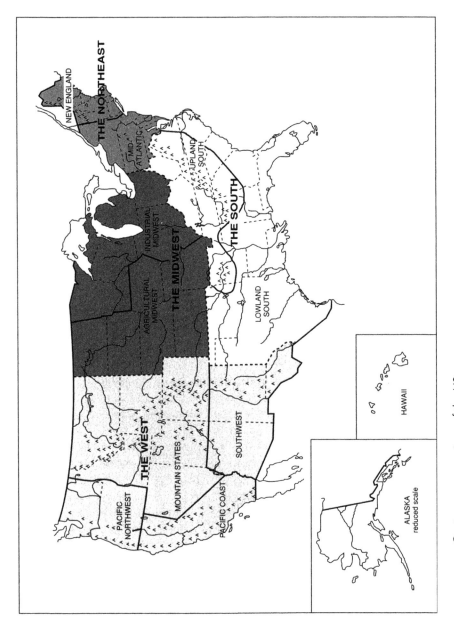

FIGURE 2.4 Contemporary regions of the US.

By the later 1800s, transportation and trade welded together New England, the Mid-Atlantic region and the big cities of the Great Lakes and inland rivers. This urban industrial core attracted people to jobs in a variety of "smokestack" industries. Although it includes agricultural areas, the distinguishing aspect of the core is still the size and closeness of its racially and ethnically mixed industrial cities. They contain many Latino and Asian groups as well today, but in popular opinion, Boston seems Irish and Italian, Buffalo is Polish, and New York City mostly Jewish, Italian, African, Asian and Caribbean. By the 1970s, the migration of heavy industries abroad and "high-tech" companies to the South and West resulted in the core being rechristened the "Rust Belt." Like New England, this region has had to develop new jobs, diversify its economy and recruit employers with tax breaks and social services. The economic tug of war between the regions continues, and the South and West still attract more jobs and people than the urban core.

The South

Traditionally, this region includes the 11 states from Virginia to Texas that formed the Confederacy during the Civil War. In addition, the "border states" from West Virginia to Oklahoma are arguably Southern. Far from homogeneous, the South has two sub-regions, the lowland South on the Coastal Plain and the upland South in the Piedmont, southern Appalachians and Ozarks. The lowland South's diversity includes the Creole and Cajun areas of Louisiana and the Caribbean–African influenced Sea Islands off the Atlantic coast. Many observers argue that much of the South, rural and urban, has lost a great deal of its traditional character because of economic transformation and migration from other parts of the nation and abroad.

The distinctiveness of the Southern lowland developed with the earliest settlement along the Atlantic coast. The first colonists, Englishmen who came for economic rather than religious or political reasons, did not find the gold and silver that Spanish discoveries made them dream about, but the climate and soil proved suitable for growing and exporting cash crops, such as tobacco and cotton, that required much manual labor but offered huge profits. Soon estates larger than the family farm (called plantations) became common and resulted in dispersed settlement with a few small urban centers. To meet the need for fieldworkers, plantation-owners imported white indentured servants (people who sold themselves into virtual slavery for four to seven years to pay for their passage to North America). By the late 1600s, however, planters turned to Africans sold into permanent slavery for labor. African slavery existed in all the American colonies, but became the main source of workers only in the plantation South.

As late as the 1830s, a proposal to end slavery failed by only one vote in the Virginia legislature. Cheap fertile land to the west, improved machinery for harvesting cotton and high prices for the crop from Northern and British textile mills made cotton the backbone of the early Industrial Revolution. This development confirmed the contrasts between the industrializing North and the slave-dependent South that led to the Civil War. The need to justify slavery and the shared memories of secession, war, defeat and occupation by Union armies reinforced Southerners' regional ties. Although slavery ended with the Civil War, cotton remained the region's main cash crop into the 1930s, and most African Americans remained dependent on their former masters for work and a place to live.

Agriculture is still important, but today the region's products are much more varied. Industry moved south because of low energy and labor costs and natural resources such as iron ore, bauxite, oil, gas and vast pine forests. An increasingly urban-industrial South forms the eastern arm of the so-called "Sunbelt," a swath of the southern and southwestern US that attracts financial, high-tech and media industries to growing population centers from Atlanta, Georgia, to Dallas, Texas. Since the Civil Rights laws and voter registration drives of the 1960s, the important roles of African Americans in public life and their support for the Democratic Party have driven most conservative white Americans to the Republicans, making the South a two-party region for the first time in a century. In response to these changes, African Americans' migration out of the region reversed in the late 1900s. The rapidly growing Latino population further complicates the picture by voting largely as Democrats. Still, surveys indicate that Southerners as a whole remain less educated, more religious, more conservative and more predominantly old-stock American than the population of the other regions.

The Midwest

The Midwest includes the states bordering the Great Lakes and two tiers of states west of the Mississippi river from Missouri and Kansas north to Canada. The Great Lakes states, with their many manufacturing centers, are the industrial Midwest, although they are also important farm states. In similar fashion, the two Western tiers of states are the agricultural Midwest, in spite of industrial cities, such as St. Louis and Minneapolis. In the national consciousness, the Midwest remains one region: the somewhat outdated picture of an American heartland of family farms and small towns, perhaps naïvely provincial and optimistic, but still the moral and social center that mediates between the other regions.

The early routes of Western migration through the Appalachians met in the Great Lakes states, making them the first place where the cultures of New England, the Mid-Atlantic and the South combined. By 1860, the Great Lakes Midwest depended on the markets of the Northeast, and during the Civil War, it gained a proud sense of its identity from having sacrificed men and wealth for the preservation of the Union. After the war, steel-plated ploughs tore up the deep-rooted buffalo grass of the prairies and Great Plains, turning them into farmland and completing the settlement of the trans-Mississippi agricultural Midwest. In the 1900s, machinery and new strains of winter wheat made these areas some of the most productive farmland in the world. Eventually this same technology rendered the American ideal of the independent small farmer obsolete, as "agribusinesses" replaced the family farm.

In recent decades, Midwestern industrial cities have made great strides toward economic and environmental recovery, despite persistent problems with the loss of manufacturing jobs, slums and urban blight that follow in the wake of deindustrialization. Today, Indianapolis, Pittsburgh, Cleveland and St. Louis, for example, can boast about glamorous downtown convention centers, museums and resurgent industries that no longer pollute the air and water. Chicago, the national hub of the commodities market, an important international seaport, and the home of widely diversified industry and cultural institutions, remains the region's premier city.

Midwestern political traditions show a mixture of pragmatic caution and organized protest. While the region has the reputation of being conservative, it was the birthplace of the Republican Party, which opposed the spread of slavery and nominated Lincoln for the presidency. Later, the agricultural Midwest was home to the Populist and Farmer-Labor parties, which protested the economic domination of the Northeast, and a center of the Progressive Movement, which strove to make American governments more honest, efficient and democratic. Midwestern states, such as Minnesota and Wisconsin, have since then been leaders in social and environmental reform. The region's population grows increasingly diverse due to arrivals from Africa, Asia and Latin America.

The West

"The West" is a myth, a popular set of values, and a region of the country. It represents possibility, freedom, self-reliance, and the future. As a region, it has three parts: the Southwest, the mountain states, and the Pacific coast. The Southwest consists of New Mexico, Arizona and parts of surrounding states with a similar climate and culture. Seized during the Mexican–American War of 1848, this area now has a mixture of old, unusually strong Spanish–Mexican and Native American communities – and a blend of people from many parts of the country and world who came in large numbers after 1945. Today cattle- and sheep-ranching are important for the economy, but dams on the major rivers and wells have transformed deserts into irrigated farmlands and metropolitan areas, such as Phoenix and Albuquerque. The warm, dry climate has proven attractive to retirees and people with respiratory ailments, as well as to electronics and aerospace companies. Mining, the petroleum industry and tourism in the Southwest's stunning national parks are also important economic supports.

The federal government is the largest landowner in the Southwest and even more clearly dominates the economy of the mountain states. The importance of its decisions about the leasing of federal lands becomes obvious when one learns that the government owns more than four-fifths of Nevada, two-thirds of Utah and vast areas of the sub-region's other states. In Colorado, for example, the national government owns 80 percent of the shale oil deposits. The lack of control over local resources increasingly frustrates traditionally independent long-time residents. Newcomers from other regions, environmentalists, business people, Native American groups and government officials now share in the debate about the use of resources. During World War II and the Cold War, the federal government used desert areas of the Southwest as test sites for a range of nuclear and conventional weapons with effects that are still the subject of heated debate. The population density is low but appears to be growing so rapidly that some Westerners think in-migration and development are nearing their acceptable limits.

Mining the mountains' mineral riches remains an economic mainstay. The mines brought the immigration, outside investment, transportation infrastructure and business that laid the financial foundation for urban areas such as Denver and Butte. Agriculture depends on ranching and forestry because other forms of farming require irrigation, and water rights have become as precious as rare metals. Las Vegas and Reno found wealth through the gambling and entertainment industries. Salt Lake City is the heart of the Mormon center in the Great Basin that is more homogeneous in population than any other cultural area in the US. Today it prospers by expertise in computer software and technology as well as by mining and irrigated agriculture.

European settlement of the Pacific coast began with the establishment of Spanish missions in California in the 1700s and included Russian and British domination of the Pacific Northwest before the US gained sovereignty over the area in the 1840s. The coastal territories attracted sizeable populations and qualified as states before the interior West because of the 1849 gold rush and reports of the lush greenness of the Oregon and Washington valleys. The San Francisco area was the first to experience rapid development because it was the port of entry for the gold rush "forty–niners." By the 1870s, the city became an industrial metropolis that successfully competed with imports from the East. Today the city is the hub of a larger area that includes Berkeley and its famous university, Oakland with its many industries, the Silicon Valley complex of computer firms, Stanford University and the Napa Valley wine district. Los Angeles has experienced rapid population growth ever since it became the terminus of a transcontinental railroad in 1885. The Los Angeles metropolis, a group of cities connected by a maze of superhighways, is home to the Hollywood film and media conglomerates as well as major energy, defense and aerospace companies. California's two largest urban areas contain every major racial and ethnic group in the nation, with especially large Asian and Latino elements. Politically, southern California has the reputation of being conservative while the northern part of the state is considered liberal.

In the Pacific Northwest, the population and culture show less Latino and more New England and northwest European influence, while Asian American groups are as prominent as they are farther south. During the past 30 years, so many people and businesses have relocated to Washington and Oregon that state authorities have attempted to limit growth. Their avowed goal is to preserve the environment and quality of life through a mixed economy based on agriculture, forestry and tourism, as well as on heavy and high-technology industries.

Resource and land-management are major issues in Hawaii and Alaska, as they are in the continental West. Hawaii's government instituted a detailed land-use system soon after it became a state in 1959. The law not only provided areas for commercial, industrial and residential building, but also protected farmland, nature reserves and tourist attractions. In the nineteenth century, settlers from the mainland recruited large numbers of Asians to work on plantations. But after 1900, when the islands became a US territory, these contract labor arrangements became illegal, and high immigration has resulted from better knowledge of the islands' attractions and easier transportation in the age of aviation. Today, the people are mostly urban and have a make-up that is unique in the nation. The majority is Asian American, with people of Japanese extraction comprising

PLATE 2.7 Vineyard in Napa Valley, California, one of the inland agricultural areas between the western arms of the Cordillera.
© *Cosmo Condina/Stock Connection/REX/Shutterstock*

the largest nationality group. Whites make up the largest minority, followed by smaller groups of Latinos, African Americans and native Polynesians.

The federal, state and Native American tribal governments own more than 99 percent of Alaska. Much of its history has involved struggles between resource-hungry developers, who lease land from government and create jobs for local residents, and conservationists, who lobby public authorities to restrict land-use because they view Alaska as the last chance to preserve an American wilderness.

Until Alaska won statehood in 1959, settlers and natives there subsisted primarily through fishing, hunting and logging. Except for the short-lived Klondike gold rush of 1898, the area seemed destined to prove right the skeptics who said the country had bought a ridiculously expensive Russian icebox containing only sealskins and salmon in 1867.

During the 1950s and 1960s, Alaska received a wave of immigrants who wanted to escape the congestion and pollution in the 48 contiguous states. At the end of the 1960s, oil strikes off the state's northern coast increased interest in developing this "empty" land. The negotiations over how to preserve the environment while profiting from the oil have been the most critical in Alaska's history. The huge amounts of land and money Native Americans received in compensation for oil lands gave them an entirely new status. The state profited so much that it replaced its income taxes with an annual oil dividend of about $1,000 per resident. To safeguard wildlife and the tundra, engineers insulated the trans-Alaska pipeline and lifted it several feet above ground.

Oil development produced mixed effects. The population grew rapidly, reaching more than half a million by 1990. The per-capita income for Alaskans is the highest in the nation, however, so is the state's unemployment rate. Much of Alaska's employment boom was temporary. In 1989, the supertanker *Exxon Valdez* ran aground and spilled millions of gallons of oil on Alaska's coasts. Clean-up efforts united environmentalists, the fishing and tourist industries, Native American organizations and ordinary citizens. Still, because the nation's economy remains largely dependent on oil, the fleets of tankers plying local coasts seem likely to grow, especially if drilling begins in the Arctic National Wildlife Refuge.

Changing public attitudes: where do we go from here?

Complex distributional and environmental issues continue to involve Americans in many-sided debates over the development and preservation of natural resources. The most prominent of these centers on the nation's management of its energy supplies. Energy independence for the nation seems achieved, according to some commentators. On the other hand, Americans remain doubtful that this situation is sustainable, given accelerating energy consumption, as well as the publicity about negative side effects of fracking and other new methods of extracting fossil fuel supplies. Oil and gas prices have plummeted in recent years, which reduces fuel costs for industry and consumers but simultaneously renders new methods of oil production unprofitable.

Few Americans are ready to give up modern lifestyles and technology, but many have understood that the quality of life in the future is dependent on reconciling environmental and pro-development interests to manage the nation's natural resources wisely. An increasing portion of those polled in opinion surveys think greater production is more important than conservation for the nation's energy situation. Detroit automakers' "gas guzzling" sports utility vehicles are still hugely popular, even though hybrid and electrically powered vehicle sales have soared. Politicians in Congress and the states have therefore mostly made political gestures, not followed through on major proposals and, as a Gallup report put it, have tried "to avoid alienating either side of the energy versus environment debate." During the 2016 election cycle, the Green Party candidate for president, Jill Klein, averaged only four percent in the polls of likely voters, where she was on the ballot, in early November of 2016. That was, however, ten times better than in 2012 when she won 0.4 percent of the popular vote.

Exercises

Explain and examine the significance of the following names and terms:

political ecology	attitudes to energy use
National Park Service	the Southwest
fall line	Native American cultural regions
Appalachians	Northwest coastal cultures
Appalachia	Environmental Protection Agency
Central Lowland	Hawaiians
glacial moraine	attitudes toward land
Great Plains	the Northeast
urban industrial core	global warming

Write short essays on the following questions.

1. Outline the main physical features of the US, describing the country's most important natural resources and commenting on the environmental cost of their use.

2. Discuss the causes of differences between Native-American and contemporary American cultural geography.

3. Investigate and comment on the development of energy sources in the US.

Further reading

Statistical Abstract of the United States, US Printing Office, annual.

The World Almanac and Book of Facts (2012), New York: World Almanac Books.

Time, weekly magazine.

US Bureau of the Census, occasional series and reports.

Grisham, J. (2015) *Grey Mountain,* London: Hodder and Stoughton. A best-selling thriller based on environmentally disastrous methods of extracting deep veins of coal in the Appalachian Mountains.

Websites

www.pollingreport.com/energy.htm

The National Park Service: www.nps.gov

The United States Geological Survey: www.usgs.gov

The United States Environmental Protection Agency: www.epa.gov

The federal commission on the Deep Horizon Oil Spill: www.oilspillcommission.gov

American environmental laws and regulations: www.epa.gov/epahome/lawregs.htm

Geographical and environmental information from the federal government: www.firstgov.gov

Chapter 3

The people
Settlement and immigration

- Mother of exiles
- Early encounters between Europeans and Native Americans
- The founders
- The first wave: colonial immigration, 1680–1776
- The second wave: the "old" immigrants, 1820–90
- Settlement patterns and nativism
- The third wave: the "new" immigrants, 1890–1930
- A renewed immigration debate and immigration restriction
- Wartime policies and the search for principle in immigration policy
- The fourth wave: 1965 to the present
- Attitudes to immigrants: the contemporary debate
- *Exercises*
- *Further reading*
- *Websites*

Mother of exiles

Immigration is a central aspect of US history. It is a major reason that the nation's total population grew to more than 325 million by 2016. Believing in the American dream, many tens of millions of people have come to live in the US. They thus changed their homelands, America and their family histories forever. They strengthened the nation's commitment to "the dream" and to its ideal of being a refuge for the poor and oppressed, a nation of nations. Gradually, over the centuries of massive immigration and the struggles of newcomers and Americans to adjust to each other, the view that the nature of the nation was and *should be* a composite of many national backgrounds, races and cultures gained popular acceptance.

This pluralistic view continues to face opposition. In 2016, Donald Trump made his promise to build a Great Southern Wall against immigrants a major part of his presidential campaign. Resistance to pluralism comes from several quarters: from those opposed to the presence of an estimated 11 million undocumented immigrants, those who believe the country is becoming "Latinized" and that newcomers should leave their homeland cultures behind, from people who feel that newcomers take "our" jobs, and those convinced that the latest wave of immigration necessitates a focus on cohesion.

Americans' (and the immigrants') core idealism, pride and naivety are embodied in Emma Lazarus' sonnet "The New Colossus," which is displayed inside the base of the Statue of Liberty (see Plate 3.1). There is some truth to the dream. Settled peoples have been able to climb a "ladder of ethnic succession" as new waves of immigrants arrive. For most of the foreign-born, life in the US has meant an improvement over their situation in the "old country," the realization of modest hopes for land or homeownership, for example. Later generations have enjoyed more progress, although "rags to riches" careers are rare indeed. Americans and newcomers to the US continue to debate and disagree strongly over the message in Emma Lazarus's poem.

"The New Colossus"

Not like the brazen giant of Greek fame,
With conquering limbs astride from land to land;
Here at our sea-washed, sunset gates shall stand
A mighty woman with a torch, whose flame

Is the imprisoned lightning, and her name
Mother of Exiles. From her beacon hand
Glows world-wide welcome: her mild eyes command
The air-bridged harbor that twin cities frame.
"Keep ancient lands, your storied pomp!" cries she
With silent lips. "Give me your tired, your poor,
Your huddled masses yearning to breathe free,
The wretched refuse of your teeming shore.
Send these, the homeless, tempest-tost, to me,
I lift my lamp beside the golden door!"

However, the meetings of newcomers and native-born have also contributed to America's history of social disorder. The contacts, conflicts and mixing of cultures have fueled widespread discrimination, economic exploitation, anti-foreign movements and debates over equality, opportunity and national identity. In a country whose history began with the meeting of Native Americans and European colonists and continued through the importation of African slaves and several waves of immigrants, there has never been a single national culture, although for centuries a majority of Anglo-Americans made vigorous efforts to establish one.

The search continues for a metaphor that captures the character of American society. Is it best understood as an Anglo-American core culture to which newcomers eventually merge into as they assimilate? On the other hand, should it be some form of cultural pluralism as suggested by, among other images, the metaphors of a "melting pot," a "salad" or a "stew"? Who, moreover, is to decide who is included or excluded from these mixtures? Some commentators reject both the claims of a unitary culture and of cultural pluralism, preferring instead forms of multiculturalism, in which multiple traditions are the ideal, and no cultural group, however old or influential historically, receives priority. Americans disagree over the nature of the process and what the ultimate goal should be: the integration, assimilation, even homogenization of newcomers, or the acceptance of a permanently pluralistic society.

Early encounters between Europeans and Native Americans

When European explorers and settlers encountered Native Americans in the late 1400s, a long history of mutual incomprehension and conflict began. These encounters amounted to a collision of worlds. Contacts between the Americas and other continents had been so rare that plants, animals, diseases and human societies evolved into different forms in the "new" and the "old" worlds. Europeans and Native Americans caught diseases from each other. Europeans survived

PLATE 3.1 Profile of the Statue of Liberty in New York Harbor against the sunset.
© *JIAN CHEN/REX/Shutterstock*

the first contacts better, but for most of the seventeenth century, well over half of them died from difficulties in adjusting to the new environment. The Native Americans fared far worse. Epidemics annihilated entire native cultures. North America's pre-Columbian population of 10 million shrank to between 2 and 3 million. The exchange of plants and animals had effects that were just as far-reaching. Horses, donkeys, sheep, pigs and cows were alien creatures to Native Americans. Potatoes, maize and tobacco were discoveries to Europeans. The potato played a key role in the great population growth that brought millions of European and smaller numbers of Asian immigrants to the US in the 1800s.

European societies were so diverse that Spaniards and the English could hardly imagine living in the same place in peace. Some Native American cultures viewed other indigenous peoples with a dislike no less intense. Yet, each continent's diversity of cultures were related, even quite similar in broad outline, when compared with cultures from the other continent. Thus, all Europeans tended to look alike to Native Americans, and most Europeans seemed incapable of seeing Native Americans as anything but a single people. To Europeans, Native Americans seemed lazy and wasteful of nature's potential. Viewing time as fluid, they had only vague concepts of the past and the future, and so seemed utterly unreliable. Because they viewed nature as a great mother, they could not comprehend how people could sell or own pieces of her. From the first European settlement until today, the focus in conflicts between these continental culture systems has been landownership.

The founders

The settlers who established the colonies are considered founders rather than immigrants because they created the customs, laws and institutions to which later arrivals (the first immigrants) had to adjust. The Spanish occupied coastal Florida, the Southwest and California in the 1500s and 1600s. The French traded with Native Americans along North America's inland rivers for animal furs in the later 1500s and set up riverside trading posts by the early 1600s. The English established their first permanent settlement at Jamestown, Virginia in 1607. Their monarch had no desire to rule distant colonies, so instead the Crown legalized companies that undertook the colonization of America as private commercial enterprises. Virginia's early residents were so preoccupied with a vain search for gold and a sea passage to Asian markets that the colony floundered until tobacco provided a profitable export. Because of the scarcity of plantation labor, in 1619 colonists imported the first African laborers as indentured servants (free people who contracted for five to seven years of servitude). Supported by tobacco profits, however, Virginia imported 1,500 free laborers a year by the 1680s and had a population of 75,000 white Americans and 10,000 Africans in hereditary slavery by 1700.

In the 1630s, Lord Baltimore established Maryland as a haven for Catholics, England's most persecuted minority. Maryland's leadership remained Catholic for some time, but its economy and population soon resembled Virginia's. In the 1660s, other English aristocrats financed Georgia and the Carolinas as commercial investments and experiments in social organization. Within a generation, these colonies too resembled Virginia, but their cash crops were rice and indigo. The Southern settlers warred with the natives within a few years of their arrival and by the 1830s drove the Native Americans from today's South.

To escape religious oppression in England, the Pilgrims, a small group of radical separatists from the Church of England, founded the first of the Northern colonies in 1620 at Plymouth, Massachusetts. The Puritans, who established the much larger Massachusetts Bay colony in 1630, wanted to purify the Church of England, not separate from it. Mostly well-educated middle-class people, they believed they could create a "city on a hill" in America to show how English society could be reformed. To that end, more than 20,000 emigrated in around ten years. By the latter 1600s, the bay colony had expanded to the coast of present-day Maine, swallowed up Plymouth, and spawned the colony of Connecticut. Flourishing through agriculture and forestry, the New England colonies also became the shippers and merchants for all of British America. Because of their intolerance toward dissenters and other religious groups, the Puritans' New England became the most homogeneous region in the colonies.

The founding of the middle colonies (New York, New Jersey and Pennsylvania) was distinctive. The earliest European communities here were Dutch and Swedish outposts of the fur trade that almost accidentally grew into colonies. New Netherlands, along the Hudson river and New York Bay, and New Sweden, along the Delaware river, recruited soldiers, farmers, craftsmen, clergymen and their families to meet the needs of the fur traders who bought pelts from the natives. New Sweden lasted from 1638 to 1655, when the Dutch annexed it.

New Netherlands itself fell to the English fleet in 1664. The Dutch maintained their culture in rural New York and New Jersey for more than 200 years. They also set the precedent of toleration for many ethnic, racial and religious groups in New Amsterdam. Although the dominant culture in colonial New York and New Jersey became English by the end of the 1600s, the English authorities continued the tolerant traditions of the Dutch.

Pennsylvania's founders were Quakers who flocked to the colony after Charles II granted the area to William Penn, an aristocratic Quaker, in 1681 as a religious refuge. As with the Pilgrims and Puritans, official English tolerance for Quakers took the form of allowing them to emigrate. Penn's publicizing of cheap land and religious freedom brought thousands of people to the colony before 1690. His toleration attracted a population whose diversity was matched only by New York's.

PLATE 3.2 King Powhatan orders the execution of the English adventurer John Smith (1580–1631) while the king's daughter Pocahontas begs for his life. Engraving from Smith's 'Generall Historie of Virginia, New England & the Summer Isles,' 1624.
© *Private Collection/Peter Newark Pictures/Bridgeman Images*

The first wave: colonial immigration, 1680–1776

The founders came for economic gain and religious freedom, but their descendants gave the first large wave of European newcomers a warm welcome only if they were willing to conform to Anglo-American culture and supply needed labor. The reception that immigrants received varied according to location from the extremes of largely hostile New England, to the more tolerant, diverse middle colonies. It was with mixed rural New York settlements of northwest Europeans in mind that St. Jean de Crévecoeur, an immigrant farmer from France, first stated in 1782 the idea that in America "individuals of all nations are melted into a new race of man." The only people who mixed in his vision, however, were northwest Europeans, and he required that the people in this first version of the melting pot had to turn their backs on their homeland cultures. Like colonists everywhere at the time, he thought that the white people along the wilderness frontier, like the Native Americans, soon descended into savage barbarism. He tolerated them mostly because they provided a protection against the natives.

Although conditions in their homelands also played a decisive role, this first wave was possible only because after 1660, the Crown opposed emigration from England and Wales but encouraged it from other nations. In 1662, King Charles II licensed the Royal African Company as the supplier of slaves to English colonies, and during the next century, about 140,000 Africans arrived after surviving the appalling conditions and brutal treatment on slave ships.

The largest group of immigrants (voluntary newcomers) was the Scots-Irish. With encouragement from the English, their ancestors left Scotland for Northern Ireland in the 1500s. They left Northern Ireland after 1680 because of economic discrimination by the English. Most paid their passage across the Atlantic by becoming indentured servants (contracting to labor without wages for four to seven years in the colonies). When their service was finished, most took their "freedom dues" (a small sum of money and tools) and settled on cheap frontier land. Constantly looking for better land, the Scots-Irish are the source of the stereotype of frontier folk, who often move if they can see the smoke from a neighbor's chimney. This westward migration scattered their settlements from western New England to the hill country of Georgia and made it difficult to preserve their cultural heritage.

The period's 200,000 German immigrants aroused more opposition than the Scots-Irish. The largest non-English speaking group in the colonies, they believed their descendants had to learn German if their religion and culture were to survive. For mutual support, they concentrated their settlements. In the middle colonies, German families lived so closely together in some areas that others found it hard to settle among them. Like the Scots-Irish, the Germans lived on the frontier, but they usually stayed behind when settlement moved farther west. Developing German-speaking towns, they kept to themselves and showed little interest in colonial politics. For some, the last straw was the Germans' prosperity. Benjamin Franklin expressed what many feared when he said they might "Germanize us instead of us Anglicizing them." In a period so near the religious wars of the Reformation, the reception Germans met also varied according to whether they were non-conformists, Lutherans or Catholics.

Other smaller groups in this wave showed contrasting ways that immigrants could adjust to new and varied conditions. England sent some 50,000 convicts and perhaps 30,000 poor people as indentured servants to ease problems at home while supplying the labor-starved colonial economy. These people formed an underclass that quickly Americanized. Immigration from Ireland included thousands of single Catholic male servants, who assimilated even more rapidly than the Scots-Irish did because of religious discrimination and the difficulty of finding Catholic wives. The Scots, perhaps because of their hatred of English attempts to suppress their culture at home, followed a pattern more like that of the Germans, using compact settlement, religion, schooling, and family networks to preserve their culture. A Catholic French enclave persisted in South Carolina, but the French Huguenots and Jews, who settled in ports, illustrated a contrasting tendency. English colonists severely limited their civil rights and sometimes attacked their churches or synagogues, but they accepted marriage with them as long as they changed their religion. As a result, their communities nearly vanished.

This first wave of immigration transformed the demography of the colonies. By 1776, English dominance had decreased from four-fifths to a bare majority (52 percent) of the population. The great diversity of the peoples in the country led Thomas Paine, the colonies' most famous political agitator, to call the US a "nation of nations" at its founding. African American slaves composed 20 percent of the population and were a majority in large parts of the southern colonies. The colonists had forced most Native American cultures inland to the Appalachians or beyond. Non-English peoples were a majority in most coastal towns, Pennsylvania, the South and parts of all the other colonies. The dominance of Anglo-Americans remained clear, but the first wave had played a major role in bequeathing America a tradition of pioneers on the frontier, a vision of itself as diverse, religious tolerance, and a federal system of government that left most power with 13 quite dissimilar states.

The second wave: the "old" immigrants, 1820–1890

Between 1776 and the late 1820s, immigration slowed to a trickle. The war for independence and founding of the nation Americanized the colonies' diverse peoples. Anglo-American culture and time weakened the old ethnic communities. Dutch and German areas of influence remained locally strong, but most ethnic groups assimilated. In the 1820s, Americans and newcomers therefore thought the situation was unprecedented when the second wave gathered strength.

A range of factors pushed Europeans from their homelands. Religious persecution drove German Jews to emigrate, and political unrest forced out some European intellectuals and political activists, but economic push factors were decisive for most of the so-called "old" northwestern immigrants. Europe's population doubled between 1750 and 1850. In Ireland and parts of Germany rural people depended on the potato, which yielded more food per acre than grain. The rapid growth of cities encouraged farmers to switch to large-scale production based on farm machinery, eliminate smallholdings and enclose common lands. With these changes, the growing population could not make a living in the countryside. As early immigrants wrote home about their experiences in the US, the alternative of solving problems by immigrating to places where friends and relatives settled became commonplace and emigration soared.

During the 1800s, the industrial revolution and an international trade boom spread from Britain to the Continent and the US, but it reached different regions at different times. If nearby cities offered work, emigration rates were lower. But the population surplus from the countryside was so large that huge numbers of people left anyway. Stage migration (moving first to the city and, after some years, from there to a foreign country) became common. Following changes in the Atlantic labor market, people moved to where the jobs were. Steamships and trains made migration abroad safer, faster and cheaper. "America letters" from family and friends in the US gave a remarkably accurate picture of economic conditions there. During the "old" immigration, 15.5 million made America home.

The largest immigrant groups, in order of size, were Germans, Irish, Britons and Scandinavians, but many other peoples, including French Canadians, Chinese, Swiss and Dutch came in large numbers. The factor that pulled most people to the US was an apparently unlimited supply of land. Few seriously considered the claims of Native Americans. Another pull factor was work. The US needed both skilled and unskilled labor. American railroad companies, as well as state and territorial governments, sent immigration agents to Europe to recruit people with promises of cheap fertile farms or jobs with wages much higher than they could earn at home. News of boom times in the US, land giveaways, such as the Homestead Act of 1862, and the discovery of gold in California brought peaks in the rising immigration.

Settlement patterns and nativism

While the newcomers settled everywhere, they were most numerous in the manufacturing centers of the Northeast and the recently settled farmlands and frontier cities of the Midwest and Pacific coast. Immigrants found many economic niches, supplying the market for domestic servants, mill and factory workers, miners, loggers, sailors, fishermen and building workers. Most came with funds to travel to countrymen who could help them adjust to American society, but after potato rot ruined the crop that supported Ireland's rural population, huge numbers of Irish immigrants arrived in the 1840s and 1850s with so little money that they initially stayed where they landed.

British immigrants seemed nearly invisible because they spoke English and the Anglo-American culture was much like theirs. White and Protestant, Scandinavians had language problems that made them seem slow to comprehend, and at times they were ridiculed for their homeland ways. Nativism (the dislike of people and things foreign) plagued many "old" immigrants, in spite of their apparent similarity to native-born Americans. Germans were welcomed for their technical knowledge and industry and admired for a culture that was Europe's most respected at that time. But they were also stereotyped as Prussian marionettes or Bavarian louts, criticized for clannishness and became the targets of temperance movements that attacked their habit of drinking in beer halls after church on Sundays. Anglo-Americans excluded German Jews from education and professions and shunned them in many social circles.

The Irish suffered many forms of discrimination. Many Americans stereotyped them as dirty, violent drunks. The most serious opposition they faced, however, came from anti-Catholic bigots, who burned convents and churches as early as the 1830s. All the large immigrant groups found themselves involved in controversies over the control and content of the public schools, but none were so critical of the schools' attempts to Americanize immigrant children as the Irish (usually through the reactions of Irish-American priests).

Anti-foreign agitation reached its first peak in the 1850s. Along with anti-Catholicism, this nativism focused on popular versions of ideas made famous by Alexis de Tocqueville's *Democracy in America*, which claimed that the basic social and political character of the US came to New England from the mother country. The Know Nothing or American Party believed that not only the Irish, with their alleged loyalty to the Pope in Rome, but also all non-British immigrants, threatened this precious heritage, and so they proposed tripling the time needed to gain US citizenship and restricting immigrants' voting rights. On that platform, Know Nothings won dozens of seats in Congress and numerous state and local offices, especially in the Northeast. Internal divisions and the coming of the Civil War defused this nativist movement. Another arose in the 1860s in the West and achieved its goal, the Chinese Exclusion Act, which ended Chinese immigration in 1882. Racism and the fear of unemployment and lower wages motivated the labor organizations that lead the campaign.

The third wave: the "new" immigrants, 1890–1930

The "new" immigration marked a change in the origin of most immigrants. Around 1890 immigration from northwestern Europe declined sharply (but did not stop), while arrivals from southern and eastern Europe rose. By 1907, four out of five newcomers were "new" immigrants. Between 1890 and 1914, the volume of immigration also soared, topping a million annually several times and equaling the 15.5 million of the old immigration in just 24 years. In numerical order, the largest "new" groups were Italians, Jews, Poles and Hungarians, but many Mexicans, Russians, Czechs, Greeks, Portuguese, Syrians, Japanese, Filipinos and others immigrated.

To most Americans, the change mostly involved the feeling that the typical immigrant had become much less like them. The religions, languages, manners and dress of the Slavic and Asian peoples seemed exotic or incomprehensible. This tidal wave of people was, however, similar to its predecessors. The economic push and pull factors had not changed. The new immigrants had the same dream of bettering their own and their children's future. Like the Puritans, European Jews emigrated because of religious persecution, chiefly the bloody Russian pogroms.

By the late 1800s, falling train and steamship ticket prices (often prepaid by relatives in America) made migration affordable even for the very poor and the young. Cheap travel also permitted people to see immigration as a short-term strategy, and many new immigrants were sojourners, "birds of passage," who stayed only long enough to save money to buy land or a small business in the old country. In general, the new immigrants were younger, more often single, and more likely to travel as individuals rather than in family groups. The opportunities in America had changed too. The closing of the frontier around 1890 signaled the end of the era of government land giveaways. Less than a quarter of the newcomers found employment in agriculture. The Japanese in California are the best example of those who succeeded by buying unwanted land and making it productive. Four-fifths of immigrants went where the jobs were, to the industries in the big cities of the Northeast and Midwest. America had an enormous need for factory workers, but due to mechanization, most jobs were unskilled and poorly paid.

A renewed immigration debate and immigration restriction

The size of the new immigration and the altered job market resulted in larger urban immigrant quarters than Americans had ever seen. Crime, overcrowding, unsanitary conditions and epidemics in immigrant ghettos caused alarm and reform before the Civil War. Now these problems seemed insurmountable, and many Americans became convinced that the more "exotic" foreigners could not be assimilated or even integrated into society. Reactions to the situation in the cities were various. Reformers established "settlement houses" and charities to help immigrants adjust, worked to Americanize them and fought for better housing and parks. Some thought that the ghettos were important buffer zones where immigrants could use their mother tongues and follow old-country traditions while gradually adjusting to the US. Others concluded that the ghettos proved that the government had to restrict immigration sharply.

In 1908, Israel Zangwill's play *The Melting Pot* popularized the idea that diverse groups in the US would eventually fuse many races and cultures through intermarriage and become a new people. To many native-born reformers, that was a radical version of the melting pot that they could not accept. To them the metaphor meant that the immigrants should conform to Anglo-American culture, for their own good. Nativists of the time could not imagine a greater calamity than such a melting pot "mongrelization" of the white race. An opposing, progressive view was that the US should be an example of what Horace Kallen called "cultural pluralism," the belief in diverse cultures united by loyalty to the same political and civic ideals. Still, pluralists had long split over the issue of race. The founding fathers, for example, made the national motto "*e pluribus unum*" (out of many, one), but in the Naturalization Act of 1790, they permitted only white foreigners to become citizens.

Restriction, even regulation of immigration, was slow to develop in the US, which encouraged immigration and, until 1875, only asked local authorities to count immigrants. Foreigners could become citizens in five years and vote as soon as they applied for citizenship. In 1891, the federal government took responsibility for regulating immigration and the next year opened Ellis Island, the famous screening depot for immigrants in New York Bay. Starting in 1910, the federal government operated a detention center to interrogate Asian immigrants before they entered the country through San Francisco Bay.

In the 1920s, those who believed the US could not successfully integrate so many immigrants won the passage of severely restrictive, racist immigration laws. The National Quota Acts represented the climax of a campaign for restriction that achieved its first result in 1875, when the federal government began a piecemeal listing of banned groups that, in time, included contract laborers, the Chinese, convicts, prostitutes, lunatics, idiots, paupers, polygamists, political radicals, the Japanese and illiterates.

The influence of eugenics, the pseudo-scientific racism of the early 1900s, which purported to prove the superiority of Anglo-Saxons over all other "races," was evident in this list and later legislation. So was the combination of First World War super-patriotism that demanded 100 percent Americanism, and the ideological insecurity that grew after the Russian Revolution of 1917. Finally in 1921, Congress passed the first general limitation on immigration, the Emergency Quota Act that drastically reduced the annual number of European newcomers to 358,000 (less than one-third of pre-war levels), and introduced nationality quotas. Each European nation's allotment of immigrant visas per year equaled 3 percent of the foreign-born in the US from that country at the federal census of 1910.

PLATE 3.3 The registration room at Ellis Island in New York Bay in 1912, where government officials decided on the eligibility of immigrants to enter the US (Underwood and Underwood). Immigrants had to identify themselves, name their sponsors in the US, pass a physical examination, and pay a head tax. The Quota Act of 1924 introduced new concepts that continue to set the rules for immigration today. Even now, law restricts entry to the country. It still defines immigrants as legal or illegal aliens, according to the numerical limits set for each sending country and how people cross US borders. To be a legal alien, each person must present documents such as a visa or a "green card" when entering or re-entering the US. Until 1965, the decision of whether people were legal or illegal depended on their "national origins" as a part of the "native" or "immigrant stock" that had accumulated in the US population by 1920. The government set a quota of visas for each country according to how large that national background had grown to be. The American residents counted to set the quotas included only Whites. The law excluded others and did not, therefore, include Native Americans, African Americans, Asians, or people of mixed racial background.
© *George Rinhart/Getty*

The dissatisfaction of restrictionists with this law revealed the groups they feared most: Asians and the new immigrants from Europe. In 1924, the Asian Exclusion Act ended all immigration from Asian nations, and a National Origins Quota Act reduced European nationality quotas to 2 percent. More important, it moved the census for counting the foreign-born of each group back to 1890, when only small numbers of "new" immigrants were in the US, so that their quotas became much smaller. The 1924 Act also introduced a new concept, national *origins* quotas. See Plate 3.3. In effect, the act cut the quotas for all European nations but the United Kingdom by one-half to two-thirds. In 1929, when the national origins quotas went into effect, Britain's was 65,361, while Italy's, for example, was 5,802 and Syria received the minimum of 100 visas. This Anglo-American definition of the national identity was the framework for immigration until 1965.

Wartime policies and the search for principle in immigration policy

Writing immigration law that functions as intended has proved difficult. The Quota Acts ended the new immigration, and arrivals of "old" immigrants fell sharply, but immigration from the United Kingdom also declined. Even the western European nations with much reduced quotas left those unfilled. Nor did Congress anticipate that arrivals from "non-quota" nations in the Western Hemisphere, such as Mexico and Puerto Rico, and entries from America's Asian colony in the Philippines would soar into the millions by 1960. Events defied governmental plans. The depression of the 1930s put a stop to mass immigration. Local authorities and "vigilantes" forcibly deported about half a million Mexican Americans, many of them US citizens, during the decade. Nazi and fascist regimes caused an enormous flow of refugees, 250,000 of whom Congress admitted as non-quota immigrants under special laws. The US turned away many more, including 20,000 Jewish children, because the government was unwilling to put aside national origins quotas during a time of high unemployment and rising anti-Semitism.

The Second World War and the Cold War caused several contrasting shifts in policy. The government imported temporary farm labor from Mexico under the "*bracero* program" due to wartime labor shortages and lifted the ban on immigration from China because it became an America ally. Yet President Franklin Roosevelt also bowed to panicky racists on the West Coast, who feared foreign spies, and confined 115,000 Japanese Americans in "internment camps," after confiscating most of their property. After the war, federal law provided for the entry of families formed by US service people abroad. In addition, acts of Congress admitted several hundred thousand displaced persons (those so uprooted by the war that they had no homes to return to). Between 1948 and 1959, Cold War refugees from communist countries, such as Hungary and Cuba, also came. The total of non-quota immigrants for those years reached 750,000, which made a mockery of the idea of regulating immigration according to national origins quotas.

Moreover, during the Cold War, when the US competed with the USSR for the allegiance of non-aligned nations, the racist principles underlying the quotas were a foreign policy embarrassment. In 1952, the McCarran–Walter

Act stated that race was no longer a reason for refusing someone an immigrant visa. Instead, it started the so-called "brain-drain" to the US by reserving the first 50 percent of visas for each country for people with needed skills. However, the law kept the national origins principle, gave many Third World countries tiny quotas, and made communist or socialist associations a bar to immigration. Pressure grew for an entirely new approach.

The Immigration Act of 1965 provided this new approach, but it also had unforeseen consequences. It replaced national origins quotas with hemispheric limits to annual immigration. To emphasize equal treatment, all nations in the eastern hemisphere had the same limit of 20,000 immigrants annually. A system of preferences set principles for selecting immigrants. Family reunification, the most important principle, reserved nearly three-quarters of immigrant visas for relatives of American citizens or resident aliens. Spouses, minor children and parents were admitted outside the limits. Grown children as well as brothers and sisters were given special preferences. The second principle continued the "brain-drain" by reserving 20 percent of visas for skilled people. Refugees received the remaining visas. Legislation made the national limit and preference system global in the 1970s.

Congress intended to make up for past injustices to southern and eastern Europeans through family reunification visas for siblings and grown children, which it hoped would lead to the reappearance of the "new" immigrants. For ten years, the plan worked, but by 1980, it became clear that the family preferences benefited people from other nations much more. In 1965, Europe and Canada provided the majority of immigrants to the US, but by 1980 less than one-sixth came from those places and four-fifths came in almost equal numbers from Asia and Latin America. Expecting Western nuclear families, American lawmakers did not anticipate how students from Third World countries, especially Asians, would adjust their legal status upon graduation and use family reunification clauses to bring extended families.

The fourth wave: 1965 to the present

The late 1990s witnessed the highest immigration totals in American history. In addition to the many immigrants allowed by the hemispheric limits (changed to a global total of 320,000 in 1980 and adjusted to 675,000 by 2016), the wave has included hundreds of thousands of immediate relatives and refugees outside those limits. It has also contained millions of illegal aliens, who cross borders without papers (or with false ones) or arrive at airports on student or tourist visas and then overstay.

Between 1961 and 2010, more than 34.5 million people secured legal permanent resident status in the US. The Census Bureau estimated that 10.8 million more were in the country as undocumented or illegal immigrants in 2010. Table 3.1 lists the ten largest nationality groups among these for 1960, 2007 and 2011. Central

Americans and Asians have long been the chief global regions sending the US people in the fourth wave. Yet important shifts have occurred in migration to the US between 2007 and 2012–13. Mexican immigration began to fall sharply in 2007 and within three years it and even the combined immigration from Latin America – including those coming in illegally – was surpassed by increased arrivals of newcomers from Asia. By mid-2012, Asian Americans had replaced Hispanics as the largest and most rapidly growing racial group in the country.

Like the earlier waves of newcomers, the fourth includes a broad range of socioeconomic groups. One result of saving visas for needed occupations is that a very noticeable minority are highly skilled workers, professionals (especially engineers, doctors and nurses), and entrepreneurs with capital. The large majority of *both* legal and illegal immigrants are similar to those who have arrived since the 1820s. They are above average educationally and economically at home but, with the exception of Asian immigrants, are below average in these areas in the US. They have come because commercialization and industrialization (now revolutionizing the Third World) have disrupted their traditional economies.

At the socioeconomic bottom of this wave are often groups of refugees from wars and other disasters. In the 1970s and 1980s, huge groups of people fled Southeast Asia to the US because of the Vietnam War. The poorest also include people who obtain visas because they are near relatives of more skilled immigrants. Latino women were recruited by agencies as live-in domestic servants and nannies. Spreading the word about these jobs and moving into better-paid

TABLE 3.1 The effects of the fourth wave on the ten largest immigrant groups, 1960 contrasted with 2007 and 2011

1960	%*	2007	%	2011	%
1 Italians	(13%)	1 Mexicans	(31%)	1 Mexicans	(29%)
2 Germans	(10%)	2 Filipinos	(4.4%)	2 Chinese**	(5%)
3 Canadians	(10%)	3 Chinese***	(4.3%)	3 Indians	(5%)
4 British	(9%)	4 Indians	(4.1%)	4 Filipinos	(4%)
5 Poles	(8%)	5 Vietnamese	(3.0%)	5 Salvadorans	(3%)
6 USSR residents	(7%)	6 Salvadorans	(2.8%)	6 Vietnamese	(3%)
7 Mexicans	(6%)	7 Koreans	(2.7%)	7 Cubans	(3%)
8 Irish	(3%)	8 Cubans	(2.5%)	8 Koreans	(3%)
9 Austrians	(3%)	9 Dominicans	(2.3%)	9 Dominicans	(2%)
10 Hungarians	(3%)	10 Canadians	(2.3%)	10 Guatemalans	(2%)

* = percent of the total foreign-born in the US
**excluding Taiwan but including Hong Kong
*** including Taiwan and Hong Kong

Sources: Migration Policy Institute, 2012; American Community Survey (ACS, 2011); Yearbook of Immigration Statistics 2007, Office of Immigration Statistics, US Department of Homeland Security.

work once they have acquired more English, they bring their families and forge the links in "chain migration" based on a network of female contacts.

The limits on authorized immigration to the US are very liberal. Immediate family members enter outside the annual cap of 675,000 and come in as additional legal immigrants. Family reunification rules alone currently allot 480,000 visas. Employment visas allow 140,000 people with needed skills to enter. Another 55,000 get their "green card" as legal immigrants through the diversity lottery, which distributes visas among nationalities that have not immigrated in large numbers recently. No individual country can receive more than 7 percent of the total visas.

The nationalities and skin colors of most people in this wave are different and more various, however, and they arrive in different ways and settle

PLATE 3.4 Children play at a newly built section of the US–Mexico border wall at Sunland Park, New Mexico, opposite the Mexican border city of Ciudad Juarez, Mexico, November 18, 2016. Picture taken from the Mexico side of the border. During his victorious campaign for the presidency in 2016, Trump found strong popular appeal in his promises to build a "great wall" to keep out Latino immigrants, deport all undocumented immigrants, and enact a ban on Muslim immigration. He also said he would require Muslims in the US country to register with the government and characterized most illegal immigrants as violent criminals. None of this anti-immigrant rhetoric caused a serious backlash against his campaign. At many of his rallies, large publics chanted, "Build the Wall!" In his first week in office, he acted on two of these promises with executive orders. In addition to partial funding for a strengthened wall along the entire Mexican border, he banned visitor and immigration visas form six "terrorist prone," mostly Muslim nations across the Middle East and North Africa. Judicial injunctions stopped the ban for some travelers within the first day of its implementation.
© Reuters/Alamy

in different places. There are colonies of Hmong in Minneapolis, Vietnamese on the Mississippi Delta, East Indian hotel-owners across the Sunbelt, and Middle-Eastern Muslims in Dearborn, Michigan and New Jersey. Large concentrations of Latinos reside not only in the Southwest and the nation's big cities, where their communities are large and long established, but also across the rural districts and small towns of the South and Midwest, where their population has grown by 70 to 80 percent between the last US federal censuses.

Attitudes to immigrants: the contemporary debate

Large foreign-born settlements have given rise to contemporary forms of racism and nativism. Groping for ways to adjust to the changes in their country's population, some Americans are again resorting to broad stereotypes. Ethnic groups' length of time in America commonly has resulted in increasing acceptance by the public, with the exception of non-white groups, whose integration takes longer. By 2016, opposition to Latinos and Muslims grew for a combination of additional reasons. Latinos had grown to be a larger minority group than African Americans. Brown skinned and culturally distinct, both groups appeared to gain increased economic, political and cultural influence, especially in the regions of their greatest concentration, such as the Southwest and Dearborn, Michigan. In the heated public rhetoric of an election year, Republicans made immigration restriction and the elimination of illegal entries major goals. Large parts of the public assumed that Latinos made up nearly all the nation's population of undocumented immigrants and did not recognize that Latin immigration declined after the late 1990s. The mass media often reinforced these views in its search for the typical or sensational.

Illegal immigration continues to cause heated debate over government policy to control entry to the US. One segment of public opinion stresses that tolerating illegal immigration encourages a general disregard for the law, lowers wages for other workers, and undermines the 1965 law that gives all nationalities an equal chance for immigrant visas. Other Americans emphasize that illegal immigrants take jobs that US citizens do not want for less than the legal minimum wage, work in substandard conditions, and, while needing the benefits of social welfare programs, dare not reveal their situation for fear of deportation.

For its own convenience, the federal government invented the word "Hispanics" to put in a single category all the Central and South American Spanish-speaking cultures arriving in the US in the fourth wave. A handy label for official statistics, the word has come to mean illegal immigrants in the popular mind because of the large number of immigrants unlawfully crossing the border with Mexico until the later 1990s. It thus contributes to prejudice against hugely diverse Latino populations. About 52 percent of "illegals" are Mexicans, but the "undocumented" come from countries as diverse as Ireland, China, Nigeria and Iran.

The federal government responded to this ongoing debate as early as 1986 by passing the Immigration Reform and Control Act (IRCA). The law attempted to reduce illegal immigration while expressing acceptance and giving rights to people already inside the US. It set fines and penalties for employers who hire illegal aliens. It also attempted to prevent employment discrimination through rules that outlawed firing or refusing to hire people because they look foreign. The law offered "amnesty" (legal immigrant status) for illegals who had stayed in the US for four years and for many temporarily resident farm workers. Almost 3 million people became legal immigrants through the IRCA. Their improved situation was the one great success of the legislation. It proved difficult to document that employers had broken the law, and the number of illegals, which declined at first, rose again to between 9 and 11 million in a few years.

Large numbers of Asian immigrants in the fourth wave arrived with capital and higher education. Those facts and popular attitudes toward some Asian cultures' emphasis on respect for parents, education and hard work have led some media commentators to lump all Asian Americans together under the label of the "model minority." This ignores the large majority of Asian immigrants who come with little money and education; the problems of Asian refugees who have experienced wartime traumas; and job discrimination and violence against Asian Americans.

PLATE 3.5 A multiethnic, multiracial crowd enjoying a recent Macy's Thanksgiving Day Parade in New York City.
© *Joseph Sohm/Getty*

Despite reactions against immigration in the 1980s, national policy became more liberal through the Immigration Act of 1990. It raised the annual total of immigrant visas, the limit for individual nations and the number of asylum seekers who could enter the US. It removed restrictions on the entry of many groups, including homosexuals, communists, people from nations adversely affected by the 1965 law, and additional family members, including the spouses and children of illegals given amnesty. During the economic boom of the 1990s, the shortage of labor made Americans willing to overlook illegal immigration. Since then, however, the stagnation of wages and disappearance of industrial jobs for Americans with a high school education or less has produced a powerful negative wave of opinion against the undocumented, especially in California, New York, New Jersey, Florida, Texas, Illinois and Arizona, where more than three-quarters of newcomers have settled. From 2009 to 2016, during Barack Obama's two terms as president, strengthened border controls against illegal immigration and sharply raised deportation of the undocumented failed to ease political discontent over the issue. Public attitudes grew increasingly negative.

After the 9/11 terrorist attacks, polls have shown that majorities of the public favor further strengthening border controls against illegal immigration and a

PLATE 3.6 After 9/11, fingerprinting and biometric identification techniques became routine for immigrants and all others entering the US.
© *Ramin Talaie/Getty*

decrease in legal immigration as well. In response, through the USA Patriot Act of 2002, the government developed new biometric identity checks to regulate entry to the country, conducted intensified surveillance of the foreign-born and called in immigrants, especially Arab Americans, for questioning and possible detention or deportation.

According to American Community Survey data, the US continued to allow the world's highest level of legal immigration in 2014–2015, when around a million entered the country annually, most of them non-white and many of them non-Western. The legal newcomers include long-term temporary residents, such as foreign students and visiting skilled and professional workers, as well as green card holders. An additional estimated half a million *illegal* entries occurred in each of those years, due to the authorities' inability or unwillingness to enforce existing law. Now, however, the largest portions of the immigrant totals come from East and South Asia (especially India, China, the Philippines, Pakistan, and Bangladesh), the Caribbean (Cuba, the Dominican Republic, and Haiti), Sub-Saharan Africa (Nigeria and Ghana), and the Middle East (Saudi Arabia, Egypt, Iraq and Iran). Immigration from Central American countries, such as El Salvador and Honduras, has recently been greater than from Mexico. The attitudes of the public seem so far little affected by the changes this situation shows. The rises in total immigration annually after 2010 – and the memory of earlier high Mexican and Latino immigration – are currently what captures attention in public debates.

Congress remained deadlocked regarding comprehensive immigration legislation between 2000 and 2016. How to deal with an estimated 10–11 million undocumented immigrants, still legally defined and publicly viewed as illegal aliens, hindered lawmakers from reaching agreement in congress. Presidents George W. Bush and Barack Obama proposed bills that would allow a path for the undocumented to become citizens. Majorities in both houses, however, refused to approve any form of "amnesty" for people who had entered the US illegally. They feared that this would encourage a later surge of illegal immigration, as had occurred after IRCA.

The DREAM Act (the Development, Relief and Education for Alien Minors Act of 2010) was the Obama administration's attempt to rally congressional majorities by carefully limiting its aid to deserving children and young people whose entry or birth in the US was not their choice but their parents'. The applicants for a path to citizenship had to have come when they were minors (under 16 years old) who could not legally decide for themselves. The proposal further stipulated that they must have lived in the same community in the US, have no criminal record, and be enrolled in school (or a graduate) or a member (or a veteran) of the American armed forces. Near the end of 2010, the DREAM bill failed by one vote in the Senate. Forty-one senators, united in a belief that once undocumented minors were legitimate residents they would use their legal status to help immediate relatives enter under the family reunification provisions of the 1965 comprehensive immigration law, voted down the proposal. They were convinced that in combination with the current law, it would cause an unacceptable surge in immigration. Supporters of the proposal thought the probable uniting of families through documented legal status and eventual citizenship was in itself an admirable goal.

Frustrated with congressional obstruction of proposals for remedying the dilemmas of undocumented immigration, the president and several states took action on their own. Alabama, Arizona, and California passed strict laws limiting the civil rights and economic opportunities of the undocumented in an attempt to drive them outside state borders. Legal challenges in the courts prevented the implementation of many of the most controversial provisions of these laws.

After his re-election, President Obama issued executive orders to provide the "dreamers" with ways to gain legal residence and citizenship without interference from congressional opponents. In 2014, he announced that his administration would give the same young people he tried to help under the DREAM Act, a new chance of a future in the US through the Deferred Action program for Childhood Arrivals (DACA). If they qualified for the program, it would delay deportation to allow them two years to adjust their status and qualify for work and education in that time. In addition, the executive order announced a planned extension that would allow undocumented parents who qualified a parallel form of delayed action on deportation. A federal judge blocked that part of Obama's executive action, but DACA operated for the rest of Obama's term. President-elect Donald Trump has promised to reverse Obama's executive orders regarding immigration. He claims that he will deport undocumented immigrants who have criminal records or are potential terrorists, and pledges to erect an effective barrier on the nation's southern boundary. In early 2017, he issued executive orders to fund the building of the wall, end the refugee flow from Syria, put a four-month pause on the entry of all other refugees, and place a three-month travel ban on all entries from seven North African and Middle-Eastern nations.

Exercises

Explain and examine the significance of the following names and terms:

indigenous peoples	middle colonies	Pluralism
bracero program	first wave	national origins quotas
"old" immigrants	1965 Immigration Act	the DREAM Act
"stage" migration	fourth wave	immigrant (contra founder)
Virginia	nativism	IRCA
push and pull factors	melting pot	executive orders on immigration
Northern colonies	2002 USA Patriot Act	DACA

Write short essays on the following topics.

1. Explain why the encounters between Native Americans and Europeans were so disastrous.

2. Describe one or more of the four major waves of immigration and discuss causes for the kind of reception the newcomers received.

3. Debate which of the metaphors for understanding the nature of American society is most accurate and enlightening.

4. Critically discuss the evolution of American immigration law and the social forces that produced it, using the text and the extended caption to Plate 3.3.

5. Use the text and Table 3.1 (percentages of Immigration from Individual Nations in 1965, 2007 and 2011) to explain and comment on the changes that have appeared in the composition of the immigrant population entering the United States during the fourth wave.

Further reading

Barkan, E.R (2013) (ed.) *Immigrants in American History: Arrival, Adaptation, and Integration*, Santa Barbara, CA: ABC-CLIO.

Bukowczyk, J. (2016) (ed.) *Immigrant Identity and the Politics of Citizen*ship, Urbana, IL: University of Illinois Press.

Lieberson, S. and Waters, M.C. (1988) *From Many Strands: Ethnic and Racial Groups in Contemporary America*, New York: Russell Sage Foundation.

Ngai, M. M. and Gjerde J. (2013) (eds.) *Major Problems in American Immigration History: Documents and Essays*, Boston, MA: Wadsworth, Cengage Learning.

Ngai, M. M. (2005) *Impossible Subjects: Illegal Aliens and the Making of Modern America*, Princeton, NJ: Princeton University Press.

Office of Immigration Statistics, US Department of Homeland Security (DHS), 2003–16.

Reimers, D.M. (2005) *Other Immigrants: The Global Origins of the American People*, New York: New York University Press.

US Bureau of the Census, decadal series and current population reports (CPR).

US Bureau of Labor Statistics, annual reports.

Zolberg, A.R. (2006) *A Nation by Design: Immigration Policy in the Fashioning of America*, New York: Russell Sage Foundation.

Websites

www.US-immigration.com/US-immigration-news
www.dhs.gov/immigration-statistics/yearbook/2015
www.migrationinformation.org/datahub

www.washingtonpost.com (archives, search and special reports)
www.uscis.gov/portal/site/uscis (US Citizenship and Immigration Services)
factfinder2.census.gov/faces/nav/jsf/pages/index.xhtml
www.census.gov/main/www/cprs.html
www.census.gov/compendia/statab/cats/population.html (the 2015 statistical abstract)

Chapter 4

The people
Women and minorities

The reason for American women's and minority history

Discrimination has given women and some minorities a special status in American society. For much of American history, male-dominated society in the US has forced women, Native Americans, African Americans, Asian Americans, Latinos and people with minority sexual orientations into inferior categories. As a result, these groups have their own histories as subjects of changing opinion and government policy, even though their experiences are integral parts of the nation's history. They have molded American history through their struggles for equality and resistance against discrimination. Inequality has led to group differences in attitudes, class, occupation, income, health, housing and crime. The gap between national ideals and the realities of prejudice has agitated the nation's conscience and prompted a very uneven but persistent progress toward greater equality.

There has been constant debate over the proper means of creating a more just society. Neither policymakers nor the subjects of policy have agreed on the course to follow. Over a century of federal civil rights laws have proved that changes in the law often do not function as intended, nor do they assure changes in attitudes. Defining what equality means has proved difficult. Most Americans have supported equality of opportunity (an equal chance to develop one's abilities and reap rewards for them) but not equality of results (an evening-out of economic, social and political power). In practice, equality of opportunity and most attempts to redistribute wealth have failed or have been short-lived. Affirmative action programs and election districts that arrange for preferential treatment of women and minorities, in order to correct the effects of past discrimination, have faced increasingly strong opposition and been discontinued, in part by Supreme Court decisions. Although Americans favor equality, they disagree about what it is and about the degree to which government can or should provide it.

Women in America

Numerically a majority, they today experience unequal treatment in significant ways. They are assigned (or are socialized to choose) prescribed roles and do not as often work in the most prestigious occupations, earn as much money or enjoy positions of equal social status as men. Popular attitudes continue to keep too many women in traditional places. Mostly working in poorly paid service jobs, they remain severely underrepresented in the highest levels of politics and business management. Women's status and roles in society continue to cause debate and change in the twenty-first century.

English judicial precedents determined women's legal status in America. Until the mid-1800s, a woman experienced a "civil death" upon marriage. She ceased to exist legally except through her spouse and had no right to own property, control her wages or sign contracts. Divorce, rarely granted, was easier to obtain for men than for women. A single woman had to submit to her father's or brother's will until she married. Men claimed that women were by nature physically frail and mentally limited, and therefore dependent on men.

The nineteenth century

Most middle and upper class white women had no paid work. Some of these women were the founders of girls' schools between 1800 and 1850 and of famous women's colleges, such as Vassar and Mount Holyoke, in the latter 1800s. These social classes also produced most of the century's female reformers, who were prominent in the crusade against alcohol abuse and in movements to improve conditions in prisons, insane asylums, hospitals, schools and immigrant ghettos. Many early female reformers integrated their advocacy for women's rights with their experiences in abolitionist (anti-slavery) campaigns. Attacked as "unwomanly" for speaking to mixed audiences of men and women, female abolitionists publicized parallels between discrimination against African Americans and women. In 1848, two abolitionists, Lucretia Mott and Elizabeth Cady Stanton, led the first women's rights convention in Seneca Falls, New York. In language taken from the Declaration of Independence, the convention's "Declaration of Sentiments" called for property and divorce rights, educational and employment opportunities and the vote.

Thereafter, the women's movement held regular conventions and worked to realize its stated goals. Before the Civil War, Susan B. Anthony led successful efforts to improve women's status in marriage and divorce cases, as well as their economic rights, under New York state law. A few years later, however, the state repealed liberal provisions. During the Civil War, women found increased acceptance as teachers and moved into nursing and government office work. Feminists joined the successful campaign for the constitutional abolition of slavery through the Thirteenth Amendment, but the movement split in two when it became clear that the Fifteenth Amendment gave only African-American men the vote.

One faction opposed broadening the franchise if that excluded women. This group championed a wide range of women's rights and pursued the vote through a *federal* women's suffrage amendment. Another group presented women's voting rights as a separate issue from suffrage for African-American men, avoided involvement in other causes that might alienate influential groups, and concentrated on winning the vote on a state-by-state basis.

The latter group first tasted victory when Wyoming Territory granted female suffrage in 1869, but of 17 states that considered women's suffrage between 1870 and 1910, only three approved it. Several other states gave women limited local voting rights. Although men continued to deny women membership in unions for skilled workers, female activists assisted unskilled women's unionization and mounted successful campaigns against child labor. On the other hand, their fight for abortion rights, birth control and membership on juries met with failure until after the Second World War.

The twentieth century

The movement united behind efforts for ratification of the Nineteenth Amendment, which granted women the right to vote in all elections in 1920. Women strongly supported campaigns to deal with political corruption, alcoholism, and urban social problems at the turn of the century, so many male politicians thought they would vote for a broad range of social reforms or form a women's party to defeat conservative male candidates.

In practice, women voters often divided over issues in much the same way as men. Many women's rights organizations disbanded soon after they won the vote, which commentators often view as the end of the first wave of feminism in the US. Women's economic position improved slowly, in part because of disagreement within the movement. Female social reformers who demanded protective measures that treated women as a special category successfully lobbied for laws limiting women's working hours and occupational choices to protect their safety and health. Until the 1970s, civil rights legislation for women and court decisions affecting their rights developed from such a protectionist approach.

Other feminists insisted that this approach keeps women in poorly paid jobs and prevents equality with men because it assumes that women are weaker than men. These activists proposed another constitutional change as early as 1923, the Equal Rights Amendment (ERA), to remove the remaining legal inequalities between men and women. Some opponents of the ERA feared it would overturn protective legislation for women. Such dissension, but even more the generally conservative mood of the country, led to the relative dormancy of the women's movement between the late 1920s and the early 1960s.

The turning point in women's employment came after World War II. Many married women who went to work during the war continued to work after it, and many more joined them in the following decades. While 15 percent of married women worked for wages in 1940, by 1970, almost 50 percent had paid jobs outside the home. By 1979, the majority of employed women was middle-aged and middle class. Husbands accepted the change because most wives did not take jobs until the children entered school and earned wages that kept the family in the middle class. Not only were larger numbers of women of all classes, married and single, working, but a larger percentage of them were getting a higher education.

Thus, when a new, "second wave" of the women's movement blossomed in the 1960s and 1970s, it challenged the view that women's place was keeping house, and many Americans agreed. The reality they lived no longer squared with conventions of the past. Again stimulated by African Americans' demands for civil rights, the women's movement lobbied effectively for the 1964 Civil Rights Act, which was the first such legislation explicitly to ban discrimination based on gender as well as on race. The more radical feminists of these decades, such as Betty Friedan, who published the best-selling *Feminine Mystique* in 1963, rejected conventional gender roles and family life as stifling, patriarchal and frequently dysfunctional. By mid-decade, women's lobbying had helped pass laws that promised women equal treatment in the job market and admission to higher education, equal pay for equal work and equal availability of loans and credit. By the late 1960's, Gloria Steinem, who exposed male exploitation of women in the Playboy Club, replaced Friedan as the movement's primary leader, and she made women's control of reproductive rights and daycare for working mother its main goals.

Advocates of women's rights often pursued their goals through court cases. In 1973, the Supreme Court allowed for limited abortion rights through the *Roe* v. *Wade* case brought by women lawyers, and since then, the court has further limited abortion rights only marginally. President elect Donald J. Trump, who marred his 2016 election campaign with sexual harassment scandals, took a strong pro-life stand and spoke of criminalizing abortion. He promises to appoint Supreme Court justices who will re-evaluate abortion rights.

In a series of rulings during the 1970s and 1980s, the court also supported affirmative action programs that aimed to increase the number of women and minorities among employees or students until it equaled their proportion in the local population. In the 1978 *Regents* v. *Bakke* case, the court struck down a policy of using numerical quotas for affirmative action, but it still supports flexible programs that actively recruit women and minorities. In the 1990s, however, rising public opposition to affirmative action was evident in a referendum in California and a federal district court decision in a Texas case that ended "positive discrimination" in favor of women and minorities in those states.

The ERA proved to be the major initiative for women's rights in the twentieth century that ultimately failed. Its text stated that neither the states nor the federal government could limit a person's rights based on gender. In 1972, Congress passed the ERA with little opposition. To become a part of the Constitution, three-quarters of the state legislatures then had to ratify it. After many states passed it in the early 1970s, however, support lagged and the ERA fell three states short of ratification in 1982. The National Organization for Women

(NOW, founded by a group of older, moderate women in 1966) asserted that the struggle for ratification was well worth the effort because it raised women's awareness of their social position, involved them in the political process on their own behalf, and helped pass equal-rights provisions to many state constitutions.

The so-called third wave of American feminism that arose in the early 1990s continues today. It has transformed the movement to a multiracial, multicultural, multi-issue network that works to support young activists and changed it from a predominately white, middle class phenomenon with leaders from the older generation.

Evaluating the contemporary situation for women

Today, court action and statutes, both state and federal, have reduced the legal hindrances to equality between the sexes. "Protective" laws based on sexual stereotypes have been repeatedly overturned. Employment ads cannot ask for applicants of one sex. State and local ordinances ban most private organizations that prohibit female membership.

Federal law set strict penalties against sexual harassment and abuse in 1994 with the Violence against Women Act. The statute also provided assistance for the victims of unwanted sexual advances and domestic violence. Congress revised VAWA in 2000 after the Supreme Court nullified its provision allowing women the right to sue their attackers in federal court. A reauthorization enacted in 2006 added help for a wide range of age, race, and ethnic groups, as well as all genders. In 2013–15, expansions of VAWA protected battered Native Americans and illegal immigrants.

Polls indicate that since law professor Anita Hill accused Supreme Court nominee Clarence Thomas of sexual harassment during Senate hearings in 1991, more women are prepared to sue men over sexual offenses, and more men expect them to do so. Judicial approval of state laws granting unpaid maternity leaves in the late 1980s led more private employers and public authorities to institute maternity leave programs. In 1993, Congress mandated unpaid leave after the birth of a child for some 42 million public workers. By the twenty-first century, many employers offered child day care centers for working mothers, but they seldom offered these facilities to women in low-wage jobs, who in addition, could not afford unpaid maternity leave.

Progress toward gender equality since the 1970s has been limited. For instance, the Department of Justice recently reported that the incidence of rape against women declined between 1990 and 2010 by 58 percent. Yet in 2016, the department continues to cite statistics showing that three of four rapes remain uninvestigated or do not lead to an arrest, in spite of changes in rape case procedures meant to protect victims. Critics in women's groups who focus on the easy availability of pornography and media violence as causes of rape have won few policy changes.

PLATE 4.1 The fight for women's rights in the United States; two suffragists put up a billboard in New York City around 1917.

© *Universal History Archive/Getty*

PLATE 4.2 Thousands of pro-choice supporters marching in New York during August 2004, when the Republicans held their convention in the city, to show their stance on the issue of abortion.
© *Sipa Press/REX/Shutterstock*

Since the 1970s, the portion of women completing higher degrees has steadily risen. They earn higher degrees mostly in fields traditional for women, such as the fine arts, foreign languages and nursing, however, which offer lower earnings. Women are making inroads in highly paid "male" professions (such as engineering, medicine and the law), but over 50 years after the Equal Pay Act (1963) became law, women's earnings on average are only four-fifths of men's. White and Asian-American men earn more than women of every race and ethnicity. When the Supreme Court turned down a woman's case against wage discrimination on a technicality in 2007, Congress passed the Lilly Ledbetter Fair Pay Act in her name and retroactive to the date of the court's decision. The act makes challenges against gender-based inequality much easier. Wage equality by gender has improved greatly. In 1967, women only earned about 58 cents to every dollar a man took home.

Some sense of recent changes in women's educational situation appears evident from yet another affirmative action case. By 1996 in *Grutter v. Bollinger*, a white woman went to court against the University of Michigan law school to prove that she had been refused admission because of the institution's affirmative action policies that gave preference to underrepresented groups in the student body, such as Native Americans, Latino Americans, and African Americans. In 2003, the US Supreme Court decided against her, declaring in a 5–4 decision that racial diversity was a "compelling interest" in the university's efforts to provide the "educational benefits that flow from a diverse student body." In 2006, however, voters ended the university's affirmative action program in a state referendum.

Between 1980 and the present, women's role in American politics has evolved. A gender gap has appeared in voting patterns. Women consistently give more support to Democratic congressional and presidential candidates, especially to those candidates who favor extensions of the social safety net and efforts for international peace. Their voting varies greatly, however, depending on the qualities of individual candidates. Women ran for and won high public office in record numbers in these years. The number of female state governors and members of state legislatures and the US congress reached new heights. In 2008, Hillary Clinton, the former First Lady, became the first seriously competitive female candidate for president. Eight years later, in the race for the presidency she won the popular vote but lost in the Electoral College. In 2016, 104 women held seats in Congress, and one in five US senators were women. Still, that fraction illustrates how far men continue to outnumber women at the higher levels of government.

The number and size of businesses owned by women has risen rapidly since the late 1990s, but the increase here is also mostly in healthcare services, where female owners controlled between half and three-quarters of facilities in 2010. Women's economic position, moreover, still seems to illustrate in exaggerated form the distance between the rich and the poor. The "feminization of poverty" continued to increase after the Great Recession of 2008–09. The income of working single mothers increased at a slower rate to that of other families during the economic recovery. In the last decade, increased numbers of single mothers were without work or day care for their children. Non-white and immigrant women in service trades were several times as likely to be living in poverty as men, and female-headed families made up nearly half of all poor families.

Native Americans

Native Americans became a small minority because of a long history of successful invasion, military conflict and pressure by Europeans and then white Americans. The conflict was always an uneven one. In the very early days, Native Americans outnumbered the invaders at the point of contact, but their opponents possessed insurmountable technological advantages, including metal weapons, textiles, written languages and books. Epidemics caused by a lack of immunity to European diseases, moreover, reduced the Native American population drastically while the influx of Europeans enormously increased. European and white American cultures were also more aggressively expansive and acquisitive than indigenous cultures.

Patterns formed in the colonial period

British settlers came in much greater numbers than other Europeans and primarily sought land, rather than trading partners or mineral riches. They presented Native Americans with a threatening front of compact settlement, brought their own women and segregated themselves from the natives. Thus, no large mixed race of "mestizos" appeared in British America.

Relations between the natives and the English involved a cycle of distrust, resentment and disastrous wars. A predictable sequence of events set the pattern for almost three hundred years of contact. First was a short period of relative peace when the settlers exchanged technology for land, furs and knowledge of the Native Americans' survival techniques. Then conflicts caused by trade disagreements, expanded white settlement and cultural misunderstanding escalated into full-scale war. In the 1620s and 1630s, the natives tried, by war, to expel the intruders and threatened the existence of the Virginia and New England colonies. During the third phase of massive retaliation, Whites militarily defeated the natives. Often the colonists received help from traditional tribal enemies of those that attacked the settlements. During the final phase, Anglo-American policies aimed at easing the expansion of settlement while minimizing the "'Indian threat." For the most part, the British Empire let colonists devise their own solutions to this threat, until the 1750s. In victory, Whites usually tried to exterminate native opponents, drive them farther inland or enslave and deport them. Often, the settlers negotiated treaties based on a policy of forced separation to free territory for colonial settlement and to end violence. The colonists moved the natives to distant lands that (the colonists promised) would be theirs permanently. In short, the "Indian reservation" system dates back to the 1630s and 1640s.

Colonial authorities promised to protect the rights of reservation natives. Some colonists also encouraged them to adopt European ways and Christianity. In New England, the Puritans recognized villages of Christianized natives as "praying towns," for example. Assimilation on distant reservations, however, failed. Native peoples further west attacked the reservations because they objected to intrusions into their territory. Colonists squatted on reservation land when it was no longer distant from colonial settlement, and colonial authorities rarely acted to limit settlement. Native Americans resented and resisted attempts to assimilate them. Thus, one cycle of violent conflict followed another, and white settlers pushed Native Americans continually further west. In outline, with the substitution of US for British authorities, this general sequence of developments continued into the early 1900s.

In the eighteenth century, Britain and France competed for power in North America. Both vied for native allies, which led Native American groups to offer their allegiance to the highest bidder. The Iroquois Confederacy in western New York and Pennsylvania, for instance, was especially successful in playing one European power against the other and, for a long time, was able to channel white settlement to the south of its territory. The French generally won support from more tribes because their trading activities seemed far less threatening. To change this, the British government established a new policy during the French and Indian War (1754–63). It gave gifts to native leaders, bypassed the colonists through direct negotiations with the Indians and, most importantly, set a western limit to colonial settlement.

The Proclamation of 1763 made a line west of the Appalachian Mountains the official boundary of British America. To the west of the line was "Indian Country," which settlers had to leave. Parliament had applied the colonists' policy of separation to both settlers and natives and created a huge Indian reservation. Its action brought enough tribes to Britain's side to defeat the French, who gave up many of their land claims in North America. The line infuriated the colonists, who ignored the proclamation but cited the limit on western settlement as a reason for rebelling against the mother country. When the American Revolution came, most tribes remained loyal to Britain. The US therefore treated several tribes as conquered nations after the war and demanded their lands without payment.

Conquest and removal, 1783–1860

Through the treaty of 1783, Britain ceded to the US all the land between Canada and Florida to the Mississippi river and asked no protection for Native American rights. With the coming of peace, tens of thousands of settlers moved into the area, but over 100,000 Native Americans blocked their way. In the Great Lakes region, a powerful native confederacy would not permit settlers north of the Ohio river. On the southern frontier, several tribes refused to give up lands, despite pressure from southern states. First, the US sent armies against the northern confederacy to take its land by conquest. When American forces suffered repeated defeats, however, the US negotiated a treaty after its first major victory. The confederacy ceded huge amounts of land but won annual payments of goods and cash in return. The US government thus set a precedent that recognized Native American land claims and the need to pay for lands taken by settlers. Abandoning reliance on military conquest, many American leaders returned to the assimilation policy. Congress sent teachers and missionaries to transform the natives into farmers who could live in American society. The US authorities did not ask Native Americans if they wanted to be "civilized," and those who favored harsher policies said their resistance was proof that assimilation was impossible.

Meanwhile, observing the rapid growth of the white population west of the Appalachians between 1800 and 1810, the Shawnee leaders Tecumseh and The Prophet worked to form a grand alliance of tribes east of the Mississippi

Tecumseh.

PLATE 4.3 Tecumseh (1768–1813), Native American chief of the Shawnee tribe, who died in the battle of the Thames in Canada, October 5, 1813, appears here wearing a British medal and tunic.
© *Bettmann/Corbis*

to limit US expansion. Tecumseh applied to the British for help when he heard that the two nations might go to war. The difficulty of unifying warring tribes defeated Native Americans' last attempt to control the land east of the river. While Tecumseh was lobbying for support among southern tribes, Americans defeated his forces in the north and discovered British guns at his headquarters. A year later Tecumseh and his allies joined the British against the USA in the war of 1812, and Tecumseh died in battle. The loss of leadership and British support led many tribes to move further west after the war.

Tribes who remained east of the Mississippi found themselves forced to accept a revival of the old separation policy, now called *removal* and defined as moving Native Americans west of the river. Thomas Jefferson supported the idea as early as 1803, when he argued for buying the area from the Mississippi to the Rocky Mountains (the Louisiana Purchase) from France. Removal gained popularity, even with so-called "friends" of the Native American who said that the policy would give the natives a chance to acquire social and political skills for assimilation away from white squatters, their diseases, and alcohol. In 1830, President Andrew Jackson, famous as a combatant against the Native Americans in the war of 1812, signed the Indian Removal Act. Many tribes north of the Ohio river had signed individual removal treaties before that time and had moved to parts of present-day Kansas. Now, federal policy required the removal of all remaining tribes to a permanent "Indian Territory," in today's Oklahoma. State authorities so terrorized southern tribes that all but two (the Seminoles and the Cherokees) accepted removal as the only alternative to extermination.

The Seminoles held out for seven years through guerrilla warfare in the Florida Everglades. The Cherokees had adopted many American institutions including industries, schools, a newspaper and an American-style government and constitution during the earlier period of federal assimilation programs. Influenced by the society around them, some Cherokees (mostly those who had intermarried with Americans) were slaveholders. The Cherokee appealed to the US federal courts to fight removal plans and the state of Georgia's seizure of their lands. The Supreme Court ruling in this case, (*Cherokee Nation v. Georgia*, 1831), set a precedent for later decisions concerning Native Americans' rights and status, even though it had little immediate effect. The court said a Native American tribe was neither an independent nation nor a state but a "domestic dependent nation." Within US borders, tribal lands were still outside American political structures. By right of first residence, Native Americans had sovereignty over their lands and could lose them only voluntarily and with just compensation. The federal government alone could negotiate with a tribe. State laws did not apply on Native American lands or reservations, where native laws took priority. American citizens could not enter Native American lands except by permission or treaty right. By implication, the decision declared the Removal Act and Georgia's actions illegal.

President Jackson and Georgia ignored the court's ruling. Federal troops and state militia in the winter of 1838 "escorted" the Cherokee to Indian Territory. Because of the weather, harassment by Americans, and poor planning for food and shelter, a quarter of the Cherokees died during the march along the path known as "The Trail of Tears." By 1840, American authorities forcibly moved nearly 100,000 Native Americans to Indian Territory. Here, the great differences in the terrain and climate required painful adjustments for eastern woodlands peoples. Put on much smaller parcels of land, groups with long traditions of mutual hostility had to live side by side. Western Indians resented the newcomers' entry into their lands and raided the territory for food and livestock. Unable to cope with the situation and often not given the protection and material aid promised by the federal government, many Native Americans in the territory sank into dependence, alcoholism and poverty.

War, concentration and forced assimilation, 1860–1934

During the Civil War, several tribes in Indian Territory supported the South by supplying Confederate armies with food. After the war, the US asked them to give up even more land by replacing its policy of removal with the concentration of Indians on reservations. Americans occupied the prairies and plains (once considered the "Great American Desert") and rushed in to profit from gold and silver strikes in the West. US government support for transcontinental railroads increased settlement and quickened the slaughter of the buffalo on which the plains natives depended. The US created new Indian reservations to free land for development.

Between 1850 and 1890, the Native Americans in the West struggled unsuccessfully to keep their land. The familiar pattern of settlement, conflict escalating to war, treaty making and treaty violation leading to new wars repeated itself. At the famous battle of the Little Big Horn, for example, Dakota warriors led by Sitting Bull and Crazy Horse killed Lieutenant Colonel Custer and his men. Custer's men were attempting to punish the Native Americans for attacking gold prospectors – white men who broke the treaty with the Dakotas by entering their sacred Black Hills. The era of open warfare ended with the so-called battle of Wounded Knee. This bloodbath resulted from clumsy attempts by American authorities to suppress the Ghost Dance religion that promised believers a return to the happy conditions before the appearance of the Whites. The US arrested Sitting Bull on accusations that he promoted the religion, and Native American police killed him while he was in custody. When US soldiers tried to disarm a nearby group of Dakotas at Wounded Knee Creek, they fought back in anger over reservation conditions and the death of Sitting Bull. The panicked troops sprayed the men, women and children with machine gun fire until all 300 were dead.

From the 1870s to the 1930s, the US tried to assimilate Native Americans quickly. The motives for this ranged from a wish to free natives from dependence and poverty to a barely disguised aim to acquire reservation lands. Assimilation programs also caused dissension within native groups. Native Americans who had white relatives or who were already practicing American-style farming tended to favor adoption of US institutions. Racially unmixed natives were often cultural traditionalists who resisted all forms of assimilation.

Efforts at Americanization took three main forms. The first was the deliberate eroding of tribes' legal authority. On reservations, agents from the US Bureau of Indian Affairs (BIA) made all final decisions. In the 1870s and 1880s, Congress removed any appearance of local control by declaring the end of tribal sovereignty and treaty-making, replacing tribal rule with the application of federal or state law and giving private companies rights to use Native Americans' land without their consent. Granting US citizenship was another way of weakening tribal authority, because it gave Native Americans individual rights they could defend in court and made them responsible as individuals to state and federal law. By 1905, over half of all Native Americans had US citizenship, and in 1924, Congress extended citizenship to the rest.

Americans who wanted to achieve assimilation in a single generation put their faith in the second major plan for assimilation: educating Native American children at boarding schools far away from their reservations. To break all ties with tribal culture, the schools forbade pupils to wear native clothing, practice native customs or religions or speak native languages. The curriculum stressed American history, customs, and government. In the 1880s and 1890s, the BIA founded some two dozen of these schools, as well as similar day and boarding schools on reservations.

Allotment programs (dissolving reservations into small farms owned by individual Native American families) were the keystone of the third method of assimilation. Tried out before the Civil War, allotment became US policy for all but a few tribes under the Dawes Act of 1887. Typically, allotment plans gave a Native American family 160 acres and single adults half as much. This nearly always left a huge amount of "surplus" reservation land available for sale to non-Native Americans.

Supporters of the Dawes Act believed that the allotment process would as effectively Americanize them as it had millions of European immigrants who became independent family farmers. Critics pointed out that Native-American farming was communal, not a collection of individual holdings. Without time to develop an American sense of landownership and farming methods, the results of allotment might be the cheap sale of "Indian family farms" to white Americans and starvation among huge numbers of landless Native Americans. To prevent this, the Dawes Act forbade the sale or leasing of allotted land for 25 years. Congress removed these restrictions after just four years, after which Native Americans' lands changed hands rapidly. By 1934, the federal government declared some 4 million acres of reservation land surplus and either sold it to white Americans or allowed failed Indian farmers to sell it to Whites. Allotment provided a bonanza for speculators and land-hungry settlers.

Tribal restoration and termination, 1934–70

By the 1930s, studies had repeatedly blamed allotment for the extreme poor health, poverty and low educational levels of Native Americans. Franklin D. Roosevelt's "Indian New Deal" attempted to correct the mistakes of the past. Native Americans shared in the relief and employment programs available for other Americans suffering from the depression. FDR's administration built new, better-staffed hospitals for Native Americans and replaced most boarding schools with local schools offering religious freedom, bilingual education and programs to nurture native culture. The Indian Reorganization Act of 1934 was the centerpiece of the reversal of public policy known as tribal restoration. It repealed allotment, supported the return of considerable "surplus" land and allotment farms to communal ownership and provided federal funds for further adding to tribal lands.

Now required to help develop self-government on reservations, the BIA funded the founding of these governments and federal credit for the conservation and economic development of local resources. Each tribe could accept or reject the act through a referendum. The Indian New Deal made effective progress toward providing social services, an economic base and self-government on reservations, until funding ended at the start of the Second World War. In response to failing government support and a growing awareness of their common cause, people from a range of Native-American cultures joined to form the nation's first large-scale national organization, the National Congress of American Indians (NCAI) in 1944 to monitor federal policies and secure the rights and benefits of all indigenous peoples.

By 1953, advocates of rapid assimilation again constituted a congressional majority, however, and pushed through three new programs. The first aimed to settle Native American claims against the US by offering financial compensation for lost lands and treaty violations. Once claims were resolved, the BIA proposed termination (dissolving the tribe/reservation as a legal entity and making Native Americans ordinary citizens of local and state governments). Then the BIA could complete the process of assimilation, the argument went, by helping former members of the tribe find work in cities. Instead of making natives "regular" Americans by transforming them into farmers, this new policy (called relocation) aimed to accomplish the same end by turning them into industrial workers. By the 1960s, the new policies reversed most of the progress of the New Deal years, and the policy of assimilation again seemed bankrupt. Termination and relocation increased welfare dependency and social alienation rather than producing self-sufficiency and social integration.

Native American interest groups formed to seek change through lobbying and court cases. Protest organizations, such as the National Indian Youth Council (NIYC) founded in 1961, worked to build Native Americans' self-respect and pride. The more radical American Indian Movement (AIM), started in 1968, focused on mobilizing urban Indians through confrontation with the authorities and used direct action to capture media attention. Claiming it as their territory, for example, thousands of AIM supporters occupied Alcatraz Island in San Francisco Bay between 1969 and 1971. In late 1972 and early 1973, AIM activists barricaded themselves for over 70 days against armored vehicles, federal marshals and the FBI at Wounded Knee, South Dakota, which they declared an independent nation. Near the end of the decade, Indian activists marched from San Francisco to Washington, DC along The "Trail of Broken Treaties" to publicize the need to compensate Indians for US treaty violations.

The situation of Native Americans in recent history

The mid-century activism bore fruit in the later 1900s and the early twenty-first century. Native American law firms won important victories in US courts. They convinced judges to view tribes according to their early nineteenth-century status as dependent domestic nations, which helped them successfully champion traditional religious practices, tribal independence, mineral, game and water rights and the return of ancient artifacts and skeletons. Court actions also returned or brought payment for vast tracts of land to honor old treaties.

An important goal of the intertribal "self-determination" movement was to lobby the federal government for equal treatment and self-government. The movement's initial success came in 1968, when the passage of the Indian Civil Rights Act guaranteed individuals living on reservations all the rights included in the US Constitution. That protected them from rights violations by American or tribal governments and allowed tribes to qualify for the welfare and poverty benefits available to other citizens. From then to the present, federal laws building on this act have made US funding and other assistance available for improving the health services, childcare, housing and education of Native Americans, on and off reservations.

In 1975, Congress confirmed this legal status in the Indian Self-Determination Act, which gave tribal councils most powers exercised by state governments. The councils develop an economy and social institutions suited to their own natural resources and values. The BIA may offer assistance, but its role ends as tribes become autonomous. Councils have developed industries, irrigation systems, tourist resorts, colleges, and tribal gambling casinos that earn Native Americans around a billion dollars a year nationally. A few tribes have grown rich from mineral deposits, for example, of oil or uranium on reservation land.

As life on the reservation improved, the flight of Native Americans to cities has reversed, but as early as the 1990 census, only one out of four Native

Americans was a "reservation Indian." The other three lived in urban areas where jobs were more plentiful and varied. The adjustment to the city has not been successful for many Native Americans. About 20 percent live below the poverty line, unemployment is high and those with jobs frequently earn low wages. A small, well-educated and integrated urban elite enjoys a much higher standard of living. In 1996, hoping that it would attract urban Indian people back to the reservations, the Native American Housing and Self-Determination Act provided reservation housing programs that allow tribes to design suitable housing for themselves.

Despite that effort, in 2015 most of America's reservation Indians lived in appalling conditions. Of all American ethnic groups, they had the highest unemployment, alcoholism, poverty and suicide rates. Many cases of malnutrition, mental illness, and a short life expectancy indicate the seriousness of the situation. Yet, at the 2010 census, 5.2 million Americans identified themselves as wholly or partly native. That is more than double the 1990 figure and far more than the birth rate alone can explain. One answer is that 2.3 million of these people indicated that their heritage was a mixture of Native American and one or more other ethnicities. Tribal leaders and experts point to a wish to share in gambling revenue and affirmative action programs, widespread interest in family history and, most encouraging, to the decline in the social stigma attached to being Native American. By 2015, after the settling of many claims and counter-claims, the census estimated that the whole or partly Native-American population was 6.6 million and that only half of this population was "American Indian and Alaska Native only."

Lesbian, gay, bisexual and transgender Americans

Until the 1950s, no advocacy organizations publicly argued that lesbian, gay, bisexual, and transgender (LGBT) Americans were minorities suffering discrimination. State laws prohibited their sexual orientation, categorized it as a form of mental illness and subjected its practice in private between consenting adults to police prosecution. The social taboos and resulting secrecy attached to these groups, as well as to bisexual and transgender people, delayed their organization and group consciousness.

Despite these conditions, gay life was a familiar dimension of city life in places such as Harlem and Greenwich Village as early as the 1920s. The mixing of many millions of people during both world wars, especially the second, made LGBT individuals (like members of other groups) more aware that they shared experiences and concerns with others. In the 1950s, support networks organized by the Mattachine Society and Daughters of Bilitis raised group and individual consciousness through publications and meetings that offered assistance and disseminated information. Social scientists' groundbreaking studies of LGBT life in the US around the same time documented the social pressures they faced and how well adjusted they were compared to the heterosexual population.

The LGBT civil rights movement of the 1960s and 1970s built upon this foundation. Gay rights demonstrations in San Francisco, Philadelphia and New York, among other cities, made public demands for equal rights. Peaceful protest famously turned to active resistance in Greenwich Village on June 28, 1969, when gay men fought back after repeated police raids on the Stonewall Inn, which they considered their local club and bar. Events in the Village inspired drag performers, minorities, and gay and transgender patrons to come together across the nation in defense of their rights.

During the 1970s, the "gay liberation movement" served as the umbrella label for the next phase of LGBT protest and a new generation of activists. In 1973, the American Medical Association (AMA) stopped categorizing homosexuality as an illness, which lessened the possibility that these minorities could be institutionalized with the mentally ill or lose parental rights, jobs, and a place in schools and civic organizations due to charges of moral turpitude. Women activists developed a wider range of lesbian organizations and demanded attention from feminist groups such as NOW. More gay associations appeared across the country. LGBT leaders worked for inclusion in the nation's religions and clergy and took public demonstration and direct political action to new heights through the National Gay and Lesbian Task Force and the march on Washington in 1979. The decade also witnessed the ordination of the first openly gay minister and the election of gay political representatives.

Meanwhile, a backlash against this open visibility and activism gained strength. Police reported that harassment and violence based on sexual orientation grew. According to polls, moreover, LGBT people experience much more such discrimination than they report. Fear and condemnation of homosexuality result in hate crimes. A man set fire to the Upstairs Lounge, a New Orleans gay bar, in 1973 and killed 32 people. At that time, local institutions and authorities offered little sympathy to survivors or the families of victims. Anti-lesbian sentiment caused the bombing of the Other Side Lounge in Atlanta in 1997. During his sentencing, the bomber said any attempt to make homosexuality socially acceptable "should be ruthlessly opposed." Reactions against such vicious attacks as the torture and murder of Matthew Shepard in 1998 eventually lead to the strengthening of federal law. Violent offenses arising from the victim's "actual or perceived gender, sexual orientation, gender identity, or disability" joined those based on race, religion, and ethnicity as hate crimes in 2009. In 2013–15, Congress expanded the law against harassment and abuse (VAWA) to include same-sex couples.

Recent public reactions, moreover, show that attitudes and social realities have changed over the decades. When a heavily armed, sexually confused Muslim attacker, shot 49 people dead and wounded 53 at the Pulse nightclub on gay night in Orlando in 2016, the national outcry and empathy was enormous.

The ongoing fight of LGBT people and their families for civil rights and social acceptance, as well as the course of events between 1973 and 2016 transformed the public response to the Orlando massacre.

The agony of AIDS-related illnesses and deaths ravaged gay communities in the 1980s and later drew attention to the great human resources of the LGBT population. Gay spokespeople spearheaded efforts to fund treatment and research to control the effects of the epidemic, prolong the health of its victims, and search for a cure. Street theater, most notably in work performed by Queer Nation and the AIDS Coalition to Unleash Power (ACT UP), as well as marches on Washington by hundreds of thousands of LGBT people and their supporters in 1987 and 1993, drew a great deal of attention. These efforts succeeded in making the medical, economic, and civil rights needs of sexual minority groups well known, as LGBT people became recognized as family members, friends, and contributors to society.

The rights of gay and lesbian soldiers, whose sexual orientation had throughout the twentieth century, if known, been cause for dishonorable discharge from military service, became a very visible political issue in the 1990s and early 2000s because of high profile court cases, documentary films and political action. By then a recognized lobby and interest group whose votes many candidates for Congress and the presidency courted, gay men and women, received support from President Clinton, who tried unsuccessfully to reverse the ban on gay members of the military because of opposition from the Joint Chiefs of Staff. The policy of "don't ask, don't tell" enacted in 1993, meant that, if concealed, LGBT service people's sexual orientation had no effect on their military service or record. The law was an unhappy stopgap compromise. Yet it remained in force for 18 years and lead to the discharge of and loss of benefits to an estimated 12,500 service people. The policy finally ended through action by Congress and President Obama at the end of 2010, despite a Republican filibuster in the senate. Open acceptance of gays in the military went into effect in mid-2011, and in early 2013, the American Civil Liberties Union (ACLU) won an agreement with the Defense Department that it would return lost benefits to gay service people participating in the ACLU's case against the government.

From the 1990s to the second decade of the twenty-first century, increasing numbers of celebrities and ordinary people have been "coming out" as polls of the public, including straight members of the military, have indicated growing levels of comfort with people of different sexual orientations and identities. The Supreme Court decision, *Lawrence v. Texas*, in 2003 ended the criminalization of homosexual relations between consenting adults. Same-sex civil unions, legal under Vermont law in 2000, were recognized by statute in six states and the District of Columbia by 2012. The US Supreme Court ended legal inequalities for married gays by ruling same sex marriage a national right in the *Obergefell v. Hodges* case of 2015. Enormous strides have been made. Self-identification as LGBT rose to 3.8 percent of Americans in 2016. Gallup polls in the five

PLATE 4.4 A symbolic rainbow flag waves above women and men marching together in the forty-third annual Gay Pride Parade in New York City in June 2012.
© *Erik Pendzich/Rex/REX/Shutterstock*

previous years show that the pace of public acceptance continues to accelerate, even as the public incorrectly estimates the country's LGBT population to be as high as 23 percent.

African Americans

In 2014, nearly 47 million Americans identified themselves as black or black in combination with one or more other races. Due to the rapid growth of the nation's Latino population, they comprised the county's second largest minority group at 13.9 percent of the population compared to the 17.4 percent composed of those the census terms "Hispanics." Mostly old-stock Americans who have been in the country for generations, the nation's Blacks also include growing populations from Caribbean and African countries. When Africans first arrived in the American South in 1619, they did not come as slaves. By the late 1600s, however, hereditary slavery became the rule and legally, whites considered African Americans to be property. Some owners treated their slaves better than other masters, but all had ultimate power over their property. For black people, slavery meant hard work, poor living conditions and humiliation. Slave labor was especially important on large tobacco and rice plantations in Virginia and Maryland. When the US became independent, slaves made up about 20 percent of the new nation's population.

Dependence on slaves diminished as tobacco and rice grew less profitable in the early 1800s. At the same time, moral indignation over the slave trade grew so strong that in 1808 the US banned the importation of slaves. New technology, however, then made slave labor more important than ever before. Eli Whitney's cotton gin, which cleaned cotton many times faster than was possible manually, greatly increased profits if plantation owners had more slave cotton-pickers to keep their cotton gins in full operation. By 1860, the slave population was just under 4 million. With a booming cotton economy (and cheap land available by "removing" the Native Americans), the south expanded westward. This often meant that slaves had to move away from family to serve masters on newly developed plantations.

Between 1820 and the Civil War, Congress compromised repeatedly to keep an equal number of slave and free states. Abolitionists felt this policy condoned slavery, while slave-owners thought each state should be able to decide whether it wished to be "slave" or "free." Compromise finally failed, and the Civil War began in 1861. Lincoln freed the slaves in the undefeated parts of the South in early 1863 through the Emancipation Proclamation and, after Union victory, amendments to the Constitution abolished slavery, granted the former slaves citizenship and gave black men the right to vote. Congress repealed the black codes that the Southern states passed to limit the rights of former slaves. However, with no land or education, most black people had to work as sharecroppers or lease land and equipment from their former masters. Rents were so high that they had little hope of getting out of debt.

The presence of the Union army enforced the new constitutional amendments from 1865 to 1877 during Reconstruction. Then, however, the US withdrew the troops and the North abandoned the cause of the former slaves. For 80 years, the federal government left the South alone. Southerners did not accept black people as equals. They passed laws to deny Blacks social, economic and political rights, and segregated almost every aspect of public life. These "Jim Crow laws" remained in effect in most Southern states until the 1960s.

The *Plessy* v. *Ferguson* case in 1896 established the court's separate-but-equal doctrine approving segregation. In 1909, a group of black and white people founded the National Association for the Advancement of Colored People (NAACP) to fight for African Americans' civil rights in general and to win repeal of the separate-but-equal doctrine in particular. At the time, Jim Crow laws affected most African Americans because about 90 percent of black people lived in the south. In 1915, the NAACP persuaded the Supreme Court to annul the grandfather clause, which denied the vote to persons whose grandfathers had not voted in the 1860s, but violent intimidation and discriminatory local laws still kept Southern black people from voting. The NAACP won the invalidation of some residential segregation laws in 1935, but again with little practical effect.

The much smaller black population in the North grew rapidly and developed vibrant urban communities around the time of the First World War. *De jure* segregation (separation of the races by law) was the rule in the South. In the North, de-facto segregation (racial separation through informal means) was almost universal and forced black people to live in ghettos, such as Harlem in New York City, the country's most famous black community. By the 1920s, black people's bitter disappointment over their limited freedom in northern centers resulted in protest movements, some demanding integration (like the NAACP) and others, such as Marcus Garvey's, promoting preparation for a return to Africa. Mass migration from the South continued. The rush for jobs in weapons industries during the Second World War accelerated the move to the North and brought Blacks to West Coast cities. By the 1950s, almost half the nation's Blacks lived in ghettos outside the South.

From 1938 the African American lawyer, Thurgood Marshall, who later became the first black Supreme Court justice, led the NAACP legal defense group; more liberals took seats on the Supreme Court during the following 20 years. These changes helped the NAACP achieve more in the courts, where it fought the separate-but-equal doctrine by showing the inequalities of school segregation. The Court did not overturn the doctrine, but its later decisions made segregation almost impossible to implement in graduate and professional schools. Not until 1954, however, did the *Brown* v. *Board of Education* decision reverse the separate-but-equal regime. The Court followed this up with the annulment of *de jure* segregation in public places and so indicated that the time was right for change.

Implementing these changes was difficult. The South offered massive resistance. The court got no help from the other branches of government. President Eisenhower had publicly supported segregation, and a conservative coalition of Southern Democrats and Republicans dominated Congress. Not until violence broke out in Little Rock, Arkansas, when nine black students tried to attend a white school in 1957, did the president send the National Guard to enforce the court's ruling. The next President, John F. Kennedy, used the guard or federal marshals several times to desegregate the schools. Defiant southerners therefore avoided desegregation in other ways. White people who had the means sent their children to private schools that were not bound by federal law. By 1964, only 2 percent of black children in the South attended desegregated schools. In 1969, the Supreme Court ordered the desegregation of all public schools and later approved measures to force integration, such as racial quotas, the grouping of non-contiguous school districts, and bussing in order to achieve racial balance in the schools. Since most black people lived in the inner cities while white people lived in the suburbs, there was strong opposition to bussing. When the court ruled against bussing between cities and suburbs in 1974, bussing declined sharply.

Other forms of *de jure* racial discrimination existed in the South in the 1950s. Blacks suffered racial exclusion from voting, employment, and the use of 'white' facilities. In 1955, police arrested Rosa Parks, a black woman from Montgomery, Alabama, for refusing to give up a seat at the front of a bus. This incident sparked a black boycott against the city's bus system led by the young Baptist minister Martin Luther King, Jr. One year later the federal courts ruled that segregated transportation violated the Fourteenth Amendment. The African American civil rights movement of the 1950s and 1960s was under way. King was one of the organizers of the Southern Christian Leadership Conference (SCLC), which coordinated civil-rights activities. His "I Have a Dream" speech to more than 250,000 people at the Lincoln Memorial in 1963 was one of the most inspiring calls for racial equality in American history.

White officials' brutal suppression of civil-rights protests in the South, newly visible on nationwide television, made Americans more conscious of racial injustice. President Kennedy addressed the problem from the White House and called fighting racism a moral issue. The Civil Rights Act of 1964 outlawed discrimination in jobs and public housing, and the following year the Voting Rights Act led to black voter registration drives that transformed politics in the South. Historians call this the non-violent revolution. However, segregationists killed peaceful protesters, both black and white, and, while Martin Luther King, Jr. advocated nonviolence, other Blacks felt change was too slow in coming. African Americans had heightened expectations, and they were disappointed with how little change civil rights laws brought to their daily lives. Frustrated residents of the black ghettos across the nation exploded in riots for three successive years in the mid-1960s.

Black radicals wanted to establish an alternate African American culture. Some of these formed the Black Power and Black Panther movements. Malcolm X became one of the most famous Black Muslims and members of the Nation of Islam, who created their own variant of Islam and rejected America's lifestyle and politics. These movements became involved in violent conflicts with the police. For many black people, nonviolence seemed defunct as a means of winning civil rights. Another Black Muslim killed Malcolm X in 1965, and three years later when an assassin killed Martin Luther King, 168 American cities erupted in racial conflict.

Nonetheless, some inspiring leaders and their supporters in this reform-minded period in the US responded to black protests. President Johnson's Great Society and War on Poverty were contested packages of reforms and took time to reach many of the people who needed assistance. Still, his dedicated staff spread out across the nation and hired tens of thousands to implement programs of assistance through relief (Supplemental Security Income), education (Head Start and Upward Bound), job training (the Job Core), medical help (Medicaid and Medicare) and public housing. African Americans have benefited greatly from these initiatives. In the 1970s and 1980s, these efforts gained wider scope.

Following President Richard Nixon, who instituted affirmative action minority preferences for federal contracts in the early 1970s, private industry and business began hiring Blacks for professional, managerial, and skilled jobs, using affirmative action employee searches and job training.

Institutions of higher education, such as the City University of New York and other public systems, offered "open admissions" to local high school graduates as well as programs of remediation to help young people enter college. In the interest of "leveling the playing field" colleges and universities across the nation offered high school and even elementary education to help minorities catch up. The black middle class grew substantially, and real progress seemed underway. In the 1990s, however, the tide of opinion turned. The public backlash against preferential treatment grew decisive as the majority on the US Supreme Court became more conservative. In 1996, Congress strictly limited the length of time the poor could benefit from welfare programs, severely affecting the poorest blacks. Court decisions or referenda limited affirmative action in higher education in several states, causing large declines in minority enrollment at the same time that blacks remained underrepresented in such high-status studies as medicine and law.

The contemporary situation for African Americans

The implementation of civil rights laws alone has not ensured racial equality. Significant differences in the quality of life for whites and blacks persist or have grown in the years after the Great Recession of late 2007 to 2012. The slow recovery that followed the crisis did not produce enough well-paying jobs, even by 2016, to end the shrinking of the economically stagnant middle class. African Americans' rate of high school completion nearly caught up prior to the recession, but residential segregation has remained great and contributes to a lower quality of public education among blacks. That in part explains why fewer African Americans complete college degrees. Less higher education results in a much lower median household income. These factors meant that blacks sooner and more often lost their jobs and homes during the financial and concomitant mortgage crisis. Since then the gap in home ownership and household wealth between the races has grown wider. Despite the Fair Housing Act of 1968, the most recent poll in 2016 showed that over four in 10 black people feel they face discrimination when they buy, borrow, or rent to find housing. As late as 2015, moreover, blacks twice as often lived below the poverty line.

Only half as many blacks *completed* a college degree as whites did in the first decade and a half of the twenty-first century. In 2003, the University of Michigan won a narrow 5–4 victory in the *Grutter v. Bollinger* case when the US Supreme Court decided that race could be a factor in admissions decisions because of the "compelling interest" of giving students the educational benefits of a diverse student body. A large majority of the Michigan public reversed the court's decision, however, by voting to end affirmative action at the state's universities in 2006. By then, polls indicated that the majority of Americans did not think the government should shoulder the responsibility for helping the disadvantaged.

Blacks documented equal qualifications with limited effect. Employers often doubted their credentials, assumed that they got special treatment in affirmative-action programs or felt alienated from black people with whom they had little contact. Government work was a mainstay of the black middle class, but budget cuts removed many such jobs after 2008.

Ironically, by 2000, most progress in residential desegregation occurred in the South, where black people left cities for suburbs at the same time as white people, instead of decades later as in the other regions. By 2012, the most racially segregated cites in the nation were in the Northeast and Midwest, including Boston, New York, Pittsburgh, Detroit, Chicago and St. Louis. Between 1990 and 2015, black people migrated into the South in record numbers, reversing their century-long flight from the region.

Passionate African American protests against stereotypical profiling of black suspects by white police, juries, and judges capture headlines today as much as it did in the 1960s. Through social media, the "#Black Lives Matter" movement

PLATE 4.5 Malcolm X, who advocated a self-sufficient Black Muslim culture within the US, addressing a crowd at a Black Muslim rally in Harlem, New York in 1963.
© *Bob Parent/Getty*

brought the injustice of police profiling of young black men to the forefront yet again. BLM originated in 2013 as a response to the acquittal of George Zimmerman, the volunteer neighborhood watch coordinator in Florida who shot and killed an unarmed black teenager, Trayvon Martin, a year earlier. BLM spokespeople characterized his death as typical of legal injustice against African Americans because, as so often before, an armed authority figure could shoot first and ask questions later when faced with a young black man – and win confirmation that his deadly action was blameless under the law.

Differences in the application of the law according to race received close attention in the commentary about a series of police shootings of black men and African Americans' retaliatory actions after Trayvon Martin's death. Two highly publicized cases of black men who died through controversial altercations with police in Missouri and New York City in 2014 led to anti-police protests and marches in BLM affiliates across the nation. In 2016, police shootings of black men in Louisiana and Minnesota led an African American man in New York and another in Dallas to kill police officers in revenge.

The spiraling racialized violence between blacks and the police brought mainstream media commentary on the spread of the BLM movement across the nation, its confrontations with city police and the resulting public debate over the need for reform of the criminal justice system. Commentators on the

PLATE 4.6 On July 17, 2016, anti-Trump organizations and Black Lives Matter protesters marched in protest through downtown Cleveland, Ohio, before the Republican convention.
© *DDP USA/REX/Shutterstock*

left noted that American blacks experienced the highest incarceration and death penalty rates of any of the nation's ethnic groups. Spokespeople on the right cited statistics showing that young blacks had the nation's highest crime rate and often threatened the lives of people in police forces, for whom recruitment was becoming increasingly difficult. Researchers analyze how inadequate legal representation of the poor and legal changes, such as many states' "stand your ground" laws to protect people who felt threatened and "three strikes" laws giving long sentences for repeat offenders, combined with "war on drugs" have disproportionately jailed poor blacks and lead to their criminalization while incarcerated.

Blacks winning elective office offered the greatest hope for attaining the dream of racial equality, in the view of some. The Black Caucus in Congress continues to grow. There are over 500 black mayors around the country, as are many other local officials. In the 2008 presidential election, Barack Obama rose above prejudice and divisive partisan politics, never running as a black man and winning a clear electoral victory on the theme of being the candidate of all the people in the United States. In 2012, he won a second term with the support of a multiracial coalition. After Obama's eight years in office, however, according to a Pew Research Center study, 32 percent of whites and 5 percent of blacks thought that his presidency resulted in worsened race relations. The partisan character of the white response to the question is evident in that 63 percent of Republican Whites judged that the first black president had made race relations worse.

Asian Americans

"Asian American" is a convenient term that lumps together a diverse collection of immigrant and American-born populations. After 2010 for example, it included rapidly growing numbers of Asian Indian, Chinese, Saudi Arabian, Nepalese, Iraqi, and Burmese newcomers, as well as Hmong tribespeople who came as refugees after the Vietnam War and the descendants of the Chinese who settled before the Civil War. The principle of common continental origins justifies putting in one category people with different religions, skin colors, socioeconomic backgrounds and historical experiences. The US census compiles information on this diverse composite group together with another such group, "Pacific Islanders," which includes native Hawaiians, Guamanians and Samoans, among others.

Between 2007 and 2016, migration from Asia rose increasingly with the result that Asian Americans became the nation's fastest growing foreign-born racial minority. Since then, Asian immigration rates have remained high, prompting demographers to estimate that if current trends continue, Asian Americans will likely be the nation's largest foreign-born population in coming decades. In

2014, Asian Americans numbered a record 20.3 million people, 32 percent of immigration to the US and 6 percent of the country's whole population.

Between the 1970s and 2016, the Asian-born population of the US has exploded in size. The Asian American community grew on average by nearly 49 percent per decade and by 200 percent or more in some cities in every region of the country. At the same time both their prominence in the fourth wave of immigrants and their diversity has grown. Hundreds of thousands of people from some 20 other Asian nations have joined the five largest Asian ancestry groups (Chinese, Asian Indian, Filipino, Vietnamese, and Korean). It is only to the old-stock American perception that all these people *look* Asian (and the different treatment that this perception has caused) that has given them related experiences in the US.

The first large group of Chinese, some 370,000 people, came with the second wave "old" immigrants between the late 1840s and 1882. One-fifth settled in Hawaii and the rest on the West Coast, mostly in California. About 400,000 Japanese immigrated between the 1880s and 1908 and settled in roughly equal numbers on the West Coast and in Hawaii, where they composed the largest Asian immigrant group. Small groups of Koreans and East Indians (about 7,000 each) came to the islands and West Coast states from 1900 to 1930. During the

PLATE 4.7 Chinatown in Manhattan with New York's City Hall in the near background.
© *Jose Fuste Raga/Getty*

same period, approximately 180,000 Filipinos immigrated, about three in five of them first arriving in Hawaii.

The situation of Asian immigrants varied greatly between Hawaii and the mainland. In the islands, most worked as recruited contract workers on plantations, where they did backbreaking stoop labor under military-style discipline and the supervision of abusive overseers. Planters segregated nationality groups in different camps and pitted them against each other to keep wages low and prevent a unified labor movement. Plantation owners depended on these workers and so provided food, housing and medical care. To get workers to stay when their contracts ended, they helped women immigrate, encouraged family life, supported religious and ethnic customs and built schools and community centers.

Discrimination against Asian Americans in Hawaii was much milder than that on the mainland because they made up a large majority of the islands' workforce. In 1920, Asian Americans comprised over half of the islands' population, and about two in five people were Japanese Americans. Thus, most Japanese Americans on the mainland, but less than 1 percent of those in Hawaii, were put in concentration camps during World War II. In the 1930s, Asian Americans started to win prominent positions in Hawaiian politics. Since 1959, Hawaii has been the only state in which they play major roles in both state and federal politics.

On the mainland, the situation of Asian Americans was fundamentally different until the mid-1940s. Always a tiny minority compared to European Americans, they much more easily became victims of systematic discrimination. Anti-Asian campaigns in the Pacific West aimed to segregate Asians from white people, prevent them from competing economically and end their immigration. Anti-miscegenation laws against racial mixing forbade marriages to white people. Many businesses refused them products and services. The only housing they could find was often in Asian American ghettos. Supreme Court decisions decided that they were non-whites and therefore ineligible for citizenship. Many western states also passed alien land laws, which prohibited non-citizens from leasing or owning land. In 1882, federal law excluded Chinese workers from immigrating. The 1908 Gentlemen's Agreement prohibited the entry of Japanese laborers, and in 1921 the "Ladies' Agreement" banned Japanese women's immigration. A national law ended all Asian immigration in 1924.

With assistance from sympathetic white people, Asian Americans fought oppression. They found loopholes in the land laws, circumvented immigration exclusion laws, created their own job opportunities by starting businesses, formed union and protest organizations and, through these, stood up for their rights through strikes and lawsuits. For all Asian American groups but Japanese Americans, World War II brought social and economic improvements. Public attitudes became positive to the Chinese, Koreans, Filipinos and East Indians, whose homelands were American allies. Members of these groups served in the US armed forces. Tens of thousands of Japanese American youths left the concentration camps to prove their loyalty in the American military. War industries gave Asian Americans professional and skilled work previously denied them. By the war's end, all four groups could immigrate and all but Koreans had won citizenship rights. Between 1945 and 1965, the US repealed laws against Asian Americans or the nation's courts struck them down.

Asian immigrants to the US after World War II are distinctive in several ways. Special laws permitted the entry of Asians who married American military personnel in that war and the Korean War. In 1965, an immigration act opened the way for the huge current wave of Asian immigration. Its provisions allow well-educated Asian students in the US to qualify to become immigrants and later bring relatives through family reunification rules. Such relatives are less accustomed to American life. Because of the Vietnam War, hundreds of thousands of Vietnamese, Laotian and Cambodian refugees settled in the US. The first wave of these refugees in the mid-1970s was comprised of mostly well-off, Westernized people who had cooperated with the colonial French and US forces. From the 1980s on, Asian refugees were often poorer and less educated.

A significant minority of fourth-wave Asian American consist of well-educated professionals. Many of them come from urban areas, where they worked in modern industry. More of the recent immigrants also arrive as families, rather than as single men, and plan to settle permanently. On the other hand, recent refugees are often destitute, poorly educated and unprepared for city life. The Hmong and Mien, pre-industrial upland peoples of Southeast Asia, have found adapting to modern conditions particularly hard. The numbers of Japanese newcomers are now small, while the totals from other Asian nations have set new records.

Asian Americans today

Since the mid-1960s, the popular media have often depicted Asian Americans as the nation's "model minority." Commentators remark on their high median family incomes, level of academic achievement and low rates of unemployment, crime, mental illness and dependence on welfare as examples to other minority groups. The emphasis on traditional family values, such as a stable marriage with children and living in multi-generation family households, is more apparent among Asian Americans than any other part of the population.

The media image of Asian Americans' success caused resentment that fed a rising wave of anti-Asian activity in the 1980s, when the US Civil Rights Commission reported many racial slurs, violent assaults, vandalism and harassment against Asian Americans. Conflicts occurred between Korean storeowners and Latino or African-American customers near their shops. In 1992 in Los Angeles, Korean shops became the target of rioters who looted and destroyed some 1,800 Korean stores. When reactions to the rapid progress of Asian immigrants cooled during the later 1990s, Asian American and African American relations improved.

The concentration of Asian Americans in a few states has been a source of benefits and drawbacks. The first wave of Asian immigration settled mostly in Hawaii, on the West Coast and in the Chinatowns of large cities. Asian new-comers established networks of mutual assistance and an ethnic economy that supported many compatriots in these places, but their visibility also fueled anti-Asian movements. Around two-thirds of all Asian Americans live in just six states today – California, New York, Texas, New Jersey, Hawaii, and Illinois. Most Japanese and Filipino Americans live in the West, while a majority of Chinese, Indian, Vietnamese and Koreans live in other regions. In California and Texas during the 1990s, the high portion of Asian Americans winning places at prestigious state universities contributed to the backlash against affirmative action programs. Still, settling close together also brought voting power on the state and federal levels. In 2016, three Senators and ten members of the House of Representatives made up the Asian American caucus in Congress.

A closer look at their situation shows that, despite their successes, sig-nificant numbers of Asian Americans have socioeconomic problems and face considerable discrimination. Asian Americans are twice as urbanized as whites. One reason for this is that their high family incomes are dependent on living in central cities with large, diverse job markets. Only these places can provide work for the number of family members who work long hours and contribute their wages to one household income, which, taken together, is higher than the family incomes of white households. In *personal* incomes, Asian Americans have not caught up with white Americans. One reason for that is that they are more concentrated in semi-skilled service trades, low-level professional, and manage-ment positions. Still, despite the large number of refugees from Asia, about half as many people in these ethnic groups lived in poverty in 2015 than was the case among Latin Americans, the other large body of recent immigrants. Asian Americans' educational attainments, moreover, were higher than those of Whites, and a higher portion of them worked in management, professional and related occupations. Still, many successful Asian Americans reported that a so-called "glass ceiling" of prejudice kept them out of the higher management levels of industries and professional firms. The slums of major American cities that have a high incidence of poverty, health problems, drug abuse and teenage gangs often overlap with the poorest parts of Asian American communities. By 2015, more Asian Americans lived in racially mixed areas than any other group, fewer in ghettos or areas dominated by one group, and more in better multicul-tural urban neighborhoods or suburbs.

Latino Americans

A Spanish language and cultural background is the inexact basis for calling peo-ple with ethnic origins in the Caribbean, Central and South America "Latinos" or

"Hispanics." The term does not apply to people from countries in the Americas, such as Brazil, Haiti or the Bahamas, whose cultural forms derive chiefly from other European cultures. Those commonly called Latinos include the Central or South American descendants of Native American peoples, African slaves, later immigrants from European and Asian nations and mixtures of these groups. In 2014, somewhat more than half of Latinos identified themselves as white. The majority are Catholic, but significant numbers are Protestant or members of other religions. Most are relatively recent immigrants to the US. Mexicans have immigrated in large numbers since around 1900. The early Spanish settlers came during the 1500s.

The Census Bureau estimated that about 56.6 million people (17.6 percent of the population) were "Hispanic or Latino" in 2015. Those figures represented well over a 100 percent increase since 1990 and mean that the Latino population continues to be the fastest growing group in the nation. Today Latinos are a larger minority than African Americans.

Two-thirds of Latinos (37.9 million people) identify as Mexican Americans. Many live in the Southwest, Los Angeles or large Midwestern cities such as Chicago. From 1990 on, Mexican American communities have appeared across the nation, especially in the rural and small-town South, Midwest and Mountain West. During 2007–14, however, Mexican immigration, both legal and illegal, fell sharply, and in some years, more Mexicans returned to their homeland than migrated to the US. The Mexican American population continued to increase, but mostly from children born in the US. Perhaps in response to political promises to build a wall along the Mexican border, Mexican immigration rose in 2015–16.

The other Latino groups are small by comparison. In 2016, Puerto Ricans, the second largest group, made up 10.1 percent of Latinos and lived mostly in New York City and other Northeastern urban areas. The two next largest groups, Cubans and Salvadoran Americans, whose largest communities are in Florida and New York City, each comprise about 4.0 percent of Latino Americans. The remaining Latinos have about 30 different national origins, the largest of which are Dominican, Guatemalan and Colombian.

Like other minorities in the US, Latinos have faced prejudice and discrimination in jobs, housing, education and politics. A combination of forces brought the first large groups of Mexican immigrants to the US in the two decades after 1900. Federal law provided funding for irrigated farming in the Southwest in 1902, and since the US excluded Asian immigration in 1924, a new source of unskilled field workers became urgent as the region's agribusinesses expanded rapidly. Filipino "nationals" provided some new laborers but could not satisfy the demand for fresh produce created by population growth, urbanization and the advent of refrigerated transportation. These magnetic factors became irresistible after 1909, when Mexico descended into a decade of revolution and violent political instability.

By 1920, nearly 100,000 Mexicans lived in California alone, and the precedent for some main features of Mexican (and Latino) immigration was set. The need for "stoop labor" to tend and harvest crops in growing acreages continued through the 1920s, when many Mexicans also worked in Southwestern mines and railroad gangs and Midwestern farms and foundries. However, in the depression of the 1930s, more than a million Mexican Americans (including many US citizens) lost their jobs and faced deportation.

Mexican laborers were welcome again during World War II. In 1942, the US and Mexico reached an agreement that legalized their temporary status in the US. This *bracero* program recruited 4.5 million Mexicans, mostly in farm work, as guest workers before it ended in 1964. The agreement's text guaranteed the *braceros'* civil rights and working conditions, but fell so far short in Texas that Mexico refused to send more of its citizens there. The program expanded during the Korean War and in the mid-1950s in response to growing needs for cheap, non-union labor. With the program's end, illegal immigration from Mexico soared until the IRCA amnesty in 1986. Until 2007, legal and illegal Mexican and Latino immigration rose to new heights and fueled the controversy over immigration restriction.

For many decades, Latino children attended segregated "Mexican" schools in the West and Southwest. When federal courts declared them to be white in the 1940s, the situation improved somewhat, but a decade later local officials used these rulings to "integrate" schools by creating districts where most pupils were Latino or African American, while non-Latino white pupils attended school elsewhere. Today the great majority of Latinos still go to school in segregated districts. To this point, race rather than English competence was decisive for their US schooling, even though, like other immigrant children, they could not speak their native language at school and met pressure to Anglicize their culture.

In the Southwest, Florida and the New York City area, Latinos achieved political influence decades ago by election to office at all levels of government. In the 1960s and 1970s, they organized "brown power" protest movements that fought for civil rights on the streets and in the courts, enhancing Latinos' pride and stimulating a variety of cultural institutions. Latinos have long been actively involved in union movements of many kinds, despite the prejudice of some white labor leaders. The largest occupational group of Latinos for many years was migratory farm workers. César Chávez became the first nationally well-known Latino leader in the 1960s through his successful five-year national boycott and strike negotiations as head of the United Farm Workers Union of California.

In the 1980s and 1990s, civil rights workers and scholars discussed how perhaps "proximity" (nearness and ease of returning to Mexico) explained Latinos' relatively low profile in electoral politics. Since 2000, however, that has changed. The Latino vote gave Obama a winning margin in swing states such as Florida, Colorado and Nevada in 2008 and 2012, but four years later, Latino turnout declined and was not decisive in the presidential election. On the other hand, the Latinos elected to the US Senate, four, exceeded the number of African Americans there, and the Hispanic caucus in the House of Representatives, 33 members, remained about the same size.

Attitudes to Latino America: the nation's largest immigrant subculture

Public opinion regarding Latinos, always mixed, grew increasingly negative as the immigration of Spanish-origin groups skyrocketed in the late 1900s and early 2000s. Reactions were particularly strong from Texas to California. Proficiency in English understandably became the center of debates over civil rights for Latinos, because the nation had never before witnessed a wave of immigration in which so many national and cultural groups shared a language. Over 20 states declared English their official language in reaction against the use of Spanish by Latinos in the 1980s. In schools, bilingual programs (teaching offered in both the pupil's mother tongue and English) became a major battle in a "culture war" centered largely on whether Latino communities would have to acquire English or have the opportunity of functioning in both it and Spanish. The compromise reached tolerates bilingual instruction only until Latino pupils reach proficiency in English. Programs for "cultural maintenance" have found little support.

Latinos won an important victory in 1982 when the Supreme Court decided that the children of illegal immigrants were entitled to public education. In 1994, however, California's voters passed Proposition 187, which would have denied the state's illegal immigrants all social services except emergency medical attention but for court actions brought by civil rights groups. In 1996, California and Texas voters ended state affirmative action programs, even knowing that these helped both Blacks and Latinos.

The issues of language competence, workers' rights and access to government services came together in the *Sandoval* case that the US Supreme Court resolved in 2001. Citing the Civil Rights Act of 1964, lawyers serving the poor in Alabama helped Martha Sandoval, a Spanish-speaker whose English was limited, sue the state for discrimination based on her cultural background, because it passed a law requiring that all driver's tests be given in English. In a 5–4 decision, the court ruled that the law did not have a disproportionately large effect on Sandoval and others in her situation. It further overturned decades of federal court decisions based on Title VI of the Civil Rights Act of 1964 that had declared unconstitutional discrimination ranging from school law to the location of polluting industries that had a disproportionate effect because of race, color or national background.

PLATE 4.8 César Chávez, leader of the United Farm Workers, speaking to union members in California in 1979.
© *Michael Salas/Getty*

Latino Americans comprised one of the youngest population groups in 2015 with a median age of 29. Often young parents with small children, Latino families contribute the most rapidly growing foreign language group and poorest prepared pupils to the nation's school systems. Close to three-quarters of these children speak Spanish at home. Their parents have by far the lowest level of education of any major ethnic or racial group and most often cannot afford pre-schooling or childhood health care. With such a poor start, Latinos became the pupils most likely to drop out of school. Unemployment and poverty rates among Latinos were also the highest among the foreign-born, which commentators blamed chiefly on their educational situation, the enormous increase in Latino immigration in past years and rising anti-Latino feeling in the regions of their greatest concentration. The high number of recent Latino arrivals still feeds rising hostility even after their immigration started declining after 2007.

In the Southwest, border patrols and local police often stop Latinos to check whether they are undocumented. In 2010, Arizona passed a law making it a state crime for foreign-born not to carry documentation of their immigration status or to seek employment if they were not "authorized." Most controversially, the law allowed state police to stop and arrest people without a warrant if they had reason to suspect they might be unauthorized. In a state where

Mexican Americans made up over 60 percent of immigrants, this seemed to target Latinos, no matter how long they had been in the US. Such "racial profiling," leads police departments to single out Latinos as suspects. Soon a half dozen other states passed similar laws.

In opinion polls, the public supported state legislation because the federal government had not stopped illegal immigration. The US Justice Department, however, won a lawsuit to stop implementation of the Arizona law. By 2012, a divided Supreme Court heard the case, struck down the state crimes it created and declared that the federal government held authority in matters of immigration and deportation. State authorities could stop people they had reasonable reason to suspect were undocumented but they could not hold them. Instead, police had to check with federal immigration agents before deciding to hold the suspects.

After 2012, there were signs of Latinos' growing political influence. Across the nation, city governments with large Latino communities declared that the undocumented were essential to the local economy and that they were "sanctuary cities," places where the authorities would not enforce state or federal laws that discriminated against undocumented residents. Since 2004, unprecedented numbers of Latino Americans have also won elected office. In 2016, however, the elimination of illegal Latino immigration became an explosive issue in Donald Trump's successful presidential election campaign.

Exercises

Explain and examine the significance of the following names and terms:

equality of opportunity	Lilly Ledbetter	abolitionists
Seneca Falls Convention	protectionist legislation	2010 Arizona immigration law
ERA	affirmative action programs	*Roe* v. *Wade*
The Stonewall riots	"domestic dependent nation"	forced assimilation
Indian New Deal	sanctuary cities	Asian contract workers
anti-miscegenation laws	urban ghettos	model minority
"glass ceiling"	black codes	same-sex marriage
Plessy v. *Ferguson*	NAACP	*de jure* segregation
non-violent revolution	illegal immigrants	Black Lives Matter
bilingual education	the *Sandoval* case	César Chávez

Write short essays on the following questions.

1. Discuss the factors that have contributed to the improved status of American women since the colonial period.

2. Evaluate the motives and effects of US policy toward Native Americans.

3. Discuss the changing situation of the LGBT community and the causes for change.

4. Give a critical review of the aspects of African Americans' struggle for equality that you find distinctive from that of other minority groups.

5. Compare and contrast early and recent Asian American immigrants and the treatment they have received in the US.

6. Describe the make-up of America's Latino population and discuss the kinds of discrimination it has faced.

Further reading

Acunã, R. (2006) *Occupied America: A History of Chicanos*, Harlow, England: Longman.

Block, S., Alexander, R.M. and Norton, M. B. (2014) *Major Problems in American Women's History*, Stamford, CT: Cengage Learning.

Hurtado, A. L. and Iverson, P. (2001) (eds.) *Major Problems in American Indian History*, Lexington, MA: D. C. Heath.

Jonas, G. (2007) *Freedom's Sword: The NAACP and the Struggle against Racism in America, 1909–1969*, New York: Routledge.

Kolchin, P. (2003) *American Slavery, 1619–1877*, New York: Hill and Wang.

McWilliams, C. and Meyer, M. S. (1990) *North from Mexico: The Spanish-speaking People of the United States*, Westport, CT: Greenwood.

Ngai, M. M. and Gjerde J, (eds.) (2013) *Major Problems in American Immigration History: Documents and Essays*, Boston, MA: Cengage Learning.

Okihiro, G. Y. (2014) *Margins and Mainstreams: Asians in American History and Culture*, Seattle, WA: University of Washington Press

PBS Broadcasting (2013) *Latino Americans*, a three-part documentary series produced by WETA, Washington, DC; Bosch and Co., Inc.; and Latino Public Broadcasting (LPB); with Independent Television Service (ITVS).

Ruiz, V. L. and DuBois, E.C. (2000) (eds.) *Unequal Sisters: A Multicultural Reader in U.S. Women's History*, London: Routledge.

Stall, R., Valdiserri, R. O. and Wolitski, R. J. (2008) (eds.) *Unequal Opportunity: Health Disparities Affecting Gay and Bisexual Men in the United States*, New York: Oxford.

Takaki, Ronald (1998) *Strangers from a Different Shore: A History of Asian Americans*, 2nd ed. Boston, MA: Little, Brown.

Townsend, Camilla (2009) (ed.) *American Indian History: A Documentary Reader*, Oxford: Wiley-Blackwell.

Websites

www.census.gov/programs-surveys/acs/technical-documentation/race-ethnicity-aian.html

www.pewresearch.org/topics/gender

census.gov/topics/population/race.html

www.census.gov/newsroom/

www.pewresearch.org/topics/african-americans/

edition.cnn.com/2015/09/28/us/pew-study-immigration-asians-hispanics/

www.nytimes.com/2016/06/15/us/upstairs-lounge-new-orleans-fire-orlando-gay-bar.
    html?_r=0

www.aclu.org/lgbt-rights

www.gallup.com/poll/158066/special-report-adults-identify-lgbt.aspx

www.pewhispanic.org/

Chapter 5

Religious culture

- Religious history
- Contemporary US religion
- Church, state and politics
- Religion and education
- Attitudes to religion
- *Exercises*
- *Further reading*
- *Websites*

This chapter discusses the role of religion in US society. It examines religious history and the diversity of contemporary denominations; considers the relationship between religion and the state; and assesses personal attitudes toward institutional religion and spiritual experience.

Many Western countries have experienced modern declines in religious observance and increased secularization (non-sacred concerns). These changes have been attributed to the effects of industrialization, consumerism, materialism, individualism and expanded education. Although Americans have historically been regarded as significantly religious, there have been recent declines in belief and practice.

The extent of US religiosity is difficult to assess since the US Census Bureau does not ask questions on religious identity. It published a *Statistical Abstract of the United States, 2012*, which gathered evidence of adult belief from the American Religious Identification Survey (ARIS) 2008–9 and church rolls. It is argued that such records may be inadequate, and there can be errors in calculating the membership of belief groups. However, opinion polls regularly publish their findings. The latter sources suggest that some 76 percent of adult Americans see themselves as "religious," which is a higher figure than for most other nations.

While religion is important for many Americans, they also believe that it is under attack and losing its influence in American life. A majority of people say they are interested in "spiritual" matters but think that beliefs are increasingly treated as arbitrary and unimportant. Religious observance may sometimes be more socially directed than devout. Spirituality may exist outside of denominational identity and can reflect a disillusionment with organized or institutional religion and a need for more personal forms of self-definition.

Formal membership or nominal identification with denominations is not always translated into active observance and religious commitment varies across the US. A Public Religion Research Institute survey in 2013 found that 31 percent of Americans attend religious services at least weekly. Other polls reported that respondents attend at varying times, with some 40 percent going a few times or once a year, while around 20 percent never attend religious services.

Significant differences are revealed at the state level. A 2014 Gallup International survey reported that Utah had a 51 percent observance rate, followed by high-scoring Southern states, a leveling-off by Midwestern, Western and Eastern states, and considerable drops by Northeastern states such as Massachusetts (22 percent), Maine (20 percent), New Hampshire (20 percent) and Vermont (17 percent).

Nevertheless, religion, in whatever form, does play a role in the US. It is illustrated in the variety of religious groups which reflect personal, communal and ethnic identities for citizens; in its influence on national institutions and morality; and in the country's history.

Religious history

Contemporary US religious life and practice derive from Native American and Viking settlement, colonial history and waves of later immigrants into the country.

This historical development is marked by certain features. First, there is a considerable religious diversity or pluralism (many different faiths) in the US. Second, religious activity with evangelical (conversion or salvation-based) and fundamentalist characteristics (strict maintenance of traditional orthodox beliefs) has been important at various times. Third, these factors have often created conflict within faiths, between different religions and with the larger society. Fourth, there has been an emphasis on the social aspects of religion and the provision of social welfare by many churches. Fifth, religion has been closely linked to a belief in democracy, freedom and egalitarianism. Sixth, religious identities and membership of specific churches have often been connected to social class and ethnicity. Seventh, there is a constitutional emphasis on the separation of religion from the state and a protection of religious belief itself.

Throughout American history, all or some of these features have been reflected in periodic religious movements (awakenings or revivals, which have varied in intensity and scope), religious activism, missionary work, utopian ideals and an interest in ecumenism (cooperation between different faiths). There has also been religious discrimination and intolerance, periods when American religiosity has been very low and increasing secularism.

Native American religion

Native American religion has historically been characterized by a diversity of beliefs and practices among many distinctive tribes or peoples. Religious principles are passed down orally (rather than in written form) as histories, stories, allegories and principles. While groups have their own belief systems, there are also common practices, traditions and ceremonies (such as feasts, dances and music). There are no unifying texts, but some spiritual stories have been transcribed and have survived. These deal with the representation of animals, the spirit world, the land and nature to tell the creation stories of individual tribes. Such activities are conducted by shamans and medicine men, and Native American religion is based on early instruction of young people in the customs of tribal communities.

In the past, Native American beliefs were not classified as religion in the US. Indian tribes were persecuted by Christian denominations and government agencies through forcible conversion, and suppression of indigenous languages and cultures continued until 1978 and the passing of the American Indian Religious Freedom Act (AIRFA). Some sacred sites are now protected by law. The communities continue to have socio/political problems, and their membership in the US has been estimated at between 9,000 and 186,000 religious persons.

The colonial period

The Spanish brought Roman Catholicism to the Americas and built the oldest European church in St Augustine, Florida in 1565, although early versions were lost until after 1786, when the surviving parish church gradually became a cathedral. The first arrivals were missionaries from Spain, Portugal and France, in addition to settlers, soldiers and traders. Catholic churches and missions were established in the South and West of the country in present-day Texas, California, Florida and New Mexico.

Many early European colonists, such as the English, were Protestants whose faiths influenced future US society. There were, however, conflicts between denominations. For example, in the early seventeenth century, after the establishment of Jamestown in 1607, Virginia's population later largely comprised members of the established Anglican Church of England. This church taxed dissenters who settled in the colony. Quakers were banned, and Baptist ministers were arrested. However, French Huguenots, German Protestants and Scots-Irish Presbyterians were allowed their own congregations.

Two groups of settlers later arrived in New England and were different from the Virginia Anglicans. A first group (102 Pilgrims and 35 Puritans) came to Plymouth, Massachusetts in 1620 from England and Holland to found their own church. The Pilgrims were separatists who had left the Church of England because they disapproved of its doctrines and suffered religious and social persecution. A second larger group of Puritans arrived in Massachusetts Bay in 1630. They were English Protestants who wanted to purify the Church of England and adopted simple church ceremonies, strict moral behavior, religious discipline and an austere way of life.

Neither group was religiously tolerant. They expelled Church of England members and restricted membership of their congregations to people who had personally experienced conversion. They believed that God had chosen or predestined specific individuals to achieve salvation. Hard work was a means of pleasing God, and any resulting prosperity was a sign that He regarded them favorably. It is argued that this Puritan (Protestant) work ethic is a factor in an American ambition to succeed materially in life. Religion was central to most people's daily and commercial lives and had an important influence on American culture.

PLATE 5.1 St Augustine's Roman Catholic Cathedral/Basilica, Florida (1793), is the oldest Roman Catholic (and European) church in the US. It was established by Don Pedro de Aviles in 1565 and developed by Spanish priests. The first churches suffered decay, warfare and disaster. The structure of the present site was completed in 1797, achieved cathedral status in 1870 and became St Augustine's Cathedral/Basilica.
© *Nikreates/Alamy*

PLATE 5.2 Jamestown, Virginia was the first English settlement in North America (1607). Conditions were bad, and many people died in the first winter following starvation and American Indian attacks. An Anglican (Church of England) church (the "golden church") was built in 1608. Archeological excavations (2010) discovered the graves of four prominent settlers in the chancel (crosses), which suggest class and power structures brought from England. The settlement survived hardships and disputes, developed a representative legislature, government, models of citizenship and defended the Church of England against Spanish Catholicism. Until 1699, it was the capital of Virginia, and its political structures were to form the base of future US government and law.
© *Jordan Oakland*

Religious diversity was most obvious in the middle colonies. These were settled by Protestant groups such as Welsh and Dutch Calvinists, Scottish Presbyterians, Swedish and German Lutherans, Baptists and English Quakers. Protestants and Roman Catholics established themselves in Maryland (formed originally in 1634 as a haven for Catholics), with religious toleration for all Christians. Puritan pressure during the English Civil War resulted in toleration for Roman Catholics becoming limited, and it ended in 1692.

A few European Jewish traders also settled in the English colonies, despite an official ban on Jewish immigration. Newport, Rhode Island, became a colonial center of Jewish life, with other groups in New York, Charleston (South Carolina) and Philadelphia.

Most of the original 13 colonies had an official established church (a link between church and state) from colonial times until the War for Independence.

PLATE 5.3 Jewish settlers first arrived in colonial Newport, Rhode Island in 1658. Touro Synagogue dates from 1763 and is the oldest existing synagogue building in the US. It was built for the Jeshuat Israel congregation and is now a small Orthodox synagogue, although there have been recent ownership disputes within the community.
© *George Oze/Alamy*

The Church of England served Virginia, Maryland, the Carolinas, Georgia and parts of New York, and the Congregational Church (Pilgrims/Puritans) settled in New England. Groups such as the Presbyterians, Lutherans and Baptists did not become the established church in any colony.

The eighteenth century

There was a change of religious emphasis in the eighteenth century. Although many early colonists had been motivated by religious beliefs, the majority of immigrants now traveled to the US for material advancement, free land or commercial adventure. There was a decline in religious influence and observation, and it is estimated that in 1750 only 17 percent of the population formally belonged to a religious group. However, some people might still have retained nominal adherence to a traditional homeland faith.

Immigrants continued to arrive in the eighteenth century, often with distinct religious identifications such as Scots-Irish Presbyterians from the north of Ireland. Some of these settled in New York and New England, where they shifted the Congregational Church toward Presbyterianism. Others went to New Jersey, Pennsylvania and western Virginia. German Lutherans continued to immigrate, and Jews arrived from Germany and Poland.

Two events affected colonial communities in the eighteenth century and produced more active religiosity, at least for a time: first, the Great Awakening (religious revival) and second, the American War for Independence. The Great Awakening affected the colonies in the 1730s and 1740s and was the forerunner of modern evangelical activities. It was an emotional reaction to the formalistic, unappealing nature of many religious practices. It began in Massachusetts among the Congregationalists and spread along the east coast from Maine to Georgia and along the western frontier to include Presbyterians, Methodists and Baptists.

Revivalist (evangelical) preachers tried to convert people to their faiths by stressing the need for repentance, rebirth and a personal experience of salvation. The Great Awakening created friction, and churches were split as ministers and congregations either supported the revivalists or opposed their emotionalism and conversion practices. The radicalism of the Great Awakening influenced revolutionary sentiment and the War for Independence.

The War for Independence from Britain was a time of religious conflict and divided loyalties among the churches. Scots-Irish Presbyterians, Lutherans, Baptists and Congregationalists were mainly on the American side of the struggle, and the Methodists were neutral. Some Church of England members supported the British and others the American cause, as did Catholics in Pennsylvania and Maryland. Pacifist religious bodies, like Moravians, Quakers and Mennonites, were persecuted during the war because of their beliefs.

Methodist and Baptist churches recovered quickly after the war, but the Church of England lost prestige and influence due to its ties with England. Its attempts to survive failed and a new (Protestant) Episcopal Church was created. This was the first American-founded church. It later became a member of the global Anglican Communion but was suspended in 2016 because of its liberal position on same-sex marriage.

However, despite the Great Awakening and the War for Independence, religiosity at the end of the eighteenth century was weak, and most Americans were not active church members. The Great Awakening did not have a lasting or deep effect, the Episcopal Church was largely inoperative, and other religious groups became either austere and intellectual or departed from their original religious doctrines. Protestant Christianity appeared to be declining with the abolition of most established churches after the War for Independence.

The nineteenth century

Religious groups recovered in the nineteenth century as further revivals occurred, the population expanded westwards, immigration increased,

PLATE 5.4 St John's Episcopal Church was one of the first colonial Episcopal churches to be built in the Georgetown Parish, Washington DC, 1796, on land provided by the Church of England, and President Thomas Jefferson was among the founders. It has a long history of change and structural renovation but largely maintains the traditional worship of the Episcopal Church.
© Jordan Oakland

missionary activities grew and the churches involved themselves in social concerns as a result of industrialization and economic growth. However, the Civil War (1861–5) was a testing time for American religion.

A second Great Awakening came at the beginning of the century on the east coast and spread westwards along the frontier. It sometimes led to superficial emotionalism and divisions within the churches, but it also increased the number of evangelical groups, such as Baptists, Presbyterians and Methodists. This growth promoted religious development and the creation of modern evangelical and fundamentalist movements. A further influence, if restricted largely to literary intellectuals, was Transcendentalism, which stressed the individual and nature as a reaction to traditional Puritanism.

Religious groups were increasingly subject to conflict within themselves and with other churches, especially between 1830 and 1860. This resulted in theological quarrels, division of churches and the formation of many sects. For example, attempts to unite the Congregationalists and Presbyterians ended in separation. There was tension between the High (east coast) and Low (frontier) Church wings of the Episcopal Church. Splits occurred among the Lutherans, but the arrival of conservative German immigrants after 1830 prevented the liberal wing from dominating the church. Norwegian and Swedish Lutheran immigrants from 1840 also supported the conservative wing. New American-founded religious movements and sects, with very contrasting beliefs, appeared as a reaction to traditional faiths in the eighteenth, nineteenth and twentieth centuries (see Table 5.1).

TABLE 5.1   Principal denominations founded in America

The Episcopal Church	1789
The New Thought Movement	1830s
Millerism and Seventh-Day Adventism	1830s
Church of Latter Day Saints (Mormonism)	1830
Churches of Christ/Disciples of Christ	1832
Southern Baptist Convention	1845
Jehovah's Witnesses	1870s
National Baptist Convention	1895
Native American Church	1890s
Christian Science	late 19th century
Pentecostalism	1904–06
Reconstructionist Judaism	1920s
Metropolitan Community Church	1920s
Nation of Islam	1930
Scientology	1954
United Church of Christ	1957

Meanwhile, the Roman Catholic Church was greatly strengthened by Irish, French and German immigration from 1830 and by immigrants from eastern and southern Europe (such as Italy) later in the century. The church, after earlier internal conflict, was eventually controlled by its hierarchy of bishops. It proved attractive to the new immigrants, and Irish settlers in particular were to influence the church in future years. But Catholic newcomers suffered considerable prejudice and hostility from the dominant Protestant groups.

Some of the more extreme Protestant groups attempted to oppose the influence of Roman Catholic immigration and to maintain strict Puritan traditions. For example, the Woman's Christian Temperance Union (1874) tried to stop the use of alcohol and campaigned to maintain the Puritan Sabbath.

Between 1840 and 1880, the Jewish population expanded from 15,000 to 225,000, because of repression and persecution in Germany and central Europe. Some Jews were Orthodox, but many became members of the new Reform movement. This adapted traditional practices to modern conditions and helped Jews to assimilate more easily to American life. Jews experienced anti-Semitism and discrimination in society, particularly from Protestants.

Despite religious tensions and the emergence of new sects, a more liberal spirit developed during the nineteenth century. Churches became involved in education and created schools and colleges with religious identifications. From 1820, further immigration promoted new outlooks and activities among the churches. Influential inner-city missions were formed on the east coast that addressed the new problems (poverty and unemployment) of a wealthier and bigger population. It is argued that these mission movements and their activism, rather than the two Great Awakenings, saved American Christianity and increased religiosity.

Slavery and the Civil War were divisive threats to religion. The anti-slavery position was based on biblical, humanitarian and democratic impulses, but there were conflicting interpretations of slavery from both anti- and pro-slavery camps. Some churches, like the Episcopal Church, tried to be neutral, while others were divided. Post-war America experienced religious uncertainty and inaction, as churches and society tried to recover morally and practically from the effects of the war and the abolition of slavery.

After 1880, US wealth increased substantially, due to industrialization and a booming economy. Divisions grew between rich and poor, and there was much social misery and inequality. There were conflicts between employees and employers, leading to strikes, unemployment and industrial unrest. Churches responded to these problems. Some emphasized social and moral commitment, supported the workers and provided for their social and economic needs, and many clergy played an active role in the community. This social concern is still a feature of some contemporary religious groups in the US.

PLATE 5.5 The National Cathedral, Washington, DC is a cathedral of the Episcopal Church in neo-Gothic design based on 14th century English Gothic style. Construction began in 1907 and some work is still continuing. It is designated as the National House of Prayer and is a center for important national occasions. The cathedral is both the episcopal seat of the Bishop of Washington and the primatial seat of the Presiding Bishop of the Episcopal Church.
Courtesy of the Carol M. Highsmith Archive, Library of Congress Prints and Photographs Division Washington, DC 20540 USA

The twentieth century

Religious variety and activity in the US increased at the end of the nineteenth century and continued during the twentieth century as large numbers of immigrants arrived from central, eastern and southern Europe, Latin America and Asia.

This influx strengthened the Roman Catholic Church, but the new arrivals also included eastern religions, such as Hinduism, Sikhism and Islam, as well as considerable numbers of Jewish immigrants fleeing persecution in Europe. Eastern Orthodox churches were also established by Greek, Russian, Armenian and Syrian immigrants. Such groups concentrated in the bigger cities, and some

PLATE 5.6 The Islamic Center of America, Dearborn, Michigan, 1949, is the largest mosque in the US. Although the original institution was founded in 1964, a new mosque was opened in 2005. It is the oldest Shia mosque in the US, and Dearborn has a large Shia Arab population (mainly Lebanese). There has been recent tension between Shia and Sunni in Dearborn. © *Dane Hilliard*

retained their own languages in religious and daily life. This produced tight-knit communities with strong ethnic identities, but it also distanced them from many Americans. The result was often intolerance directed against new arrivals.

It is argued that a diversity of religions led to competing pressures in US life in the twentieth century between pluralism (separatism) and ecumenism (closer relations between faiths), social action and spiritual renewal, and secularism and religious growth.

Religious pluralism can indicate vitality and toleration of different religions, but it may also be divisive as denominations quarrel with each other. The dominant Protestant majority in early US history promoted basic national characteristics and institutions, but it often treated Roman Catholic, Jewish and other faiths with suspicion and hostility. This situation slowly changed in the early twentieth century and considerably since the 1950s, due to immigration, population growth in ethnic communities, improved social attitudes and a decrease in the Protestant majority. Three major faiths (Protestant, Catholic and Jewish) then shared American religious life with many other churches, groups and sects, such as Islam.

The pluralistic and somewhat divisive nature of US religion has been offset by ecumenical movements among different faiths, which have become more tolerant and cooperative. Traditional churches divided by historical disputes, like Congregationalists, Lutherans, Presbyterians and Methodists, became closer. Cooperation has occurred at local and national levels between Protestants, Catholics, Jews and Orthodox groups with the creation of ecumenical organizations. For example, the Anti-Defamation League (1913) and the National Conference of Christians and Jews (1928) reduced anti-Semitic tension in the early twentieth century. There was also a greater assimilation of immigrants into the larger society as homeland languages declined and "national" churches and synods merged. Internationally, American Protestants helped to found the World Council of Churches in 1948, and ecumenism was treated positively by the Second Vatican Council (1962–5,) which encouraged Catholics to be more open to other religions and modern developments.

By the 1970s, ecumenism declined. There was a concern that individual faiths might become weaker through cooperation and an increasing conservatism caused divisions in some church groups. Nevertheless, Protestants, Catholics and Jews have become less divisive, and anti-Catholicism and anti-Semitism are not as virulent or as widespread as they once were. Catholics and Jews have achieved greater status and recognition in American life, and religions such as Islam, Buddhism and Hinduism have been generally accepted. The emphasis has turned to coexistence among many faiths, rather than ecumenism. However, suspicion still exists between a majority of Americans toward Mormonism and Islam.

There are also areas of tension that are reflected in opposed views of social action and spiritual renewal. Social action stresses religion's public role and follows American traditions of liberal theology and social commitment. Some churches have campaigned for social change, provided welfare services and have debated social problems and moral concerns such as starvation, racial inequality, poverty, refugees, the Vietnam, Iraq and Afghan wars, industrial relations, abortion, same-sex relationships and educational issues. This liberal social position has often necessitated new theological interpretations of belief and practice.

Some evangelical and fundamentalist groups within Protestantism emphasize spiritual renewal and reflect a desire among many Americans for more personal religious commitment and simple faith. Such movements are founded on a close reading and literal interpretation of the Bible, although they do vary in their practices and beliefs. Generally, they are traditional and orthodox in a strict maintenance of their values, stress the importance of personal salvation, are suspicious of social action and oppose liberalizing trends. Their emphasis on fundamental beliefs and fellowship has led them to reject not only evolutionary theories (Darwinism) in favor of creationism (the literal Bible story), but also new radical interpretations of the Bible and what they consider to be corrupt forms of modern life. Protestant churches in the twentieth century, and especially since the 1960s, consequently experienced battles between liberals, modernists, evangelicals and fundamentalists.

Some fundamentalists left their churches to form new groups where they could practice their beliefs. Other people have joined evangelical churches. These groups are connected to earlier traditions of revivalism with their espousal of the Christian gospel, conversion, emotional experiences and personal salvation through admission of one's sins. Evangelicals and fundamentalists have become a powerful social and political force in recent decades, have attracted media and popular attention and have grown strongly. Nevertheless, some of these churches have collapsed because of limited support, fraud or internal scandals.

The terms "evangelical," "conservative," "the Christian Right," and "fundamentalist" tend to be used interchangeably and somewhat loosely. "Fundamentalist" can be applied to Protestant groups with absolutist orthodox beliefs, which are based on the Bible as the authoritative word of God. "Evangelical" can be applied to Christian denominations with very varied titles, but which may be based on the doctrine of salvation and converting people to their beliefs in a "born-again" experience or personal relationship with Christ. Evangelicalism emphasizes the role of scriptural authority but can include modernist interpretations of biblical faith. Both groups may have a conservative message that is based on moral values, the role of the family and education. They provide certainties for many Americans and stress individual responsibility and commitment.

Evangelical ministers and fundamentalist movements often use television and radio to spread their message and have become very skilled in their use of the media. They own or control some 1,300 radio and television stations. Preachers can become very popular celebrities, their media performances attract large audiences and advertising revenues and religious broadcasting has become very profitable. After a fall in popularity and influence in the late 1980s, the evangelical churches recovered in the mid-1990s and again have a significant voice on the political right.

Spiritual renewal has also led people to join a wide variety of sects, cults and churches. Common to them all is an attempt to create a sense of belonging through close emotional fellowship. Groups, such as the Moonies and some guru-led organizations, have aroused hostility among many Americans. Their techniques of recruitment, alleged brainwashing of members and religious fanaticism are heavily criticized.

Some Americans, in the search for personal spiritual growth, ethnic identity and answers to modern problems, have joined or converted to eastern religions, such as Islam, Hinduism and Buddhism, and founded the African American Nation of Islam. Others seek religious or spiritual satisfaction in a wide range of alternative beliefs such as the occult, Native American religions, astrology and witchcraft.

It is argued that the emergence of so many religious and pseudo-religious groups and the possible diffusion of national identity in this amorphous situation have led concerned Americans to embrace a "civil religion" centered on US political traditions. It is a mixture of religion, morality and nationalism that emphasizes symbols, emblems and traditions, such as the national motto ("In God We Trust") and the pledge of allegiance to the flag ("One Nation, Under God"). "Civil religion" supposedly overarches the varieties of belief, although the Christian emphasis is evident, and arguably gives the US a moral character and sacred mission. Although this may be a source of national integration, it can also be divisive, and its contemporary influence, while formerly evident in the public-school system, is debatable.

There has also been an increased secularism in twentieth-century US life, which has conflicted with religious growth. Personal decisions are made without recourse to religious teachings or interpretations. Secularism has particularly affected education. Some private schools and colleges had previously been created by churches as a way of promoting religious belief, but in the twentieth century public schools were increasingly secularized by state authorities. A more relaxed and informal American society, with increased leisure and entertainment opportunities, has also contributed to the growth of secularization.

However, Americans were still involved with religious groups and activities in the mid-twentieth century. This coincided with greater interest in religion after the Second World War. Since then, there has been decline in some churches and growth in others.

Contemporary US religion

US religion underwent significant changes after the post-war revival. The influence and membership of mainstream Protestant and traditional denominations declined in the liberal social climate of the 1960s and 1970s. Increased immigration and religious reorganization in the later twentieth and twenty-first centuries led to new religious communities, such as fundamentalist and evangelical churches (which attracted large numbers of members), sects, cults and eastern religions, such as Islam, Hinduism and Buddhism.

Despite these changes, the majority of religious Americans today are still within the Judeo-Christian tradition, and US religion consists of three main faiths in terms of their history, numbers and influence: Protestantism, Catholicism and Judaism.

When respondents to polls and surveys say they belong to specific US denominations, some may be nominal or preferential rather than active adherents. Religious organizations differ in their counting methods, and statistics should be regarded as approximate. Polls also report movements in US religiosity as people change (or "switch") religions. Many belong to a different tradition than their birth affiliation, others reject organized religion and some embrace different forms of spirituality. But a Pew Research Center survey in

PLATE 5.7 Malibu Hindu Temple, Calabasas, California, built in 1981 in the Santa Monica mountains is a temple of the Hindu god Venkateswarma. It is visited by many Hindus throughout southern California and is one of the largest Hindu temples in the West.
© *Allstar Picture Library/Alamy*

2014 reported that there had been falls in contemporary religious affiliation in the adult US population since 2007 (with some increases, such as evangelical Protestants and non-Christian groups like Hindus and Muslims) and large increases in the unaffiliated (see Table 5.2).

The Pew survey showed that 70.6 percent of adults in the US self-defined themselves as Christian (a decrease of 2.4 percent from 2012), of whom 46.5 percent were Protestant (decrease of 1.5 percent), but with evangelical Protestants at 25.4 percent (up 6.4 percent), mainline Protestants at 14.7 percent (down 0.3 percent) and Black Churches at 6.5 percent (down 1.5 percent). Roman Catholics amounted to 20.8 percent (a decrease of 1.2 percent), 1.6 were Mormon (down 0.4) and one percent was Orthodox. Six other faiths, such as Jews, Buddhists, Muslims and Hindus, totaled 5.9 percent. Unaffiliated respondents were 22.8 percent (up 3.2 percent), such as atheists, agnostics and "nothing in particular."

The poll nevertheless reported that 76.5 percent of respondents still identified with a religious faith, a drop of 3.5 percent from 2012. Another Pew Poll in 2012 found that 80 percent of respondents said that religion was "very" or "somewhat" important in their lives; 25 percent reported that they rarely

TABLE 5.2 Religious affiliation in the US, 2014

Affiliation	% of US population
Christian denominations	70.6
Protestant	46.5
Evangelical Protestant	25.4
Mainline Protestant	14.7
Black churches	6.5
Catholic	20.8
Mormon	1.6
Jehovah's Witnesses	0.8
Eastern Orthodox	0.5
Other Christian	0.4
Unaffiliated	22.8
Nothing in particular	15.8
Agnostic	4.0
Atheist	3.1
Non-Christian faiths	5.9
Jewish	1.9
Muslim	0.9
Buddhist	0.7
Hindu	0.7
Other Non-Christian faiths	1.8
Don't Know	0.6

Source: adapted from Religious Affiliation in the US, 2014 Pew Research Center

attended religious services. The poll characterized the US as a "competitive religious marketplace," and the nation was said to be highly religious with different churches competing for new members.

Protestants

Protestantism is the largest and most diverse of the US faiths. Although a majority of adult Americans identify themselves as Protestants, they are divided into many churches and sects, representing Mainline, Evangelical and Black Church traditions. There is no one denomination for all Protestants. Each church is independent, supports itself financially, has its own ministers, constructs its own buildings and follows its own beliefs and practices.

Mainline Protestantism includes the United Methodist Church, the American Baptist Churches USA, the Evangelical Lutheran Church in America, the Presbyterian Church (USA) and the Episcopal Church. These represent

Protestantism from early US religious history and numbered some 36 million adult members in 2014, a decline of about 5 million from 2007.

The Black Protestant tradition, which includes the large National Baptist Convention, the Church of God in Christ, the African Methodist Episcopal Church and the Progressive Baptist Convention had some 16 million adult members in 2014 and has experienced no substantial losses since 2007.

The churches in the Evangelical Protestant tradition, such as the Southern Baptist Convention, the Assemblies of God, Churches of Christ, the Lutheran Church–Missouri Synod, the Presbyterian Church in America and a range of other denominations, had an adult membership in 2014 of some 62 million, an increase of about 2 million from 2007.

Mainline churches have primarily traditional values and some liberal theological and social attitudes, are composed largely of middle- or upper-class people and have formal worship and service patterns. Some Evangelical and Black Church Protestantism often represents fundamentalist or conservative religious and social views, while others such as the mainly White Southern Baptist Convention and the Black National Baptist Convention may consist of lower-income groups and encourage emotional responses to religion, such as "born-again" conversions. These congregations can vary in their directions and messages.

While some traditional mainline churches have lost members since the 1970s, black and Evangelical churches, such as the Seventh-Day Adventists, Churches of Christ, Mormon/Latter-Day Saints, the Church of the Nazarene, the Assemblies of God, Evangelical /Born Again and Jehovah's Witnesses have increased their membership, as have some Pentecostal/Charismatic churches, such as Assemblies of God and Church of God. They offer absolutist moral instruction and traditional values and appeal to those who want moral direction and religious certainty.

Roman Catholics

Although there was significant Catholic immigration into the US in the nineteenth and twentieth centuries, the country was still mainly Protestant in religion and national attitudes.

The Roman Catholic Church is the largest religion after Protestantism but the biggest in terms of a single denomination. It has about 19,000 churches, and Latino population growth and southeast Asian immigration from 1990 to 2008 appeared to have maintained its numbers. But there were 51 million Catholic adults in 2014, 3 million fewer than in 2007.

Catholicism was historically confined to ethnic groups such as the Irish, Polish, Italians and Germans in the big cities and was initially largely working class. This urban concentration enabled Catholics to achieve political influence at the local, if not the national, level. After the Second World War, Catholics

PLATE 5.8 The Salt Lake Temple of the Church of Latter Day Saints (LDS), Salt Lake City, Utah, also known as the Mormon Church, is situated on Temple Square in Salt Lake City, Utah, which is the base of the Church. It is the largest LDS temple and was dedicated in 1893. It is the fourth temple built since the Mormon exodus from Nauvoo, Illinois, in 1846.
© *Steven Milne/Alamy*

built more churches and schools for their growing population, improved their income and class status, and many moved to the suburbs.

The movement of Catholics from tightly knit urban communities to the suburbs has arguably meant a decline in Catholic identity. Catholics are now more willing, after years of discrimination against them, to mix with non-Catholics. Hostility toward them has largely disappeared, illustrated by the election of Catholic John F. Kennedy as President in 1960. American Catholics are also influential in international campaigns and domestic social projects and tend to be more ecumenically minded today than in the past.

However, religious and social change has caused internal tensions within the community. Members are not as active in church activities as they were, attendance at weekly mass has declined and many have left the faith. The church is divided between liberals and conservatives with opposed opinions on birth control, abortion, the celibacy of priests, gay and lesbian relationships, same-sex marriage and the question of women priests. These concerns have clashed with conservative Vatican views. A serious development in recent years has been evidence of Catholic priests abusing young people and the alleged cover-up of such behavior by the Catholic leadership. This has provoked criticism within the church and by outsiders, which has resulted in Court cases and compensation for victims.

The Jewish community

Jews have historically settled mainly on the east coast (New York and Florida), in California and in the big cities. After immigration, their religious practices changed somewhat and now range from traditional Orthodox to moderate Conservative and liberal Reform groups. Most groups, religious or not, have been concerned to preserve their Jewish heritage and traditions.

As the Jewish population grew, they established Hebrew schools and synagogues and contributed to Jewish charities. The creation of the state of Israel in 1948 was an additional focus for Jewish identity. Although anti-Semitism increased in the early-twentieth century, this has now been reduced because of changing social attitudes, ecumenism and sympathy for Jewish suffering in the Second World War. Jews have assimilated into American society and are more accepted than they once were. They have also become more secularized with increased intermarriage between Jews and non-Jews, leading to fears of a decrease in the religious community. There are 4.2 million adult self-defined religious Jews divided into the Reform, Conservative and Orthodox traditions. But an estimated 2.1 million ethnic or cultural Jews are secular or non-religious or have become members of a faith other than Judaism.

Other religious groups

There are other US non-Christian religious groups (amounting to 8.8 million adults) in addition to the three main faiths, such as Buddhism (1.2 million), Hinduism (1 million,), Islam (3.3 million) and Sikhism (78,000). It is argued that Islam today is a fourth major faith in the US which, combined with other Asian religions, has a growing representative importance.

Examples of other religious communities are Native American (estimates between 9,000 and 186,000), Wiccan (342,000), Pagan (340,000) and Spiritualist (426,000).

Unaffiliated

The 2014 Pew Research poll reported that 56 million adult respondents described themselves as religiously unaffiliated, an increase of 19 percent since 2007, amounting to 22.8 percent of the US population. These Americans did not identify themselves with any organized religion. They include atheists, agnostics and those of no religion or "nothing in particular" and are collectively more numerous than Catholics or mainline Protestants. The American Religious Identification Survey (2008–9) argued that the challenge to Christianity in the US does not come so much from other religions, but rather from a rejection of organized religion.

Church, state and politics

The First Amendment of the Bill of Rights, 1791, provides that "Congress shall make no law respecting an establishment of religion, or prohibiting the free exercise thereof." This separation of church and state forbids state-supported religion, the creation of a state church, state promotion of religion, and the favoring of one religion over another but gives individuals the right to freely practice their faiths. The Constitution's Article V1 also has a prohibition on religious tests as a condition for holding public office. The First Amendment originally applied to the federal government, not to the states. But the US Supreme Court has ruled that the Fourteenth Amendment (1868) also covers states and local government.

The Court has held that the right to the free exercise of religion is not absolute. For example, a 19th century decision upheld the criminal conviction of a member of the Church of Jesus Christ of Latter-day Saints for practicing polygamy (allowing a man to have several wives), which was against federal law. The law cannot interfere with religious belief, but it may ban resultant practices that affect the rest of society, such as human sacrifice. But section one of the Fourteenth Amendment grants legal protection and due process, so that religious practices and beliefs that incur penalties may be exempted if they do not obstruct other people. States and the federal government have prohibited or regulated practices such as prostitution, gambling, alcohol and drug use. Religious liberty is a contentious issue in areas such as abortion, contraception, gay rights and business owners/serving assistants refusing service to customers on religious, moral or personal grounds (*Stormans v. Wiesman*, 2016).

Religion, or its lack, is supposedly a private matter. Respondents to a Brookings Institution poll in September 2011 supported the principles of religious freedom, religious tolerance and strict separation of church and state. Eighty-eight percent agreed that the US was founded on the idea of religious freedom for all, including unpopular religious groups. Ninety-five percent accepted that all religious books should be treated with respect even if individuals did not share their religious beliefs. But respondents disagreed about whether Islam is incompatible with US standards (47 percent agreed/48 percent disagreed) and 54 percent agreed (43 percent disagreed) that Muslims are an important part of US religious life.

But majorities of poll respondents have felt that the promotion of religion should not be banned; many have supported a more direct role for religion in public life, such as organized school prayers, the teaching of creationism (God-directed evolution), allowing religious symbols like the Ten Commandments to be displayed in public buildings and continuing the use of "One Nation, Under God" in the Pledge of Allegiance to the flag.

These findings might suggest that Americans are divided on the question of religion in public life and that strict church-state separation may be questioned. Some Americans feel that religion should play a bigger role in US politics, but an AP/IPSOS survey in 2005 found that 61 percent of respondents were against attempts by religious leaders to influence government decisions and public policy.

There were established official churches before the War for Independence, but eventually churches were separated from the state. There are now no church taxes; churches are not supposed to receive any direct state or federal support; there are no legal or official religious holidays; and no political party is formally affiliated to a specific denomination. Any attempt to introduce religious roles or practices in these areas would be regarded as violating the Constitution, unless the courts allowed exemptions.

Religious groups are self-supporting independent organizations. They depend on members' and public financial contributions for their existence and payment of expenses. Americans' charitable donations are generous and 33 percent of household contributions in 2015 went to religion. Fundamentalist and evangelical churches are reckoned to attract the greatest amounts. Local religious buildings and their congregations are the strengths and centers of US religion. They also provide social, cultural and community activities, supply relief aid for the poor and needy and engage in missionary work domestically and overseas.

As society has become more complex and government more pervasive, church and state do interfere with each other. States have historically restricted freedom of religion by prohibiting Catholics and Jews from voting or holding public office. Courts have ruled on special working practices for minority religions, such as Mormons and Seventh-Day Adventists. It is argued that permitting exceptions to the general rule suggest that decisions may depend upon fine distinctions or interpretations.

Since public and private lives are not inseparable, the diversity of denominations in American life suggests that religion and its moral concerns may influence political debates on issues such as abortion, the death penalty, same-sex marriage and armed conflicts. For example, Pew polls in 2003 found that although 53 percent of respondents opposed gay marriage, this was a decrease from 65 percent in 1996, and in June 2015, the Supreme Court ruled that states cannot ban same-sex marriage. Americans have also become more liberal on abortion, and there are conflicting opinions about the death penalty.

A religious (or "civil religion") sensibility is arguably reflected in national symbols and emblems such as the US seal, the currency ("In God We Trust") and the Pledge of Allegiance to the flag. US presidents may belong to a religious group, politicians refer to God and the Bible in their speeches, and presidential election campaign addresses and State of the Union Messages end with "God bless America." US presidents swear the inaugural oath of office on the Bible, sessions of Congress commence with prayers and both Houses of Congress have chaplains.

However, formal religion probably has little direct influence in political matters, or has not as yet reached the stage where it could seriously do so. Politicians are generally conscious of the constitutional position and its restrictions upon government action, as well as the restraints imposed on religious tolerance. Nevertheless, personal religious beliefs and values may affect the way in which individuals react to political and social issues.

A source of national debate about religion and politics has revolved around the role of evangelical groups and their leaders. Many of them are very visible, actively propagate their beliefs and attempt to influence public opinion, social institutions and political processes. They do not restrict themselves to moral and religious matters, but campaign on political issues such as anti-abortion legislation and prayers in public schools. The evangelical right, sometimes known as "the moral majority" or the "Christian coalition/right" because of its absolutism and stress upon alleged American values, has supported conservative politicians in election campaigns, and some of its leaders have also attempted to gain political office.

The role of religion in politics and social issues is problematic. Majorities of poll respondents think that churches should be able to express political and social views; others consider that churches should not favor any one candidate in a political election over another.

Religion and education

Administrative and financial organization of public schools is generally carried out by local districts, and school boards composed of elected citizens oversee the schools in their area. They influence school policy, often decide what is to be taught, and battles between religious fundamentalists and modernizers are fought at this level.

Education is supposed to be neutral. The constitutional separation of church from state means that public schools can teach about religion, but cannot promote it or endorse a particular religion. Any attempt to do so would be regarded as an infringement of the First Amendment. This has often been tested in court cases dealing with religious holidays; religious dress; the school curriculum; the Ten Commandments; the Pledge of Allegiance; school prayers; and proposals to teach creationism and evolution in public schools. In 1963, the Supreme Court ruled that religion could be taught in the public school curriculum as long as it was objective instruction about religion rather than promotion.

After the colonial period, when schools were often run by different denominations, most public schools supported a historically dominant Protestant Christianity by means of school prayers, religious instruction and activities, and denominational identity. But concern about Catholic growth in the nineteenth century led some states to ban schools from obtaining public funding for religious purposes, and public schools were gradually secularized.

The Pledge of Allegiance and school prayers have been central to education debates. The Supreme Court ruled in 1942 that students cannot be compelled to recite the pledge, or be punished for refusing. In March 2010, the US Court of Appeals for the Ninth Circuit upheld the words "one nation under God" in the pledge, arguing that they were of a "ceremonial and patriotic nature" and not promotion of religion. Use of the pledge in the school day varies, with about half of the states committed to it. However, some critics argue that this practice effectively indoctrinates schoolchildren with "civil religion."

In 1962, the Supreme Court in *Engel v. Vitale* removed elements of school religion. It ruled that school-sponsored non-denominational prayers in public schools were unconstitutional because they violated the principle of separation between church and state by promoting religion. In 1984, the US Senate banned prayers in public schools by rejecting two constitutional amendments, and the division of church and state remains.

However, a 2003 *USA Today*/Gallup/CNN poll reported that 78 percent of respondents supported the reciting of non-denominational prayers in public schools. An Anti-Defamation League (ADL) poll in 2005 found that 47 percent of respondents believed that public school students should be able to express religious beliefs/group prayers during the school day, while 44 percent thought that public schools should allow a moment of silence for individual prayer. Sixty-nine percent of fundamentalist/evangelical Christians believed that group prayer is appropriate, while 25 percent supported individual prayer only.

In trying to reconcile school prayers and activities with state funding, the question is whether or not religious organizations may use government money, grants and school vouchers, to subsidize (and thus promote) religious schooling. In June 2002, the Supreme Court ruled in *Zelman v. Simmons-Harris* that Cleveland, Ohio's voucher program did not promote the establishment of religion because the decision to use voucher funds to attend a religious school was at the personal discretion of the family to affect their children's education and was not dictated by the state. The issue of private schools receiving public money is vigorously debated, and the private sector generally receives no direct funding from federal or state sources. Two 1985 Supreme Court decisions prohibited public-school teachers from teaching courses in private religious schools.

Nevertheless, the 2001 Supreme Court decision in *Good News Club v. Milford Central School* ruled that publicly funded schools must allow religious groups to use their facilities for religious activities during non-school hours if such usage is provided for other organizations. Court rulings have also allowed state and university property to be used by students for religious purposes, as long as that property can also be used by others for other purposes. But, in 1992 the Supreme Court banned clergy from offering prayers at graduation ceremonies in public schools. These decisions partly distinguish between state recognition of religion by the participation of officials at public ceremonies and the participation of students or others in voluntary religious activities on state property.

A 2001 Gallup poll reported that the use of school property after teaching hours for student religious meetings was favored by 72 percent (26 percent opposed); 80 percent also believed that students should be allowed to recite a spoken prayer at school graduations; 66 percent thought spoken prayer should be allowed in the classroom (opposed by 34 percent); and 62 percent felt that religion had too little presence in public schools.

Parents send their children to religious, faith or private schools because they feel that public schools do not reflect their values. They often provide an academic education with a religious orientation. The secular public school curriculum, the controversies over evolution and creationism and parents' disillusionment with the quality of the public school system have arguably contributed to more home school teaching and private alternatives.

However, many private schools founded in the 1970s and 1980s had no religious identification and little if any federal grants. It is argued that while religious people should be able to choose and pay for such schools, public money should not support them. It is also felt that public schools have established a system that teaches students of all faiths and cultures and enables them to live with differences without the promotion of religion.

In education there is conflict between those people who support the teaching in public schools of creationism (human beings created by God as expressed in the Bible) and those who favor evolution (humans evolved naturally without God from lower forms of life). A YouGov poll in 2013 reported that 40 percent of respondents said that creationism should be taught in schools, while 32 percent opposed it. But the Supreme Court ruled in 1987 in *Edwards v. Aguillard* that teaching creationism promoted religion and violated the First Amendment position that publicly-funded schools must be religiously neutral. The debate continues about the teaching of creationism and evolution in public schools; whether or not they should be taught only in science or biology classes; that either both should be taught or both omitted completely from the public curriculum.

Attitudes to religion

Historically, American attitudes to religion have been generally positive, although there have been recent declines in belief (see Table 5.2). A Gallup poll in 2015 showed that 52 percent of respondents felt that religion was very important in their lives (a decrease of 6 percent since 2012), 26 percent thought it fairly important, (decrease of 3 percent), and 22 percent thought that it was not very important.

However, 76 percent of respondents felt that religion was losing its influence in the US (an increase of 4 percent from 2012), and only 20 percent thought that it was increasing its impact. Although polls traditionally showed that most respondents believed that religion could solve life's problems, only 52 percent now thought that faith could provide answers to most national and personal difficulties (a decrease of 5 percent since 2014), and 33 percent felt that religion was old-fashioned and out of date (an increase of 3 percent).

A *Newsweek* poll in 2009 reported that changing perceptions about the religious and social composition of the US suggested that since the 2008 inauguration of Barak Obama, 62 percent of respondents considered the US to be a Christian nation, compared with 69 and 71 percent during the two George W. Bush administrations. Those who claimed to have "old-fashioned values about family and marriage" had decreased to 74 percent.

It is argued that Americans were more religious in the 1940s and 1950s. A declining formal church or synagogue membership is reflected in a Gallup poll where 54 percent of respondents reported being a church or synagogue member in 2015, with 46 percent saying they were not. However, a Gallup poll in 2013 reported that 75 percent of respondents thought that if more Americans were religious, this would be positive for American society.

But the poll also found that Americans' more basic personal beliefs have not changed much in the last 20 years. Nine in ten Americans still have faith in a superior spiritual being or creator, and 78 percent said prayer was an important part of daily life. Forty eight percent described themselves as both "religious and spiritual"; 30 percent said they were "spiritual but not religious"; and 9 percent said they were neither religious nor spiritual.

A Gallup poll in June 2015 reported that only 42 percent of respondents had a great deal or quite a lot of confidence in "the church or organized religion," which was a decrease from 68 percent in 1975 and arguably illustrates a long-time decline in Americans' trust in institutional religion since the 1970s. Confidence fell in the mid- to late 1980s as a possible reaction to scandals involving clergy and preachers. These findings reflected a negativity toward other US social institutions, such as banks, television news and public schools, and were also illustrated in a January 2015 Gallup poll, which found that only 13 percent of respondents were "very satisfied" about the influence of organized religion in the US and 40 percent were "somewhat satisfied."

A lack of confidence in organized religion does not necessarily indicate a decrease in Americans' personal attachment to spirituality and its importance

TABLE 5.3 American personal beliefs, % change between 2009 and 2013

	2009	2013	
	Believe (%)	Believe (%)	Change (%)
God	82	74	−8
Miracles	76	72	−4
Heaven	75	68	−7
Jesus is God (or son of God)	73	68	−5
Angels	72	68	−4
Survival of soul after death	71	64	−7
Resurrection of Jesus	70	65	−5
Hell	61	58	−3
Virgin birth (of Jesus to Mary)	61	57	−4
The devil	60	58	−2
Darwin's theory of evolution	45	47	+2
Ghosts	42	42	0
Creationism	40	36	−4
Unidentified flying objects (UFOs)	32	36	+4
Astrology	26	29	+3
Witches	23	26	+3
Reincarnation and rebirth	20	24	+4

Source: Adapted from The Harris Poll, December 2009 and 2013

in their lives. However, a Harris poll in 2013 reported that only 19 percent of respondents said that they were "very" religious, and 40 percent said that they were "somewhat" religious, a decline of 9 percent since 2007. The number of Americans who say that they are not religious at all has almost doubled since 2007, from 12 percent to 23 percent.

Personal beliefs of Americans include expressions of traditional faith, such as God, miracles, heaven, angels, the soul, the devil; a sense of spirituality outside organized religion; and some support for alternative belief systems (see Table 5.3). Although such findings scored relatively highly in earlier Harris surveys, the 2009 and 2013 Harris polls showed a decline in most items. Many people were nominal adherents to a faith without subscribing to all its beliefs, and unaffiliated individuals might include elements from several faiths. Large minorities of adults believe in ghosts, UFOs, astrology, witches and reincarnation.

Evolution and creationism continue to be debated. Polls reach differing conclusions depending upon the methodology and questions used, the volatile state of the subject in the US over the past 40 years and interpretations of poll results. A Gallup poll in 2014 reported that 42 percent of respondents believed that God created human beings in their present form (biblical creationism); 31 percent believed in God-guided evolution from less advanced forms of life; and 19 percent accepted naturalistic human evolution without the guidance of God. Support for biblical creationism has remained steady between 40 and 47 percent in Gallup polls since 1982. However, a 2007 poll found that the number of people who believed that the Bible is the actual word of God had decreased to 31 from 38 percent.

Consistent themes run through US opinion polls. Many respondents think that religion plays too small a role in most people's lives today. Others do not think that the ethical and moral standards of Americans are as high as they should be; that morals are one of the top problems facing the country; and that the country's moral and cultural values have changed for the worse since the 1960s because the US has become too permissive and/or liberal.

Exercises

Explain and examine the significance of the following names and terms:

secularization	*Protestantism*	*evangelicalism*
civil religion	pluralism	school prayers
Puritans	fundamentalism	Congregationalists
Episcopal Church	social action	sectarianism
ecumenism	Great Awakenings	denomination
creationism	evolution	Fourteenth Amendment

Quakers   dissenters   Awakenings/revivals

sect/cult   established church Darwin

      permissive   graduation and prayers

      Mormons   Pledge of Allegiance

Write short essays on the following questions.

1. How is the diversity of contemporary denominations reflected in, and due to, American religious history?

2. Describe and examine the ways in which American religion has been traditionally characterized by division and conflict.

3. Briefly analyze the growth and present position of one of America's main faiths: Protestantism, Catholicism or Judaism.

4. Examine the public-opinion poll findings in the text and evaluate, in your view, whether they are significant illustrations of US religious life.

5. With reference to Plate 5.2, what significance does the Jamestown settlement have for religious and political life in the US?

Further reading

Abrams, E. (1997) *Faith or Fear: How Jews Can Survive in a Christian America*, New York, NY: Free Press.

Ahlstrom, S. (1972, 2004) *A Religious History of the American People*, New Haven, CT: Yale University Press.

Buck, C. (2009) *Religious Myths and Visions of America: How Minority Faiths Redefined America's World Role*, Westport, CT: Praeger Publishers.

Corbett-Hemeyer, J. (2016) *Religion in America*, London: Routledge.

Dionne, E., Elshtain, J. and Drogosz, K. M. (2004) *One Electorate Under God? A Dialogue on Religion and American Politics*, Washington, DC: Brookings Institution Press.

Eck, D, (2002) *A New Religious America: The World's Most Religiously Diverse Nation*, New York, NY: HarperOne.

Fowler, R. B. and Hertzke, A.D. et al., (2004) (eds.) *Religion and Politics in America*, Boulder, CO: Westview Press.

Goldstein, N. and Brown-Foster, Walton (2007) *Religion and the State*, New York, NY: Infobase Publishing.

Haddad, R. T. and Lummis, A.T. (1987) *Islamic Values in the United States*, Oxford: Oxford University Press.

Jocks, C. (2001) *Native American Religions*, London: Routledge.

Lambert, F. (2010) *Religion in American Politics: A Short History*, Princeton, NJ: Princeton University Press.

Melton, J. G. (2009) *Encyclopedia of American Religions*, Gale: Gale Directory Library.

Putnam, R. D. and Campbell, D. E. (2010) *American Grace: How Religion Divides and Unites Us*, New York: Simon & Schuster.

Queen, E. L. et al., (2009) (eds.) *Encyclopedia of American Religious History*, New York: Facts on File.

Witte Jr, J. (2000) *Religion and the American Constitutional Experiment: Essential Rights and Liberties*, Boulder, CO: Westview Press.

The World Almanac and Book of Facts (2015) New York, NY: World Almanac Books.

Wuthnow, R. (2007) *America and the Challenge of Religious Diversity*, Princeton, NJ: Princeton University Press.

Websites

Pew Research Center: pewforum.org/2015/05/12/americas-changing-religious-landscape/pf_15-5-05_rls2_1_310px/

usinfo.state.gov/usa/infousa/facts/factover/homepage.htm

www.usia.gov/journals/journals.htm

religiousmovements.lib.virginia.edu/profile/profiles.htm

www.dallasnews.com/religion

Chapter 6

Political institutions
The federal government

Stable political institutions have been essential in a nation of immigrants. Commentators feel that loyalty to the basic structures and principles of government acted as the cement that held together so large and diverse a nation. The US holds several records for political stability and longevity. The world's oldest functioning democracy, the nation also has its oldest written constitution and political party (the Democratic Party).

Much has changed in American government and politics since the nation declared its independence. The Constitution of 1787 has endured because it has proven amenable to changing interpretations and important extra-constitutional elements. Political institutions in the US continue to be the subject of heated debate. In 2017, as Barack Obama ended his second term, 8 years of divided government (a president of one party and majorities of the other major party in one or both houses of congress) ended with the inauguration of Donald John Trump and Republican majorities in Congress. An "outsider" candidate with no experience in elected office or the military, Trump used his campaign and inaugural address to criticize the entire Washington, DC establishment, including his own party leadership. Thus, whether the election brought "unified" government between the president and Congress remains uncertain.

Historical origins

The English authorities allowed the American colonists to evolve political institutions with little outside interference. Partially based on local control and the consent of the inhabitants, these traditions of self-government later inspired the independence movement, formed the foundation for the constitutions of the independent states after 1776 and served as the model for the federal government erected through the Constitution of 1787.

Americans opposed a strong central government, which they identified with British oppression. The first US Constitution, the Articles of Confederation (1781–8), established a loose league of independent states under a very weak central government, a one-house legislature that lacked significant power. Much like the United Nations, the confederation had to ask the states for everything, from military forces to money for operating expenses.

Soon chaos in the nation's economy and international relations made members of the merchant classes support stronger central government. These "federalists" argued for the adoption of the new constitution drafted in Philadelphia in 1787. The anti-federalists, who pictured the country's future as largely agri-cultural, opposed the new constitution because it endangered the sovereignty of the states and lacked a list of protections for individuals. Only with ten amend-ments to satisfy these objections (later called the Bill of Rights) did enough states ratify the constitution. The new national government reflected both sides of the debate.

This constitution returned to the colonial tradition of a government with three branches (the legislative, executive and judicial), but it did not make the legislature paramount. Instead, it provided branches that had to cooperate to govern. It also changed the nature of the union. The loose confederacy became a federation whose national government had powers that remedied the weak-nesses of the Articles. Federal law became supreme in areas covered by those powers, but the states' kept their territorial integrity and sovereignty in all other areas.

Three compromises secured the states' approval for the new government. The first balanced the representation of small and large states in Congress. In the House of Representatives, the number of seats per state was proportional to population to please the states with many residents. In the Senate, every state had two seats, regardless of population, to please the small states. The second compromise patched over conflicts between the North and South regarding slavery. Once representation in one chamber of Congress depended on pop-ulation, the issue was how to count the large number of slaves in the South, who were not citizens and who were legally property rather than people. In the North, the states had abolished slavery or contained very few slaves. The com-promise stated that three-fifths of the slaves would count for representation in the House, but that the US could ban the importing of slaves by 1808. In the early years of the nation, this compromise gave the slave states additional power in the House of Representatives and the Electoral College that chose the presi-dent. The drafters also compromised on economic disagreements by permitting Congress to tax imports but not exports, which simultaneously kept the prices of Southern agricultural exports low and opened the door for tariffs to protect Northern manufacturers from cheap imported goods. Critics point out that two of these compromises tacitly approved slavery by giving it advantages in the framework of the federal government.

The constitutional framework

Four-fifths of the original text of the Constitution remains unchanged. Only 17 amendments have followed the Bill of Rights. Yet succeeding generations have interpreted the constitutional thought and language in satisfying ways. The changes in US constitutionalism have been significant but few. They have come through amendments and judicial review, rather than revolutionary upheavals.

PLATE 6.1 The Capitol, Washington, DC.
© *Wes Thompson/Getty*

The enduring principles in the Constitution are republicanism, federalism, the separation of powers and the system of checks and balances.

A republican form of government

Republicanism is the belief in a government without people privileged by birth (no royal family or aristocracy) or occupational class (no privileged class of clergy, for example). The constitution prohibits inherited titles and a state religion. Article IV, Section 4 of the document, moreover, guarantees each state a republican form of government.

The constitution defines federalism through the concepts of "reserved" and "delegated" powers in the Tenth Amendment. It reserves to the states or people those powers not specified in or reasonably inferred as federal from the constitution's wording. American federalism is a system in which the national government and the states share the governing power (sovereignty). The states delegated some powers to the national government in 1787 but reserved most powers to themselves. The rights reserved for the people in the Preamble of the Constitution and the Bill of Rights limit the powers of the federal government and the states. The preamble stresses popular sovereignty (the idea that "the people" are the power behind government). The people created the government and can alter or replace it.

Judicial review

The US has a hierarchy of law. The federal constitution is the supreme law. Acts of Congress signed by the president, as well as state and local laws, must conform to it. State and local laws must also conform to federal statutes and the state constitution. This legal hierarchy led the federal Supreme Court to assume the role of final interpreter of the US Constitution through "judicial review." Connecting state and national law, the court decides what government activity is permissible on any level. The US Constitution limits judicial review, however, to "cases and controversies." This means the court cannot interpret the constitutionality of a law unless someone brings legal charges against that law to a lower court and appeals the case to the US Supreme Court.

The constitution's broad language has allowed the Supreme Court to expand federal power into areas originally reserved to the states. Congress, for example, has extended its activities through clauses giving it broad power to regulate commerce, provide for the general welfare and create all laws that are "necessary and proper" to carry out the other powers granted to the federal government in the constitution. In practice, therefore, government activity in the US today falls into three categories: that allowed the states alone, that permitted only to the national government and that shared by both levels of government.

The separation of powers

The third basic principle in the Constitution is the separation of powers between the legislative (Congress and support agencies), executive (the president and executive bureaucracy) and judicial (the US Supreme Court and other federal courts) branches. In this non-parliamentary system, no person may serve in more than one branch at the same time. Thus the president and the heads of the executive departments, as well as federal judges, may *not* sit in Congress. The one exception to this rule is the vice president's power to preside over the Senate. Other arrangements further separate governing powers. The people choose the president, senators and representatives through independent elections that do not all occur at the same time. The areas that elect them (the nation, states and congressional districts) and the lengths of their terms of office are different. Thus, they each feel responsible to different constituencies and develop dissimilar political loyalties and priorities. As a result, one party often controls one or both houses of Congress while another holds the presidency.

The Constitution also separates the branches by listing the powers of each. It thus outlines the limits of legislative, executive and judicial action. Separating the branches prevents the concentration of power in any one and creates cooperation and tension between them. Federal judges sit in an independent judicial branch protected by the separation of powers and their lifetime terms of office. This constitutional framework removes them from current politics and suits the role of reviewing the actions of the other branches and levels of government.

Checks and balances

The branches share power through a system of checks and balances. The president nominates federal judges, including justices of the Supreme Court, but the Senate must confirm their appointment. The senate must also approve treaties negotiated by the executive and the president's candidates for other high federal offices. The president can veto legislation passed by Congress, but it can override a veto with a two-thirds majority in each house. One house of Congress balances and checks the other in that bills must pass both. Congress can remove members of the other branches from office through impeachment, but the president can pardon people accused of federal crimes. Supreme Court justices serve for life terms, dependent on "good behavior," however, there has never been an impeachment of a Supreme Court justice.

Congress can raise money through taxes and spend it on government programs. When implementing laws, however, the president and executive departments control the use of funds by setting rules that interpret the language of federal law. Congress can create, regulate or eliminate elements of the executive branch below the vice president and of the judicial branch below the Supreme Court. It can thus respond to the other branches' attempts to frustrate its intentions. As noted, if someone challenges a law, the Supreme Court can declare it unconstitutional and can force the other branches to revise their actions. In these ways, the Constitution checks each branch's power and balances power between the branches.

Constitutional change

The provisions for amending the federal Constitution stress the federal principle by involving both the national and the state governments. Two-thirds majorities in Congress or a constitutional convention called by two-thirds of the states can propose amendments. The legislatures or conventions in three-quarters of the states must ratify constitutional changes.

Important changes in the constitutional framework have come through both formal and informal means, that is, through the amendment process as well as through evolving customs and changing historical circumstances. Amendments have generally enhanced federal power at the expense of the states, and have democratized participation in government. The three Civil War Amendments written by the victorious North contributed to both these general trends. They abolished slavery (the Thirteenth), gave all former slaves citizenship (the Fourteenth), and permitted former male slaves to vote (the Fifteenth).

In the twentieth century, the Fourteenth Amendment, which requires states to respect the rights of US citizens by extending to them "due process of law" and "equal protection of the laws," proved essential to protect the civil rights of individuals. From the 1950s to the 1980s, the Supreme Court read these phrases in a way that greatly broadened minorities' access to legal remedies against discrimination. In the first 16 years of the twenty-first century, the Court had a mixed record of extending and restricting the rights of minorities.

Other amendments that democratized American politics are the Seventeenth (1913), which provided for the selection of US senators by a popular vote rather than by the state legislature; the Nineteenth (1920), which granted women the vote; and the Twenty-Sixth (1971), which lowered the voting age to 18. The Sixteenth Amendment (1913) gave the federal government much greater financial power than the states have by granting Congress the right to tax incomes.

So-called "extra constitutional" changes in the political system (those that occur without the amendment process) have been even more important. Among these are political parties, primary elections, the congressional committee and subcommittee system, the Executive Office of the President (EOP) and the Supreme Court's power of judicial review.

The political parties

The founding fathers viewed political parties as factions (interest groups that pursue narrow private interests rather than the common good). They designed a constitutional system to keep factions so divided that no one of them could gain significant power. Yet, parties emerged quickly and the Constitution was one cause of their appearance.

The separate and staggered elections required for senators, representatives, and the president, as well as the republican form of government guaranteed the states, ensure many and frequent elections. Parties arose in part because traditionally, at least, they recruit, screen and nominate candidates for elections. The separation of powers also helped create parties because the disparate policy initiatives of separated branches required a coordinating tool. The founders set up a system that encourages two parties, rather than no parties. Only one person is elected from each electoral district and that person needs only a plurality (more votes than any other candidate gets) to win the election. Thus, coalitions form *before* elections. Political parties are few in number and are coalitions of interests with middle-of-the-road programs whose vagueness results from compromises made to unify dissimilar elements. Since 1856, there have been two major national parties: the Democrats and the Republicans.

Two other factors have been important for the development of a two-party system in the US. First, winning the presidency is so important that it has inspired two broadly based national coalitions, one consisting of the party in the White House and the other of everybody else. Second, there has usually been a division of voters into two camps on the important issues, such as slavery or government regulation of the economy.

Differences between the parties

Despite their broad diversity and the diffuseness of their ideologies, the two major parties represent different political orientations. Their differences are clear in the view the voters and activists for each have of themselves. For example, Republicans much more frequently identify themselves as conservatives. Until recently, the major parties were also distinct because of their strength in different regions of the nation. In the decades after the Civil War, both parties were competitive in only a few states. The South blamed the party of Lincoln for the war and so voted almost exclusively for the Democrats. The rest of the nation tended to be heavily Republican. From the 1890s to 1930s, this regional division deepened as discriminatory state election laws disenfranchised African Americans in the South and the Republican Party became more associated with big business. In all but name, the nation consisted of one-party regions.

Franklin D. Roosevelt's New Deal Coalition complicated the picture. He forged a national majority by appealing to pluralities in the South, the Northeast and Midwest. From 1932, when Roosevelt was first elected president, until 1968, Democrats were conservative in the South but often liberal in other regions of the nation. Republicans were conservative in the rural Midwest and the West as a whole, but frequently moderate or liberal in the Northeast. Since 1968, white conservative Southerners have increasingly voted Republican, first in presidential elections, but since the late 1980s also in congressional and state contests.

The growth of African American voting, the influx of people from other regions and the modernization and urbanization of the South have made it a two-party region. The weight of white opinion is conservative Republican but Blacks, Latinos, the elderly and people from other regions are potentially decisive political "swing" groups. In the 2008 and 2012 presidential elections the Democrats were stronger on both coasts, three states in the Southwest, in big cities, their inner suburbs, the Great Lakes Midwest and the Northeast. They also broke the "solid" Republican South by winning in Virginia and Florida in 2012, and in those two states plus North Carolina in 2008. Republicans did best in rural areas, small towns, outer "white" suburbs, the rest of the South, and the Great Plains and Rocky Mountain states. In 2016, Donald J. Trump won in these areas under the Republican label, but also in the Southern "swing" states and narrowly, in Pennsylvania, Ohio, Michigan and Wisconsin.

Today, Democrats tend to represent a moderate-to-liberal political orientation. Republicans are now more uniformly conservative as the party's moderate-to-liberal wing in the Northeast, Upper Midwest and Pacific Northwest has shrunk and lost influence. The ideological center of the Republican Party supports a small federal government, states' rights, minimal business regulation, low taxes, and private solutions to social problems.

To win the party nomination during the primary season, presidential candidates usually move toward its more radical activist base on the left or right. In the general election afterwards, they shift toward the center of the party and electorate to assemble a winning coalition nationally. In 2008 and 2012, John McCain and Mitt Romney took positions associated with the right-wing Tea Party Movement during the primary campaign and then edged toward the center of the electorate as the voting neared. Hillary Clinton adjusted her policy proposals to the left during primary contests with Bernie Sanders and then returned closer to mainstream positions.

Democrats are more in favor of government management of the economy, a public social safety net and unions. Bill Clinton moved the party to the political center in the 1990s but nearly alienated his party's liberal wing. Since the 1970s, the parties divided over a number of social issues. More Democrats have favored civil rights, affirmative action programs, gun control, abortion rights and equal rights for the LGBT population. More Republicans have favored reducing government spending and balancing the federal budget.

A range of economic and social indicators also shows differences between the parties. Democrats have, on average, lower incomes, less education and less prestigious occupations. They are more often female, Jewish, urban and members of racial minority groups. Until the 1980s, most white Catholic ethnics were also Democrats, but now they more often split their allegiance. In the 2016 election "outsider" candidates, Sanders and especially Trump, campaigned with ideological views and positions on central issues, such as trade and immigration, that were different from the parties' traditional profiles.

Party organization

The federal system results in parties on three distinct levels. State and local party organizations vary a great deal. They affiliate with the national parties, which usually do not interfere in their activities except to offer funds or services. The parties have organizing committees on every level with the Republican and Democratic National Committees (DNC and RNC) and their chairs at the top. The state and local parties are active on a continuous basis, while the national organizations, until recently, have lain dormant between presidential elections. The party that loses presidential elections can sustain its strength in Congress and state governments. Both parties seem weak compared with European parties. Nearly all candidates label themselves as Democrat or Republican, but the party no longer chooses them, controls their election campaigns or formulates

PLATE 6.2 The 2016 Republican convention in Cleveland, Ohio, July 18–21 at the Quicken Loans Arena, where Donald J. Trump officially became the presidential nominee of the party and delivered his acceptance speech.
© *REX/Shutterstock*

the policies they advocate. The Trump and Sanders candidacies exemplified all these recent trends.

Independent candidates and "third" parties

Independent candidates and minor or splinter parties (so-called "third" parties) have a long history in the US. They seldom win federal elections because of election rules and about half the voters' loyalty to one of the major parties. Independents' victories usually occur in state or local contests.

There are several types of third parties. In national elections, independents such as Ralph Nader (in 2000 and 2004) and some third parties attract votes from people who are dissatisfied with the major parties and the government in general. Other third parties, such as the Socialist and Libertarian parties, represent ideologies that have only small followings in the US. Yet others are single-issue organizations, such as the Prohibition, Women's, Right to Life and Green Parties. The most important third parties have been those that result from splits in the major parties. From the 1990s to 2016 third parties very likely were a factor in deciding who became president in close elections. The impact of third parties has most often been evident in the adoption of their policy suggestions, such as primary elections, the direct election of senators, women's suffrage, and the income tax by the major parties.

The legislative branch

In addition to the staffs of members and committees, Congress draws expertise from its own library, research service, and accounting, budget and technology assessment offices.

During the Cold War, the president seemed more important than Congress because of the executive's capacity for quick and decisive action. Since the 1970s, Congress has attempted, with limited success, to reassert its authority. A very powerful institution, it is no longer the dominant branch of the federal government, as the founders intended. Its main functions are law making (mostly dealing with the president's legislative agenda), forming structures and programs to implement policy, overseeing the bureaucracy, raising and allocating funds and advising the president.

Differences between the chambers

While the chambers of Congress are in theory equally powerful, there are several significant differences in their membership, organization and practices. As intended, the House responds more quickly than the Senate to the electorate's mood. Elections every two years in smaller geographical units allow representatives to more closely reflect the current views of local voters than do senators, who serve six-year terms and represent whole states. The large majority of both chambers consists of middle-aged white men, many of whom are lawyers. After the 2016 elections, for example, (a record) 21 senators were women.

The House contains a much more diverse membership. For example, when the new Congress (the 115th) took office in 2017, it included record numbers of women and members of minority groups: 104 women, 49 African Americans, 39 Latinos, 15 Asian Americans, and 2 Native Americans. In 2007, the House chose Californian Nancy Pelosi as its first woman speaker. Since the mid-1990s, the number of women and minority group members in Congress has continued to rise, although their representation remains far below their portion of the nation's population.

There are constitutional differences between the chambers as well. To qualify for a seat in the Senate, a person must be 30 years old, a citizen for nine years and a resident of the state where elected. Representatives must be 25, seven

PLATE 6.3 Former Speaker of the House of Representatives (current Minority Leader), Democrat Nancy Pelosi, who represents the eighth district of California – much of San Francisco and vicinity – and her successor, Republican Paul Ryan, who represents the first district of Wisconsin, which includes Milwaukee suburbs and counties to the city's west.
© *DPA Picture Alliance/Alamy*

years a citizen and (by custom) a resident of their district. Financial bills must begin in the House, although the Senate usually amends them. The Senate must approve treaties and presidential appointments. Size, however, is the constitutional difference that has the most important effect on the chambers.

Because of its much greater size, the House must regulate its business carefully. The Speaker of the House and the Rules Committee have considerable power to schedule the work of the chamber, limit debate and restrict amendments to a bill from the floor. The speaker also influences the assignment of members and bills to committees, decides which bills come up for a vote and determines who speaks during debate. The majority party chooses the speaker, who in turn chooses the party's members on the Rules Committee. The majority party also elects a majority leader as the speaker's next in command and a whip to help round up votes. The other party selects a minority leader and whip.

The smaller Senate has much more relaxed procedures and no officer with power comparable to the speaker's. Bills come up for debate in any order and whenever a majority of the chamber wishes. There are majority and minority leaders, and both parties use the whip system to get out the vote. The Constitution appoints the vice president as the presiding officer of the Senate and requires the senators to elect a president *pro tempore* to chair the chamber in the vice president's absence. The vice president is often absent, attending mostly for ceremonial occasions.

When there is a tie vote, the Constitution gives the vice president the power to break a senatorial deadlock. The George W. Bush presidency set a precedent for reinterpreting the customary meaning of "presiding" over the Senate. Bush asked Vice President Dick Cheney to lead the chamber on a regular basis, and because the parties had equal numbers of seats during Bush's terms, Cheney broke tie votes more often than most vice presidents. After the 2016 elections, the Senate held 52 Republicans, 46 Democrats and 2 independents who usually vote with the Democrats. In a closely divided chamber, it will be interesting to see the role Vice President Mike Pence assumes.

Members usually find the position of president *pro tempore* of the Senate so powerless that they turn it over to a junior senator. The real leader of the chamber is customarily the majority leader, but even he has no formal power to limit debate or amendments. Members can therefore engage in a filibuster (an attempt to defeat a bill by talking until its supporters withdraw it so that other business can be finished). Only if 60 members vote for closure, which limits speeches to one hour, can the Senate stop a filibuster. Filibusters seldom occur. When they do, it signals an issue (or presidential appointment) so controversial that senators are unable to compromise, and therefore filibusters receive considerable notice. Amendments to a bill during Senate debates can be irrelevant to its subject or purpose. Senators sometimes attach these "riders" in an attempt to ensure the bill's defeat. They also add them to secure the passage of proposals that would have great difficulty passing if forwarded separately.

PLATE 6.4 Former Secretary of State Hillary Clinton and Republican presidential nominee Donald Trump during the third presidential debate, which took place at the University of Nevada, Las Vegas, on October 19, 2016.
© *WENN UK/Alamy*

Congressional organization

Members of Congress organize themselves in several ways. The most important of these is by party. Members divide along party lines on between two-fifths and two-thirds of the votes that take place in Congress. Special party groups pick the officers of each chamber and decide which committee's members will work on. Each party gets a number of committee members equal to the percentage of seats it won in the last elections. The majority party wins the leadership positions and the largest committee staffing.

Members also act based on other loyalties. In the House, state delegations are important, especially since the members from states with large populations represent big, potentially unified voting blocks on some issues. Congress has over 100 caucuses (interest groups formed to lobby other members) that allow members to gather in groups that are important rivals to the parties as the source of policy proposals. There are conservative, moderate and liberal caucuses for each party, as well as caucuses formed to promote regional, economic, ethnic, racial and women's issues that cross both party and chamber divisions. Three decades ago, Congress had only four caucuses. Today some commentators claim they cause the fragmentation of congressional planning.

Powers and functions of congress

The Constitution grants Congress "all legislative powers" in the federal government. The president, interest groups and private citizens may want laws passed by Congress, but a member of *each* chamber must introduce the proposal for it to become federal law.

Law making is only the best known of the legislative branch's duties. Members are truly representatives; so much of their work involves "casework" (handling pressure groups' and voters' complaints and requests). The national legislature alone can make the federal budget, raise funds, allocate, or spend US government money. Congress also has the constitutional authority to regulate foreign and interstate commerce. Only it has the power to raise, finance and regulate military forces and to declare war. The legislative branch has great power over the other arms of the national government. It created all the federal courts below the Supreme Court, can (and has) changed the number of Supreme Court justices and decides which cases the federal courts can hear by defining jurisdictions. Congress, not the president, established the departments and the executive bureaucracy.

The committee system

Congress does most of its work in committees in which members gain the expertise and power to make their mark on public policy. The amount of legislation introduced annually made committees an indispensable tool for the division of labor. The committee system assigns members to specific legislative work, the supervision of executive departments and agencies, hearings on public issues and (in Senate committees) on presidential appointments.

Members strive for assignments on committees of the greatest concern to their states or districts. As government became involved in wider areas of life, the two dozen or so standing (permanent) committees in each chamber spawned many subcommittees. Thus, for example, a House member from Mississippi works to become the chair of the subcommittee dealing with cotton. The most senior member of the majority party traditionally becomes chair of a committee and through this position exercises control over its power to "kill" or promote a bill. However, subcommittees have multiplied and won greater independence. Moreover, they now choose the chair by secret ballot, which does not always result in election by seniority.

How a bill becomes an act of Congress

The lawmaking process in the two chambers is parallel. Bills can be introduced in one chamber first or in both simultaneously. After that, a committee takes charge of the bill and usually refers it to a subcommittee. There members air their views, gather reports from experts and lobbyists and hold hearings. Then in a "mark-up session," the subcommittee agrees on changes in the bill and returns it to the committee for another mark-up session before it goes to the whole chamber for debate and a vote on passage.

Most bills "die" in committee or subcommittee because they served only to publicize a member's willingness to "do something" about an issue, or because they are too flawed or controversial for passage. If a bill passes both chambers, amendments added in one or both houses may result in different texts. Then a conference committee with members from both chambers writes a compromise text. If it passes a vote in the House and Senate, the president receives the bill, may sign or veto it, and sends it back with a signing or veto message.

Congressional elections

Elections for Congress take place in different subdivisions: congressional districts, each of which chooses one member of the House of Representatives, and states, each of which selects two members of the Senate. Congressional elections take place every two years, when all members of the House of Representatives and one-third of the Senate face re-election.

Redistricting (reapportionment of congressional seats)

The House expanded as new states entered the union and their populations grew. Then in 1929, its size was fixed at 435 (with three additional non-voting delegates from the District of Columbia). States now receive seats according to their population relative to other states' by a process called reapportionment (reassignment of the number of House seats to each state) after every ten-year federal census. The Constitution guarantees each state a minimum of one representative. The number any state has above this minimum depends on how large its population is, compared to that of the other states. Since the size of the House is constant, states with declining or slowly growing populations lose seats, and those with more rapidly growing populations gain seats. From 1950 to 2010, the political power of the Northeastern and Great Lakes states in the House declined while that of parts of the South, Southwest and Pacific coast rose. At the last redistricting, for example, New York and Ohio lost two seats, Florida gained two, and Texas added four.

The 1962 Supreme Court ruling in *Baker* v. *Carr* required redistricting (the redrawing of the geographical lines between districts) to follow the one-person-one-vote principle by creating congressional districts with equal populations. In 2012, districts contained about 710,000 people, a number adjusted up after the 2010 census. Amendments to the Voting Rights Act in the 1980s required that states redraw district lines must make it likely that minority group members would win elections to the House in numbers equivalent to the group's portion of the population of the state, but court challenges to the constitutionality of "minority majority" districts reduced their number greatly. The protests to that were few, however, because by the 1990s, record numbers of minorities won seats in Congress.

Today, the use of sophisticated statistical computer models allows the majority in state legislatures to design a redistricting plan that satisfies any political priorities it has. In the redistricting based on the 2010 census, on the one hand, in six states (Maryland, Pennsylvania, Georgia, Florida, Michigan and Texas) the legislature created "safe" districts for the majority party that effectively eliminated competition from the other major party. On the other hand, another six states (New Jersey, Arizona, California, Idaho, Washington and Hawaii) chose a bi- or non-partisan commission to protect candidates from both parties.

Elections for one-member districts in a non-parliamentary system

The two-member constituencies for the Senate are a major exception to the principle of single-member election districts in the US. Even these *function* as one-member districts because only one of a state's senators stands for election at a time. A key to understanding the nature of Congress lies in remembering that the US does not have a parliamentary form of government. In a parliament, the prime minister is usually the leader of the majority party in the legislature after a general election. Members of a parliament keep in line with party policies because voting independently can cause the fall of the government. In that kind of system, members owe their seats to political parties, and voters choose between parties rather than candidates. Voting independently can lead to de-selection by the party at election time.

Congress does not choose the chief executive. Its members can vote without fear that the government will fall if they do not support their party. This means they can give first allegiance to their state or congressional district, rather than to the party or the chief executive. Members of Congress owe their seats to elections in which their personalities and positions on issues matter more than party labels. The parties cannot control who enters congressional elections or directs these campaigns. Most candidates choose their campaign staff and finance their election campaigns. The party is but one of several sources of support.

To run for a seat in Congress, usually a candidate must first win a primary election. Two or more candidates from the same party compete in a primary for the right to represent the party in the general election. They may put themselves forward or be recruited by the party. State laws require people to document the seriousness of their candidacy by collecting a certain number of signatures supporting it before the party puts their names on the primary ballot. Victory in a primary comes with a plurality rather than a majority of the votes, because the field of candidates is often between three and five. In some states, the two frontrunners compete in a run-off primary between when no candidate wins a majority. In the general election, there are usually two candidates, a Democrat and a Republican, although independent or third party candidates sometimes run.

Being a member of Congress has become a career. Between 1946 and 2016, over 90 percent of House members and about 85 percent of senators won re-election. Incumbents (sitting members) have advantages over challengers. They use their office for media attention, their names and faces are consequently better known, and they can take credit for helping to pass government programs that benefit the state or district. In 2016, opinion polls showed that voter dissatisfaction with Congress was much greater than it was with President Obama. In surveys, large majorities of the public repeatedly support congressional term limits. Still, members of Congress won re-election at only slightly lower rates in 2016. Of course, a large staff, name recognition, gerrymandering, fundraising, and voter turnout also greatly contribute to reelection.

The Democrats had majorities in both houses of Congress for almost the entire time from 1954 to 1994, losing control only of the Senate between 1980 and 1986. The advantages of incumbency helped the party stay in power, but backfired in 1994–6 as voters made Democrats the target of their discontent with government. The mid-term elections (those between presidential election years) usually result in losses for the majority party and in 1994 cost the Democrats control of both chambers. The Republicans won majorities in both houses for the first time in 40 years then and kept a majority in both houses, except for a short period early in George W. Bush's first term, consolidating their control in Congress after 2000 and gaining increasing majorities through the 2004 elections. The partisan tide turned at that point, however. The Democrats won majorities in both houses in 2006 and strengthened them considerably two years later, giving Obama the majorities he needed for health reform early in his first term.

The pendulum swung again in favor of the Republicans at the 2010 mid-term elections, in part because of the surge of the rightist Tea Party movement, which successfully targeted vulnerable Democrats and moderate Republicans. The Republicans dominated the House of Representatives and stalled the president's agenda, while a slim Democratic majority in the Senate tempered House action. After the 2012 elections, Congress remained split between a Republican House and a Democratic Senate. Two years later, a Republican "landslide" gave the party control of both houses, enough to stop Obama's initiatives completely but not the 60 seats needed in the Senate to stop a filibuster. Strife with the Tea Party wing of the party grew so sharp that House Speaker John Boehner resigned. Still, the Republicans won majorities in both houses as well as the presidency in 2016. With the end of divided government at that point, it remained unclear how well the two Republican-controlled branches would cooperate.

The executive branch

Some 2.1 million civilians and 1.4 million active-duty military employees work in this largest branch of the federal government. The degree of control the president has over the 15 departments, 90 independent agencies, 4 branches of the military and numerable government corporations in the federal bureaucracy depends on the rules set up by Congress. More than 99 percent of civilian federal bureaucrats, for example, get their jobs through competitive examinations required by the Civil Service Act, rather than by presidential appointment. The president nominates the highest officials in the executive branch: the secretaries and assistant secretaries who lead the departments, the chief administrators of agencies and commissions and the ranking officers of American embassies. The Senate must approve these appointments. The roughly 2,000 high-level positions in the EOP do not require congressional approval.

The Executive Office of the President

The main components of the EOP that operate outside the White House are the Council of Economic Advisers, the National Security Council, the Office of Management and Budget, and the Central Intelligence Agency. Inside the White House are the first lady's staff and the president's own staff, which includes personal advisors, the press secretary, the congressional liaison officer and the chief of staff. The structure and operation of the EOP and the upper levels of the executive branch vary, depending on the style and character of the president. For instance, the cabinet, although it is composed of department secretaries and other key officials, has played a smaller role in most recent administrations.

Qualifications for and powers of the presidency

Constitutional clauses provide for a strong executive but include checks to prevent the development of presidential government. The president must be born in the US, at least 35 years old, and a resident of the US for 14 years. He is more independent of the legislature than the chief executives of most democratic governments because his election is separate from Congress and a vote of no confidence cannot remove him from office.

The price of his independence is having no guarantee of majorities in the Houses of Congress, the difficulties of lobbying for support in an institution of which he is not a part and the limits put on his powers by the system of checks and balances. Still, the chief executive is the only official elected by voters in all the states, and on that basis, the president can claim to be the sole politician who sets an agenda in the *national* interest.

Presidential duties arise from constitutional clauses, congressional delegation or circumstances. The most important extra-constitutional duties are acting
as chief of state and party leader. The president is the nation's ceremonial head
of state by default, because the Constitution provides no office for that purpose. He became the national leader of his party as parties developed into the
organizers of the nation's political life and the presidency became increasingly
powerful. The president's popularity often affects the success of his party's candidates for other offices.

The office's constitutional powers are the result of interpreting rather vague
phrases in the document. The president is the administrative head of the nation,
for example, because the Constitution states that "executive power shall be
vested in a President." What that and other constitutional phrases mean in practice has evolved from the claims that presidents have made without provoking
Congress or the courts to effectively oppose them. As one political scientist
has famously put it, in a system of checks and balances with branches sharing
powers, the president's power is not to command but to *persuade* – to convince other political actors that what the president wants is what they want.
The vague constitutional powers give the chief executive great leeway but not
nearly so many or so specific powers as those enumerated for Congress in the
Constitution.

PLATE 6.5 Donald Trump took the oath of office for president from Supreme Court Chief
Justice John Roberts during the inauguration ceremony in Washington, DC on January 20,
2017, with his family and notables of both parties looking on.
© *MediaPunch Inc/Alamy*

As chief administrator, the president must carry out the laws written by Congress. This means managing the bureaucracy and enforcing existing policies, but interpreted broadly, it has enabled presidents to break a strike or send troops to integrate a public school. Presidents have thus been able to read current conditions, the Constitution or both as justification for the expansion of executive powers at the expense of the balance among the three branches.

George W. Bush, for example, attempted to persuade politicians and the public that his view of the "unitary executive" reflected the intent of the drafters of the Constitution and was essential after the terrorist attacks of September 11, 2001. With this theory of presidential power, he asserted that the executive branch should not be subject to congressional oversight (inspection) and that the president and his high-level appointees should be able to hire and fire government officials without senatorial interference. He also claimed his administration's right to redefine of the Geneva Conventions, the international understanding of "torture," and civil rights at home without questioning by the courts. As long as the nation felt acutely threatened by the 9/11 attacks, the administration remained popular with the public, and criticism of the "unitary" executive remained muted. Facing an international economic crisis, two ongoing wars, terrorism, and domestic problems, Barack Obama found the temptation to expand presidential powers difficult to resist, and, for example, reauthorized the Patriot Act.

Chief lawmaker

The president's role as legislative leader also developed from constitutional clauses requiring him to inform Congress about the "state of the nation" and suggest the "measures" he considers "necessary or expedient." Another clause allows him to convene a special session of Congress if he deems it necessary. However, the president did not usually set the legislative agenda until the twentieth century.

In 1921, Congress weakened its control over the "power of the purse" by enacting the Budget and Accounting Act, which delegated to the president the power to screen the budget proposals of executive-branch departments and agencies. As a result, the White House routinely sets policy priorities by proposing how much money government programs should receive. Not until the Great Depression of the 1930s, however, did the president draft a coordinated "package" of bills for congressional action. The New Deal proposals of Franklin D. Roosevelt marked a new era in presidential legislative activity, but then the president sent bills to Congress and let it decide what to do with them. Today, presidents follow their progress through Congress closely and use legislative aides to lobby hard for their passage. Obama thus received criticism for not guiding his health reform proposals more closely.

A president who is an effective legislative initiator and lobbyist has less need of his veto power to stop the passage of bills. Vetoes can take place in two ways: with a veto message giving presidential objections or by the executive's taking no action on bills that come to the White House within ten days of the adjournment of Congress (the so-called pocket veto). The president's veto power is limited. Congress may override it with two-thirds majorities. In addition, only from 1995 to 1997 did the executive have a line-item veto on financial bills to annul objectionable *parts* of legislation. Thus, members of Congress can add unwanted "riders" to bills the executive wants passed without fear of a veto on just those lines of text.

To counter such tactics by members of Congress, presidents since Ronald Reagan have made expanded use of the "signing statement," a signed legal opinion from the president included with the text of the new law. Clinton found somewhat less need for these statements, but George W. Bush's extensive reliance on them in controversial situations, especially with regard to the treatment of military prisoners and financing for defense, resulted in mounting opposition. The signing statement often defines how the executive intends to implement the law. It can identify provisions that the president finds unclear, politically unacceptable or unconstitutional and so announces that the executive may not implement these. Bush defended his position by claiming that a "unitary" executive branch required these powers. On the other hand, opponents of his way of using the signing statement say that it restores the president's line-item veto. Setting a historic precedent, it allows the executive to replace Congress as the branch that interprets a law's intent and the Supreme Court as the judge of constitutionality.

The president and foreign policy

The Constitution names the president as commander-in-chief, making him the highest-ranking officer in the military, but it gives Congress the power to declare war. The founders' attempt to give the legislature control over the executive's military power proved so limited that in 1973 Congress passed the War Powers Act to restrain the president. It requires congressional approval within specified time limits for deployment of American troops abroad. Presidents call the Act unconstitutional and follow its notification procedure only when it suits them. Since World War II, the US has mostly engaged in undeclared wars. Congress has instead passed resolutions giving the executive nearly carte blanche on the conduct of these "armed conflicts."

The president's military power is one of several factors that strengthen the position as foreign policy leader. This is the arena where the executive branch has most clearly developed its dominance. Presidents have learned to circumvent constitutional clauses that require approval by two-thirds of the Senate for ratification of a treaty and a simple majority for confirmation of diplomatic appointments. Today, the executive usually carries out international decisions not with treaties but with executive agreements, which do not need Senatorial approval. The national security advisor, an EOP staffer who owes the position solely to the president's choice, has become most presidents' main advisor in formulating foreign policy.

The president has four major organizations to support conduct in foreign affairs: the Departments of State and Defense, the CIA and the National Security Council. Faced with these facts, Congress continues to assert its role in foreign policy but recognizes presidential leadership. In addition, since 2002, the chief executive has a new division of the executive branch, the Department of Homeland Security (DHS), to assist in the mobilization and discipline of the public for national defense during the global war on terrorism, an open-ended period of national crisis that some commentators have christened the "second cold war."

Presidential elections

The selection of the incoming chief executive and vice president occur at the end of the sitting president's four-year term. The constitution further specifies that the election for those two offices must take place on the first Tuesday after November 1. Although the process of picking the executive team consumes more than 18 months, the vote for president is on the same day as that year's local, state, and congressional elections. The tenth amendment of the federal constitution states that the states set the "times, places, and manner" of elections, but the constitution makes important exceptions to that rule for the election of the president.

The process is *federal* because the voters make their choice in separate elections in each state – and more recently – in the District of Columbia (Washington DC), US territories, and units of American citizens living abroad. The president is the only official whose electoral district includes all these units. When tallied together, the results of these separate elections determine who the next president of the federation is. The constitution establishes a special assembly from the units, the Electoral College, to count who has won the majority of the unit elections across the US federation. The constitution states that each unit will have a delegation in the College equal to the number of its representatives in Congress. After the ten-year census, the number of electors per state changes to reflect the shifting size of their populations and congressional delegations (see Figure 6.1). For example, California, the most populous state in 2016, has 55 – 2 delegates for its senators and 53 for its representatives in the House.

The constitution sets up an *indirect* method of electing the president by reaching the final tally in the College. In November, the "popular vote" takes place in the unit elections, and the media report which candidate does best in each of those contests. These voting publics, however, do not choose one of the candidates nominated by the parties. Instead, they vote for the unit's delegation

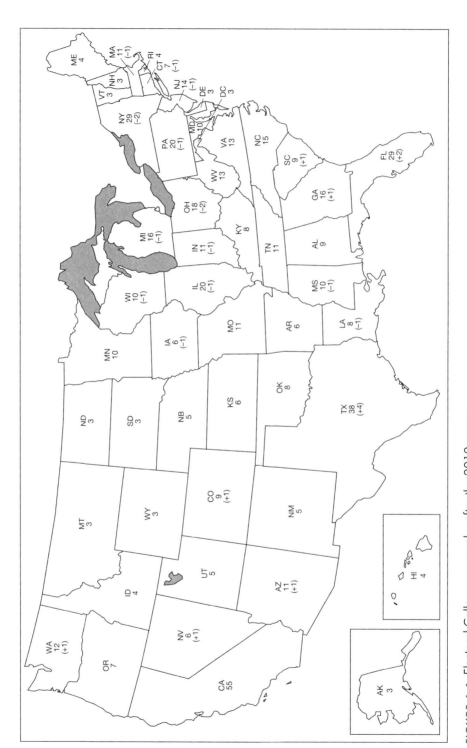

FIGURE 6.1 Electoral College geography after the 2010 census.

Note: Changes in states' electoral votes because of the 2010 census are in parenthesis.

of "electors" in the College. In all but two units (Maine and Nebraska), those electors form a winner-take-all block that gives all its "electoral votes" to the candidate who won the most votes within the unit. Thus, all of California's 55 electors voted for Hillary Clinton in 2016 because she won the state with 61.6 percent of the vote. On interactive maps, the media keeps track of the accumulated electoral vote. For victory in the Electoral College, a presidential candidate must have a majority (270) of the 538 electoral votes.

According to the constitution, the Electoral College vote must be in the state capitals on the first Monday after the second Wednesday in December, which in 2016 was on the nineteenth of the month. The President of the Senate had to receive the electoral votes by December 28. On January 6, Congress met in joint session to confirm the election of Donald J. Trump, who officially began his term of office with the inauguration ceremonies on January 20, 2017.

Non-constitutional practices: an evolving, multi-stage process

The Constitution provides no instructions for the nominating process of choosing candidates for president and vice president. It makes no mention of political parties, whose invention resulted in part to find candidates for office and develop arrangements for choosing among them. As noted, however, it does assign the states the job of deciding when, where, and how elections occur as well as stipulating important elements of the timing and method of electing the president. Together, the parties and states set up the rest of the election process, which evolves to meet their priorities and changing circumstances.

Today, electing the president is a long, costly, several-stage affair. The year before, the first stage begins when candidates hold press conferences to announce that they are running for the office. Several people from each party commonly propose themselves. Over six to nine months, these candidates "test the waters" to see if support for their candidacy across the nation is warm enough to raise the hundreds of millions of dollars necessary to pay for the primary caucus campaign. Most drop out during this demanding "invisible primary," which seemed to decisively favor those with support among the nation's wealthiest until 2004, when Democrat Howard Dean raised sufficient funds for the next stage through small donations made over the Internet.

Barack Obama's campaign in 2008 and Bernie Sanders' in 2016 followed Dean's lead, both becoming Internet movements with funding from hosts of small contributors. The pre-primary stage started earlier and was more visible in the 2012 and 2016 elections. A record 17 Republicans competed for their party's nomination in 2015–16. They engaged each other in five debates in late 2015. One cartoonist pictured these as showdowns with 16 pistol-shooting cowboys in a circle firing at Donald Trump. A billionaire entrepreneur without political or military experience, Trump attacked both party elites and the

Washington establishment. He branded his opponents with demeaning nick-names, such as "lyin' Ted" (Cruz), "little Marco" (Rubio) or "low energy" (Jeb Bush)" and won growing support and free media attention through confident unpredictable brashness.

Five Democrats, including two who dropped out early, vied for their par-ty's nomination. The party's three debates in 2015 drew few viewers and little media attention. The Democratic establishment gave Clinton overwhelming backing, both from the party machinery and private donors. A unique major party candidate, as a woman, former first lady, US Senator, and former secretary of state, Clinton faced unexpectedly strong opposition, in 2008 from Obama and in 2016 from Sanders, a charismatic Jewish socialist who registered as a Democrat one year earlier to run for president with the party label. Sanders' message got little media attention compared to Trump in 2015, even though they both were party outsiders leading populist movements.

From January to June of the presidential election year, the states narrow the field of candidates from each party to one through caucuses or primaries. Both procedures are indirect: party voters choose delegates to the party's national convention and give these delegates the authority to make its official nomina-tion of a candidate. Most states use presidential primaries, but 15 held party meetings called presidential caucuses in 2016. Because they result in the choice of roughly 70 percent of convention delegates, primaries attract much more attention.

The campaign funds needed to campaign across the US lead most would-be party nominees to withdraw relatively early. Public debates also serve to reduce the number of candidates. The Republicans held 6 more televised debates during the second stage of the election, the primary-caucus period from January to June of 2016. By the last debate in March, only three candidates remained – Trump, Ted Cruz and John Kasich. The Democratic candidates debated seven times in the spring, and Martin O'Malley dropped out after two of these.

Changes in the primary-caucus stage result from shifting party rules and states' right to set rules for choosing convention delegates. Recently, states have "front loaded" their primaries or caucuses by moving them to earlier dates to get more attention. In 2016, states choose to hold these elections on the same date to be part of turning points in the nomination contest. After two 'super' Tuesdays, one on March 1 with 14 contests (mostly in small states) and another 6 on March 15 (mostly in big ones), Trump secured the Republican nomina-tion. He did this amid opposition from leading party figures and a "stop Trump" movement led by Mitt Romney, its nominee in 2012. Trump defied polls and expectations, winning a loyal following even as his daily "tweets" and televised remarks provoked women, Latinos, Muslims, Blacks, the disabled, foreign policy experts, libertarians, neo-conservatives and environmentalists.

The Democratic race was a contest between Clinton and Sanders from early February, when she won the first caucuses in Iowa by a tiny margin and he won the first primary in New Hampshire decisively. She had an inbuilt lead, however. Almost the entire party elite of "super delegates" had joined her camp before the caucus/primary season began. The candidates won almost equal numbers of nomination contests in different regions of the nation until June. Clinton swept the South and Sanders showed strength in Vermont, parts of the Midwest and the Pacific Northwest. Sanders' hopes grew with the number of his victories, especially because he believed they might persuade some of the party elite's "super delegates" to join him.

The Democrats more often divided convention delegates between the candidates in proportion to the part of the vote each won, instead of assigning them in winner-take-all blocks. As a result, Clinton could keep a lead in the delegate count even as she lost more contests. Nearly all the 400 or so party super delegates, moreover, remained loyal to Clinton. In June, she swept 7 of 9 contests and won the nomination with a clear majority of delegate votes at the convention. Yet Sanders did not withdraw from the race. Instead, he led his movement's negotiations with Clinton to promote its agenda at the convention.

Stages three and four: the conventions and general election season

The media keep count of the pledged convention delegates for each candidate and track the front-runners' progress toward a majority of votes at the party conventions in July or August. In recent decades, each party's choice was clear before the convention. The party "in the White House" re-nominated the incumbent (the person in the office), and a single "out party" candidate won a delegate majority at the convention before the end of the primaries and caucuses. Still, proportional representation in growing numbers of nomination contests now sends more divided blocks of delegates to the conventions. Caucuses and primaries bind delegates only on the first roll-call vote of the states. If no candidate wins a majority, delegates can switch loyalties on later votes, so the final choice could be unexpected. No such surprises occurred at recent conventions.

Conventions are usually well-orchestrated media events designed to demonstrate the healing of internal disagreements from the primary season. In 2016, both parties experienced strife at the conventions. The Democrats had to replace the leader of their national committee, put several planks of the Sanders agenda in the party platform, and roundly praise his campaign to keep peace. The Republicans' presidential family, the Bushes, and other leaders boycotted their party's convention, so Trump and his children played the leading roles. Ted Cruz, Trump's closest competitor, gave an address but received loud boos when he did not endorse Trump.

Candidates now announce their vice presidential "running mates" in advance of the conventions. In 2008 and 2012, Obama chose Joe Biden, an experienced elder senator, who "balanced the ticket." Romney waited until close to the Republican convention before choosing Paul Ryan, a much younger man to his political right with Tea Party support. In 2016, Democrat Tim Kaine and Republican Mike Pence balanced the presidential candidates by coming from other regions and elements of their parties. Pence also had long government experience. The party conventions offer competing media presentations of the parties and their candidates. The key question is which of these mass appeals is more successful at convincing the voting public.

The post-convention campaign runs from late August until the voters go to the polls at the beginning of November. Candidates crisscross the country to make themselves and their stands on the issues known, but they stay in a city only long enough to arrange for the media to take them into the public's living rooms. The major parties, candidates and super PACs buy hugely expensive television ads to portray the faults of their opponents and put themselves in the best possible light. Because of the high cost of television campaigning, candidates also depend on getting free coverage by making the evening news with campaign activities. Television advertisements from independent partisan groups have played an especially visible role in this stage of presidential elections. In 2012, super PAC ads questioned Obama's birthplace, his un-American ideology, and "Obamacare," which would allegedly destroy the country's economy. In 2016, prominent ads claimed that Trump's unstable temperament or Clinton's Wall Street connections were disqualifying.

In the closing months of the campaign, televised live debates (three presidential debates and one vice-presidential debate) offer the candidates a chance to contact a mass audience. A bigger audience watches the debates than any other event in the campaign, and many voters say the debates influence their choice. Candidates are wary of making mistakes in front of this enormous audience and so prepare to meet any question with a well-informed answer. Trump joked about not preparing for the first debate, but changed tactics after the media declared Clinton the winner. The debates are an unreliable predictor of who will win. A combination of other factors, such as the economic situation, the public's division over key issues and the candidates' performance in un-televised campaign activities, are often decisive.

Election day

On election day, the television networks display maps of the country to track two tallies of the results. One is the "popular vote" across the nation of people that have supported each candidate. These figures are estimates from polling companies who ask people how they voted as they exit the polling stations. Because of the difference in time zones, there is no estimate from the Pacific West until very late. The second tally is the Electoral College vote. The media "call" states for one of the candidates as soon as a plurality for one seems clear. The Supreme Court has determined that states cannot *require* electors to vote for that candidate, but few electors have not. The plurality system has its most dramatic effect in the Electoral College vote.

Today, most people are concentrated in a dozen or so "big states," and only a few of these are "competitive" (divided in their support for the major parties). Candidates spend most time and money in the campaign in states like Florida and Ohio to win large blocks of highly contested Electoral College votes. When an election is exceptionally close, as in 2000, even electoral votes of the smallest states can be decisive.

Trump won a shocking upset victory in 2016. Polls showed Clinton winning by large margins in the popular and electoral votes. Yet, he won traditionally

TABLE 6.1 Selection of US presidential elections between 1932 and 2016

Year	Candidates	Parties	% of popular vote	Electoral College vote
1932	Franklin D. Roosevelt	Democratic	57.4	472
	Herbert C. Hoover	Republican	39.7	59
(Roosevelt won in 1936, 1940 and 1944, serving until his death in 1945, when vice president Harry S. Truman succeeded him.)				
1948	Harry S. Truman	Democratic	49.6	303
	Thomas E. Dewey	Republican	45.1	189
1960	John F. Kennedy	Democratic	49.7	303
	Richard M. Nixon	Republican	49.5	219
1964	Lyndon B. Johnson	Democratic	61.1	486
	Barry M. Goldwater	Republican	38.5	52
1980	Ronald Reagan	Republican	50.8	489
	Jimmy Carter	Democratic	41.0	49
1988	George Bush	Republican	53.4	426
	Michael Dukakis	Democratic	45.6	111
1992	Bill Clinton	Democratic	43.0	370
	George H. W. Bush	Republican	38.0	168
	H. Ross Perot	Independent	19.0	0
2000	George W. Bush	Republican	47.9	271
	Albert Gore, Jr.	Democratic	48.4	266
2008	Barack Obama	Democratic	53.0	365
	John McCain	Republican	46.0	173
2012	Barack Obama	Democratic	51.0	332
	Mitt Romney	Republican	47.0	206
2016	Donald Trump	Republican	46.1	306
	Hillary Clinton	Democratic	48.3	232
	Gary Johnson	Libertarian	3.3	0
	Jill Stein	Green	1.1	0

Notes: Victors in italics third-party candidates shown only occasionally

Democratic states, such as Pennsylvania, Michigan, and Wisconsin, and big competitive states, such as Florida and North Carolina. As the results came in over several days, it was clear that he had won a decisive electoral victory, while she won close to a 3 million popular vote plurality.

Commentators provided a multi-factor explanation for his success. She should have campaigned more in the rust belt. He touched the nerve of discontent in the working and middle classes there, whose wages have stagnated for decades. Especially in the post-industrial Midwest, many voters wanted change, which Hilary's long career in politics and close ties to Obama did not represent to them. Trump, on the other hand, sharply criticized the entire established leadership and Democratic, Republican, military, bureaucratic, and intelligence communities. A few days before the election, FBI Director James Comey raised questions about Clinton's culpability as secretary of state for using a private e-mail server and potentially causing national security leaks. In a close election, the Libertarian and, to a lesser degree, the Green Party won a decisive protest vote in crucial state contests from Florida to Wisconsin.

Campaign financing

The funding of campaigning for elections, not only for the presidency but also for all federal elective offices became a major issue in 2015–16. On the Republican side, billionaire Donald Trump contrasted his independence from donors with his rivals' need to seek money from contributors, who he said would naturally expect policy favors from the person elected. Both Bernie Sanders and Trump criticized Hillary Clinton for fund-raising through the exorbitant fees Wall Street firms paid her for lectures to their audiences. Trump and his allies also alleged that when she served as Secretary of State she was guilty of trading government favors for contributions to the Clinton Foundation, which she and Bill Clinton established as a global charity. Trump, however, accepted money from large donors and superPACs (large political action committees) during the last stage of the campaign. New York State found that his Trump Foundation had broken state laws for charities.

Influence peddling has long been a vital concern for reformers who want to prevent "special interests" from using contributions to exercise undemocratic control over how elected members of government vote on policy issues. The federal government has passed laws to regulate campaign funding since the mid-1800s. The modern regime of regulations dates from the 1970s, when presidential candidates could win matching public funds for the campaign on the condition that they accepted a spending cap and demonstrated that they had broad citizen support though small donations in 20 states. In the last four election cycles, most pre-primary candidates refused public funds because they needed to spend more than the cap.

The government stopped funding the nominating conventions in 2014. It still offers full public funding for the post-convention campaigns of each major party's nominee up to a spending cap ($9.14 million for each candidate in 2016), if they opt for government funding. No candidate chose public funding in the last several elections, because they spent far in excess of the cap. The estimated cost of the 2016 presidential election was $5 billion.

PLATE 6.6 A polling place at Salina Elementary School on November 8, 2016, in Dearborn, Michigan, the nation's most heavily Arab American and Muslim neighborhood. A local official checks voters' qualifications with a computer and registration printouts. Approved voters stand nearby at voting booths separated by partitions to cast their ballots. Some critics of state registration procedures, mostly Republicans (including Donald Trump), claimed that voting fraud by millions of ineligible people gave Hillary Clinton the victory in the popular vote for president. Outdated lists of local voters, they said, included many people who were deceased or had moved to another district and so could vote in two places. Republicans called for updated voter rolls and stricter registration rules. Democratic commentators responded that studies by non-partisan political scientists found so little voting fraud that it could not have changed the outcome of the election. Democrats emphasized that "voter suppression," caused by the stricter voter identification laws in many states, was the real problem. Requiring specified kinds of picture identification, the relocation of voting places, and reductions of the length of the period of early voting, they asserted, kept legitimate voters from casting a ballot, especially among the poor, elderly, poorly educated, unemployed, or foreign-born, who often voted for Democratic candidates.

© *Jim West/Alamy*

Central provisions of the Bipartisan Campaign Reform Act (BCRA) of 2002 established rules to control the ways candidates and supporting groups use public or private money during the election. Most important, the Act banned the use of "soft money" raised in a party's name, and limited funding by independent political action committees (PACs).

In January 2010, the Supreme Court ruled on several provisions of the BCRA in *Citizens United* v. *the FEC*. The court held that corporations have the same First Amendment rights to freedom of expression as individuals, including contributions to campaign communications such as advertisements and films. In effect, this eliminated BCRA's limits on campaign spending. While the court upheld the Act's disclosure provisions, its decision led to greatly increased spending by so-called super PACs, which are no longer subject to spending limits. In 2014, the Court further weakened the BCRA by banning limits on the total amount *individuals* can contribute to campaigns or parties. Election costs continue to soar, and the contributions of the very wealthy increase. On the other hand, some argue that Trump's largely self-funded populist campaign, and Sanders and Obama's success in Internet funding campaigns with vast numbers of small contributions suggest that the effects of money on elections are complex. Clinton, for example, raised much more than Trump but lost the election.

Reform the system?

The 2000 and 2016 presidential campaigns drew attention to controversial aspects of the electoral system. In both years, Americans divided their support so evenly for the major candidates that one of them won the electoral vote and the other the popular vote. The constitutional definition of the electoral vote as decisive and determined by state blocks seemed increasingly undemocratic. The population's growing concentration on the coasts and in cities has, since 2000, twice brought a popular vote victory to the candidate who lost in the Electoral College. There has long been debate about the College, but no concerted effort for change has emerged. Critics of the present system reject the constitutional rule that if no candidate wins a majority in the College, the House of Representatives decides the election by an undemocratic one vote per state ballot. Only because of a Supreme Court decision was this avoided in 2000. Supporters of the status quo note that in the American federal system, the college properly gives weight to states and produces a clearer result. Those effects were evident in 2016, but hardly in a satisfying way, considering that Clinton won nearly 3 million votes more than the victorious Trump. The debate over campaign financing has also resurfaced with increased intensity. By the end of 2016, referenda passed in 19 states had asked Congress to overturn *Citizens United* and amend the US Constitution to allow control over the influence of money in elections.

Flaws in the *practice* of the system are also a matter of concern. In 2000, former President Jimmy Carter, who had inspected and critiqued elections in many parts of the world, reported a 5 percent error rate in the decisive race in Florida, a rate that fell below international election commission standards. In 2002, Congress passed the Help America Vote Act (HAVA) that required each state to submit a plan for uniform voting procedures and standards to improve the reliability of its reported election results. Since then only a minority of states have implemented the requested changes. In 2012 and 2016, inequalities in the voting systems in some states, such as Michigan and North Carolina, still appeared when voters in poorer city districts had to wait for hours to cast their ballots.

The judicial branch

The only court specifically mentioned in the Constitution is the US Supreme Court. Congress established lesser federal courts in a three-tier system. Among these, the district courts have original jurisdiction (the first court hearing) in most federal cases. Only about one-sixth of the decisions of these courts are appealed to the next tier, the US courts of appeals.

Most of the US Supreme Court's work consists of hearing cases from US courts of appeals or state supreme courts. The cases raise federal questions (controversies arising under the Constitution, federal law or treaties). In addition, it has original jurisdiction in cases that involve a state or officials of the federal government. Presently, in a year, the court gives around 80 of the cases it accepts a plenary review with attorneys' oral arguments. It then writes a formal written decision in 60–70 of these cases. The decisions of lower federal courts become final in cases it refuses to hear, which means those judges also exercise judicial review, although usually that means following earlier decisions set by the US Supreme Court.

The Constitution creates a separate judicial branch with a Supreme Court that has an unspecified number of justices with terms of office dependent only on their "good behavior." In recent history, the court has had nine justices, including a chief justice. Since early February 2016, following the death of Justice Antonin Scalia, the court had only eight members, which sometimes made reaching a majority decision difficult. Because the Republican-controlled Senate refused consider a candidate for Scalia's seat during the last year of Obama's term, it remained vacant for over a year. In practice, terms of office have been for life or until voluntary retirement. Because Congress has never impeached a justice, life terms have given justices an impressive degree of independence.

PLATE 6.7 In 2016, the US Supreme Court had only eight justices after Antonin Scalia's death. Supreme Court Justices made the sign of the cross during prayers at a private ceremony in the Great Hall of the Supreme Court where late Supreme Court Justice Antonin Scalia lay in repose on February 19, 2016 in Washington, DC. From back left were Counselor to the Chief Justice Jeffrey Minear and Supreme Court Justices Elena Kagan, Samuel Anthony Alito, Jr., Ruth Bader Ginsburg, Anthony M. Kennedy, Chief Justice John G. Roberts, Jr., Clarence Thomas, Stephen G. Breyer, and Sonia Sotomayor.
© *Pool/Getty*

Exercises

Explain and examine the following names and terms:

Articles of Confederation	"third" parties	campaign finance
popular sovereignty	Speaker of the House	presidential appointments
"reserved" powers	majority leader	presidential veto
filibuster	presidential caucuses	"necessary and proper" clause
the separation of powers	"unitary executive"	electoral college
winner-takes-all system	reapportionment	original jurisdiction
a two-party region	judicial review	primary and caucus elections
Citizens United	presidential debates	divided government

Write short essays on the following questions.

1. How are the principles of federalism and limited government protected by the Constitution of 1787 and its amendments?

2. Compare and contrast the chambers of Congress, giving particular attention to the effects of their different size, membership and terms of office.

3. Discuss the powers of the president and contrast his position with that of a prime minister in a parliamentary government.

4. Describe American parties and elections and discuss the causes and effects of their most distinctive elements.

5. Critically discuss the stages in the presidential election system, defending in a balanced fashion how democratic you think the process is.

Further reading

Barone, M. and Ujifusa, G. (annual) *The Almanac of American Politics*, Washington, DC: National Journal.

Ceaser, J.W. and Busch, A. (2001) *The Perfect Tie: The True Story of the 2000 Presidential Election*, Lanham, MD: Rowman & Littlefield.

Fisher, L. (1995) *Presidential War Power*, Lawrence, KS: University Press of Kansas.

Freeman, J. (2002) *A Room at a Time: How Women Entered Party Politics*, Lanham, MD: Rowman & Littlefield.

Hudson, William E. (2017) *American Democracy in Peril: Eight Challenges to America's Future*, Washington, DC: Congressional Quarterly Press.

Websites

www.justice.gov
www.congress.org/congressorg/home
www.whitehouse.gov
www.supremecourt.gov
www.nytimes.com/interactive/2016/us/elections/election-2016.html?_r=0
www.opensecrets.org/pacs/superpacs.php
thomas.loc.gov
fpc.state.gov
www.politics1.com
www.oyez.org/cases/2000-2009/2008/2008_08_205
c-span.org
www.latimes.com
www.washingtonpost.com/wp-dyn/politics

Chapter 7

Political institutions
State and local government

- The place of state government in American federalism
- The evolution of state government and federalism in the US
- The structure of state government
- Local government
- *Exercises*
- *Further reading*
- *Websites*

Both advocates and critics of the European Union have compared it to a "United States of Europe." Europeans grapple with dilemmas of constitutionality and government structure similar to those weighed by the drafters of the Constitution of 1787. The vastly different historical situation of European nations today makes comparison dubious. Nonetheless, political leaders in both times and places wrestle with the issues of how the EU and US should balance power between the federal and the national ("state" in the US) governments. How should we maintain sovereignty, control the movement of people in and out of borders, and deal with tensions that threaten the stability of federal unions?

The answers the founding fathers gave to these and related questions defined the particular brand of federalism originally established in the US. Such issues are not decided finally. They are part of an ongoing debate about the nature and purposes of government. The answers given at different times provide a map of the evolving character of American federalism and state and local government in the US.

The place of state government in American federalism

One whole article of the Constitution is devoted to the states. Article 4 recognizes the limited sovereignty of the states by denying federal authorities the power to alter the boundaries of existing states without their permission. A federal capital, Washington, DC, became a reality only because the states of Maryland and Virginia agreed to give up some of their territory to create the District of Columbia. Constitutional procedures for the admission of new states on an equal footing (having "full faith and credit") with the original 13 and a clause guaranteeing them a republican form of government recognize *states* as the main building blocks of the American system. The importance of the states is in the weave of other provisions of the Constitution as well, such as the rule that states elect the members of both chambers of Congress and the president. In addition, amendments to the US Constitution require the approval of three-quarters of the states. These protections and privileges alone go a long way toward explaining the movements for statehood in Puerto Rico and the District of Columbia.

At the time, the drafters of the Constitution thought that it provided for an appropriate division of powers between the national authorities, the states and the people. James Madison, a Founding Father, explained, "the great and aggregate interests" were "referred to the national, and the local and particular to state governments." Thus some powers are prohibited to the states by the Constitution. They can neither coin money, nor conduct their own foreign policy, keep their own military services, make war or set their own customs duties.

All these were recognized as "delegated powers," aggregate interests that had to be exclusively the national government's to prevent conflicts among the states and between them and the federal government. In addition, the Constitution gives national authorities the responsibility of protecting the states from foreign invasion and internal rebellion. To protect the rights of the people from both levels of government, it includes clauses such as the right to a jury trial, and the first ten amendments, the Bill of Rights, secured many more rights.

A considerable list of powers remained that were "reserved" and considered local and particular interests inappropriate for the federal government. To the states were reserved the establishment of local governments and protecting public safety and morals, which came to mean providing police, fire and sanitation departments, among other institutions. States also took responsibility for furnishing educational and health facilities as well as for levying taxes and borrowing to fund all these activities.

States wrote their own codes of civil and criminal law. The maintenance of internal transportation networks, issuing of licenses for activities within the state (marriage licenses and certification for the professions, for example), and incorporation of businesses were taken to be parts of their regulation of state commerce. Not least, state legislatures determined voting qualifications and conducted elections for all levels of government. Moreover, the Tenth Amendment, which reserves to the states or people those powers not granted the federal government, was an important constitutional guarantee of the states' sovereignty.

Some government activities are *concurrent powers*, those shared by the states and national authorities, because the Constitution does not designate one level of government as primarily responsible. These functions include lawmaking, establishing courts, taxing, borrowing and providing for the general welfare. A basic principle of federalism is that two levels of government exercise authority and powers over the same territory. That apparent overlapping has not usually been problematic, because the national government applies these powers to relations between the states, while each state exercises them only within its borders.

The growth of federal power

Over time, however, the existence of concurrent powers and disputes concerning them have worked to the advantage of the federal authorities. Despite the kind of federalism the Constitution defines, power has shifted dramatically from the states to the federal government for those and several other reasons. Historical circumstances and practical politics have determined the balance of power between the states and the nation more than theory has. The debate goes on. Republican leaders and President Trump want to return powers to the states.

The defeat of states' rights advocates in the Civil War and a series of historical crises, such as the world wars, the Depression, the problems of urbanization and industrialization, the Cold War, common standards in education nationally and, today, the war on terrorism, have proved to be beyond the capacities of the states and so have strengthened the national government. In these crises, the accepted limits of national power were too confining for the solution of the problems at hand. Therefore, the federal government has interpreted its constitutional powers quite broadly, and the states (and usually the federal courts) have accepted the transfer of power to the national authorities.

A number of changes that increased national power resulted from constitutional amendments. For example, until after the Civil War, the Bill of Rights only applied to relations between citizens and the *national* government. Two phrases in the Fourteenth Amendment (1868), however, require *states* to offer citizens "due process of law" and "equal protection of the laws." The US Supreme Court interpreted these phrases to mean that states too must meet the standards set in the Bill of Rights. The Court has therefore upheld federal civil-rights legislation as well as the demands of individuals for protection from state actions. Other amendments have limited states' power over tax revenues, voting rights and elections.

Most of the growth in federal power has come through lawmaking and political pressure. Congress used the so-called "elastic clause" of the Constitution to set precedents for federal legislation in almost every area of life. That clause gives Congress the right to make any laws that are "necessary and proper" to carry out its other powers. The president lobbied Congress to invoke this and other broad constitutional phrases, because the public expects the chief executive to lead the nation out of troubled times. Both these federal branches cited their concurrent power of promoting the "general welfare" to encroach on state authority.

Federal laws often include grants-in-aid (funding earmarked for specific purposes) as a means of persuading states to give the national government a say in their internal affairs. Grants-in-aid hold out the possibility of gaining resources to solve pressing problems, but they require states to accept federal regulations determining how they will use the money. Because grants are "matching funds," a state receives no more support from Washington for a project than it contributes itself. This was the case for the No Child Left Behind Act in 2001, the Help American Vote Act in 2002, and the Affordable Health Act of 2010.

The promise of funding operates as a powerful incentive. The threat to *deny* funds is a powerful pressure to get states to give up their own standards for federal standards. By choosing to fund some kinds of activities and not others, the federal government often sets states' policy agenda. The combined effects of concurrent powers, national crises, constitutional amendments, Supreme Court decisions, congressional legislation and grants-in-aid has been a strong trend toward centralized government over the past two centuries.

The evolution of state government and federalism in the US

Between 1803 and 1865, the federal government laid the foundation for the expansion of its powers when it allowed the Supreme Court to establish its power of judicial review and the tradition of broadly interpreting the federal government's constitutional powers. Even so, both the national and the state governments exercised their powers in a small way for most of the nineteenth century. Until the 1930s, the main way the federal government affected most citizens was through help in promoting the development of the frontier. Its armies fought Native Americans and forced them farther west. It gave new states federal land for schools and joined states and private entrepreneurs to build roads and canals. From the 1860s on, Congress wrote legislation providing free or cheap land on the frontier for settlers homesteading in the wilderness and companies engaged in building transcontinental railroads.

Dual federalism

When the federal government attempted to legislate in the areas of public health, safety and order in the 1800s, the Supreme Court ruled that these were *solely* the concern of the states. Likewise, it decided that the regulation of business was purely a matter for the states. Overall, the Court acted in accordance with the theory known as "dual federalism." The court asserted that state and federal governments have clearly separated spheres in which each is sovereign. It interpreted the Constitution narrowly, limiting government activity on any level to explicitly granted powers. Thus, it commonly approved neither federal nor state laws regulating industry and labor. Strongly influenced by laissez-faire economic theory, from the 1880s through to the 1920s, the court refused to accept laws to regulate child labor, minimum wages and working hours, safety or working conditions.

At the start of the Great Depression, states were the sole provider of most services reserved to them by the drafters of the Constitution. Washington, DC did not regulate citizens' behavior and provided them with very few services beyond the post office. The combination of the economic crisis, Franklin D.

Roosevelt's New Deal legislation and the court's advocacy of a new theory of federalism changed the governmental landscape by 1939.

Cooperative federalism

By the late 1930s, the national authorities' regulation of the economy and creation of a social-security safety net ushered in the era of "cooperative federalism." The court interpreted the Tenth Amendment and elastic clause broadly. It viewed the division of powers between state and federal governments as less distinct and less important than the ways they might work together. Many vital activities of the authorities seemed to be among the concurrent powers of government. Sweeping expansions of both state and federal powers resulted from the change in the court's philosophy, but Washington's share of all money spent on domestic needs nearly tripled while the states' expenditures on these problems remained the same.

Grants-in-aid programs began with the New Deal laws and grew rapidly in number for almost 40 years. In the 1950s, such grants resulted in heavy federal involvement in secondary and higher education to compete with the Soviet Union's technological progress. They also supplied states with funds for the interstate highway system built at the time. In the 1960s, grants helped pay for enforcement of civil- and voting-rights legislation and the ambitious goals of Lyndon B. Johnson's Great Society and War on Poverty programs. Johnson aimed at equal opportunity and a better quality of life for all Americans.

Grants-in-aid mushroomed in kind, number and expense. The federal government became active in local law enforcement, low-rent housing projects, urban mass transit, health services and job training. It *shared* responsibility for virtually all services that had been exclusively the functions of the states. For the first time, moreover, it encouraged applications for aid directly from local governments and private community groups, frequently bypassing the state authorities in its decisions on financing.

"New federalism"

By the early 1970s, a counter reaction set in. State and local governments complained of over-regulation, red tape and the tendency of the national government to legislate "unfunded mandates" (laws that place duties on the states without supplying sufficient funding). Conservatives in both parties called for a return to dual federalism. Many said President Nixon's proposals in 1972 amounted to just that, although he called them "New Federalism." His revenue sharing cut most strings attached to federal grants so that the lower levels of government could gain more power in setting priorities and standards. Combining many grant programs into large block grants for sectors such as health or education aimed to accomplish the same purposes. New Federalism had little success in stopping the shift of power to the national government. Members of Congress were unwilling to give up taking credit for exercising control over bringing federal money to their districts or states. Revenue sharing ended in 1986, and most grant programs returned to their former pattern even earlier.

President Reagan promised to revive New Federalism, but the main effect of his administration was to reverse the trend of increasing federal aid to state and local government. Such aid dropped by 25 percent in the early 1980s, and to date has grown only slightly, in spite of the federal budget surpluses of the 1990s (which turned into many trillions in red ink by 2009). Federal grant programs grew in the 1990s and next decade, but state and local governments had to bear more of the cost of new programs. In exchange, congressional leaders and all presidents since Nixon have agreed to set fewer binding federal regulations on grant programs. They often did not keep those promises. Unfunded mandates have multiplied.

American devolution and deregulation

During the past decade or so, the federal government has left the solution of growing numbers of national problems to the states through an American form of devolution. That decentralization inevitably means that inequalities among the states grow, because cuts in federal grants hurt poor states most. During the 1990s boom, the wealthier states made up for the loss of federal funds through increased state incomes, while the poorer states cut services and hovered near bankruptcy. In the 2000s, all states alike cut services in worsening economic conditions to satisfy their constitutions' balanced budget clauses. Since 2010, some states have built up the economy with undocumented labor, fracking, green energy, and social media.

Political commentators viewed the Republican triumphs of the 1990s as a sign that the national mood favored the devolution of power from the national government. In 1996, Democratic President Clinton approved the devolution of federal aid for needy families to the states. By 2000, Clinton agreed with Congress on the removal or relaxation of federal regulation of telecommunications, agriculture, civil rights, pollution prevention, environmental protection, and stock and investment markets. In the same years, Supreme Court decisions disallowed acts of Congress that would have enforced national regulations through clauses permitting citizens to sue the government. Instead, either the states regulated private institutions dealing with these areas of life or institutions regulated themselves.

The rebirth of big federal government

During his first term, George W. Bush, a self-proclaimed "compassionate conservative," met some conventional expectations of conservatives in the debate over federalism but not others. By 2005, he had pressed through two large tax-reduction packages and promised wholesale tax reform in his second term. Thus, he apparently aimed both to reduce the size of the national government by starving it of funds and to free the public (especially those with capital) of the burden of federal taxation. On the other hand, some called him America's first "big-government conservative" because he intruded into policy areas traditionally belonging to the states, especially education, and enlarged federal spending by some 29 percent (triple its rate of growth during the 1990s).

President Bush also implemented a very ambitious and costly domestic agenda for national school standards, faith-based federal social services, programs from the Department of Education promoting abstinence, and a Medicare prescription drug plan. He pursued these goals simultaneously with foreign policy and national security initiatives requiring a military build-up, the astronomic costs of wars in Afghanistan and Iraq and the costs and regulations of homeland security arrangements since the attacks of 9/11. Then in late 2008, the greatest economic crisis struck the nation since the stock market crash of 1929.

To prevent a decline into another Great Depression, the Obama administration bought the nation's largest insurer to save it from bankruptcy, rescued leading financial institutions to prevent the collapse of banking, lent billions to failing automakers in Detroit, spent billions on stimulus packages, and launched universal health care for the first time in the nation's history. The federal government thus bought or invested in private businesses and negotiated long-term involvement in the private sector. A combination of the domestic ambitions of the Bush and Obama presidencies, their foreign policy and the economic crisis produced a situation in which the imbalance between federal and state power was arguably as great as in the 1930s or even greater. In spite of the economy's strong recovery, during the 2012 and 2016 elections, public concern focused on the stagnant wages of the "99 percent," the growing wealth of the "1 percent," and the need to reduce federal spending. The feeling that the states should assume more responsibility for policy in these circumstances aided Republican candidates' successes.

The structure of state government

The original states developed the fundamental principles of all American governments. It is therefore not surprising that the structure of state and federal governments are similar. Each state has a written constitution, a separation of powers among three branches, and a system of checks and balances.

All state legislatures, except Nebraska's, have the same format as Congress with two houses, usually called the state senate and state assembly. State legislatures also work through committees and pass laws through a process very like that used in Congress. Like the president, the chief executive of a state, the governor, enjoys the powers of administration, appointment and veto. The structure of a state judiciary is also broadly parallel to the federal court system. In most states, there is a state supreme court and under it appeals courts and (parallel to the US district courts) county or municipal courts.

There are, however, important differences in the structure of state governments. State constitutions are typically several times longer than the US Constitution because they contain provisions that are more detailed. Instead of reserving undefined powers to a lower level of government or the people, the drafters of state constitutions attempt to be as explicit as possible. Such detailed documents less easily adapt themselves to broad interpretation and consequently need more frequent amending. New York State has amended its constitution over 200 times in the past century, for example, while the federal government has added only 27 amendments to the US Constitution since 1787. Most states have written entirely new constitutions or extensively rewritten their old ones not once but several times.

The branches of government also have distinctive elements at the state level. Most state legislators are part-time lawmakers. They often divide their time between the legislature and a law practice or business in their home districts. State legislators have fixed terms of office like members of Congress, but they do not choose to run for re-election as often. Instead, they go back to full-time work in their current private jobs or use their government experience to enter a new line of work. Thus, well over a third of all members in state legislatures are newcomers at any time and as many are relatively inexperienced.

State legislators' interest in careers in government is low for several reasons. Compared to what they can earn in the private sector, the annual salary is low. Traveling between the capital and the member's district as well as maintaining an office in both places requires considerable time and expense. Sitting in the state legislature does not bring much prestige, even though it disrupts family life and leads to the forced neglect of members' other part-time profession or business. Some experts on American government argue that the states should change to full-time, professional, well-paid legislatures. Tradition and the enormous cost of converting to full-time lawmakers make the present situation likely to persist. The traditional view is that having part-time legislators is an advantage. Their businesses or jobs in local districts keep them concerned about the well-being of the community they represent. As one political scientist explained, "Part-time legislators really have something at home, unlike congressmen who don't have anything to come home for except trying to get votes."

In practice, the debate may be moot, however, because the federal government's increasing withdrawal from grants-in-aid programs has forced state governments to assume more responsibility. The increased workload of state lawmakers has already produced a strong movement toward full-time legislatures in the more populous states.

There are also important differences between a governor's situation and that of the president. On the one hand, most governors have two powers the president lacks. They usually have more control over the state budget. Most also have the line-item veto, which allows them to accept some parts of a bill passed by the legislature while vetoing other parts. On the other hand, in many states, the governor's power is weaker than the president's is in four important ways. First, many are not free to make as many appointments as the president does. More state officials are elected than at the federal level of government. Second, many states have a tradition of electing several of a governor's department heads. For example, elections often select the State Treasurer, Attorney General and Commissioner of Education.

These other state executives are part of the governor's "team" at election time, but each must run for office separately, which makes them more independent of the governor. Many times, these department heads do not even belong to the governor's party. State parties often seem less important to voters than selecting a team of state executives that represent a range of different races, ethnic groups and economic interests.

Third, governors have less control over suggestions for new laws. Starting early in this century, many states developed two procedures for taking suggestions for new laws (or changes in old laws) directly to the voters, bypassing the governor and usually the legislature. The "initiative" allows citizens to call for a vote on a state law or constitutional amendment, either in the legislature or by the public at the next election. Those proposing the initiative must petition the state for this vote by collecting signatures from somewhere between 5 to 10 percent of the state's registered voters. A little under half of the states currently permit some form of voter initiative. The referendum, known as a "proposition," is a direct vote of the public on an issue. It may be the result of a successful initiative, a requirement for amending the state constitution, or an item put on the ballot by the state legislature. Half the states allow referenda on many issues, and all but one state require them for constitutional changes.

It is politically dangerous for governors to oppose procedures that make state government more democratic by giving ordinary voters a say in state law-making, even though some propositions may have harmful effects. Thus state executives have found it difficult to speak out against proposals similar to Proposition 13, passed in California in 1978, which so reduce taxes that state and local governments must cut back on basic services. In the 1970s, the use of referenda grew rapidly and, in the 1980s, numbered nearly 250 in every congressional election year, leading some critics to doubt whether the public could be informed enough to vote intelligently on so many issues. In the 1990s, the trend continued and politicians made little protest, even though the most common and successful proposal put limits on the number of terms they could run for office. By 2000, however, term limits had been found unconstitutional for federal offices, and the tide of propositions at election time had started to abate somewhat. Between 2010 and 2016, voters could decide many different issues. Among the most controversial were proposals to impose stricter gun laws, permit or ban same-sex marriage, and to legalize assisted suicide or the use of marijuana.

The fourth important way governors have lost power is through special district governments, authorities designed to deal with a specific problem that crosses governmental boundaries. Some special districts have become so powerful that the public calls them regional governments. Most special districts have appeared since the First World War. Federal authorities suggested some but, like all forms of local government, special districts are creations of the states.

State legislatures do not aim to weaken the governor's position by founding special districts; rather, legislatures simply recognize that growing problems, such as air pollution, land and water shortages, refuse disposal and regional traffic jams, cannot be efficiently handled within one legal jurisdiction. Several states and often many local governments share the responsibility for dealing with these problems. Coordination between so many separate authorities becomes difficult if not impossible. Many of America's big cities are merely the centers of much larger metropolitan areas that include many suburbs, several satellite cites and even "pockets" of rural territory. The states create most special districts in just these areas, where the need for coordinated public services is greatest.

Official representatives from the various local and state governments in the area where regional problems exist govern special districts. Special districts also have their own staffs and budgets. Grants from the federal government usually fund both, and they are therefore outside the governor's control. Presidents Ronald Reagan and George H. W. Bush said they intended to reduce the role and importance of special districts. Though the number of special districts reached nearly 30,000 by the beginning of the 1990s, however, neither they nor later presidents have taken any significant action in the matter, because the problems districts are set up to solve have only become more serious. Thus, it is instead likely that special districts will gradually take more planning initiative from state governors and state governments generally.

The judiciary branch of state government is different from the federal judiciary in two important ways. First, many state and local judges win seats on the bench through election, rather than appointment, to terms of office that vary from four to 15 years. In many states, voters choose their Supreme Court justices. Generally, the intention of electing judges is to make them more responsive to changes in public opinion and make the removal of unpopular or incompetent judges easier. Of course, as a result of their election, state and local judges are more frequently accused of being swayed by political pressures. Once on the bench, judges by law must be impartial. Therefore, it is common that both major parties endorse the same person for judge, if the candidate has a record as a fair and competent jurist.

PLATE 7.1 Florida Supreme Court Justices listen to a response from attorney David Boies, who represents Vice President Al Gore, in the Florida Supreme Court during an appeal of an election contest ruling in Tallahassee, Florida on December 7, 2000. The state high court heard arguments from attorneys representing both presidential candidates concerning the state's November 7 election.
© *REUTERS/Alamy*

Second, the state supreme court cannot be sure of handing down the final decision in the most important cases that come to it. Of course, that is because the federal constitution takes precedence over all other law, and the US Supreme Court has the power to review the constitutionality of both federal and state laws. In practice, it much more often overturns state law and the decisions of state courts. The importance of this fact became particularly evident in 2000, when the US Supreme Court reversed the decision of the supreme court of Florida to allow manual recounts of the presidential election in the state, and thus determined the outcome of the presidential election as a whole.

Local government

The 50 states contain some 83,000 units of local government. In addition to the special districts, there are counties, towns, cities, boroughs and school districts.

The states create these (and other) kinds of local governments and determine their powers. No local government in the US has sovereignty, that is, power in its own right. Units of local government receive no mention in the federal constitution. They exist because the states create them as instruments, tools to help the state carry out its responsibilities. State constitutions establish some local governments some local, while others came into being through acts of state legislatures. Special districts often result from agreements among two or more states.

Local governments vary tremendously across the country, because each state has developed its own system of local authority. Most states are divided into counties, although in Louisiana, the parallel unit of government is called a "parish" and in Alaska a "borough." Counties also vary greatly in population, size and function. Still, most counties share several general responsibilities. They are usually the main units of government in rural areas. Counties rarely have any lawmaking power but instead act as agents of the state. They serve as administrative units that carry out some statewide programs in local areas, such as keeping records and issuing different kinds of licenses.

All powers of local government are really powers of the state. The state just delegates the work of providing local facilities and services to smaller units of government. Thus the states often set general standards and guidelines but ask counties to carry out the functions that are delegated. Typically, these functions include providing local transportation systems, schools, fire and police protection, water and sanitation systems and medical programs and buildings. Counties also collect the local property taxes to pay for these services.

County government usually consists of a board of between three and 12 members, a county court and the chief officers of county departments. Board members (or commissioners) run for election and serve on a part-time basis in counties that are more populous. Their powers usually include deciding how to raise local taxes and spend funds for county programs, as well as the authority to establish zoning codes.

The boards have no influence over the county court, but their power of the purse and zoning gives them significant control over local department heads. The county superintendent of schools, for example, must have the board's support to raise more money for local schools or to have a site for a new school approved. Other administrative officers commonly found in a county include the county sheriff, the medical examiner or coroner, commissioner of health, the recorder or registrar of property deeds and the clerk (who issues licenses and keeps population records). Because they carry out state law on a daily basis, all these officers of county government usually determine what the law means in practice for most residents.

In built-up, heavily populated areas, the states have usually created substitutes for county government. In urban areas, cities, towns, villages, boroughs or special districts take over most tasks performed by counties. The meaning of

PLATE 7.2 A street sign outside Los Angeles' City Hall shows its sister cities.
© *Yevgenia Gorbulsky/Alamy*

these common terms varies widely, according to the legal definitions established by each state. For example, "city" usually indicates an urban unit of local government with a population of at least several tens of thousands. Most states define smaller built-up areas as villages, towns or boroughs. There are, however, many exceptions to this rule of thumb. In Kansas, a "city" may have a population of only 200 people. In Illinois, the suburban "village" of Oak Park has a population of over 50,000. The term "town" also has various meanings in different parts of the country. In New England, towns existed *before* national independence resulted in state governments. Counties appeared later and never became as important as towns in the New England states.

The US Census Bureau has exacerbated the confusion of terms by developing its own vocabulary for analyzing units of population. Documents from the federal government often discuss "metropolitan statistical areas" (MSAs) and "consolidated metropolitan statistical areas" (CMSAs). These terms are very useful for mapping the population concentrations that cross the boundaries of state and local governments. They often demonstrate the need for special districts, but they have no legal status as units of government.

Most states have granted urban units of government some form of home rule, a legal status amounting to limited local autonomy. This gives them a degree of legislative power to establish local law and usually a municipal charter that functions as a kind of local constitution. Ordinarily, the approval of local residents is necessary to alter this charter of incorporation. However, if there is disagreement with the state or federal government over the limits of the powers granted in the charter, state and federal courts usually interpret the municipal government's powers in a narrow way.

The structure of municipal governments varies widely. In most, a mayor is the chief executive, and the mayor decides policy together with a city council. The amount of power allowed to the office under the city charter may make the

PLATE 7.3 An aerial view of Dallas, Texas, a "sanctuary city" which, like scores of states, counties, and cities, refused to cooperate with federal authorities to detain or turn over undocumented immigrants in 2017. President Donald Trump threatened to withhold funding for the operation of federal programs in these areas. Resistance to federal law or executive actions has a long history in the US. Some Americans provided sanctuary to runaway slaves in the 1850s, and others shielded draft avoiders from federal marshals during the Vietnam War in the 1960s and 1970s. Today the mayors of cities like Dallas, Minneapolis, Denver, New York, and Los Angeles assert that the president's announced mass deportations of the undocumented are unacceptable when their cities' economies depend on these immigrants' contributions.
© *Universal Images Group North America LLC/DeAgostini/Alamy*

mayor merely a figurehead or the primary decision-maker in local affairs. Since the early 1900s, a large number of cities have experimented with or adopted "city-manager government," in which the city council is the chief political organ of government and a professional administrator, the city manager, carries out its decisions.

The council writes local laws, called "ordinances," in the policy areas granted it by the state charter. The mayor may or may not have the veto power over such council legislation. As in counties, a range of officials carries out local policy in specific sectors of local government activity. The mayor or city manager usually prepares an annual budget proposal based of these officials' requests for money and available sources of income and submits it to the council for approval.

Until recently, the financing of both county and municipal government came primarily from real-estate taxes, but by 1990, property taxes supplied only about a third of funding. Another third came from state governments, and a tenth came from the federal government. Both state and federal financing was generally tied to grants-in-aid programs that gave these other authorities an important role in local decision-making and often aimed to alleviate the effects of local poverty or socioeconomic inequality. The remainder of local funding generally came from a variety of fees and charges. To make ends meet and launch new programs, large cities have increasingly raised additional revenue through sales and income taxes.

The meanings and powers of local governments vary so much for three main reasons. First, local authorities developed in several different historical periods. Second, these governments reflect the effects of local conditions, such as climate, natural resources and the various population groups that have settled there over time, bringing with them a variety of traditions for handling local affairs. Third and most important, each state is free to give local governments whatever powers and functions it chooses.

To citizens, the state's definition of local government is very significant. Local governments have the job of providing most of the vital services citizens expect today. The territory of local governments often overlaps. Towns, villages and cities often have authority inside parts of a county. Therefore, citizens must learn which local government is responsible for each necessary service. Otherwise, it becomes impossible to apply for the local services state law gives people a right to expect. A citizen cannot even complain effectively about problems with the water supply, refuse removal, the school system and so on without knowing which unit of local government to contact.

There are arguments for and against the great number, variety and overlapping authority of governments in the US. Some observers maintain that the situation is quite democratic in that it gives many citizens opportunities to participate in government and to affect the making of policy. Critics, however, note that voter participation is highest in national elections and lowest in local elections. Some suggest that US voters participate less in *all* elections than people in

FIGURE 7.1 Local governments and cities in the Great Lakes region.

other developed countries because there are more opportunities for participation than the public has the capacity to focus on.

Another disadvantage often cited is that the complex sharing of powers and functions by all levels of government has become too difficult to disentangle for many people, so that they have great difficulties securing the very services government is instituted to offer. The same complexity makes individuals turn to organized lobbies that have the time and resources to influence policy. Thus, instead of bringing government to the people, some pundits complain, the current situation encourages the growth and power of special-interest groups.

Other commentators emphasize benefits of multiple governments. Some believe state and local governments with significant powers allow the nation to experiment with alternate solutions to problems on a small scale. That is why the states have long been termed "50 laboratories for democracy." In recent years, both states and cities have pioneered new plans for public education, health-service management, pollution control and welfare reform, to name just a few examples. Many, if not most, governmental reforms since late in the twentieth century have been tested out at lower levels of government before being adopted nationally.

Other observers insist that only such varied and overlapping governments can respond to the sharply contrasting conditions that exist in a country as diverse as the US. Smaller units of government can respond more quickly and appropriately to such differences. Local solutions generate inequality as well, in this view of the situation, and that is why the federal government must step in to protect minority rights and to even out economic disparities.

Exercises

Explain and examine the significance of the following terms:

delegated powers	dual federalism	propositions
concurrent powers	cooperative federalism	special districts
elastic clause	New Federalism	ordinances
grants-in-aid	state constitutions	local governments
full faith and credit	devolution	unfunded mandates

Write short essays on the following questions.

1. Discuss the reasons for and the effects of the changes in American federalism since 1787.

2. Compare and contrast the structure of the state and federal governments.

3. Give a critical evaluation of the use of the initiative and referendum in state government.

4. What are some arguments for and against the election of judges?

5. In your opinion, does the variety of overlapping governments in the US represent a factor for increased democracy?

6. Investigate the origins of sanctuary cities (counties, and states) and argue the merits of allowing this form of civil disobedience. See the extended caption of Plate 7.3 for information to begin the work.

Further reading

State of the States (annually published) Washington, DC: The PEW Center on the States.

Book of the States (biennially published) Lexington, KY: Council of State Governments.

Bowman, A. O. and Kearny, R. (1986) *The Resurgence of the States,* Englewood Cliffs, NJ: Prentice-Hall.

Census of Governments (published every fifth year) Washington, DC: US Government Printing Office.

Dye, T. R. (1990) *American Federalism: Competition among Governments,* Lexington, MA: Lexington Books.

Websites

www.whitehouse.gov/1600/state-and-local-government

www.stateline.org/live

www.access.wa.gov

www.state.ny.us

www.state.tx.us

www.state.ne.us

www.state.me.us

.

Chapter 8

Foreign policy

A nation apart? American attitudes to world affairs

On the one hand, the foreign policy of the US is like that of all nations: it has been a mixture of self-interest and an attempt to act according to commonly held ideals. On the other hand, a factor that makes America's (and all nations') foreign policy distinctive is the size and strength of each relative to other nations at critical times in its history. In the beginning of its history, the US, then a weak and inconsequential actor on the world stage, emphasized what the American political scientist Joseph S. Nye terms "soft power" (attracting support by example, ideals and diplomacy) to the near exclusion of other means of handling international affairs. Today, the nation is the world's only superpower, and in the view of some commentators, it too seldom uses soft power, especially since the terrorist attacks of September 11, 2001, and relies too frequently or hastily instead on "hard power" (achieving goals through economic sanctions and military threats or force). During the Obama administration's two terms, the president, intent on concluding the Iraq and Afghanistan wars, tried to redress the balance with a greater willingness to talk and negotiate through what he and his Secretaries of State Hillary Clinton and John Kerry called "smart" power.

President Donald J. Trump claimed that the post-Cold War period was over. The old alliances, such as the North Atlantic Treaty Organization (NATO), he asserted, were perhaps obsolete and needed renegotiation so that European allies paid their fair share. Touting a new nationalism that would make America regain its unique position in the world, Trump promised to put America first in his economic, military and political dealings with the world.

For the US, the nation's vulnerability in relation to the European nations involved in the settlement of North America was decisive in its foreign relations until 1900 or, some argue, 1945. Only from the twentieth century on did other nations significantly challenge the Euro-centered character of American foreign relations. This situation, of course, also generally resulted from Europe's leadership in world affairs during much of American history and the predominance of Europeans among immigrants to the US until the 1970s.

Its history of settlement and immigration is another major influence on the character of US foreign policy. European colonists and later immigrants have usually had mixed feelings toward their homelands. They emigrated to escape aspects of their home societies but simultaneously harbored deep attachments to the old country. Consequently, immigration has produced both isolationism and internationalism in American foreign policy, as Americans expressed their wish to avoid or cultivate contacts with former homelands. Immigrants brought with them their homelands' history of international relations and often lobbied the American government to fight the old country's enemies and help its friends. Longer-settled Americans have periodically doubted the loyalty of recent immigrants. The US has a history of perceiving threats to national security from foreign agitators that has caused repression at home and strained its relations abroad.

From the earliest colonists, migrants to America have wanted to prove the "promise of America" true to justify their decision to emigrate. Thus grew up the faith in American exceptionalism. This is the belief (rhetorical or sincere) that America's foreign affairs, unlike those of other nations, are not self-interested but are based on a mission to offer the world a better form of society characterized by the ideals of "the American creed": the US version of a republican form of government, economic and political freedom, egalitarian social relations and democracy. When he spoke of a "City on a Hill that the eyes of all people are upon" in 1630, the Puritan leader John Winthrop had in mind a religiously reformed community that would be a model for change in England. Later American leaders, from George Washington to Donald Trump in his inaugural address, have echoed Winthrop's words or sentiment to confirm Americans' sense that they had a unique mission to set an example for the rest of the world and conduct a foreign policy unlike that of any other nation. Whether real or imagined, American exceptionalism has had palpable effects on the history of US foreign relations.

In reality, the concerns that influence the foreign relations of other nations have also played major roles in the formulation of American policy. Of necessity, the US too has protected what it saw as its vital interests: economic success at home and abroad, access to important natural resources, support for its ideological views, respect for its military power and assistance in times of crisis. The US has often seemed as concerned with "realpolitik" as other nations, in spite of sincere and rhetorical devotion to ideals like those previously described.

A third factor, the nation's geographical position, has also made its foreign relations unique. If one looks at the globe as Americans do, with the US in the center, two "facts" that have colored much of US foreign-policy history seem clear. First, broad oceans separate the Americas from the other continents. Second, most of the world's population and farmland, and *all* the other great powers, are located in Europe and Asia.

For over 300 years, the relative physical isolation created by the oceans encouraged those migrating to North America to believe they were leaving behind whatever they disliked in their home societies. Here was the basis for US isolationism, the belief that Americans could withdraw from involvement with the rest of the world and focus on domestic (internal) affairs. As the country expanded across the continent, its size offered another excuse to believe the US "was world enough" for its inhabitants. Transportation, communication and arms revolutions, as well as the globalization of the economy, however, made isolationism founded on geographical separation an indefensible foreign-policy position. Still, traditional attitudes continue to influence the views of many Americans. President Trump's "America First" foreign policy, for example, is in some respects a return to a more isolationist stance.

Paradoxically, geographical separation has also contributed to a tradition of national insecurity. Looking outward and seeing the great powers of Europe and Asia on all sides, Americans have periodically felt surrounded. That anxiety resulted in a determination to create national security in the North American quarter of the globe. The US has driven European powers out and controlled the land, sea, air and, outer space approaches to North America to become a quarter-sphere hegemon – the only great power on the continent.

Americans have used the perceived need for continental security to justify territorial expansion through war, purchase or negotiation. The peoples who first bore the brunt of this preoccupation with security were Native Americans. Success in driving them westward fueled Americans' ambitions and sense that they had a destiny to "civilize" the continent.

Security was the rationale for a ring of military bases and, later, of radar stations beyond the country's borders. The US entered the world wars because of threats to its control of continental sea approaches. In the 1980s President Reagan's strategic defense initiative (SDI) sought to extend this 200-year-old principle of quarter-sphere security to space approaches. He envisioned using high-tech weaponry placed in space to shoot down missiles armed with nuclear warheads that might attack the US. At first, supporters of the SDI viewed the likely attacker as the USSR, but since the end of the Cold War, so-called "rogue nations" who ignore international law and support terrorism appear to be the most serious threat.

In the 1990s and early twenty-first century, American presidents supported research and development for a "national missile shield" against such threats. Shortly after taking office, George W. Bush announced a vastly bigger shield and offered America's allies protection behind it. Just months later, terrorists used American passenger jets as bombs to destroy the World Trade Center in Manhattan and one side of the Pentagon in Washington, DC. Not since 1812 had a foreign force attacked the North American mainland, killed thousands, and wrecked symbols of US military and economic power.

The sudden vulnerability felt by the public made a mockery of the long search for security at the root of US foreign policy. Commentators asked why the FBI and CIA had not discovered the terrorists' plans. Their representatives and foreign-policy specialists in Congress, it appeared, had been warning of such "low tech" terrorism for years. A car bomber attacked the Twin Towers some years earlier. In the immediate aftermath, some observers reckoned that the tragedy proved that a missile shield could not make the nation safe, but the president and public polls showed increased determination to regain the nation's former sense of safety by all possible means, including SDI, whatever the cost. As the "War on Terror" grew into wars in Afghanistan and Iraq and security measures that limited civil liberties and privacy at home, a small but growing number of voices asked what in America's foreign relations contributed to the catastrophic events of 9/11 and weighed alternative foreign-policy futures. Still, many interpreted Bush's 2004 election victory as a mandate to stay the course in the War on Terror he declared. Four years later, when the sitting president's foreign policy was very unpopular, several Democratic candidates vying to replace him said the nation needed to restore its global soft power, and the victory went to Obama, the only competitive aspirant for the office who had opposed the Iraq War before the election. He, however, fought the Afghanistan War vigorously as he withdrew troops from Iraq and often used diplomacy, multilateral cooperation, and drones in pursuing its goals.

PLATE 8.1 REUTERS On the morning of September 11, 2001, terrorists piloted United Airlines Flight 175, its crew and passengers into the World Trade Center in New York City. The World Trade Center south tower (L) burst into flames after being struck by Flight 175. The north tower burns following an earlier attack by a hijacked airliner on the same morning.
© *Sean Adair/Reuters/Corbis*

From neutrality to isolationism, 1776–1830

The first period in the history of American foreign affairs covers the years from 1776 until around 1830. During this time, US policy toward other countries (especially the European powers) resembled that of the newly established Third World nations in the twentieth century. Like those nations, the US tried to avoid alliances with great powers and instead strove to keep neutral in foreign affairs and act unilaterally. Fear of becoming a pawn of British or French expansionist schemes was the mainspring of American policy in this period.

Around 1800, the US was a political and economic midget. Americans felt hemmed in by British colonies to the north, French Louisiana in the west and, in the south, the rich and powerful Spanish Empire that included Florida and today's Southwest. During the colonial period, every war between the European powers had its American phase, and the new nation could not afford to have that pattern continue if it was to stabilize its political institutions and economy. Thus, the US stayed aloof from the Napoleonic Wars and refused to become involved in the French Revolution, even though the French had been an indispensable ally in the War of Independence with Britain.

After serving as the nation's first president, George Washington stated the existing policy in general terms in his Farewell Address (1796). Its main principle consisted of avoiding political and military alliances while cultivating trading relations with other countries. President Washington also advised the nation to remember its uniqueness and resulting need for unilateral action. When the US strayed from these principles by entering the Napoleonic Wars on the side of France in 1812, the results were disastrous. British forces burned Washington, DC, the US did not win a single important victory, and the cost was enormous. After that object lesson, the core ideas of the Address remained a pillar of American foreign policy until after the Second World War.

The Alien and Sedition Acts (1798) were more evidence of the American fear of becoming a pawn of European powers. These laws established presidential powers to deport or imprison foreign subversives. Fear of French sympathizers inspired the Acts, which allowed the President to punish a foreigner who seemed dangerous to national security. The Acts were an early sign of insecurity about the loyalties of newcomers in a nation of immigrants.

The foreign-policy statement from the early period that contributed most to the development of later policy was the Monroe Doctrine. Between 1800 and the 1820s, many Spanish colonies in Central and South America rebelled and declared their independence. The US wanted to recognize these new nations but feared conflict with Spain and the possibility that Britain or France would intervene and return them to Spanish control. America was too weak to prevent European interference in Latin America, but it formally expressed its opposition to outside meddling in the Americas through the (1823) Monroe Doctrine.

The Doctrine centers on three basic principles. The first (called non-colo-nization) is that the US opposed any new colonies in the Americas. The second (non-intervention) demanded that the European powers remain uninvolved in the affairs of New World nations. In return for Europe's compliance with these rules, the US would observe a third principle (non-interference) that amounted to accepting the presence of the remaining European colonies in the Ameri-cas and keeping aloof from European affairs. The US could not enforce any of these principles until around 1900, when it had constructed a powerful navy. Until then, the British navy prevented other European nations from violating the Doctrine and opened Latin America for British economic influence.

The Monroe Doctrine transformed American neutrality into isolationism and combined it with the country's sense of having a special mission in the world. It declared the Americas the US's exclusive sphere of interest. Euro-pean kingdoms and old-world politics were to have no place in the hemisphere, so that only the US's brand of government would influence Latin America. In short, the Doctrine expressed the mixture of idealism and ideological domina-tion that was to become typical of US relations with Latin America.

From expansionism to imperialism, 1783–1914

The second period of American foreign policy overlaps with the first but extends into the early years of the twentieth century. During this time, the US was pre-occupied with developments that Americans often viewed as internal affairs: the settlement of a frontier that constantly moved further west, the struggle over whether slavery should spread into new states or be abolished, and the construction of transportation systems to bind the continent together and ease the exploitation of natural resources. All these processes consisted of, or were related to, territorial expansion, and, therefore, central to the conduct of foreign affairs.

Early in the nineteenth century, the US roughly tripled its territory through treaty and purchase. Agreements with Britain added the land between the Appa-lachians and the Mississippi river, the northern section of Maine and parts of Minnesota and the Dakotas. America bought Florida from Spain. France offered the US the land from the Mississippi to the Rocky Mountains in the Louisiana Purchase. Most Americans viewed these as legal and unaggressive ways to con-solidate US territory and minimize the dangers of European interference. They assumed that the European powers could legally transfer hegemony over the Native Americans to the US. In reality, much of American foreign policy until 1900 consisted of war and treaty negotiations with these native peoples.

Such enormous increases in the country's size inspired the growth of an intense national pride. The feats of frontier settlers evolved into myth and a set of idealized character traits. The farther west people and institutions were, the more truly American they appeared in the popular mind. Some advocates of expansion emphasized that only a nation spanning the continent could effectively isolate itself from external threats. Others told themselves that they were extending the benefits of democracy to less advanced peoples. Most Americans and European immigrants felt certain that they developed the land and made it bear fruit more than the Native Americans did and simultaneously gave little or no attention to the destruction of the natural environment that this development brought. Forthrightly racist expansionists said the "red and brown" peoples were inferior. Whites had to conquer them.

By the 1840s, the idea of America's expansion to the Pacific was popular as the nation's Manifest Destiny (its apparently inevitable, divinely determined fate). Since it was the "natural order," that expansion was also right, argued the expansionists. "Oregon fever" sent thousands trekking across the plains and mountains. Facing threats of armed conflict, Britain gave up its claims to the present Pacific Northwest and parts of the mountain states in border negotiations. Americans were more militantly aggressive toward Mexico. American settlers seized power in Texas and asked the US to annex it.

When the Texans disputed the border with Mexico in 1846, the US offered to buy the territory in question but took the first excuse to take it by war after Mexico refused to sell. Expansion in the Southwest aroused strong opposition, especially in New England. Many argued against acquiring Texas (a slave-owning republic) and against endangering US troops to make more territory available for slavery. Texans waited ten years for annexation. The Mexican War was the source of violent congressional debate. In 1848, the treaty at its end added the Southwest, California and most of the southern mountain states to the US.

In the decades after the Civil War, expansionists gained support from several sources. Businessmen and farmers demanded the opening of new markets abroad to prevent overproduction causing economic depressions at home. Military strategists pointed out that a strong navy and overseas bases were necessary to keep these markets open and protect US shipping. Religious leaders fused the ideas of Manifest Destiny and the "white man's burden" to support overseas missions and the "civilizing" of foreign peoples. Nationalists, now using the language of Social Darwinism, claimed Americans were surely the fittest to survive in the international competition for territory and influence. When the federal government declared the western frontier closed in 1890, some people feared that Americans would lose their strength and endurance if they did not find frontiers abroad. In a trendsetting essay, the University of Wisconsin historian Fredrick Jackson Turner claimed that the frontier was essentially "American" and had been responsible for Americanizing immigrants.

Buoyed up on this wave of public opinion, US foreign policy became territorially and economically imperialist around the turn of the century. That is to say, America used hard power to impose its control on overseas peoples, both formally (through colonization, annexation, and military occupation) and informally (through military threats, economic domination, and political sub-version). In 1898, the US declared war on Spain as an imperialist power that was stifling Cuban freedom. Having won that "splendid little war" (as the American secretary of state called it), the US acquired economic control over Cuba and the right to intervene in its affairs. It also acquired (as colonies) Puerto Rico, Guam Island and the Philippine Islands, where Filipino nationalists fought a war for independence from the US.

American trade expanded rapidly, especially in Asia and Latin America. The US annexed Hawaii, Samoa and Wake Island, which served as suitable bases for further economic expansion eastward. To protect its growing trade in China, the US contributed troops to an alliance of European powers that put down a Chinese rebellion. It also announced the "Open Door Policy," which demanded equal access to Chinese markets to counter the Europeans' claim to exclusive trade rights in China. In Latin America, President Theodore Roosevelt insti-gated and ensured the success of a Panamanian revolt against Colombia in 1903 in order to secure the right to build and control the Panama Canal. A year later, he announced the revision of the Monroe Doctrine known as the Roosevelt Corollary. According to the corollary, the US was justified in intervening in the internal affairs of Latin American nations if their politics or economies became unstable. He warned the European powers that America would not passively permit their intervention in the western hemisphere. Between 1900 and 1917, the US intervened in six different Latin American countries through presiden-tial action.

Critics known as the "anti-imperialists" actively opposed overseas expan-sion. Because of their efforts, for example, Cuba remained independent, and the US promised Philippines independence as early as 1916 (although the promise remained unkempt until 1934). Some anti-imperialists claimed that unilateral executive action sending US military forces abroad for intervention or coloni-zation upset the balance of power in foreign policy between the president and Congress by increasing his importance as commander-in-chief. Other opponents of imperialism stressed that America could gain access to foreign markets with-out oppressing other peoples. Prominent leaders of the Progressive Movement protested that America ought to clean up its political corruption and inequali-ties at home instead of exhausting its energies abroad. Both traditionalists and the Progressives also asked Americans to remember their historic commitment to self-determination in the Declaration of Independence.

Isolationism and internationalism, 1914–1945

For nearly three years, the US maintained the fiction that the First World War was a European conflict that did not concern America. President Woodrow Wil-son held that neutral pose because it reflected the traditional isolationist views of the US electorate. Neutrality was impossible to preserve for three reasons. Wilson, along with many other US politicians, felt strong sympathies for the Allies. The majority of Americans shared his belief in loyalty to Anglo-American traditions, despite vocal German American and Irish American minorities opposed to an alliance with Britain. Finally, the US economy depended on trade with the warring nations, who each tried to prevent goods from reaching its enemy.

Most Americans took sides but were reluctant to commit their fortunes and lives to intervention. Both Wilson and the public needed to believe they were entering the war for high moral reasons rather than for the country's economic interests. Some two months before the US declared war, Wilson provided that rationale through a new vision of collective security in his famous Fourteen Points, which appealed to the tradition of the American mission to create a new world order.

The essential elements of the Fourteen Points fit into three major categories. The first was all nations' right to self-determination. Every "people" was to draw its own national boundaries after the war so that each could freely determine whether it wished to be an independent country. The principle of self-determination amounted to a plan for popular referenda on ethnic nationhood in Europe with no formula for determining how nations and peoples would implement the project. The second category was a general set of principles for governing international conduct after the war. These provided the means of preventing a return to the European balance-of-power strategies that Wilson believed had caused the war. Among the main principles included were free trade, freedom of the seas, global disarmament and the outlawing of secret alliances. Making efforts for these ideals, but especially for the remaining points, would implement the third category, Wilson's proposal for *collective security*, a League of Nations that would put self-determination and the other principles into effect and defend them. The key provision here was the commitment of each League member to defend the principles and each other by diplomatic and military means. Except for the League, most of the points were cornerstones of the US's traditional rhetoric if not of its practical policy.

The Fourteen Points constituted Wilson's public justification for participating in the war, and were but one set of conditions meant to limit US involvement. American troops remained separate from the Allied armies and fought under American commanders. Wilson called the US an "associate" rather than an ally to emphasize that it was in an emergency coalition, not a lasting alliance (and therefore remained true to the injunction against such alliances in Washington's Farewell Address).

When it finally came, American participation in the war was decisive but very limited. Significant numbers of American troops fought in Europe only during the last eight months of the war. About 110,000 US soldiers died in that time, compared to the 900,000 British, 1.4 million French and almost 2 million German troops that died in four years.

The conditions on American aid to the Allied war effort, combined with the Allies' very different experience with a long and destructive conflict, made the US position seem arrogant. Although America claimed to be materially disinterested, its call for freedom of the seas and free trade would benefit the US most since its industrial plant was booming and its fleet the least damaged. The Allies wanted revenge and to make Germany pay for war damages. They rejected all Fourteen Points but the League.

The US Senate failed to ratify the treaty Wilson brought home from the Paris peace conference. Many senators rejected the idea of the League because they were unwilling to bind the US to membership in a permanent international alliance that could limit US sovereignty. The foreign policymakers who took over after Wilson were not isolationists. Rather, they wanted to design safeguards for peace that would not limit America's traditional freedom to act unilaterally in world affairs. In 1921, the US negotiated separate treaties with the defeated central powers. The League functioned without US participation but never became an effective international force.

During the rest of the 1920s, US foreign policy centered on eliminating obstacles to trade. International peace and stability were essential so that US trade would remain free of interference. Many Americans also believed free trade fostered peace by making nations more open and familiar with each other. However, the US and European nations failed to agree on a plan to revive European economies by cancelling or easing their war debts to America, and in 1930 Congress passed the protectionist Smoot–Hawley Tariff, which effectively closed the US market to most European goods.

In the same years, the country advocated peace through disarmament and called for arms reductions and the destruction of some 2 million tons of navy ships. It reaffirmed and extended the Open Door Policy. Finally, it initiated the Kellogg–Briand Pact in 1928 under which 62 nations signed a pledge not to use war as an instrument of national policy. Critics called this pact and others the US entered at the time, a "paper peace" since it depended on voluntary compliance.

In the 1930s, however, isolationism replaced this limited internationalism. As the German war machine marched into land after land and the rest of Europe rearmed, American voters made it clear that they would not support another old-world war. Over four-fifths of the people surveyed in a Gallup poll in March of 1941 were opposed to US intervention. At about that time, President Franklin D. Roosevelt had won congressional approval for the Lend-Lease Act, a disguised giveaway plan he invented because domestic opposition to open aid to the Allies was massive. Under Lend-Lease, the President could sell, but also let the Allies borrow or lease, war material, on the promise that they would return it after the war.

The Japanese surprise attack on Pearl Harbor on December 7, 1941, accomplished overnight what Roosevelt could not in years of effort: it united

PLATE 8.2 Fred Martin Torrey's statue "Abraham Lincoln Walks at Midnight" (1933) dedicated by the state governor on the grounds of the capital of West Virginia, in Charlestown. Vachel Lindsay's poem with that title inspired the creation of the statue during World War I. The figure portrays Lincoln eternally wandering the streets of his hometown, Springfield, Illinois, because even in death, the tragedy of America at war does not allow him to rest in peace. Lincoln, the Civil War president, embodies the burden of the modern American chief executive, whose foreign policy responsibilities include sending American service people into harm's way on missions of maintaining national security.

© *Jordan Oakland*

the American people in a fervent commitment to war. In a few days, Congress had declared war on all the Axis powers and announced its support of the Allies. Almost as quickly, Roosevelt constructed a vision of a new world order for the post-war period. Determined to succeed where Wilson had failed, Roosevelt called the Allies the "United Nations" almost from the start. He also ensured that American troops fought together with the British and French. Joint command and cooperation, he decided, would prevent complaints about American arrogance.

Roosevelt expressed his vision for world order after the war in the so-called Four Freedoms and proposal for the United Nations (UN). Cleansed of advantages to US business, the Four Freedoms were essentially the rights contained in the American Bill of Rights (freedom of religion, speech and expression) or broad extensions of those, such as freedom from want and fear, that amount to a version of the American dream. The UN was to make the Four Freedoms realities. A number of the UN's features aimed to make it a more effective organization than the League. Unlike its predecessor, the UN can take preventive action, ask members to contribute troops to an international "peacekeeping" force and act against aggressors without approval from all its members. The UN's weaknesses, for example, in dealing with wars within nations, human rights, and genocide, would become clear over time.

At the Yalta Conference in February 1945, Roosevelt won Stalin's and Churchill's support for the UN. On other issues, the results of the conference were less clear. Roosevelt could not convince the other leaders to give up the concept of spheres of influence in Europe. He thought, however, that they had agreed to the establishment of democratic governments under no other nation's direct control in Eastern Europe. All three leaders agreed that Germany should not become a military power again quickly, but they could not resolve their differences on how to prevent that. The conference made no plans for post-war Germany.

The Cold War era, 1946–1992

As Soviet forces set up pro-Communist governments in Eastern Europe in the weeks after the Yalta Conference, Roosevelt discovered how differently he and Stalin interpreted its results. Before he could establish a policy to deal with the new situation, Roosevelt died of a sudden heart attack. In August 1945, President Truman ordered the dropping of atomic bombs on Hiroshima and Nagasaki. He justified the mass slaughter of civilians by saying the attack would save many more lives (both American and Japanese) by bringing the war's close without an invasion of the Japanese home islands. The events dividing the globe into the Cold War blocks were under way. A year later, Churchill said an "iron curtain" divided Soviet-controlled Eastern Europe and Western Europe with its American ally.

PLATE 8.3 US President Franklin D. Roosevelt, British Prime Minister Winston Churchill, and Soviet leader Josef Stalin at the Yalta Conference, February 1945, where the leaders agreed on post-war "spheres of interest."
© *Hulton Archive/Keystone/Getty*

As the former allies struggled to influence the governments emerging on the borders of the Soviet Union after the war, American policymakers became convinced that the Soviets were intent on establishing communist regimes around the world. In 1947, President Truman announced the Truman Doctrine. In a speech to Congress, he asked for funds to fight communist aggression in Turkey and Greece. According to the Doctrine, the US had to follow a policy of *containment* to prevent communist expansion anywhere in the world. The Soviets spread their ideology, inherently a threat to the US and to democratic institutions, through internal subversion as well as outside pressure. In a "domino effect," one nation after another would fall to Soviet domination unless the US led the "free world" by actively intervening to prevent it. Thus, the stage was set for American involvement in internal conflicts and wars, not only in Latin America (where the Roosevelt Corollary justified intervention) but also around the world. Containment became the cornerstone of American foreign policy throughout the Cold War. Pursuing containment protected and expanded US interests abroad and its implementation contributed to the formulation of other foreign-policy initiatives.

In the late 1940s, by working to meet the communist threat, the US revolutionized its foreign policy. It kept its military forces near wartime levels, extended mandatory military service into peacetime, and continued its military build-up. When the Soviets rejected international inspection plans to enforce a ban on nuclear weapons, the US expanded atomic research and gave nuclear weapons a central place in its arsenal. The National Security Act of 1947 reorganized the federal government to meet Cold War threats by centralizing control over all branches of the military in a new Department of Defense (the "Pentagon") and creating the National Security Council (NSC) and the Central Intelligence Agency (CIA).

In a sense, the Act put the country in a state of permanent military readiness by transferring enlarged powers over defense to the president and making it easier for him to take aggressive action internationally without a declaration

PLATE 8.4 Atomic mushroom cloud from a US military detonation in the country's isolated southwestern desert testing grounds after World War II, Nevada, 1951.
© *Photo Researchers, Inc/Alamy*

of war. By 1950, a NSC report known as NSC-68 defined the US stance: more than ever, America had an important mission in the world; on the US lay the responsibility to lead the free world. To that end, the nation had to quadruple its military budget so that it could take the initiative in containing communism.

Meanwhile, Secretary of State George Marshall became convinced that the US ought to fund the economic revival of Europe. The motives for the so-called Marshall Plan were several. In general, the hope was to learn from the mistakes of US policy after the First World War. Humanitarian concerns and ethnic ties played important roles in building congressional and public support of the plan. Economic concerns also inspired approval. Assisting Europe could absorb surpluses that threatened to cause an economic recession in the US, and a revitalized Europe would provide markets for American goods. Finally, Marshall believed that prosperous economies would strengthen European resistance to communism and so contribute to containment. The US spent about $15 billion on the program from 1948 to 1951.

The vision of one world united through the Four Freedoms faded. Instead, the world seemed to consist of two warring camps threatening each other with nuclear destruction. Therefore, the United States reversed its historic refusal to form permanent military alliances. The US joined in the first of these, the Organization of American States (OAS), in 1948 and NATO in 1950, and similar mutual defense pacts eventually covered the globe. Commitment to internationalism replaced isolationism.

When Soviet troops entered Hungary in 1956 and crushed the revolt against Soviet domination, Hungarian Americans protested strongly. President Eisenhower announced that the United States would not intervene in their homeland because the Truman Doctrine did not extend to nations in the Warsaw Pact (the Eastern European–Soviet alliance organized as a counterforce to NATO). In 1968 when the Soviet Union and Warsaw Pact nations put down a popular revolt in Czechoslovakia, the US followed the same policy of noninvolvement.

In the early 1950s, the fear of communism set the stage for Senator Joseph McCarthy's hunt for Americans involved in "un-American activities" as spies or tools of the Soviets. In a general sense, "McCarthyism" was nothing new, although his blatant accusations against government officials as well as Hollywood stars through guilt by association with suspected members of leftist organizations were unprecedented. Fear of communist influence and Bolshevik immigrants appeared in the "Red Scare" of the 1920s and was part of the old distrust of the foreign that stretched, in some form, all the way back to the Alien and Sedition Acts. McCarthy and his supporters did not create anti-communist hysteria. They merely exploited the public anxieties built up by the Cold War and the threat of nuclear destruction.

These anxieties led to historic changes in the position of the military in American society. Before the arms race during the Cold War, the US had always greatly reduced the size of its arsenal and standing forces after a major war. From the early 1950s, that has not happened. Instead, the economic, governmental, and military organizations involved with weapons (raw material producers, manufacturers of weapon systems, executive agencies, congressional committees, and branches of the military) have expanded and developed into a mutually supportive network. As early as January 1961, Dwight Eisenhower warned of the dangers this could pose for a democracy in his farewell address saying, "In the councils of government, we must guard against the acquisition of unwarranted influence, whether sought or unsought, by the military–industrial complex." Today, economic prosperity in widely scattered parts of the country depends on the complex. Lobbyists, bureaucrats, generals and members of congress have stakes in its further development. With the Cold War replaced by the War on Terror in the early 2000s, critics have continued to analyze what some call the militarization of America and decry its consequences.

The CIA's covert involvement in the Bay of Pigs affair and the Cuban Missile Crisis raised Cold War tensions to new heights. The superpowers' nuclear arsenals made mutual assured destruction (MAD), the basis for deterrence the best chance of avoiding war. Still, after the missile crisis, relations between the two superpowers began to improve. Developments furthering this trend included the Nuclear Test Ban Treaty of 1963 and the decision that neither superpower would intervene in the Israeli–Arab war. In the 1970s, President Nixon initiated the policy known as détente (peaceful coexistence) and the gradual reduction of nuclear arsenals that later presidents continued. Despite unstable periods in the superpowers' relationship in the decades to come, a similar understanding appeared during the Gulf War almost 30 years later in 1991, when both countries condemned the Iraqi occupation of Kuwait in the United Nations and joined in contributing forces to drive President Saddam Hussein's troops back into Iraq.

In Asia, the United States committed itself to containing communism in Korea, Vietnam, Cambodia and Laos. The Vietnam War, the first the US lost since the war of 1812, produced massive anti-war protests at home and widespread anti-American demonstrations abroad. The conduct of the war demoralized the young at home as well as US combat troops. The cost of the war drained funds from President Johnson's programs to deal with domestic poverty and inequality. The frustrations of trying to win a "limited war" led President Nixon to authorize the secret bombing of Laos and Cambodia without congressional approval.

The Vietnam War became a traumatic experience to the American people and inhibited later involvement in other countries. During the Gulf and Afghanistan Wars, the US chose to act in a multinational coalition after securing approval from the UN, even though Americans constituted the largest group of participants. Low-intensity warfare and short engagements executed with precision through technological weaponry, the US hoped, could replace the prolonged military engagement and high casualty levels of the Korean and Vietnam Wars.

An important turning point in US foreign relations came when President Nixon opened talks with the leaders of mainland China, taking advantage of a split between China and the Soviet Union, and thus reduced the apparent threat of communism. In the following years, American policy was less concerned with military control and, especially during the Carter presidency, emphasized support for human rights in other countries. This angered the Soviets, as stories of dissidents confined in psychiatric "hospitals" appeared in the work of Aleksandr Solzhenitsyn. In the later 1970s, the relationship between the two powers grew tenser.

The US–Soviet relationship went through several pendulum swings. American policy toward Latin America, for example, varied with the temperature of the Cold War. Still, the commitment to containment has generally led to US support to right-wing regimes in America's "backyard," where apparent stability has often seemed more vital than human rights. In that frame of mind, covert American operations helped unseat the democratically elected Salvador Allende in Chile during the Nixon administration, and in the 1980s, the Reagan administration refused to stop giving the right-wing Contra rebels aid in their guerrilla war against the Sandinista government of Nicaragua when Congress cut off funding for the Contras. The Iran–Contras scandal revealed that Oliver North and others among Reagan's officials had secretly sold weapons to Iran and used the profits to aid the Contras, in direct contradiction of congressional policy and the administration's public statements. Some commentators said the Cold War produced an "imperial presidency" that undermined both the balance of power between the branches of government and the constitution.

After proclaiming strong opposition to the communists' "evil empire" and carrying out a massive military build-up, President Reagan pursued peaceful coexistence. On the Asian scene, he extended the détente of previous presidents when he signed a series of agreements with the People's Republic of China in 1984. He accepted friendly overtures from the general secretary of the Communist Party in the USSR, Mikhail Gorbachev, which led to disarmament treaties in his second term and agreements on increasing trade and cultural relations under President George Bush, Sr.

In November 1989, cheering crowds from both sides tore down the Berlin Wall, the symbol of a divided Europe, and in the following summer, the two Germanys reunited through a treaty signed by the four allies from the Second World War. In 1992, due to internal ethnic conflicts and economic strains, the Soviet Union split into a loose federation of republics, and in the following years, some of its subordinate parts and nations in the Warsaw Pact declared their independence.

The sole superpower in the post-Cold War era and beyond

In the first two decades after 1989, some contours of the post-Cold War world and America's place in it became apparent. The elimination of the Iron Curtain and lowered nuclear tension caused jubilation and optimistic attempts to fashion a better future. European leaders moved quickly to include ten of the recently independent Eastern European countries in the European Union (EU) by 2004 and two more by 2007. These countries thus grew less dependent on America for trade and military needs.

Many former East Bloc nations exhibited strong support for US foreign-policy views, partly perhaps in gratitude for America's long record of opposing their Soviet oppressors. Several of these nations indicated a wish to become members of NATO and some (most notably Poland and the Baltic nations) did, which reaffirmed their ties to the US even as that organization struggled to redefine its purpose and took on military duties outside the territory covered by the alliance. On the one hand, NATO took responsibility for winning the campaign against Osama bin Laden's terrorists and the Taliban in Afghanistan, and on the other, Georgia's wish to join the organization led to loud sabre rattling from Russia.

In the first decade of the twenty-first century, US relations with Europe were sometimes tense. When the continent's nations divided sharply over the approach to war with Iraq, most former East Bloc countries were prominent in their agreement with the US position and later sent considerable numbers of troops and equipment as part of George W. Bush's "coalition of the willing." US Secretary of Defense Donald Rumsfeld famously contrasted this "new" Europe with the "old" one that felt that UN inspectors should have more time to search for weapons of mass destruction (WMD) in Iraq and questioned the need to depose Saddam Hussein. Between 2002–3 and 2008, friction between the US and many of its traditional allies grew. Explanations for this focused on several policies of the Bush presidency: its tendency to act unilaterally or covertly, insistence on preventive war in Iraq, and use of imprisonment and brutal interrogation of "enemy combatants" at Guantanamo in violation of the Geneva Conventions.

Military conflicts and political unrest continued within the Russian federation and in newly independent neighboring nations. The US wanted to aid these nations with their reconstruction, just as the Marshall Plan had helped war-torn Western Europe but debated on how to do so without interfering too much in their internal affairs or provoking Russia. The initial attempt to do this came through the loose cooperation of the Partnership for Peace, but the US largely left the handling of these problems to Russia. A more constructive result of superpower rivalry appeared in the US–Russian agreement during the Gulf War of 1991 that drove Saddam Hussein's invaders out of Kuwait.

By the end of the first Iraq War, the world generally viewed the US as the sole superpower, and during much of the 1990s, the USSR's economy, military and empire continued to implode. From then on, however, through wrenching economic adjustments, conflicts, and agreements internally and with neighboring states, a new Russian federation emerged that asserted itself on the world stage and flexed economic power through its gas and petroleum resources. Although the second President Bush and Prime Minister (former president) Vladimir Putin functioned amiably together through personal diplomacy at the start of the 2000s, the US–Russian relationship remains uneasy. Russia dislikes the eastern expansion of NATO and is convinced that the plans to place advanced radar-satellite installations for a missile shield in the Czech Republic and Poland, announced as a protection for the US, Russia, and European allies alike against "rogue" states in the Middle East or central Asia, is actually further evidence of American expansionism.

US–Russian relations worsened during Obama's two terms for these and other reasons. In 2014, the US and its European allies enforced economic sanctions against Russia after it seized and annexed the Crimean peninsula and a portion of far eastern Ukraine. During the next two years, its military cooperation with President Bashar al-Assad's regime in the Syrian civil war brought the danger of direct conflict between the Russian and American air forces. In the 2016 elections, US intelligence agencies asserted that the highest levels of Russia's government approved cyber-attacks to assist Donald Trump's campaign efforts. For his part, Trump studiously avoided offending Prime Minister Putin and after his election hoped for more friendly relations between the two nations, but did not remove the Crimea sanctions.

The economic dimension of American foreign affairs witnessed a pendulum swing in favor of free trade through multinational treaties and a backlash against these agreements between 1995 and 2017. In his first term, centrist Democrat President Bill Clinton made strengthening the domestic economy by increasing free trade his primary foreign-policy goal. By 1995, the Senate had ratified both the North American Free Trade Agreement (NAFTA), between Canada, Mexico and the US, and the Uruguay General Agreement on Tariffs and Trade (GATT). During the second Bush presidency, trade negotiations proved more difficult as the interests of unions at home, developing nations abroad and the concerns of the world's environmentalists about pollution and global warming complicated the process. Nevertheless, the Bush administration successfully revised NAFTA. President Obama's distinctive aim was to make the US less Euro-centered and instead a "Pacific rim" power. Economic goals and countering Chinese economic expansion inspired American negotiations for the Trans-Pacific Partnership (TPP), which involved nearly all the major Pacific Coast nations except China.

George H. W. Bush and Clinton also attempted to define America's role in dealing with a major after-effect of the Cold War: the increasing disorder in Asia, Africa and Central America that involved former "client states" of the superpowers. As the sole remaining superpower, the US faced mounting pressure at home and abroad to act in these crises, but American policymakers in the 1990s were at first reluctant to be on call as the world's police. In the hope that neighboring countries would step in (the Europeans in the former Yugoslavia and other African nations in that continent's many "trouble spots"), the US delayed too long during Clinton's presidency, according to some critics. Then America initiated a series of multilateral strategic interventions in humanitarian crises (in Bosnia, Somalia and Haiti) and efforts for peace in long-standing conflicts (in Northern Ireland, North Korea and Palestine).

Mixed results followed the "new interventionism." American participation seemed effective in ending "ethnic cleansing" in the Balkan conflict, for example, but the mission to feed starving civilians in Somalia changed into ill-executed efforts at "nation-building" that ended in the death and post-mortem humiliation of US soldiers followed by American withdrawal. Commentators debated over how often and how forcibly the superpower should act, those abroad generally wanting international leadership from America but expecting it to act in concert, most often through the UN. A prominent group of critics at home, supported by the Clinton administration, took this same view, but there was heated disagreement, especially from the so-called neo-conservatives, about how much the US should allow other nations and international organizations to influence its foreign policy. Agreement appeared only about regret at America's not having intervened to end the genocide in Rwanda. While in Africa, former President Clinton called that his administration's worst error, and in 2003 George W. Bush was prompt in asking for international action to stop the slaughter in Sudan's civil war. Later he traveled to Africa and allocated large resources to fighting the AIDS epidemic there.

On taking office in 2001, George W. Bush formed a team of foreign-policy officials and advisors that included moderates, such as Secretary of State Colin Powell, "pragmatists," such as National Security Advisor Condoleezza Rice, and leaders associated with neo-conservative views, such as Vice President Dick Cheney, Secretary of Defense Donald Rumsfeld and his chief assistant, Paul Wolfowitz. On the one hand, neo-conservative policy commentators urged a new foreign-policy realism, which meant acting energetically to achieve key objectives and rejecting or scaling down less vital involvements interests. Early in his first term, Bush's administration withdrew from the Anti-Ballistic Missile Treaty and the Kyoto Protocol on global warming, rejected the International Criminal Court, and disengaged from diplomatic efforts in Korea and the Middle East. In agreement with neo-conservative advisors, Bush also embarked on a major military build-up.

Until the terrorist attacks of 9/11, the Bush regime repudiated the Clinton administration's willingness to engage US troops abroad. From that day, however, other parts of the neo-conservative agenda grew prominent. The president announced a global war on terrorism, and within weeks, the US military was engaged in pursuing Osama bin Laden, eliminating the al-Qaeda terrorist training camps in Afghanistan, and replacing the Taliban regime that sheltered them. The US took note of its unchallenged status as the sole superpower and acted accordingly. It adopted an interventionist stance to change the world to suit American ideals and interests, rather than merely to manage the world's crises as a global police officer. It used military force to bring regime change where it seemed necessary. In retrospect, it is clear that in this new global war Bush and his advisors reacted excessively.

In an age of global terrorism, President Bush announced, the US could no longer wait for threats to materialize. Instead, it had to use its intelligence gathering capacities to discover threats and then strike enemies first, abroad, before they could attack the American homeland. The US would take "pre-emptive action," attacking an enemy as it prepared to strike, and "preventative action," attacking even without evidence of an imminent enemy strike. With advice from White House lawyers, Bush instituted higher levels of government secrecy and conducted massive surveillance at home and abroad to detain terrorists and their allies.

His administration established secret prisons in foreign countries and converted the US base in Guantanamo, Cuba to locations for the detention, interrogation and torture of terrorist suspects who Bush classified as "enemy

PLATE 8.5 Coalition soldiers in central Baghdad during the Iraq War in 2003.
© *Sipa Press/REX/Shutterstock*

combatants" outside the provisions of the Geneva Conventions to protect the rights of war prisoners. Bush's administration held these people outside the US so that they could not claim rights under American law. When the Supreme Court declared these actions illegal, the administration set up especially designed military commissions outside the US to try prisoners.

As early as the 1980s, neo-conservatives identified "rogue states" as the dispensers of terrorism and, therefore, as the prime candidates for US-led change. Bush identified some of these nations as an "axis of evil" stretching from North Korea through Iran to Iraq. His administration convinced Congress of the imminent threat of Iraq's plans to use WMD (weapons of mass destruction) and of its connections with al-Qaeda. Despite entrenched opposition, both at home and in the UN, the US and its allies occupied Iraq in early 2003. The president declared victory in less than three months, but the war wore on and American casualties rose as the "coalition of the willing" attempted to restore public order and put in place a stable democratic government. Senator Obama, one of few members to vote against the Second Iraq War, as president, made ending the war a major goal. Still, in 2017, American advisors remained and Iraqi government and society were fragile.

The view policy experts emphasized after the Obama years stressed that armed conflicts would be protracted and continuous with a complex role for the US military, involving less frequent use of force and more negotiation and empowerment of local allies in "stability operations." Critics doubted that any orthodoxy of approach could suit the variety of international conflicts around the globe. Meeting the challenge of terrorism, much of it arising from radical Islamic groups, US leaders could only credit the war on terrorism with preventing additional attacks by external groups on America's home soil. Its successes became controversial due to the high financial burdens and serious limitations on individuals' civil liberties that resulted from the US Patriot Act. Nonetheless, George W. Bush won re-election on a promise to continue vigorously prosecuting the war on terror.

In office, Obama shared that commitment but eschewed many of the legally dubious powers Bush asserted. The new president closed the secret prisons, but Congress' and foreign nations' concerns about accepting Guantanamo prisoners kept the Cuban detainment center open. He ended the use of torture and indefinite detention but continued using military commissions, though in reformed form. He lowered the secrecy level but went on with massive surveillance. He pursued no legal actions against his predecessor's excesses.

Obama aimed to set the nation's foreign relations on a course relying more on soft power. He hoped to open new opportunities for multilateral talks to work out agreements based on shared interests. This was the purpose of his speech to the Islamic nations of the world at Cairo University, the reopening of talks with North Korea, and trips to Europe. The administration's actions brought less open hostility, but relations remained intractable with North Korea,

Iran, nations experiencing uprisings to overthrow dictatorships during the "Arab spring," and non-state actors like the Islamic terrorist cells in northwest Africa.

America could not change complex international relations and the resentment of American policies going back to before the Cold War through verbal demonstrations of good will – or even the avoidance of hostile action. Obama's use of robot drone planes and the successful military action to kill Osama Bin Laden in Pakistan proved that the US was still willing to kill civilians and violate another country's sovereignty to achieve its goals. His most important foreign policy project, halting Iran's development of nuclear weapons, consumed years of multilateral negotiations that, though much contested, reached success in 2015. The US, UK, France, Germany, Russia, and China enforced crippling economic sanctions on Iran until it agreed to reduce its atomic programs to civilian energy facilities and maintain them on that level for 15 to 25 years. Israel and many Republicans fought the treaty.

On taking office, President Trump made efforts to fulfill campaign promises to change US foreign policy with regard to the Iran agreement, immigration, and trade agreements. He put Iran on notice that the US monitored its actions closely and announced new economic sanctions when it continued to

PLATE 8.6 President Donald Trump points to British Prime Minister Theresa May in the White House Oval Office in Washington, DC on, January 27, 2017.
© *REUTERS/Alamy*

test missiles. Engaging in an acerbic exchange with the Mexican president, he signed an executive order to fund the wall on the Mexican border. He insisted that eventually the Mexicans would pay for the wall, despite their president's denials of that. Trump's national security travel ban on visitors and immigrants in early 2017 excluded only people from majority-Muslim countries in the Middle East. After its first day, court injunctions suspended the travel ban and left the implementation of the national security dimension of Trump's immigration policy uncertain.

President Trump proclaimed his aim of relocating the US embassy in Israel to Jerusalem, promised Israel steadfast support and met the country's prime minister very early. He gave no commensurate signs to the Palestinians. The signals from the new administration regarding the Middle East, however, were mixed. The White House also announced that the US viewed the expansion of Israeli settlements on Palestinian lands as a barrier to peace.

During the years of successful negotiation of the TPP, critiques of multinational trade deals grew sharper in the US. A consensus developed among union members and conservatives that such treaties cost working-class Americans jobs and favored other nations with cheap labor. As promised during his campaign, Trump withdrew the country from the TPP on taking office. An opponent of globalization, he pledged a protectionist approach and indicated publicly his intention to renegotiate or withdraw from NAFTA. He applied his motto, "America First," to economic relations, which he asserted US presidents before him bungled badly. The Trump administration planned to have bilateral rather than multilateral agreements.

The foreign policy establishment debate

The governmental structures of the US are another factor that make American foreign affairs distinctive. The system of checks and balances requires the executive and legislative branches to share responsibility for the nation's foreign relations. The dispersion of power in these branches, moreover, has resulted in opportunities for other institutions and groups to influence foreign policy decision-making. As a result, the official and unofficial groups that play a part in the foreign-policy establishment are many and varied. Several competing centers of power interact in ways that change over time and according to the situation.

The balance of power between the two branches over foreign policy has shifted. Congress was the dominant partner for most of the nineteenth century, except for the Civil War years. A strong shift toward greater executive power since the 1900s resulted from the near constant international crises involving the US. The president grew increasingly dominant until failures of executive policy involved with the Vietnam War provoked congressional attempts to correct the balance between the branches and greater presidential caution in making foreign commitments. Because of the Reagan presidency's initiatives and the 9/11 crisis, however, a high degree of executive dominance in foreign policy has returned.

The president has powers that make him the most important figure in US foreign policy. He must share these, however, with other groups. Constitutionally the commander-in-chief, he is usually a civilian with little military experience. He depends on the advice of the leaders of the armed forces and other experts in international relations to meet national security needs. Even if convinced that the vital interests of the US are threatened, he cannot declare war. Only Congress can do that, and since the Second World War, it has been especially reluctant to do so. Consequently, presidents increasingly commit the nation to military action in other ways when they perceive crises of national security. Recently, the common pattern is that the president commits US military personnel or otherwise responds to an attack on American interests, and soon after informs Congress, asking for a joint resolution of support if the "military conflict" is likely to be of longer duration.

As the chief executive, one of the President's primary duties is to carry out foreign policy, but the Constitution requires the approval of both houses of Congress for the governmental expenditures that all foreign policy initiatives depend on. Not only must the President win majorities for his policies, therefore, but he can also expect military leaders and bureaucrats to lobby Congress in favor of competing programs. Congressional involvement does not stop there. It exercises its investigatory power to evaluate if the executive spends money as Congress stipulated and stops funding or repeals those acts if it is dissatisfied.

The chief executive has escaped some of the most important checks on his foreign policy powers. No other official can nominate people to ambassadorial and other high-level positions in American foreign service, but all such appointments must be approved by a majority in the Senate. Congress removed this limit in 1939 by creating the Executive Office of the President (EOP), which allows presidents to rely on White House advisors, who do not need Senate approval. The EOP's National Security Council eclipsed the Departments of State and Defense as the center of policymaking in foreign relations by the mid-1960s and diminished congressional influence in foreign policy. The president alone can negotiate treaties, but the Senate must ratify treaties by a two-thirds majority. Approval from so many senators often seems doubtful, especially since the First World War, and so presidents often depend on executive agreements, which do not require Senate approval.

Two foreign-policy roles of the President, acting as chief diplomat and ceremonial head of state, have grown greatly in importance since the beginning of high-speed air travel, electronic communication and supersonic weaponry. The possibility for extensive personal diplomacy between world leaders and the media attention it commands have made the president the visible maker of foreign policy. During the Cold War with the threat of nuclear destruction and, since 2001 the possibility of a catastrophic terrorist attack, the greater speed of executive action is a convincing argument for presidential control of foreign affairs.

The organization of the congressional and executive institutions in the foreign-policy establishment create opportunities for many interest groups to exercise influence. Each chamber of Congress has a permanent committee that specializes in foreign policy with subcommittees to deal with the major regions of the world and important international issues. Both chambers also have other committees (with subcommittees) that are part of foreign policy decisions, such as the armed services, energy, commerce and intelligence committees.

The State Department and Department of Defense are, like Congress, organized into groups of specialists that focus on particular issues or areas of the world. These groups formulate policy suggestions that they send through bureaucratic channels to the secretary of state or the secretary of defense, who forward them to the EOP and Congress. The president usually decides on major policy concerns, but bureaucrats manage the implementation of policy. They

PLATE 8.7 Secretary of State John Kerry speaking with former Secretary of State Hillary Clinton at the reception before the groundbreaking ceremony for the US Diplomacy Center at the State Department in Washington DC on September 3, 2014. Secretary of State Kerry and five former secretaries of state attended the reception and groundbreaking of the Center, whose mission is demonstrating the ways that diplomacy has mattered throughout American history. © *Michael Reynolds/Epa/REX/Shutterstock*

also hold investigative hearings. For these reasons, the full range of pressure groups and members of Congress try to catch the ear of influential officials in the State Department and Department of Defense.

There has long been debate about the foreign-policy establishment. According to some critics, deliberation and lobbying in roughly parallel structures in Congress and the departments produce wasteful redundancy, lost information and unnecessary confusion over policy alternatives. These observers emphasize that the foreign-policy establishment has yet another component, the personal advisors and agencies in the EOP. The 'president's national security advisor, the National Security Agency (NSA), the joint chiefs of staff of the military and the Central Intelligence Agency (CIA) and other intelligence agencies often evolve a third set of priorities and policies. Is it any wonder that over the half century of the Cold War some 45 separate national security and intelligence gathering units grew up? This situation was partly to blame for the intelligence failures leading to the 9/11 terrorist attacks. One of the chief governmental changes in the wake of the tragedies consolidated many of those programs into a single new structure, the Department of Homeland Security (DHS), in 2002.

Exercises

Explain and examine the significance of the following names and terms:

isolationism	Washington's Farewell Address	exceptionalism
soft power	hard power	Alien and Sedition Acts
Monroe Doctrine	expansionism	Roosevelt Corollary
manifest destiny	imperialism	NAFTA and the TPP
anti-imperialists	Fourteen Points	limited internationalism
Four Freedoms	Yalta Conference	Truman Doctrine
Marshall Plan	McCarthyism	National Security Act
Vietnam War	détente	Gulf War
9/11	Iran – Contras scandal	post-Cold War era
hegemony	Department of Homeland Security	USA Patriot Act
Iraq War	Islamic terrorist cells	"America first"

Write short essays on the following questions.

1. Critically evaluate the degree to which US foreign policy is (or has been) distinct from that of other nations.

2. Summarize what you think are the important historical trends and turning points in the evolution of America's relations with the rest of the world.

3. Critically evaluate the significant changes in US foreign policy from 1945 to 1989. Evaluate the most important changes from 1989 to the present.

4. Describe the institutional structures in America's foreign-policy establishment and critically discuss how well they serve as a basis for the formulation of the nation's foreign policy.

Further reading

Dobson, A. P. and Marsh, S. (2006) *American Foreign Policy since 1945* 2nd ed, London: Routledge.

Haass, R. N. (2009) *War of Necessity, War of Choice: A Memoir of Two Iraq Wars*, New York: Simon & Schuster.

Johnson, L. K. (2007) *Seven Sins of American Foreign Policy*, London: Longman.

Kennedy, P. M. (1987) *The Rise and Fall of the Great Powers: Economic Change and Military Conflict from 1500 to 2000*, New York: Random House.

Lipset, S. M. (1996) *American Exceptionalism: A Double-edged Sword*, New York: W. W. Norton.

Magstadt, T. M. (2004) *An Empire if You Can Keep It: Power and Principle in American Foreign Policy*, Washington, DC: Congressional Quarterly Press.

Merrill, Dennis and Paterson, T. G. (2009) *Major Problems in American Foreign Relations, Vol. I: To 1920.*, Boston, MA: Boston, MA: Wadsworth-Cengage.

Merrill, D. and Paterson, T. G. (2009) *Major Problems in American Foreign Relations, Volume II: Since 1914.* Boston, MA: Wadsworth-Cengage.

Nye, J. S., Jr. (2004) *Soft Power: The Means to Success in World Politics*, New York: Public Affairs.

Foreign Affairs (1922 to the present) *The Council on Foreign Relations*. New York, New York.

Websites

www.whitehouse.gov/
www.foreignaffairs.com/
www.cfr.org/publication/
www.thomas.loc.gov
www.CarnegieEndowment.com
latimes.com
www.washingtonpost.com
www.cnn.com
www.nytimes.com
www.georgetown.edu/crossroads/index.html
usinfo.state.gov/journals/journala.htm
news.bbc.co.uk/2/hi/americas/6249565.stm

The legal system

This chapter examines the historical development of the US legal system; describes the court apparatus, and federal and state court proceedings; considers the role of the legal profession; comments upon crime and punishment; and concludes with attitudes to the legal system.

The legal system consists for practical purposes of judges and lawyers who service independent state and federal courts, which are concerned with two main types of law (civil law and criminal law). The individual cases which are dealt with by the courts and other institutions are accordingly classified as either civil or criminal.

Civil law involves claims for compensation (often financial) by individuals (or groups) who have suffered loss or damage through the acts of others. Domestic actions (divorce, children and custody), automobile accidents, personal injury cases, libel and corporate matters are the main civil actions. Civil law has a service role and tries to secure social harmony by settling disputes between individuals or organizations. This is achieved preferably by settlement during the course of litigation and negotiations. If no settlement is agreed, the case goes to a full trial.

Criminal law involves the trial and punishment of persons who have committed crimes against society, such as theft, assault or homicide (murder). State, local and federal authorities prosecute groups or individuals in an attempt to establish guilt, which may result in a fine, imprisonment or (in serious cases) execution. This is the control aspect of the legal system, and the criminal law protects society by punishing those who have broken social codes embodied in the law. The trial and any punishment are also supposed to act as deterrents to potential offenders, although the effectiveness of deterrence is hotly debated.

The legal system plays a central role on public and private levels of American society, to a greater extent than in other countries. Legal issues and court decisions are of widespread interest, concern and comment. They are also intertwined with the nation's political, social and economic life. Americans make active use of their legal system and, according to Current Population Survey, had 1.2 million lawyers in 2015 to assist them with their cases.

There are several reasons for this cultural behavior. First, participation in the legal process derives from a colonial and frontier tradition of individualism in which Americans defended their own interests and rights. However, legal actions can also result from group causes or class actions. The American War for Independence, for example, began with collective legal complaints by some colonists against British rule and showed that law could protect individuals and communities against oppression by government and other authorities.

Second, public and private life is influenced by a constitutionalism which stems from the Declaration of Independence (1776), the US Constitution (1787) and the Bill of Rights (1789). These documents provide a framework for the good society; guarantee civil rights and freedoms for citizens; and stipulate a separation of powers between an independent judiciary and the executive and legislative branches of government. Americans' expectations of social and political justice depend on the safeguards in these documents, irrespective of whether they are actually achieved in all cases.

Third, such constitutional features are founded on a tradition of legalism (the belief that conflicts can be legally and fairly resolved at individual and national levels), which also stems from colonial times. Civil disputes between citizens, institutions and groups, as well as criminal cases have to be legally decided by the federal and state court systems.

Issues of justice and rights are therefore a basic concern for Americans. They expect action from the criminal law, and go to the courts for satisfaction if they feel that their civil rights have been infringed by federal or state governments, doctors, hospitals, airlines, neighbors, employers, the educational system, manufacturers or companies. But, although an American "legal rights culture" has grown, this does not mean that all such cases succeed.

A large number of civil and criminal cases are handled annually by the courts. Most are determined at state and local (rather than federal) levels. Americans have a constitutional right to have their cases quickly determined by settlement or in a trial by an impartial judge or jury (a selected number of citizens who decide the facts in many court cases).

However, despite a need for correct legal procedure and claims that US society is humane and moral, fair treatment and appropriate outcomes are not always achieved. The ideal may not be matched by the reality, raising questions about the quality of the legal system and justice. The crucial question is one of access to the courts, which often depends upon the nature of a case, wealth, social class, the level of court and legal practices.

It is argued that the criminal and civil systems and police forces must be reformed; that the disadvantaged, poor and ethnic minorities do not receive satisfaction despite legal aid (federal or state help to those who cannot afford legal fees); that the legal system is biased toward the powerful and the wealthy; that high legal costs are an obstacle to litigants seeking help; and that the legal system is not living up to its founding ideals.

The law can be brought into disrepute by dubious or inadequate defense procedures by trial lawyers in criminal and civil cases: by prosecution inadequacy; by plea-bargaining, which allows an accused person to avoid heavier criminal and civil penalties by pleading guilty to lesser charges; by contingency fees, which specify high percentage payments to lawyers for successful results; by juries that may be biased on racial, social or political grounds; by tampering with or fabrication of evidence; by suspect police procedures and conduct; by lawyers who are accused of driving up costs; and by allegedly partial judges. The question of victims' rights of access to law and compensation is also a contentious issue.

Legal history

The legal system is founded on customs brought to the US by European colonists. Many elements were English, such as the common law (judge-made law), parliamentary/royal statutes and judges. These were later added to by American features like the US Constitution, the relationship between state and federal government, and judicial review (the power of superior courts to invalidate laws and actions that violate federal and state constitutions).

When the British colonized parts of North America in the seventeenth century, the English common law, statute law and judges were adopted by some colonies. But other settlers had left their homelands to avoid oppressive institutions and to create a better society. They rejected the common law and created a simple rules system in 1634 in Massachusetts.

However, as life stabilized in the colonies and as the population grew, such rules were insufficient to govern a more complex society. English legal structures became more acceptable. Significantly, colonists in pre-independence America protested that the British Crown had denied them their traditional common-law rights and the Declaration of Independence (1776) contained legal grievances based upon those rights.

After the American War for Independence, the 13 original states used the common law in their legal systems. But, since some states contained settlers such as the Dutch, Germans and Swedes, the common law had to accommodate other legal customs. This process was repeated when the US incorporated territories like California (1850). Each state interpreted and developed the common law in individual ways. But it was not adopted when the US purchased Louisiana (1803), which had its own French law.

The War for Independence involved discussions about the independent role of state governments. Federal government developed later and led to a division of authority between state and federal institutions. Most laws today operate at the state and local level. The 50 states have their own legal systems, create their own laws in their own legislatures, and have their own police forces and law courts. All (except Louisiana) apply their versions of the common law, and most lawyers are qualified to practice in only one state.

New political factors evolved after independence, which alleviated some criticisms of the common law, lawyers and judges. In 1787, delegates from the 13 states at the Constitutional Convention in Philadelphia framed a Constitution for the US, which became law in 1789. This stipulated that, while states remained sovereign in many areas, a new federal union of the states was also sovereign in its own sphere of competence.

PLATE 9.1 The Supreme Court building, Washington DC is adjacent to the US Capitol and is the seat of the US Supreme Court, completed in 1935 in neo-classical style. It is the highest court in the US, serves as a court of appeal from lower courts and has decided many historic cases which have affected fundamental aspects of US life.
© *Kjetil Ree*

Article 111 of the Constitution created a third branch of government, the independent federal judiciary: "The judicial power of the United States shall be vested in one Supreme Court and in such inferior courts as the Congress may from time to time ordain and establish." The founders of the US considered the judiciary to be the weakest branch of government, restricted to applying the Constitution and the laws. But it later developed a central importance, particularly the Supreme Court in Washington, DC.

The Judiciary Act (1789) created new federal courts with two roles. They interpret the meaning of laws and administrative acts (statutory construction) and examine laws and administrative action by national or state authorities in the light of the US Constitution (judicial review). This latter function was initially contested by states' rights activists. But it was finally conceded and was an important factor in establishing a united nation.

These developments created a legal organization for the whole country, and authority was divided between state and federal courts. The states had their own courts, constitutions, statutes and jurisdiction over state law. But if a state-court decision violated federal laws or involved a federal question, the US Supreme Court could ultimately review and overturn it. Some matters may thus proceed from local courts to the Supreme Court, and federal laws and the Constitution have a uniform application throughout the country.

The independent judiciary was gradually strengthened. It is regarded as an essential safeguard against potential abuse by the executive and legislative branches and fits into the US system of separation of powers and checks and balances. Some 3,679 federal judges were formally appointed in 2012 by the president, subject to approval by the Senate. They serve until retirement and can only be removed for gross misconduct. All other judges at various levels are appointed by methods peculiar to individual states or are elected by voters. A further development increased the status of the judiciary, courts and legal system. Since the Constitution contained few rights for individual citizens, a Bill of Rights was voted by Congress in 1789, ratified by the states in 1791, but applicable only at the federal level until the 1920s. The Bill of Rights (and Amendments) protects citizens against imprisonment without just cause, excessive fines or other oppression. However, the courts still have to interpret the Bill and amendments in individual court cases.

Two other new features have strengthened the place of law in US society. First, Congress (given limited power by the Constitution) later regulated American life through interstate commerce Acts. The authority to "regulate commerce among the several States" (the commerce clause) and to create laws "necessary and proper" to carry out its powers enables Congress to pass social and economic legislation for the whole country. These laws may be examined by federal courts, although traditionally they have not interfered overmuch.

Second, law has become complex due to increases in federal and state legislation. This means that business people, consumers and other individuals are now more concerned with and directly affected by the law. They are very cautious about their legal transactions, contracts and court appearances and frequently need the assistance of professional lawyers.

Courts and judges in the US, especially at the federal level, make policy to some degree as they interpret and apply the law. It is argued that the courts are therefore political and legislative institutions, and the judiciary is part of these processes. But judges do not make law or policy in the explicit way that politicians do. They function indirectly in the process of resolving disputes brought to their courts and may use different forms of legal reasoning to reach their verdicts.

The sources of US law

The two most important sources of contemporary US law are common (judge-made or case) law and statutory law.

Versions of the English common law were accepted in all American states (except Louisiana) and much state law is now common law. It is administered and interpreted by the courts and is found in court decisions of judges, who generally decide matters by adopting principles of law and decisions (precedents) from previous similar cases.

Generally, American judges at all levels now decide cases pragmatically, in terms of existing law and a sense of justice, so that the decision is fair and reasonable in the light of contemporary conditions (a process that is often described as "American Realism.") They follow the precedents unless there are good reasons for ignoring them. Some judges, however, may follow particular readings of law such as "originalism" (reading the Constitution as its framers intended and as it was understood when it was written).

Statutory law consists of laws which have been passed by state or federal legislatures. This legislation is now very important. It expanded from the nineteenth century as state and federal government intruded increasingly into everyday affairs. The meaning and application of legislation is interpreted and determined by the courts. Many social, economic and family matters are provided for by state statutes and handled by state courts. At federal levels, statutory law is virtually the only type of law and includes the Constitution, treaties, Acts of Congress, presidential proclamations, executive orders and rules of federal departments.

The court system

The courts play a central and influential role in US society. They affect the daily lives of citizens; social and personal struggles are reflected in civil and criminal court battles; and the courts attract both positive and negative criticism.

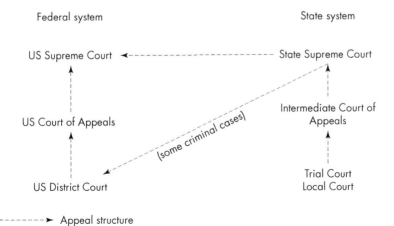

FIGURE 9.1 The main US courts.

US courts operate at federal and state/local levels and have their own areas of authority or jurisdiction. State and local courts handle much of the legal work and are the most immediate for Americans. Federal courts account for some two percent of cases tried annually. But the existence of separate court systems can make litigation complicated.

Parties in a case may, in certain circumstances, appeal a court decision to a higher court. An appeal is an examination of procedures and legal principles on which the decision was based in the previous trial, and may include any new admissible evidence.

The federal court system

Federal courts deal with cases that arise under the Constitution, federal law and disputes involving the federal government. They also hear matters concerning authorities and citizens of different states and thus play a part in state law. If a case in the highest state court of appeal involves a federal question, it may be appealed to the US Supreme Court. The three levels of courts in the federal system are, in ascending order of appeal:

1.   US District Courts
2.   US Courts of Appeals ("Circuit Courts")
3.   The Supreme Court in Washington, DC

A case involving federal jurisdiction is heard first in a district court. An appeal may (rarely) be made to a US Court of Appeal and, in the last resort, to the US Supreme Court. Most federal cases are settled in the US District Courts. There are 94 of these courts in the US (with states having at least one court) organized into 12 regional circuits. They are trial courts in which a judge (sometimes with a jury) decides cases on evidence presented.

District Courts have jurisdiction to hear most categories of federal civil and criminal matters and have a large caseload. They try breaches of federal criminal law, such as bank robbery, drug dealing, kidnapping, mail fraud, interstate crime, currency fraud and assassination. Much of the work of the District Courts, however, is in areas of civil law, such as taxation, civil rights, administrative regulations, disputes between states, bankruptcy, and special cases dealing with international trade, customs and claims against the US.

At the next federal level, there are 12 US appeals courts, and each court belongs to a regional circuit of three to nine states (except for one court which serves only the District of Columbia). These courts (with from three to five judges examining a case) mainly hear appeals from decisions of the US District Courts and federal administrative agencies within the relevant circuits. Most of their decisions are final and set a precedent for future similar cases. It is argued that they are the most important judicial-policymakers in the US. They are not, however, the ultimate authority because their decisions can be overturned by the US Supreme Court on appeal. There is also an additional US Court of

Appeals, which specializes in patents, federal employment law and international trade.

The US Supreme Court in Washington DC is the apex of the federal court system. It comprises a chief justice and eight associate justices, assisted by law clerks. It has jurisdiction in national and federal matters and its main role is as an appeal court, hearing cases from lower federal and state courts. Appeals usually involve constitutional issues, questions of federal law and conflicts between two or more of the states.

The court has authority to review any executive and legislative action or law passed by a level of government (if challenged in a court case) and can declare it unconstitutional after judging its compatibility with the Constitution. Although not specifically given power of judicial review by the Constitution, the Supreme Court developed this jurisdiction from the Judiciary Act in 1789. It enables the court to influence many aspects of American life.

Its decisions have given protection and rights to African Americans and other minorities and written influential rulings on education, religion, the death penalty, gun law and abortion. However, it has ruled that a relatively small number of federal laws have been unconstitutional, compared to the greater invalidation of state and local laws. Supreme Court decisions can be overturned by the court itself, a constitutional amendment or by Congress introducing legislation to overturn a decision of the Court.

The Court rules on about 100 cases each year out of some 7,000 submitted to it, and decides itself whether or not it will hear particular cases. It usually accepts cases that involve a constitutional principle, an important question of federal law or a conflict between state and federal law. It does not have the power to make laws. However, since its authority is largely independent of the other branches of government and it interprets the constitution, its decisions often have a legislative, policymaking (and arguably political) force, in which individual justices may demonstrate their personal views and legal philosophies.

The court usually plays a conservative role, following legal tradition and precedent. But it has had periods of controversial "liberal activism" and been criticized for exceeding its job of interpreting statutory law and the Constitution; usurping the powers of Congress; obstructing the popular will; and preventing the passing of economic and social legislation. It has chosen to rule on high-profile cases and declined to act in other matters that might have seemed more appropriate for review. Nevertheless, its caseload has expanded due to new legislation in civil-rights and federal regulations. This has increased its "political" profile.

The state and local court system

State and local courts constitute a large, complicated and individualistic system. They have a wider jurisdiction than federal courts and much heavier workloads. They determine the guilt or innocence of persons accused of violating

PLATE 9.2 Athens County Courthouse, 1880, Athens, Ohio. A historic landmark in the town, it is the third courthouse to have been built on the site and remains in use. Currently, it is fourth District Court of Appeals for Ohio and the Athens County Court of Common Pleas. The Athens County Municipal Court is on another site and has civil and criminal law functions.
© *Jordan Oakland*

state criminal laws and decide civil disputes. Most criminal and civil cases, like assaults, theft (larceny), homicide (murder), divorce and property disputes are settled within the state system.

The Constitution stipulates that the states have areas of authority (or sovereignty) outside the federal system. They have their own criminal and civil legal systems, laws, prisons, police forces, courts and associations of lawyers. Court systems and laws are similar in most states. But there are differences, such as the number of courts, court structures and names, procedure, the appointment or election of judges and some variation in laws and punishment for crimes. The states guard their independence and are self-contained legal units whose courts deliver judgements from which there is often no further appeal. But jurisdiction can be shared between federal and state bodies if an issue or appeal has federal implications.

Local courts are the lowest state courts and have limited jurisdiction. They hear minor civil and criminal cases (misdemeanors) that often cannot be appealed and mostly do not need a jury to decide the issue. Their names vary according to locality and the nature of the case. They may be known as police courts, town or city courts or justice of the peace courts. Trial courts are the next highest and handle criminal matters (except misdemeanors) which will usually be heard before a judge and jury, and some civil cases. They may consist of the following in different states:

- district, county or municipal courts, which decide civil and criminal cases,
- juvenile or family courts, which hear domestic, juvenile and delinquency cases,
- probate courts, which rule on wills and hear claims against estates, and
- criminal courts, which determine criminal cases.

About three-quarters of the states have intermediate appeal courts that hear appeals from lower courts. But the highest court is the State Supreme Court, which hears civil and criminal appeals from inferior state courts and can employ judicial review. Federal and constitutional matters may be appealed from this court to the US Supreme Court, and some criminal cases can be appealed to the federal District Courts.

PLATE 9.3 A traditional local court with wooden paneling and a judge's bench with Tiffany glass canopy, at Pacific County Courthouse, South Bend, WA. A judge would preside and could hear and decide cases, with or without a jury.
© *Dorothy Alexander/Alamy*

Federal and state court proceedings

American legal proceedings in both criminal and civil cases are based on due process (basic legal rights, accepted procedures, formal trial and correct information) and the adversary system. The latter enables competing parties to present their views to an impartial third party, under procedural rules that allow the evidence to be given in a fair and structured manner. A trial under the adversary process is designed to determine the facts according to the appropriate law and to resolve cases by producing a judgement. It is the third party (judge or jury) who decides the case based on the evidence presented to the court.

The legal language and emphasis on correct procedure in court are supposed to safeguard the rights of citizens and to ensure equal protection under the law. In practice, most civil disputes and some criminal cases are not resolved through court trials and many legal problems do not result in lawsuits. Lawyers may try to avoid civil and criminal contests in court by arranging settlements during the course of negotiation and litigation or by other devices, such as plea bargaining (guilty plea to a lesser offense and punishment).

Criminal proceedings

A range of rights and protections for citizens in criminal cases is provided by amendments to the Bill of Rights and by later judicial decisions (see Figure 9.2).

These stipulate that individuals shall not be deprived of life, liberty or property without due process of law and should be given a speedy and public trial, usually by jury, in the location of the alleged crime. Accused persons can question witnesses and compel most witnesses to appear on their behalf. They have the right to a lawyer for their defense (often at public expense if necessary), the right to remain silent and a right against self-incrimination.

There is protection against excessive bail (payment to secure freedom prior to trial); the police cannot force a confession from a suspect by duress or threats and may not hold persons for more than two days without charging them with a criminal offense. Long imprisonment in isolation prior to trial is illegal and a confession obtained by the police in these circumstances is unacceptable to a court. It is argued, however, that such safeguards are not always observed by the criminal justice system and individuals' rights may be abused.

Trial by jury is a basic tradition in the US and is guaranteed in indictable (serious) criminal cases. It may also be employed in other criminal trials. A defendant charged with a criminal offense may have been previously indicted by a grand jury or sometimes by a process of information at state level. The trial jury consists of between six and 12 ordinary citizens (depending on the level of the court), who make a decision based on the facts before them in court. A unanimous decision is needed in federal criminal cases and in most criminal cases in all states (although majority verdicts may sometimes be allowed).

Pre-trial procedure

1. Arrest of suspect by police (*Miranda* v. *Arizona, 1966;* rights must be read to suspect).
2. Custody (suspect may be held for up to 48 hours without formal charge).
3. Initial appearance of suspect before a judge. Judge determines whether there is sufficient evidence of a crime (probable cause) to charge the defendant, who is informed of the charge details and his/her legal rights. If no charge is preferred, the defendant is released. If defendant is charged, the judge will set bail (the amount of money or conditions to release defendant from custody until trial) and determine legal representation.
4. Arraignment. Defendant appears in court for the reading of the indictment/information/charge. Their rights are explained and they enter a plea. On a not-guilty plea, a trial date is set. On a guilty plea, a date is set for sentencing.
5. Plea bargaining. Both sides come to an agreement on the charges without a full trial (for example, plead guilty to a lesser offence).
6. Discovery. If a case is set for trial, prosecution and defense disclose their witnesses and prosecution must generally produce all evidence against the defendant to the defense.

Trial procedure in court

1. Trial held before a judge, who presides, and a jury, which decides the facts of the case.
2. Selection of (usually) 12 jurors to form the jury.
3. Opening statements firstly by the state (prosecution) followed by the defense.
4. Presentation of evidence and examination of witnesses by the prosecution. At close, the defense may seek a motion to dismiss the action. If unsuccessful, the defense presents its evidence. At close, rebuttal evidence may be called by the prosecution.
5. Objections to the nature of the questioning may be made by either side. Questioning may consist of examination, cross-examination and additional questioning.
6. After all the evidence has been presented, there are final motions in the absence of the jury for a directed verdict from the judge. If this fails, the jury returns to listen to closing arguments first by the defense and then by the prosecution.
7. These are followed by the judge's instructions to the jury, the jury deliberation and the jury decision (verdict). Motions after verdict may be submitted (for example, for a new trial). If unsuccessful, the judge then enters a judgment on this decision and sets a date for sentencing.

Source: adapted from ABA, *Law and the Courts: A Handbook of Courtroom Procedures.*

FIGURE 9.2 Outline of procedure in criminal cases.

After trial, the Seventh Amendment guarantees that the accepted facts on which a trial was based cannot be re-examined in appeal to a higher court and the appeal must be based on other grounds, such as new evidence. The Eighth Amendment provides protection for the guilty from cruel and unusual punishment (see the death penalty debate).

District attorneys conduct criminal prosecutions under these rules at the local (county or city) levels. At the federal level, prosecuting attorneys from the Department of Justice and the offices of the attorney general and solicitor general represent the government in initiating and trying criminal cases and suggest cases to the courts.

Civil proceedings

Civil cases in federal and state courts are divided into categories. The majority deal with matters such as accident and personal injury claims. The plaintiff serves documents on the defendant and, unless the case is settled out of court by negotiation, it goes to trial before a judge and, sometimes, a jury. In more expensive cases, a jury trial must be held. A majority (rather than a unanimous) jury decision is permitted in civil cases in some states. A current concern is the amount of punitive damages being awarded in some cases by the civil courts.

The legal profession

Hostility was shown toward judges after independence because of anti-British feeling, and in the nineteenth century attempts were made to democratize and de-professionalize the legal system. It is argued that some judges have been too political or have bowed to pressure, and others have been accused of incompetence and corruption. However, generally US judges are now given respect. But lawyers (such as corporate, divorce and "celebrity" trial lawyers) can be treated with suspicion or antagonism. Defense and prosecution trial lawyers have attracted negative comment for their alleged manipulation of evidence and the jury.

The judiciary

Federal judges are nominated by the president, confirmed by the Senate and appointed for life. Selection may reflect political and legal considerations. They hold office during good behavior and can be removed by impeachment (trial by the Senate for gross misconduct). This process has been rarely used and never successfully against a Supreme Court justice.

State and local judges may now be appointed, selected or elected (by the people) depending on the practices of individual states. They may also be investigated by state commissions, which may recommend their disciplining or removal.

The judiciary has a range of functions and duties. It enforces legitimate laws and regulations of the legislative and executive branches of government, but it also protects citizens against arbitrary acts by either executive or legislature. Judicial review gives the higher judiciary a crucial authority and judges' freedom from control by the other branches of government means that they are independent and theoretically "above politics."

The authority of judges is generally supported by the public. The justices of the Supreme Court, for example, can be very influential (if not always trusted) and their decisions affect ordinary people's lives. Judges may, however, vary in their political inclinations and legal philosophies and this may be reflected in their decisions.

Lawyers

Americans have tended to distrust lawyers, although they do often need their services. This antagonism today might be due to their courtroom behavior in some cases, to the perception that they drive up legal costs or to the large number of lawyers in society. In addition to their legal roles, their numbers make them very visible in business, politics and public life, and the American Bar Association (ABA) reported that there were 1.2 million licensed lawyers in 2011. The number of lawyers was expected to grow by 10 percent between 2010 and 2020, and competition for legal jobs is intense.

Members of the legal profession, known as "attorneys-at-law," "counselors" or simply "lawyers," exercise broad functions in the law, although many now specialize in one particular area of expertise. They act as advocates (presenting criminal and civil cases in court) and advisors (giving legal assistance such as the drafting of contracts, trusts, wills and settlements). They advise and represent individuals, businesses or government agencies.

Most lawyers today have obtained a law degree from the law school of a university, usually after a 4-year bachelor's degree in another subject. The value of the 3-year law degree varies with the status of the school, although the best (such as Harvard and Yale) are world-famous and high-quality. The degree gives the lawyer a general grounding in American law through academic lectures and practical course work. But lawyers also have to know the law of the state in which they will practice and must pass the state bar examination.

Lawyers work for federal, local and state government or in industry and commerce, but the majority operate from private or corporate legal offices and cater to individual and corporate clients. Some work on their own account (48 percent) and serve a range of clients. However, others practice in firms. Some 15 percent work in small firms with 2–5 lawyers, consisting of office attorneys and trial lawyers, who perform different functions. The remainder work in bigger firms, which have many lawyers and may have offices worldwide. The three categories of lawyers in big firms are senior partners and junior partners, who receive a share of the profits, and associates, who are paid a fixed salary.

The lawyer's income is frequently a high one in the medium-to-large firms and is, on average, one of the highest in the country, with a median annual wage of $114,970 in 2014. Top students of the best law schools are normally able to join a prestigious law firm at a good salary and may quickly proceed to a partnership.

The financing of a law firm, in addition to ordinary commercial fees, may include other features. The contingency fee (payment upon results in personal injury cases) can be charged at rates which may reach over 50 percent of the damages awarded. But *pro-bono* legal help without fees may be provided for those who cannot afford to pay for legal services, and firms can participate in formal state and federal legal aid programs for the poor. The provision of legal aid is an important and expensive federal program, particularly since fees for legal services are generally very high. The public also seem to think that lawyers are overly concerned with money and that they drive up costs and their fees.

Lawyers have organized themselves at national and state levels into bar associations, which supervise the profession, protect professional interests and discipline their members. The ABA was created nationally in 1878. Most states require that lawyers be members of the state bar association, which is affiliated to the ABA, in order to practice law in that state.

The ABA is regarded as a conservative organization and is often criticized. But its lobbying has improved the status of lawyers. It has fought for improvements in the law, legal education and the legal system. It also serves as a source of legal information to the public. The expert opinion and special status of the ABA are influential in the nomination of judges and in proposing changes in criminal and civil law.

Crime and punishment

Crime

Legal history, official statistics and media reports often suggest that the US has a high crime rate in comparison with other countries. Much of this is associated with professional crime organizations, street gangs, drugs, race-related disturbances and low-level offenses. However, crime is spread unevenly across the country and among victims, and international comparisons indicate that US crime statistics are not exceptional in all cases, and rates for some crimes are lower than in other jurisdictions.

It is argued that crime rates in the US have declined overall since the 1970s and 1990s. But there are two measurements of the statistics that may give different results. The Federal Bureau of Investigation (FBI) produces primary Uniform Crime Reports (UCRs), which include serious crime reported to the police. In 2014, the estimated number of violent crimes decreased by 0.2 percent when compared to 2013. There were an estimated 1,165,383 violent crimes. Murder and non-negligent manslaughter decreased by 0.5 percent, but rape and aggravated assault increased by 2.4 and 2.0 percent, respectively. Property crimes decreased by 4.3 percent and showed an annual decline over the previous 12 years to an estimated 8,277,829 crimes. Burglaries dropped 10.5 percent, larceny thefts decreased by 2.7 percent and motor vehicle thefts declined by1.5 percent.

The second crime measure is based on the Bureau of Justice (BJS) National Crime Victimization Survey (NCVS), which examines criminal victimization through interviews with persons who actually experience crime. Unlike the UCR, the NCVS does not cover homicide, arson, commercial crimes and crimes against children under age 12. It includes non-fatal violent offenses (rape or sexual assault, robbery, aggravated assault, and simple assault) and property victimization (burglary, motor vehicle theft, and property theft). It also includes information on domestic violence, injury and use of weapons. No significant increase had occurred in the rate of violent crime from 2013 to 2014. The rate of property crime decreased from 2013 to 2014.

The majority of persistent offenses are property crimes, and a smaller proportion is violent crime against individuals. It is estimated that firearms are used in three-quarters of such cases. The US murder rate has recently declined, but the figure was high among industrialized nations at 4.6/4.5 per 100,000 population between 2011 and 2013 (with 13,716 victims in the latter year). The latest figures suggest that violent crimes and murders increased in 2015, but that overall crime decreased. The incidence of crime is higher in some states, cities and regions; many offenses are still unreported; and only 20 percent of reported crimes are solved and their perpetrators convicted. It is estimated that 60 percent of all crimes are committed by 5 percent of the population and the majority of these persons have a prior criminal record.

Young people aged between 15 and 19 are statistically the most criminally inclined age group. But the number of offenders has declined as increased jobs, prosperity and "zero tolerance" police policies in the 1990s reduced crime statistics, although recession and rising unemployment have since hindered this progress. In some urban areas, murder is the main cause of death among non-White males between the ages of 24 and 45, and overall, non-Whites have a higher victimization rate than Whites.

The reasons for crime are notoriously arguable and varied. Some critics maintain that the police and courts are too lenient in their treatment of criminal suspects and sentencing patterns, while the police criticize the courts and defense lawyers. Others blame slums, social deprivation, poverty, bad schools, lack of opportunities and role models, unemployment, lack of discipline, unstable or dysfunctional families, inadequate or non-existent parenting skills, drugs, organized crime, teenage gangs and the availability of guns and other weapons.

Law enforcement

In 2014, FBI law enforcement statistics reported staffing levels from 12,656 city, county, state, college, university and Native American agencies that employed 627,949 sworn officers with arrest powers and some 271,263 civilians, a rate of 3.4 employees per 1,000 inhabitants. State law is implemented by the police and detectives in the cities and by sheriffs or marshals and constables (deputies) in rural areas. Federal crimes are the responsibility of the FBI, which also provides technical assistance to state and local law enforcement agencies.

Crime prevention is a difficult job for law-enforcement officials and the courts. Public demands for stronger punishment for criminals and increased rights and compensation for crime victims and their families create cost pressure and are expensive. Overcrowded prisons, accessibility of guns, uncertain civil rights and arguments about the death penalty influence the crime debate. Courts and law-enforcement officers face criticism and have difficulties in coping with the legitimate needs and demands of society and the rights of suspects.

Rights of criminal suspects

The Constitution ideally guarantees equal justice under the law for all citizens and the individual's right to freedom and security. Constitutional Amendments and court decisions have also strengthened the rights of criminal suspects.

The Fourth Amendment protects citizens against unreasonable search and seizure. It is generally illegal for the police to search people's homes, persons or papers unless they have a warrant. The Supreme Court has created exceptions so that the police can in some circumstances search and act without a warrant. However, incriminating evidence that results from an illegal police search is excluded from a criminal trial.

Another important rule established by the Supreme Court in *Miranda v. Arizona* (1966) extended the protection of criminal suspects. The police must read suspects their legal rights upon arrest and under custody. These include the right to remain silent, to have an attorney present during questioning and to consult a lawyer before making a statement. If the police proceed incorrectly, any evidence obtained from questioning cannot be used in court.

Many protections for criminal suspects stem from liberal Supreme Court decisions in the 1960s. Conservatives campaign for the reversal of these rulings and other provisions that arguably overprotect suspects. They maintain that such rules hinder law enforcement and the protection of society and shift the balance of doubt toward suspects. Liberals argue that any reduction in the rights of criminal suspects may affect innocent people and leaves too much power and control in the hands of the police and the criminal justice system.

The death penalty

Capital punishment is hotly debated in the US. In 1972, the Supreme Court ruled in *Furman v. Georgia* that the death penalty for convicted murderers was "cruel and unusual punishment" (Eighth Amendment) and unconstitutional. This decision was reversed in 1976 in *Gregg v. Georgia*, which ruled that the death penalty was constitutional if it is applied in a fair and impartial manner. Critics argue that the Court decided this case in a narrow legal sense and ignored the ethical implications of the "cruel and unusual" clause. For them, the death penalty illustrates the gap between law and justice in American society: it is unconstitutional as a cruel and unusual punishment and does not serve as a deterrent. Thirty-one states, the Federal Government and the US Military retain the death penalty (2016), but seven states have repealed the punishment since 2004. Given the uncertain state of the law and opposition to capital punishment, the number of executions fluctuated after 1976; there are some 600 fewer prisoners on death row than at the end of 2000, and death sentences have become rarer. Execution is more prevalent in the South (such as Texas with 524 cumulative deaths by 2015), and California has the largest death row population. Department of Justice statistics showed that 1,312 convicted murderers were executed in the US between 1976 and 2012. Of these, according to the Death Penalty Information Center, 740 (56 percent) were White, 452 (35 percent) were Black, 101 (7 percent) were Latino, 24 (2 percent) were other races/ethnic groups and 12 (0.9 percent) were female.

The most common method of applying capital punishment is lethal injection by a triple mixture of drugs. This system arguably lacks adequate supplies, has application weaknesses and risks and is considered to be a cruel, unusual and unconstitutional punishment. The concern about executing the wrong person had led to more complex and expensive appeals, and executions continue to decline. But in 2008, the Supreme Court ruled that execution by lethal injection had to present a "substantial" or "objectively intolerable" risk of serious harm for it to constitute cruel and unusual punishment. A divided Court (5–4) upheld Oklahoma's lethal injection process in June 2015.

The death penalty for people convicted of murder has fluctuating support. A Pew Research Center survey in April 2015 reported that 56 percent of respondents favored the punishment, but this was the lowest majority in 40 years and 38 percent were opposed. Forty percent of Democrats, 77 percent of Republicans, and fewer women than men supported the death penalty. But Pew found in October 2016 that only 49 percent of respondents were now in favor, a 7-point decline since 2015.

PLATE 9.4 Aerial view of San Quentin State Prison, located north of San Francisco, in Marin County, California, opened in 1852 and is one of the largest prisons in the US with 4,223 inmates in 2013. It has the state's only death row for males, and executions are by lethal injection.
© *Aerial Archives/Alamy*

The 2015 survey found widespread doubts about how the death penalty is applied and whether it actually deters serious crime, with 61 percent of respondents thinking that it did not. Nevertheless, a majority (63 percent) said that the death penalty is morally justified when a person commits a crime like murder, and 31 percent said that it is morally wrong. But while 63 percent of respondents felt that there is some risk that an innocent person will be executed, only 26 percent said that there were adequate safeguards in place to prevent such an outcome. Fifty-two percent thought that minorities are more likely than Whites to be sentenced to death for similar crimes. An American Values Survey in November 2015 for the Public Religion Research Institute found that a small majority of respondents preferred life without parole as a substitute for execution. A decline in death penalty support since the mid-1990s coincided with falls in violent crime, better examination of wrongful convictions, and more convicts being exonerated through DNA evidence and faulty forensic work.

A majority of Americans report that although an innocent person might be executed, they would still defend the death penalty. However, support for execution can vary, depending on the alternatives and the circumstances of individual cases. For example, support declines to about half of the population when Americans are given the opportunity to choose the alternative of life imprisonment with no possibility of parole. On the other hand, in instances of horrific crimes (such as child killing), support can rise to 80 percent.

Prisons

The US has a higher percentage of its population behind bars than any other country and spends billions of dollars a year on its prisons. According to the BJS, there were 2,222,300 adult prisoners in US federal, state and county jails in 2013. There were also 4,751,400 adults on probation and parole and 54,148 young people in juvenile detention. The incarceration figures in prison and jail have climbed sharply since the mid-1970s and have remained consistently high. Florida, Louisiana, California, Texas and Illinois have recently housed the most prisoners in their correctional facilities.

American administrations, in response to public concern about crime, have followed "tough-on-crime" policies in the last 35 years and favored the following:

- keeping the death penalty in most states,
- putting more police on the streets,
- building more prisons,
- enabling more prisons to be run by private firms,
- stressing punishment above rehabilitation,
- reducing parole,
- giving longer and tougher sentences for serious crimes and
- imposing immediate custodial sentences on criminals who repeat serious crimes ("three strikes and you're out").

It is argued that mass incarceration cannot solely explain recent falling crime rates, although US governments maintain that tactics of tough and effective policies to tackle crime are working. But a relatively healthy economy until 2007–8 and from 2010, demographic changes (with an ageing population and declining numbers of 15- to 19-year-olds on the crime scene), community policing and zero toleration of crime are contributory factors.

However, critics say that tough crime laws since the 1980s have filled US prisons with mainly non-violent offenders, moved the US penal system away from rehabilitation, are creating problems for the future, and have failed to rehabilitate prisoners. Reformers advocate improved cost-effective welfare systems, better education and drug treatment programs, with prevention, rather than punishment and detention, being the aims. Many prisons tend to be old;

they do not serve as positive examples of rehabilitation, and the US public is allegedly ignorant of the violence, abuse and overcrowding in US prisons.

Gun control

The ownership and legal control of guns in the US are controversial issues with conflicting opinions from different interest groups. Gun control activists stress the need to fight crime and maintain public safety by restricting public possession of guns, while those who insist on the right to own guns claim support from American history, law and need for self-protection.

The Congressional Research Service in 2016 estimated that there were 300 million privately owned guns in the US. A *Pew Research Center* survey in December 2013 reported that 37 percent of US households contained an adult who owned a gun. Twenty-six percent of respondents in a 2014 *Gallup* poll felt that this makes a house safer, but 30 percent thought that it made it dangerous. Sixty percent of respondents in a 2013 *Gallup* poll owned a gun for protection but a later poll in October 2015 found that concern over guns and gun control had increased to third place in a list of non-economic problems facing the US. It is argued that federal and state governments have a responsibility to protect citizens from misuse of guns and against crime, civil unrest and violence. But official control is weakened by ineffective laws, and gun rights supporters promote firearms for self-defense, traditional hunting activities, sporting events and security and claim that gun ownership reduces crime. It is also alleged that US gun laws and controls do not prevent violence.

Gun culture in the US is subject to judicial interpretations of the Constitution, and specifically to the Second Amendment (1791) and the Fourteenth Amendment (1868) of the Bill of Rights, which cover federal and state jurisdictions. The Second Amendment states that "A well-regulated Militia, being necessary to the security of a free State, the right of the people to keep and bear arms, shall not be infringed." This raises questions as to whether all "the people" may legally own guns for security reasons, or only those who serve in a militia, and whether there should be any restrictions on the possession of weapons. The Supreme Court in June 2008 in *District of Columbia v. Heller* decided that a handgun ban by Washington, DC was an unconstitutional infringement of the Second Amendment.

The Court ruled by a majority of 5–4 that the constitution "protects an individual right to possess a firearm unconnected with service in a militia, and to use that arm for traditionally lawful purposes, such as self-defense within the home." However, the Court's ruling also stated that the right was not unlimited. "It is not a right to keep and carry any weapon whatsoever in any manner whatsoever and for whatever purpose." The Court thus impliedly gave authorities the means to combat gun abuse and to regulate gun use. The issue is how far the right to possess guns can be constrained.

It is difficult to pass gun control legislation, despite the fact that guns are used in murders, rapes, robberies and assaults; there have been frequent killings and interracial attacks in recent years, including shootings in schools (such as Newtown, Connecticut 2012 when 20 children and 6 teachers were killed), universities, cinemas and shopping centers.

The influential National Rifle Association (NRA), militias and hunting groups against gun control vigorously oppose restrictions on the sale and use of firearms as a violation of the Constitution. After Newtown, the NRA argued that there should be armed guards in all schools. A *Gallup* poll in 2014 found that 26 percent of respondents regarded the NRA very favorably and 32 percent as mostly favorable.

Gun control laws have been passed that include the imposition of waiting periods for the purchase of handguns to allow checks into the buyer's background; registration of guns; bans on semi-automatic assault weapons and machine guns; stronger penalties for gun offenses; tighter licensing rules for gun-dealers; limitations and regulations on the sale and possession of weapons; and prohibiting certain categories of people from buying guns. But these laws allegedly have not been stringent, were for trial periods, could be circumvented, might be variously applied in different states and did not seriously challenge the "right-to-guns" culture. The Obama Administration proposed action in 2013 to reduce gun violence by closing background check loopholes, banning assault weapons and large capacity magazines, creating an ownership database, making schools safer and checking buyers' convictions and mental health. Meanwhile, gun violence continues.

Recent polls indicate mixed attitudes to guns and control. A Pew Research Center poll in February 2013 found that 48 percent of respondents felt that personal protection was the main reason for owning a gun, although many supported stricter gun laws. A Pew Survey in July 2015 supported expanded background checks of private gun sales (85 percent); laws to prevent the mentally ill from buying guns (79 percent); the creation of a federal database to track gun sales (70 percent;) and a ban on assault-style weapons (57 percent).

However, respondents in many polls feel that mass shootings are isolated acts of troubled individuals rather than reflecting problems in US society. It is also argued that although concern and requests for action increased after violent events, these were followed by public apathy about guns and falling support for stricter gun laws. More radical suggestions such as banning guns completely for private use are apparently un-American and do not reflect the national culture.

The polls have discussed changes in opinion about guns over time. Two years after the Newtown shootings (2014), it seemed that respondents favored the right of Americans to own guns as opposed to increasing control of gun ownership. For much of the 1990s and into the 2000s, most Americans believed it was more important to control gun ownership than to protect gun owners' rights. From 2014, opinion changed with more Americans saying that protecting

gun rights (some 52 percent) was more important than controlling gun ownership (some 46 percent). These percentages are finely balanced and may be
reversed.

Self-defense

The issue of gun control is connected to self-defense and perceived fears about
crime. Historically, people's right to defend themselves, families and property
against crime has been a basic (and often necessary) tradition in American life.

Despite the apparent decline in recent crime figures, there is still a lack
of public confidence in the ability of the courts, legislators and police to cope
with crime or to adequately and effectively protect individual citizens. People
consequently feel that they must safeguard themselves in the face of people
determined to commit criminal acts. Security has become a priority for many
individuals, who devise ways (such as neighborhood watch schemes) to protect
themselves and their homes from attacks, violence and burglaries. They also
tend to avoid certain areas because of crime concerns.

Attitudes to the legal system

Opinion polls between the 1970s and the 1990s suggested that crime, guns,
violence, gangs, assaults and drugs consistently appeared as leading concerns
among Americans and were reflected in high crime statistics. In the early 2000s,
the economy, healthcare, terrorism, the war in Iraq and dissatisfaction with the
government, rather than crime and violence, were seen as the most important
problems facing the US. However, this pattern changed when 70 percent of
respondents to a Gallup poll in October 2015 thought that there was more
crime in the US than in 2014; 18 percent said there was less crime; and 8 percent said the amount had remained at the same level. A later Gallup poll on
April 6, 2016 found that 53 percent of respondents reported that they "worried
a great deal" about crime, compared with 39 percent in 2014, which was the
highest level of concern about crime for 15 years.

Although it is argued that fear of crime is historically considered to be
greater than its actuality and that perceptions about crime are volatile, some
Americans believe that crime and violence might affect their lives and feel
threatened. Gallup analysts argued in November 2015 that Americans' perceptions of crime may conflict with government and FBI data that point to a
decline in violent crime. The poll showed differences in fear between groups
and regions of the country but reported that 35 percent of respondents overall
were afraid to walk alone at night in their neighborhood, and 46 percent were
aware of local crime.

There are opposing attitudes about how to deal with crime. A Gallup poll in January 2012 found that 50 percent of respondents were very/somewhat satisfied with official policies to reduce or control crime, and 45 percent were somewhat dissatisfied/very dissatisfied. Many Americans wish for tough responses to crime, but others want to fight it through better rehabilitation programs, education courses, jobs and job training.

Historically, US legal institutions and their personnel have not attracted great public support for their efforts. For example, a Gallup poll in June 2016 reported that 21 percent of respondents had a great deal of confidence in the police and 31 percent had quite a lot. The figures for the Supreme Court were respectively 15 percent and 21 percent. Those for the criminal justice system were 9 percent and 14 percent. A Gallup poll in September 2015 found that 53 percent of respondents had a great deal or fair amount of trust in the judicial branch of government, while a Gallup poll in December 2015 reported that only 21 percent of respondents thought very highly or highly of the honesty and ethical standards of lawyers.

Attitudes to the legal system vary and may be influenced by publicity about police matters and high-profile cases, as well as the established views of liberals and conservatives. Conservatives are strong on law and order, feel that the rights of criminal suspects and defendants should be restricted, favor strong criminal penalties, harsh punishment and the death penalty, and seek to overturn liberal legislation. Liberals tend to be suspicious of the police and law-enforcement agencies, are against what they see as tough criminal legislation and penalties, and favor extended civil rights for individuals.

Variable attitudes to crime and violence can create a self-perpetuating image of the US as a conflicted, crime-ridden, lawless and violent society. Some professionals and academics seem to suggest that America's fundamental problem is the cult of violence itself and feel that one way to counter this image is to restrict access to, or ban, guns. Others argue that the American media concentrates on a simplistic portrayal of violence, which is copied and replicated by individuals and groups in society and can impact many innocent people.

Exercises

Explain and examine the significance of the following names and terms:

legalism	precedent	impeachment
common law	jurisdiction	civil law
judicial review	constitutionalism	US District Courts

legal aid	plea-bargaining	State Supreme Court
statutory law	ABA	adversary system
judiciary	Bill of Rights	contingency fees
Miranda v. Arizona	rights culture	pro-bono
litigation	commerce clause	jury
Supreme Court	NRA	militia
criminal law	prosecutor	legal appeal

Write short essays on the following questions.

1. Why is law such an important part of American life?

2. Briefly discuss the historical evolution of American law and the legal system.

3. Examine the arguments for and against either the death penalty or gun control.

4. Attempt to explain attitudes to crime in the USA by analyzing the polls in the text and the websites.

5. What is the role of the US Supreme Court justices?

Further reading

Abadinsky, H. (1995) *Law and Justice: An Introduction to the American Legal System*, Chicago, IL: Nelson-Hall.

American Bar Association (latest edition) *Law and the Courts: a handbook of courtroom procedures*, Chicago, IL: ABA Press.

Apple, J. G. and Deyling, R.P. (1995) *A Primer on the Civil-Law System*, Washington, DC: Federal Judicial Center.

Bedau, H. (2003) (ed.) *Debating the Death Penalty: Should America Have Capital Punishment? The Experts on Both Sides Make Their Best Case*, Oxford: Oxford University Press.

Biskupic, J. and Witt, E. (1997) *Guide to the US Supreme Court*, Washington, DC: Congressional Quarterly Press.

Carp, R. A. and Stidham, R. (1998) *Judicial Process in America*, Washington, DC: Congressional Quarterly Press.

Fine, T. M. (1997) *American Legal Systems: A Resource and Reference Guide*, Cincinnati, OH: Anderson.

Friedman, L. M. (1986) *A History of American Law*, Safety Harbor, FL: Touchstone Books.

Friedman, L. M. (2004) *Law in America: A Short History*, New York, NY: Random House, Modern Library Chronicles.

Hall, K. L. et al. (2010) *American Legal History: Cases and Materials*, Oxford: Oxford University Press.

Hart, P.D. Research Associates, Inc. (2002) *Changing Public Attitudes toward the Criminal Justice System*, New York, NY: The Open Society Institute.

Stumpf, H. P. and Culver, J. H. (1992) *The Politics of State Courts,* New York: Longman Press.
Tushnet, M. V. (1999) *Taking the Constitution Away from the Courts*, Princeton, NJ: Princeton
   University Press.

Websites

Gallup: www.gallup.com/poll/186308/americans-say-crime-rising.aspx
Gateway and links to judicial branch/courts/crime statistics/civil rights/government etc.:
   usinfo.state.gov/usa/infousa
An alternative gateway is www.firstgov.gov
Bureau of Justice Statistics (BJS): bjs.gov/index
Collected polls on crime: www.pollingreport.com/crime.htm
Crime: www.fbi.gov/about-us/cjis/ucr/crime-in-the-us/
Crime: www.gallup.com/poll/186308/americans-say-crime-rising.aspx
Death penalty: www.deathpenaltyinfo.org
Death penalty: www.clarkprosecutor.org/html/death/usexecute.htm
Death penalty (PRRI): http://publicreligion.org/research/20ll
Gallup: www.gallup.com
Gun control: CNN/ORC POLL 7, August 7–8, 2012 http://politicalticker.blogs.cnn.com/2012/
   08/09/cnnorc-poll-august-7-8-guns
National Crime Survey: http://bjs.gov
Roper Center Public Opinion Archives: www.ropercenter.uconn

Chapter 10

The economy

- Economic history
- American economic liberalism: theory and practice
- Social class and economic inequality
- The contemporary economy
- Industry and manufacturing
- Service industries
- Agriculture, forestry and fisheries
- Environmental issues
- Financial and industrial institutions
- Attitudes to the economic system
- *Exercises*
- *Further reading*
- *Websites*

This chapter describes US economic history and social class; examines the contemporary economy; and discusses American attitudes to the economic system.

Historically, the US economy has been characterized by technological change from basic beginnings, and periods of recession, adaptation and growth. Agriculture, hunting and fisheries were the main economic activities until the mid-nineteenth century, when they became more mechanized, efficient and used fewer workers. Industrial and manufacturing output increased rapidly from the nineteenth century and resulted in the US becoming the world's richest country by the early twentieth century.

Between 1945 and 1970, the US achieved a large degree of self-sufficiency and economic dominance. Since the 1970s, major changes have been the growth of service and financial industries; a decline in traditional manufacturing industry; a relative weakening in the US position as other countries became more competitive; instability in trade; and fluctuating budget deficits and dollar values. Globalization (interdependence of world trade and business) has affected the US as it adapts to the changing international economic order. The US is no longer the only global economy and faces competition from Japan, China, India, other Asian Rim countries, Central and South America, and the European Union (EU).

The US economic system has recently experienced the serious effects of a 2007–10 financial crisis and Great Recession when median household income fell; the poverty rate rose; household wealth decreased; the labor market was weak; unemployment increased; the housing market suffered; and GDP growth was flat. Recovery in many sectors was gradual.

Economic history

US economic expansion from the nineteenth century can be explained by the country's size, its natural resources, commercial structures, population growth, characteristics of the people, political independence and the ideological principles that support economic activity.

The indigenous Native American inhabitants of North America had varied economies, ranging from nomadic gathering, fishing and hunting to small settled agricultural communities. A similar basic economy was adopted by colonial Americans and other immigrants, who later developed sophisticated agricultural systems based on farms.

British settlers in the seventeenth century were employed by British companies that were granted trading charters by the English Crown, such as the Virginia

Company, which established Jamestown in 1607. The colonies provided Britain with raw materials but could not compete in manufactured exports with the mother country. This relationship collapsed when Britain imposed tax and trade restrictions. After the War for Independence (1776–83), the US developed its own economic markets. New technology led to a greater variety of goods as Americans expanded agriculture, farmed the prairies and exported more products.

A belief in possibilities and personal advancement encouraged pragmatism, hard work and individual initiative in the people. These qualities have been linked to religion (the Protestant work ethic) and the pioneer spirit of early settlers, whose survival lay in their own ingenuity and efforts. Many Americans today embrace these values: retrain if unemployment occurs, create new jobs or businesses and move to fresh opportunities.

The US in 1800 was still an agricultural society. Some 95 percent of the people lived in rural areas, and the economy was based largely on self-sufficiency. But nineteenth-century growth combined agricultural advances with expanding industrial and manufacturing bases. These were aided by government financial support, economic protectionism and a transport revolution that established railway, canal and road infrastructures.

Agricultural productivity increased as small farmers made use of the transportation system, specialized in selected crops or animals, sold their products to a wider internal market and developed their export potential. But this growth led to overproduction and reduced prices. By the start of the twentieth century, some farmers were having difficulties.

Economic progress in the nineteenth century was also affected by the Civil War (1861–5), as 23 states of the industrializing North opposed 11 Southern agricultural states on issues of slavery and secession from the Union. A Northern victory led to a greater emphasis on the nation's industrial base, with advances in the production of manufactured goods.

Between the Civil War and the First World War (1914–18), the US rapidly industrialized and developed urban and suburban areas. Expansion was based on natural resources, iron and steel production, and steam and electrical power. It was later helped by technical advances and inventions such as the internal combustion engine, the telegraph and telephone, radio, typewriters, assembly-line production and interchangeable-parts technology. Economies of scale in production and distribution led to the growth of large manufacturing units, and the export of manufactured goods became more important than raw materials.

Economic activity was largely free from restrictions. Business operated for profit in a "market economy" that determined the need for and price of goods and conditioned the activity of independent buyers and sellers. There were few restrictions (such as government regulation), and people were largely able to pursue their own economic interests. But this led to unregulated capitalism as big business and the profit motive became central features of American life. Industrial and commercial progress was accompanied by slumps, unemployment and harsh job and living conditions for the expanding population (including African

Americans from Southern states and European immigrants between 1890 and 1910).

The growing economy resulted in the development of new products and the creation of large business corporations in most economic sectors. These based their production and competition policies on marketing, advertising, advanced technology, cheap products, rationalization of the work process, efficient management organization and good service. The growth of corporations enabled the US to export many types of manufactured items abroad, and consumer goods were also spread throughout the domestic American market.

Larger corporations (trusts) were formed by mergers and takeovers, which controlled competition. They were associated with owners like Rockefeller (oil) and Carnegie (steel), whose economic and political power influenced the whole economy. But it was gradually felt that government should regulate these monopolies, which were seen as anti-competitive.

Some anti-trust legislation (e.g., the 1890 Sherman Anti-Trust Law) was passed. But trusts still controlled many areas of production. President Theodore Roosevelt (1901–8) tried to regulate them by preventing restrictive deals

PLATE 10.1 Aerial view of Silicon Valley (from "silicon chips"), southern California and the San Francisco Bay area where a large concentrated number of high-tech companies, such as Google, Facebook, Intel, eBay, Hewlett Packard and Amazon have their corporate headquarters. The photo looks toward San Jose Airport and downtown San Jose.
© *Aerial Archives/Alamy*

between companies on products, prices, output levels and market shares; by limiting mergers that minimized competition; and by improving employment conditions (such as an eight-hour working day). President Woodrow Wilson (1913–21) also attempted to control corporate markets. He passed an anti-trust law, reduced tariffs against foreign competition and reformed agricultural and labor sectors.

However, corporations still had great power and the 1920s ("the Roaring Twenties") created instability and hardship for many people. Low taxes led to a rise in living standards, but too much money circulated in the economy and the consumption of services and goods increased. There was overproduction by factories and farms; overprotection of business against foreign competition through tariff barriers; and financial speculation. The economy collapsed in October 1929 with the Wall Street Crash on the stock market, and many corporate and individual bankruptcies. This marked the beginning of the worst economic depression in US history (the Great Depression).

Demands were made for more government regulation of business activity and for help to those who were suffering socially and economically. President Franklin D. Roosevelt (1933–45) argued that the depression was due to faults in the capitalist system, tried to remedy the situation with his New Deal and was the first President to substantially intervene in the economy by trying to balance public sector services and the private sector market. New regulatory powers over the stock market were initiated by a Securities and Exchange Commission (SEC) and other commissions supervised public utilities such as electricity. The unemployed were given jobs in public-works projects, and government finance was granted to farmers who were suffering badly. A Social Security Act (1935) was the first major federal legislation to provide security against unemployment, job-related accidents and old age. These measures aimed to stabilize the economy, regulate commercial institutions, create internal demand for American products and prevent social and economic hardship.

The New Deal did not solve all the problems. Consequently, governments since the 1930s have intervened in the economy by using legislation and regulatory powers to influence commerce. But US governments are not generally opposed to business and have invested in private sectors such as research, aerospace, development and defense. They have aided economic growth; protected US industry, farmers and manufacturers against foreign competition; used public money to encourage private business; and given land to private interests to develop transport systems. The economy grew and competed successfully with European countries. Despite their acceptance of some free trade and global agreements, US governments do protect the national economy by granting subsidies and imposing tariff barriers on foreign imports, while themselves also experiencing foreign trade restrictions.

The 1944 Bretton Woods Conference in New Hampshire was an attempt at international cooperation, economic liberalization and free trade after the experiences of the two world wars and the Great Depression. It tried to create a system of monetary management among the world's major industrial states, which would stabilize economies, currencies and relations between countries. It established the International Monetary Fund (IMF) and the International Bank for Reconstruction and Development (now part of the World Bank). The Bretton Woods system was relatively effective until the early 1970s but then declined because of inherent weaknesses and the role of dominant currencies, such as the American dollar. However, the IMF and World Bank continue to function.

The US economy grew after the Second World War (1939–45) and, by the 1950s, had achieved global dominance. Large technological, financial, commercial and manufacturing corporations, such as Exxon Mobil, Walmart, General Motors, Chevron, ConocoPhillips, Boeing, General Electric, Ford Motor, IBM, Bank of America Corp, Citi Group, AT&T, Verizon Communications, JP Morgan Chase, Microsoft, Amazon and Google now influence American and overseas business. Some are multinational organizations owned by financial groups with diversified interests and plants worldwide. Others are smaller companies (three-quarters of the US corporate market) that create most jobs, are often owned by individuals and can be very successful and influential.

However, since the mid-twentieth century, the performance of the US economy has fluctuated with periods of inflation (increase in prices and fall in money purchasing values), increased global competition, recessions, weak gross domestic product (GDP) growth and productivity, job shortages, low wages, unemployment and high energy and oil prices.

American economic liberalism: theory and practice

The founders of the US stressed economic freedom. They were influenced by philosophers such as Adam Smith and argued that consumers and producers should pursue their own self-interest and profit-making in a free enterprise economy. The market (not central government) decided what should be produced and what prices should be charged for goods and services based on supply and demand. It was felt that greater competition and trade would result, society would benefit, the economy could produce what was needed, consumers could buy at competitive prices and market forces would control production and efficient distribution.

Many areas of the economy, such as industry, business, airlines, telephone and media systems, energy supplies and railways, are in private rather than public ownership, and US governments are confined to a regulatory role in the economy. Since the 1930s, they have used anti-monopoly and deregulation measures (removal of restrictions on free markets) to promote competition in services and prices in public and private sectors.

Governments (chiefly Democratic) and official bodies intervene more actively in business. They try to influence monetary and fiscal policy such as interest rate changes by the Federal Reserve; subsidies and controls on prices; legislation; and as purchasers of goods and equipment from private industries. Regulation includes safety standards for manufactured goods, labor, welfare and equal employment reforms, environmental and factory protection, training schemes and pro-union improvements in working conditions (such as the federal minimum wage, which in 2016 was $7.25 an hour) and restrictions on banks. Federal regulation may curb freedom of operation for employers (and states) and illustrates the more intrusive role of contemporary government.

Economic restrictions are fiercely debated. Conservatives and corporations argue that there is too much regulation, bureaucracy, government interference and taxation. Liberals generally support an interventionist role in economic matters. But many Americans have a traditional distrust of "big government," disagree about the appropriate role of government in the economy and are skeptical about the ability of government to solve economic and social problems. But they also dislike the near-monopolistic nature of some "big business," which may dominate consumer choice and provide bad service and products. A Gallup poll in June 2016 found that only 18 percent of respondents had a great deal or quite a lot of confidence in big business. But 68 percent of respondents had a great deal or quite a lot of confidence in small business (an increase from 62 percent in 2014).

The US has a relatively large public sector involving state and federal government, the police, fire protection, public education, public health, parks, roads, airports and social security benefits. Since the public sector depends on taxation receipts to operate, the US does not have an absolute "free market" system. Although Americans may support free enterprise, individual initiative and the ability of a competitive market to deliver goods, services and resources means that not all individuals can pursue economic success because of differing circumstances and the influence of factors such as corporate power. But historically it has been generally felt that achievement and material prosperity may result from personal hard work.

Debates are concerned with how much government regulation and corporate power there should be in the economy and whether public and private sectors work efficiently and deliver results. US attitudes were tested when the Great Recession (2010) followed a credit squeeze, consumer debt and the collapse of banks, insurance houses and the housing market. Many people opposed the $700 billion government rescue of the private financial sector.

Corporate behavior can seriously affect the economy, such as insider dealing on the stock exchange and the failure of corporations, such as Enron, WorldCom and Tyco. It can also result in government takeover of banks and the nationalization of insurance/mortgage houses, or the collapse of banks, such as Lehman Brothers in 2008. Historically, Americans have been very skeptical of the stock market, banks and insurance houses, and the Wall Street crash of 1929 casts a long shadow. A June 2014 Gallup poll found that only 26 percent of respondents had a great deal or quite a lot of confidence in banks (from 21 percent in 2012).

A 2008 study by American Human Development Index concluded that the US economic system fails to provide opportunity and choices to all Americans to advance themselves economically and that a belief in free enterprise as the best way to help people out of poverty does not fundamentally reduce inequalities. A Measure of America study in 2013–14 researched aspects of well-being and gave the US a Human Development Index score of 5.03 out of a total of 10. This reflected the severe effects of the Great Recession but also suggested underlying weaknesses of the US economic model to advance well-being.

Social class and economic inequality

Although the US is often portrayed as a classless and egalitarian society, there have always been social and economic inequalities between Americans. These originally formed a class model divided into working, middle and upper classes based on jobs, income, capital and birth. Nineteenth-century industrialization increased the class and wealth gaps between industrialists, manufacturers, financiers and landowners on the one hand and workers on the other. It was argued that class divisions were a natural result of the freedom of competition.

In the twentieth century, American workers were increasingly placed either in the white-collar service sector or the industrial blue-collar sector. It was felt that these groups fell outside European notions of the "working class" and should more appropriately be seen as "lower middle class." But a reduced manufacturing and industrial base has led to a decline in blue-collar workers and service-sector white-collar employees decreased in status and wages. The middle class was also affected by changing conditions and expectations.

A Pew Research Center poll in January 2014 used "lower class" to include those who self-defined themselves as lower or lower-middle classes, and "upper class" for those who perceived themselves as upper or upper-middle class. Lower class respondents had increased to 25 percent of the adult population in 2008 and to 40 percent in 2014 (see Table 10.1), with 44 percent self-identifying themselves as middle class (53 percent in 2008) and 15 percent registering as upper class (21 percent in 2008). The lower class had increased numerically over the other classes and more Democrats than Republicans saw themselves as lower class.

The changes in the period 2008–14 coincided with social and economic shifts, such as the Great Recession (2010), stagnating wages, a decrease in median household income, a lack of opportunities in middle-skilled, middle-income jobs, a growth of low-skilled jobs and a decline in social status for young adults and the elderly. It was widely reported in 2015 that the important American middle class had been squeezed over the past 40 years relative to upper- and

TABLE 10.1 Self-defined class in the US, 2014

Class	% 2014	% 2008
Lower	40	25
Middle class	44	53
Upper	15	21

Source: adapted from the Pew Research Center, January 27, 2014

lower-income groups, and the middle-class share of workers, incomes and jobs declined.

The US is a wealthy country and provides most of its people with one of the world's highest living standards. According to the US Bureau of the Census, the annual median family income of all races was $53,657 in 2014 (half of families received above this figure and half received less). But median income for Black ($35,398) and Latino families ($42,491) fell behind that of White ($60,256) and Asian families ($74,297), creating relative income inequality.

Income inequality is tied to wealth and poverty levels. It is estimated that the top one percent of US households own 34.6 percent of the nation's wealth, the next highest four percent have 27.3 percent, the next highest five percent have 11.2 percent, the next 10 percent have 10 percent, the upper middle 20 percent own 10.9 percent, the middle 20 percent 4 percent, while the bottom 40 percent of households own 0.2 percent of national wealth. The gap between rich and poor in the US is considerable. Inequality of income and wealth was seen in 2013 when 45.3 million Americans (14.5 percent of the population) lived below the annual poverty lines of $23,834 for a family of four and $11,888 for one person. Of these, 27.1 percent were Blacks, 10.4 percent Asians, 23.5 percent Latinos and 12.3 percent Whites.

The contemporary economy

Taxation and federal budgets

Most of the US government's income (used for public spending) comes from income tax paid by individuals and social-security contributions paid by firms and workers. Corporate taxes (by companies on profits) and excise duties are a relatively small part of total federal receipts.

Americans pay federal income tax and also property tax, sales tax and state income tax, in addition to private medical and dental costs. Tax increases to pay for government spending arouse opposition, especially from the middle class and the rich, and they may determine election results. But tax cuts can significantly reduce the provision of public services.

A family with an annual median income in 2014 of $53,657 (half of households below and half above this figure) paid about 25 percent of income in various taxes. Those with higher incomes pay proportionally more taxes. The amount of tax people pay depends on tax cuts, tax breaks and their claims for a range of deductions, such as interest on home mortgages (loans to buy property) and medical bills.

Features of the contemporary economy

The US was the world's biggest economic power in terms of its share of global GDP for over a hundred years until it dropped into second place behind China in 2014. US GDP comprises the goods, services, capital and income the country produces, and in 2015, it was an estimated $17.97 trillion with per capita GDP of $56,300.

The GDP shows that the US has a diversified economy. Its wealth reflects large natural resources (coal, oil, gas, shale, copper, lead, phosphates, uranium, bauxite, iron, timber and hydroelectricity), agricultural output, industrial production and service-sector income. The US supplies 25 percent of the world's agricultural products and manufactured goods (such as machinery, automotive components and vehicles, aircraft, chemicals and high-tech hardware). Traditional heavy manufacturing industries (such as automobiles) have had setbacks and agriculture is under threat, but service sectors have expanded.

The US is one of the world's biggest importers and exporters. This fact and the size of its economy mean that the US is a crucial factor in global trade and business. But the US economy no longer dominates, as it did after the Second World War.

Internationally, the US balance of trade with other countries has been in deficit (importing more goods than it has exported) since 1980. In 2015, for example, exports were worth $1.598 trillion million, while imports were $2.347 trillion. These imports are in traditionally strong American sectors such as automobiles, petroleum, food and drink, machinery, iron and steel and consumer goods such as television sets, cameras and computers. The sectors have suffered because of stronger and cheaper foreign competition.

Globalization and weaknesses in the internal economy have undercut US advantages and forced it to become more interdependent with the economies of other countries and to reduce its protection of home products. American investment capital and assets are an important element in the Canadian,

Latin-American, European and Asian economies. But there is also considerable foreign investment and asset-holding in the US domestic economy.

US governments and corporations generally aim at a cooperative and stable international trading environment. In 2014, America's main export partners were Canada (19.2 percent), Mexico (14.8 percent), China (7.6 percent) and Japan (4.1 percent), while it imported primarily from China (19.9 percent), Canada (14.8 percent), Mexico (12.5 percent), Japan (5.7 percent) and Germany (5.3 percent).

The US finalized the General Agreement on Tariffs and Trade (GATT) in 1994, which tried to promote freer and less protectionist world trade. US attempts to balance world trading blocs included NAFTA in 1994 with Canada and Mexico. The Central American–Dominican Republic Free Trade Agreement (CAFTA-DR) between the US, Costa Rica, the Dominican Republic, El Salvador, Guatemala, Honduras and Nicaragua was in force in 2009. The TPP was signed in 2016 between the US, Australia, Brunei, Canada, Chile, Japan, Malaysia, Mexico, New Zealand, Peru, Singapore and Vietnam, but it is not in force. The US has tried to stabilize its relationships with the European Union, China and India. But there are conflicts between free trade and protectionism, and these agreements may be reevaluated.

The US economy experienced difficulties from the 1970s until the early 1990s due to international competition, domestic conditions and recession. The country had not adapted to a "post-industrial age," in which high-technology and service industries were a dominant part of GDP or to a globalized economy. But industry was restructured and productivity increased with reductions in the workforce, new technology, freer trade and strong corporate management. Investment increased, unemployment and inflation fell, new jobs were created and many people prospered in the mid- to late-1990s.

TABLE 10.2 US average annual inflation rate, 2000–2016 (CPI)

Year	%	Year	%	Year	%
2000	3.4	2006	3.2	2012	2.1
2001	2.8	2007	2.8	2013	1.5
2002	1.6	2008	3.8	2014	1.6
2003	2.3	2009	0.4	2015	0.1
2004	2.7	2010	1.6	2016 (Feb)	1.0
2005	3.4	2011	3.2		

Source: adapted from US Bureau of Labor Statistics (BLS), 2016

However, the early twenty-first century saw another downturn with growth, consumer confidence and manufacturing weak and unemployment and inflation increasing. Moderate recovery took place in 2002 with the GDP growth rate rising to 2.4 percent, although the stock market declined sharply. In 2003, the recovery of the stock market and GDP growth at 3.1 percent were promising signs. But in early 2004, job creation remained weak, jobs were lost, interest rates rose and economic expansion was in doubt. Long-term problems included inadequate investment in economic infrastructure, manufacturing decline, trade and budget deficits, weak wages, low consumer spending and reduced factory output.

The economy shrank and unemployment increased from 7.3 percent in 2008. In 2007–10, the US experienced a severe credit (loans) and banking crisis, financial market turmoil, a collapsed housing sector, a budget deficit, rising unemployment and the Great Recession of 2010. The government was forced to rescue the financial markets. Interest rates were cut to one percent in October 2008 to stimulate credit, promote economic growth and counter the threat of deflation (where falling prices conflict with low or no consumer spending). Deflation of -2.10 was registered in the first quarter of 2009–10.

By 2012, the economy was still weak, although some positive signs were detected in consumer spending, growth, employment and the housing market. It was argued that economic recovery needed a balanced budget package of increased taxes on the rich and spending cuts in order to avoid a US and global recession. The US economy still suffers from austerity measures and the effects of the Recession, and there is dissatisfaction with the government's management of the economy. The US faces geopolitical tensions and volatile economic conditions, the risks and advantages of globalization, and competitive economies in China, India, Japan and Western Europe. American workers are worried about the effects of both globalization and free trade on jobs and wages and many want protectionist solutions. They are pessimistic about the economic future, low wages and stagnation.

The workforce

The workforce of 156.4 million in 2015 was divided by occupation into managerial, professional and technical (37.3 percent), sales and office (24.2 percent), other services (17.6 percent), manufacturing, extraction, transportation and crafts (20.3 percent), and farming, forestry and fishing (0.7 percent). It has mobility and flexibility, but not all workers have gained from economic growth. Arguably, the expansion of technology has led to a "two-tier" labor market in which those at the bottom lack the professional, educational and technical skills of those at the top. The former may not be union members and do not receive pay rises, health coverage and other benefits comparable to the latter. Most gains in household income have gone to the top 20 percent of households. Less-skilled

TABLE 10.3 US annual unemployment rate (percent of workforce), 2000–16

Year	%	Year	%	Year	%
2000	4.0	2006	4.6	2012	8.1
2001	4.7	2007	4.6	2013	7.4
2002	5.8	2008	5.8	2014	6.2
2003	6.0	2009	9.3	2015	5.3
2004	5.5	2010	9.6	2016 (Feb)	4.9
2005	5.1	2011	8.9		

Source: adapted from US BLS, 2016

male workers have seen weak wage growth, job insecurity, unemployment and falling living standards. Unemployment was high from 2000 and during the economic difficulties of 2007–15.

The economic status of women as employees and employers has improved. More women (47.5 percent of the workforce in 2013) work than in the 1960s and males form 52.5 percent. While the proportion of men with jobs has fallen, that of working women has risen. Male average earnings have fallen while those of women have grown. However, although women's wages gained on men's for the first time in the 1980s, women's annual median earnings in 2013 were $27,627 (70 percent of males) and those of men were $39,530. Women in part-time or unskilled work have the lowest rewards but have suffered less than unskilled men because low-skilled men and women have different jobs and differentials.

US labor statistics in 2013 showed the range of large and small percentages of women employed in the following occupations: educational services, health care and social assistance (74.2); finance, insurance, real estate, rental and leasing information (54.7); other services, except public administration (53); arts, entertainment, accommodation and food services (51.2); retail trade (49.3); public administration (44.1); professional, scientific, management, administrative and waste management services (41.9); information (41.7); wholesale trade (29.5); manufacturing (28.9); forestry, agriculture, hunting, fishing and mining (18.5); and construction (9.2). Some occupations comprise over 90 percent of women workers, such as dental hygienists, preschool and kindergarten teachers, hairdressers, administrative assistants and secretaries, speech-language pathologists and licensed practical and vocational nurses.

Well-educated women who continue working after marriage receive the highest rewards (especially those married to high-income husbands) and earnings of the top 5 percent of working women have risen. But fewer wives of lower-skilled men have joined the workforce and wages of lower-skilled working wives have risen more slowly than those of better-educated women. Family income has thus risen at top levels and fallen at the bottom.

There has also been an increase in women business-owners. Their businesses are a growing and influential part of the corporate economy and are often entrepreneurial, small, home-operated and in the service or retail sector. Such firms can suffer from adverse economic conditions and a downturn. But women-owned businesses in the manufacturing and construction sectors are growing and more women are attending business schools.

Industry and manufacturing

Historically, manufacturing and industrial production has been a crucial factor in the US economy. Today, the sector, although suffering problems is still a leading global power, technologically advanced, very diversified and had 20.8 percent of US GDP in 2015. Important areas are the manufacture of heavy transport and automotive equipment (vehicles, aircraft and aerospace components), non-electrical goods, electrical machinery, food products, chemicals, steel, consumer goods, mining, lumber/timber, oil, telecommunications, electronics and high-tech hardware.

The traditional industrial and manufacturing heartland of the US is the Midwest region of the Great Lakes, southern Michigan, northern Ohio and Pennsylvania around Pittsburgh. Growth and production here has fluctuated, declined in some "rust-belt" areas or switched to high-technology industry, and other compensating industrial regions have grown in the Northeast, Northwest and Southwest (California). These specialize in high-tech and computer manufactures. Other fast-growing industrial regions are the Southeast and Texas, where steel, chemical and high-tech industries have developed. But some US businesses have moved their production facilities overseas to save on costs.

The manufacturing and technological base is represented by corporations, such as General Motors (Detroit) and Ford (Michigan) in vehicles, Exxon (New York) in oil-refining, IBM (International Business Machines) (New York) and Microsoft (Washington State) in computing, General Electric (Connecticut) in electronics and Boeing (Seattle) in aerospace and defense. However, the automobile industry had serious problems in 2008, with General Motors, Ford and Chrysler facing bankruptcy and requiring government bailouts, and car cities such as Detroit have suffered.

Although industrial production growth rates fluctuated in the 2000s, the US is the world's second largest producer of industrial goods. In 2013, 15.2 million Americans were employed in manufacturing and 8.9 million in construction. But recession forces have reduced the number of blue-collar workers and

PLATE 10.2 Aerial view of computer and high-technology company Microsoft, with its West Campus at Redmond, near Seattle, Washington State. The photo looks toward the southeast. © *Jelson*

industrial plants, although the US was in 2014 the world's third largest producer of crude oil and the largest producer of natural gas. It is a leader in shale oil and gas production but suffered from falls in oil prices in 2016.

Service industries

Service industries have expanded significantly since the 1950s and are now the leading economic sector with 77.6 percent of GDP in 2015, despite the recession. This process is echoed in other industrialized countries and has encouraged debates about "post-industrial" societies.

The service industries vary in size from small firms to large corporations. They have developed nationwide, but particularly in the Northeast, Northwest and Southwest. They include government services, business and health, banking, finance and taxation consultancy, computer and data processing, hotels, restaurants, leisure activities, trade, personal services (including child day care) and communications. But, although more people are employed in the service sector, many of them are in unskilled or semi-skilled and part-time positions and many aspects of the sector tend to be manager-intensive rather than labor-intensive. However, US service companies are forecast to be the fastest-growing industries in the future and many managed to survive the worst effects of recession in 2008–10.

Agriculture, forestry and fisheries

Although US agriculture, forestry and fisheries have large productivity, they contributed only some 1.6 percent to the GDP and formed 0.7 percent of the labor force in 2015, with 124,000 employed persons in 2013 in these industries.

Agriculture

About 47 percent of the US land area is farmland devoted to crops and livestock. The Midwest is still an important agricultural region, with corn (maize) and wheat as its main crops and large scale livestock and dairy farming in the upper Midwest states.

The South is a center of traditional crops, like tobacco (the Southeast and Kentucky), corn and cotton (the South and Southwest). Its economy has now diversified and grown, so that Texas and Florida are the US's main providers of cattle, sheep, cotton and rice. The West is important for cattle and wheat farming in the Great Plains, fruit and vineyards in the Pacific states and livestock herds in the Southwestern and Rocky Mountain states.

The US is a large food producer and exporter (corn, wheat, soybeans) and is largely self-sufficient in farm products, although there are some imports. In 2013, there were 2.1 million farms in the US. Small subsistence farms have declined, farm sizes have increased (agri-businesses) and labor has been reduced as competition, mechanization, technological advances and specialized farms have increased. High productivity has resulted in occasional surpluses and reduced prices.

US agricultural exports declined in the 1980s as other world markets expanded. Farmers had difficulties because of import restrictions by foreign countries and high dollar values. But free-trade GATT and World Trade Organization (WTO) agreements that reduced tariff barriers have helped to stabilize the world position of American agriculture. However, global tariffs and protectionism continue and liberalization of world trade is problematic.

Forestry

The US ranks fourth in forestry after Russia, Brazil and Canada. Forests cover 32.4 percent of the land area. Most of the forests are in the West, but some are in the South and the North. About 80 percent of the forests are softwoods, and 20 percent are hardwoods; two-thirds produce wood items and timber commercially. Some 70 percent of forests are privately owned, the federal government owns 20 percent and state or local government supervises the rest. In recent years, the environmental aspect of forestry has grown, with an emphasis on eco-system management and increased recreational and wildlife uses of the public forests.

Fisheries

The US ranked third in 2012 after China and Indonesia among world fishing nations in fish catches. Fishing fleets operate from ports on the Atlantic, the Pacific, the Gulf of Mexico and the Great Lakes. Alaska is the leading state, and Louisiana has a large catch (chiefly shellfish), as do Texas and California. Massachusetts and Maine, important fishing centers since the colonial era, are major players in the fisheries industry. But their traditional fishing grounds (shared with the Atlantic provinces of Canada) face potential depletion.

Environmental issues

Public concerns about the environment are influenced by opposing ideologies of Democrats and Republicans and the activities of business and industry. Vehicle, industrial and domestic burning of fossil fuels (such as coal and oil) resulted in the US becoming the world's second largest producer of carbon dioxide emissions after China in 2011. Air pollution and acid rain are widespread, and pollution also results from the run-off of industrial waste, agricultural pesticides and fertilizers. There are limited freshwater resources in much of the West, and desertification has occurred. Farmers have suffered from "dust bowl" conditions due to drought, high temperatures and over-use of the land. Frequent storms, hurricanes, heat waves, wildfires and flooding have increased fears about the potential results of global warming.

Despite signing the Kyoto Climate Change Protocol in 1997, critics argued that the US had not tackled domestic and international environmental concerns. Nevertheless, in 2012 carbon dioxide emissions in the US were at their lowest level for 20 years and the country led the world in reducing emissions over the previous six years from a peak in 2007. These improvements were partly due to a US switch to heating by natural gas, which emits less carbon and partly to a retreat from coal usage. Hydraulic fracturing ("fracking") has accessed shale gas and oil locked in underground rocks and arguably reduced pollution. Renewable energy resources, such as wind turbines, biofuels and solar panels have also contributed to reduced emissions. But the burning of fossil fuels still contributes to global warming, and it is uncertain how permanent the effects of recent innovations, such as fracking, will be.

An impetus for global action resulted in the December 2015 United Climate Change Conference in Paris, where a consensus of participants agreed to limit global warning to less than 2°C compared to pre-industrial levels and to limit temperature increase to 1.5°C. The Paris Agreement would be legally binding if joined by 55 countries that represent 55 percent of global greenhouse emissions between April 2016 and April 2017. China and the US, which account for about 40 percent of total emissions, ratified the Agreement on 3 September, 2016 although there are doubts about future US participation.

International agreements coincide with relatively positively positive findings in US polls, although historically there have been conflicting and very varied responses to the environment. However, a Gallup poll in March 2015 reported that 48 percent of American respondents felt that the US government was doing too little to protect the environment; 34 percent thought that it was doing about the right amount; and 16 percent thought there was too much emphasis on environmental concerns. Later polls suggest that a small majority of people support protection of the environment over the provision of energy supplies.

Financial and industrial institutions

Early American economic development did not require national financial institutions. The economic system slowly became more centralized from the late eighteenth, and most financial and industrial institutions initially operated as private and local concerns.

Corporations and entrepreneurs

The corporations of the nineteenth and twentieth centuries, which were owned by individuals like Henry Ford (automobiles), John D. Rockefeller (oil) and Andrew Carnegie (steel), and smaller corporations under personal or family proprietors, have decreased in numbers, although huge companies such as Microsoft, Apple and Amazon were originally founded by small groups or individuals. Some businesses today are owned by financial conglomerates and multinational companies, which invest in company shares for profit.

The actual running of the businesses is often done by professional accountants, executives or managers who may own only a small percentage of the corporation's stock or shares. The rise of an American executive and managerial culture was aided by the creation of business management schools, which may be independent institutions or sometimes attached to universities, and initiated degrees such as the master of business administration (MBA) and taught business techniques to their students.

Big corporations, such as Exxon, Walmart, General Motors, Ford Motor, General Electric, Citigroup, IBM and AT&T now dominate American business and influence consumer patterns. Smaller corporations may be taken over by

PLATE 10.3 The New York Stock Exchange (under the "Stars and Stripes" in the photo) on 11 Wall Street, New York City. Founded in 1817, it is in Lower Manhattan's Financial District. © *Sean Pavone/Alamy*

larger ones and large corporations expand through mergers in the pursuit of markets and profits.

However, small and medium-sized companies account for some three-quarters of the corporate system and are an important part of the business world. They have historically generated more new jobs than larger corporations, tend to be created by entrepreneurs or are family concerns and are often associated with the service sector. Some succeed and some fail, but all are important in employment statistics as indicators of the state of the national economy.

The ethos of American business attracts people who want to succeed and are prepared to work hard to achieve material success, careers and status, although some Americans are not sympathetic to this culture. Workers and business people had problems in the early 1990s under the pressures of domestic and international recession. Although the financial and business markets improved with the upturn in the economy from 1994, they experienced difficulties in 2000–4 and more seriously with the subprime credit crisis in 2007–8. Banks and financial institutions suffered, and there was large unemployment among employees. Among those affected was Citigroup, once the biggest and most powerful company and bank in the world. It suffered huge losses in the global financial crisis of 2008; was rescued in a stimulus package by the US government; and now ranks third among US banks.

Wall Street

"Wall Street" is the financial center of the US, and it is situated in lower and midtown Manhattan, in New York City. It comprises business institutions, such as stockbrokers and financial companies, banks, insurance corporations, commodity exchanges (that deal in coffee, cotton, metal or corn) and the New York Stock Exchange (NYSE). These institutions deal with huge sums of money and control and invest much of Americans' capital. Corporate America's performance in 2000–08 left much to be desired, and there was evidence of fraud, dubious accounting practices, insider dealing, greed and incompetence. Despite help by a government bailout in 2008, many banks still went out of business, and others were not eager to start lending again, particularly to small businesses that needed aid. A Pew Research Center poll in June 2014 reported that 45 percent of respondents felt that Wall Street helps more than it hurts the economy, but 42 percent had an opposite view.

Large corporations are dependent for their financing and prosperity upon exchanges in which stocks and shares in selected businesses are bought and sold. This system, as well as raising investment money, is an important indicator of businesses' financial standing. New York City's two stock exchanges (the NYSE and the American Stock Exchange) handle the majority of stock sales and purchases in the US. The computerized NASDAQ in New York deals with hi-tech shares but does not have a trading floor like the NYSE. The performance of the stock market has varied considerably in the 2000s, and it has been increasingly influenced by international factors, such as falling oil prices and recession.

The NYSE (founded by the Buttonwood Agreement in 1792) comprises about 1,300 members who trade in stocks and bonds for themselves or as agents for clients. It is a market for the buying and selling of these instruments that are listed on the exchange's trading register and the value of which can fluctuate. A company must have a specified amount of stock and a minimum turnover of trade before it can be listed on the NYSE. The NYSE is internationally known for its Dow Jones Average. This is a list that contains the prices of stocks and bonds in selected industrial and commercial companies on the exchange. It is adjusted throughout the working day and its movements are shown in points. The Dow Jones is influential and international financiers, investors and governments see it as an accurate indicator of the US's economic health.

The banking system

Americans have long been suspicious of banks and market traders. The 1929 Wall Street Crash, when banks collapsed and clients lost money, still affects

PLATE 10.4 General view of traders working on the floor of the New York Stock Exchange, 2011, the world's largest stock exchange, where stocks and bonds are bought and sold.

© *Gerald Holubowicz/Alamy*

PLATE 10.5 The computerized NASDAQ MarketSite stock market in Times Square, New York City, 1971, does not have a traditional trading floor but deals with the hi-tech buying and selling of shares from video displays on a telecommunications network that provide market quotes, financial news and advertisements. It is the world's second largest stock market after NYSE.

© *Sueddeutsche Zeitung Photo/Alamy*

people, and fears revive when the stock market performs badly as in 1987, in 2001 after the 9/11 terrorist attacks on New York and in 2008 with the credit crisis. A Gallup poll in June 2016 found that only 27 percent of respondents had a great deal, or a lot of confidence in the banks.

US law is supposed to regulate the banking system and curb any excessive growth of individual banks. There are about 8,600 different commercial banks in the US, which provide personal and corporate financial services for clients. Some banks are incorporated (or licensed) under national charter and are known as National Banks. Others are regulated under state charters. The banking system has been increasingly deregulated to allow other financial competitors, and banks have moved into new (and riskier) areas such as securities trading, currency dealing and insurance. There are also many non-bank institutions, such as personal credit groups and savings-and-loans associations. The largest banks in 2014 were JPMorgan Chase, Bank of America Corp, Citigroup Inc, Wells Fargo and Goldman Sachs.

It is argued that the banking system is not as closely regulated at federal and state level as it should be, particularly at a time when financial institutions are expanding and when fraud and bank collapses still regularly occur. Some critics argue for more accountability and increased control and regulation over American financial markets. Others want to preserve an unrestricted market and the free enterprise economic system.

Federal Reserve System (The Fed)

The Federal Reserve System (created in 1913) is similar to central or national banks in other countries. Its banking framework comprises 12 Federal Reserve Districts throughout the US, each with its individual Federal Reserve Bank. The system is supervised in Washington by a board of governors and headed by a chairman, who arguably may be more influential in the management of the US economy than politicians and presidents. The governors are appointed by the president and confirmed by the Senate. As independent appointees and custodians of the monetary system, they do not always agree with government economic policies. However, the US Treasury Department (the federal financial department) does generally work closely with the Federal Reserve. The latter influences the financial markets by its supervision of the national debt, adjusts the amount of credit in the monetary sector by changing its deposits with the Federal Reserve Banks and crucially sets the inflation rate.

The Fed decides the minimum financial reserves that must be held by commercial banks for them to operate, adjusts interest rates, issues bank notes, implements US monetary policy and tries to create a stable environment for corporate activity. Most commercial banks are members of the Federal Reserve and hold three-quarters of total bank deposits.

PLATE 10.6 The Fed is the central bank of the US and was created in 1913 to organize a safe and efficient monetary and financial system for the US. The Marriner S. Eccles Federal Reserve Board Building was completed in classical style in 1937 and houses the main offices of the board of governors of the Federal Reserve System in Washington, DC.
© Roman Babakin/Alamy

Trade/labor unions

The Knights of Labor was formed in 1869 to organize workers and to press for better employment and social conditions. Further efforts to create labor organizations led in 1886 to the American Federation of Labor (AFL), which was a collection of independent craft unions.

More effective frameworks for worker representation and collective bargaining between employers and employees were established in the 1930s, after strikes and often violent struggles between unions, the police, government and employers. The Congress of Industrial Organizations (CIO), which was based on manufacturing industry, was formed in 1935. The AFL and the CIO then merged in 1955 to form an umbrella institution, the AFL–CIO. A majority of unions and their members are now affiliated with the AFL–CIO.

American unionism is more associated with construction and manufacturing industries than white-collar jobs and the service sector. Unions lost members and influence after being a powerful economic force from the 1930s to the 1950s. A minority of the labor force are now union members (11.3 percent in 2013) compared with 35.5 percent in 1945.

The decline in union membership stems from economic trends, such as the growth of service and high-technology industries in a post-industrial economy, foreign competition, recession, increased automation and advanced equipment, less need for blue-collar workers, increased unemployment among union members, the cost of unionization, downsizing of firms and outsourcing to cheaper labor and factories overseas. The failure of unions to protect the jobs of white- and blue-collar workers in the 1970s and 1980s also led to a drop in union influence. Companies restructured the labor market, sacked full-time staff and employed cheap contract freelancers. A two-tier workforce was created with skilled, highly paid top staff and a poorly paid membership with limited industrial strength.

American unions have the right to strike, but this may be restricted by cooling-off periods and compulsory arbitration. Work stoppages can be unpopular and counterproductive since strikers may lose their jobs. After a period when industrial action was low, the number of strikes increased in 2011–12 but fell to 15 in 2013 involving 55,000 workers.

US unions have achieved pay and insurance benefits for members, but some workers regard job security as more important since there are few company redundancy payments, workers have little job security and minimum wages are low and unevenly applied.

Many American unions are not highly organized, do not have the historical influence or political motivation of European labor and have not attracted a mass membership. There are several reasons for this situation. First, the political and economic power of employers and anti-union legislation by Congress (such as the Taft–Hartley Act of 1947) have minimized union impact. Second, the laissez-faire attitudes of the US economy and a trust in individualism encourage workers to believe in the possibility of upward mobility, which limits political identification with union activity. Third, blue-collar workers often look to the Republicans for economic answers. Fourth, the "Red Scare" of the 1920s and anti-Communist agitation in the 1950s neutralized potential left-wing influences, and union membership tends to be at variance with the more politicized goals and ideology of union leaders. Fifth, corruption and scandals in the unions have alienated workers. Sixth, immigration to the US and the formation of ethnic groups has detracted from the solidarity of trade unionism. Seventh, there have been divisions between skilled and unskilled workers and between different craft unions. Workers have not been closely involved in corporate policymaking and unions have not consistently influenced the national economy. A Gallup poll in June 2015 found that 58 percent of respondents approved of labor unions, 36 percent disapproved and 53 percent thought that unions would become weaker.

There has been a slight increase in union membership among African and Asian Americans in recent years, and the AFL–CIO leadership is stronger. Although shortages of skilled and unskilled workers in prosperous times allow unions to press for wage increases and better conditions, workers do suffer from recessionary cutbacks and unemployment.

Attitudes to the economic system

A Gallup poll of 13–17 July, 2016 prior to the presidential election reported that the economy was seen by 27 percent of respondents as the most important problem facing the country. Areas of particular concern were the economy in general (12 percent); unemployment/jobs (7 percent); the federal budget deficit (4 percent); the gap between rich and poor (2 percent); lack of money (2 percent); and wage issues and corporate corruption (1 percent each). Such worries influence people's voting behavior.

An Allstate/*National Journal* Heartland Monitor Poll XXV in January 2016 found that respondents were divided over the economy. They felt that government, politicians and financial institutions do not satisfactorily confront economic problems. Twenty-five percent of respondents believed that the US was headed in the right direction, and 62 percent thought it was on the wrong track. The threat of unemployment, cuts in wages and working hours, the minimum and living wages, job stress and lack of finance were concerns for many people. The Gallup US Economic Confidence Index of July 12, 2016 showed that some job creation and industrial market results since 2010 had not greatly increased American optimism about the economy. Twenty-five percent of respondents rated the economy as "good" or "excellent," while 31 percent said it was "poor." The Index suggested a downward movement in 2016 and falling expectations for the economy. It was felt that only significant improvement in the labor market and economic growth would encourage greater public confidence. The public supported a combination of spending cuts and tax increases and thought that raising taxes on the richest incomes would benefit the US economy, protect the middle class and cut the budget deficit.

The performance of the economy was linked to doubts about trade and globalization. While many Americans think that international trade is largely good for the US economy, others are protectionist and believe that free trade costs jobs, undermines wages and does not always reduce prices. A Gallup poll in April 2016 found that 58 percent of respondents thought that foreign trade is good for economic growth by producing increased US exports, but 34 percent saw it as a threat to the US economy from receiving foreign imports.

A Pew Research Center poll of February 10, 2016 addressed traditional questions about the US economy. Sixty-five percent of respondents said that the system "unfairly favors powerful interests," while 34 percent thought it was "generally fair to most Americans." A May 4, 2015 Gallup poll found that while 31 percent of respondents thought that the distribution of wealth in the US was fair, 63 percent felt that it should be more evenly spread among a larger percentage of the people. Fifty-two percent of respondents agreed that the government should redistribute wealth by heavy taxes on the rich, while 45 percent thought that it should not.

However, a Gallup poll in October 25, 2013 showed that fewer Americans now feel they have the opportunity to progress, with 52 percent of respondents having plenty of possibilities and 43 percent having few. The polls suggest that the American dream of economic success has been undermined by rising income inequality, high unemployment and less mobility. The belief that each generation would improve on their parents' achievements was seen as likely by 51 percent of respondents and unlikely by 48 percent. Only half of respondents now accept the American dream that hard work and effort will bring success.

Inequality of income and opportunity in the US invited the question of government aid for the poor in the form of benefits or welfare. Historically, many Americans have thought that they do more harm than good and that the government cannot afford to do more to help the needy.

Government aid to the poor and who or what is to blame for poverty have been divisive issues on both the right and the left. In the 2014 Pew poll, while 44 percent said that the poor can easily get government benefits without doing anything in return, 47 percent believed poor people "have hard lives because government benefits do not go far enough to help them to live decently." The Conservative right tend to believe in the first position and a Democratic liberal majority supports the second. The blame for a person being poor was due to lack of effort on his or her part (39 percent) or because of circumstances beyond his or her control (50 percent).

Exercises

Explain and examine the significance of the following names and terms:

AFL–CIO	Wall Street	entrepreneurs
Federal Reserve	NYSE	New Deal
Dow Jones Average	anti-trust laws	corporations
recession	inflation	monopoly
service industries	arbitration	trade balance
budget deficit	GDP	deregulation
Rockefeller	NASDAQ	Roaring Twenties
blue-collar workers	Bretton Woods	raw materials
the Great Depression	globalization	free trade
tariffs	median income	Knights of Labor
environmentalism	fracking	social mobility

Write short essays on the following questions.

1. What is meant by the American "free enterprise" economic system? Examine its claimed advantages and disadvantages.

2. Comment critically on the present state of the US economy.

3. What do the opinion polls in this chapter tell us about people's attitudes to the US economic system?

4. What are the strengths and weaknesses of the US trade-union movement?

Further reading

Brenner, R. (2002) *The Boom and the Bubble: The US Economy Today*, London: Verso.

Chandler, A. D. Jr (1993) *The Visible Hand: The Managerial Revolution in American Business*, Cambridge, MA: Belknap Press of Harvard University Press.

Dethloff, H. C. (1997) *The United States and the Global Economy since 1945*, New York: Harcourt Brace.

GfK Roper Consulting Green Gauge US Survey/ Johnson, S. C., (2011), The Environment: Public Attitudes and Individual Behavior – A Twenty-Year Evolution.

Gordon, J. S. (2005) *Empire of Wealth: The Epic History of American Economic Power*, New York: Harper Perennial.

Heilbroner, R. and Singer, A. (1999) *The Economic Transformation of America: 1600 to the present*, New York: Harcourt Brace.

Krugman, P. (2004) *The Great Unravelling: From Boom to Bust in Three Scandalous Years*, London: Penguin.

Lind, M. (2012) *Land of Promise: An Economic History of the United States*, New York: Harper.

Mansfield, E.D., Mutz, D.C. and Brackbill, D. (2014) *Effects of the Great Recession on American Attitudes Toward Trade*, Annenberg, University of Pennsylvania (download).

Stiglitz, J. (2002) *Globalization and its Discontents*, New York: Norton.

The World Almanac and Book of Facts (2015) New York: World Almanac Books (Infobase Learning).

Websites

AFL–CIO: www.alfcio.org/

Class and social trends: www.pewsocialtrends.org

Economic statistics, income and poverty: www.census.gov/

Effects of Recession on American Attitudes Toward Trade: https://www.google.co.uk/search?q=great+recession+and+trade%3A+pdf&ie=utf-8&oe=utf-8&client=firefox-b-ab&gfe_rd=cr&ei=p2s2WfSOKfPv8AeT_5rwCA#q="great+recession+and+trade:+PDF+November+10,+2014Environment: www.brookings.edu/papers/2012/02_climate_change_rabe_borick.aspx

Fairness in the economic system: www.pewresearch.org/fact-tank/2016/02/10/

Gallup Special Report on American Economy: www.gallup.com/opinion/polling-matters/184586/special-report-proposals-fix-american-economy.aspx

Institute for Policy Studies – Reports: www.ips-dc.org/

New York Stock Exchange: www.nyse.com

US Bureau of Labor Statistics: www.bls.gov

US Bureau of Economic Analysis (BEA): www.bea.gov/

US Federal Reserve: www.federalreserve.gov/

US Department of Labor: www.dol.gov/

US Government's Official Web Portal: www.usa.gov/

US Department of State (US Economy): http://usinfo.org/enus/

US Government Printing Office: www.access.gpo.gov/su_docs/budget/index.html

usinfo.state.gov/usa/infousa/trade/tradeovr.html

usinfo.state.gov/products/pubs/oecon/html

American views on the Economy and Obama: www.theatlantic.com/politics/archive/2016/02/america-economic-outlook

Chapter 11

Social services

- Social services history
- The organization of contemporary social services
- Public social services
- The needy and the poverty line
- Voluntary services
- Healthcare
- Housing
- Attitudes to social services
- *Exercises*
- *Further reading*
- *Websites*

This chapter examines the history of US social services, which are now provided by the public, private and voluntary sectors. Together they cover healthcare, pensions, housing, disability, unemployment and other needs.

The public sector supplies state and federal benefits and aid on both contributory and non-contributory bases. The private sector consists of businesses, such as hospitals, doctors and the housing market, that deliver services to people who pay for them with their own capital or from insurance policies. The voluntary nonprofit sector and charities are additional to the public and private frameworks; are funded mainly from personal and corporate donations; and provide help to those in need, often without payment.

The availability and nature of US social services has changed under the influence of historical events and the attitudes of citizens and politicians. They are also conditioned by experiences with the actual workings of institutions and the demands of social life.

Americans have traditionally seen themselves as self-reliant and independent. Social provision has been a personal matter and the responsibility of individuals or families rather than state or federal institutions. People are still generally expected to look after themselves or to buy services from the private enterprise market, which is supposed to satisfy demand.

However, since the 1930s, there was a greater awareness that some people were unable to provide for themselves because of economic and personal circumstances. Reformers felt that the delivery of social help should be a national responsibility. The scope of many services has consequently changed and been extended to new areas of social security, welfare assistance, insurance, healthcare and housing needs. But such provisions have not created a welfare state similar to models in some nations, which have centrally organized, comprehensive and universally (freely) accessible social services financed by taxation and workers' national insurance contributions in areas of need such as healthcare.

Although the social services have grown and are now diverse and complex, some critics feel that coverage is patchy, expensive and unequal. It is argued that a truly universal system would be more rational, responsive to need and cover all citizens. Others oppose such proposals on the traditional grounds of self-reliance, private markets and funding. Spending on public and welfare services has increased since the 1960s, and the country does help some of its neediest inhabitants, such as people with disabilities, children, the sick, war veterans, the unemployed and pensioners. Nevertheless, Americans generally still expect other individuals to provide for themselves out of their own resources.

Government policies in 1996 restricted some existing welfare programs, suggesting that the US was moving further away from universal models and toward more privatized services. But calls for improvement resulted in a reworking of social security, and legislation in March 2010 for a reformed healthcare system that has attracted debates on its scope and outcome.

Social services history

Three hundred years ago, the newly emerging country had few large urban centers and was primarily a rural society in which most people worked in farming. Until the 1930s, there were no widespread public services for the population. The large majority had to be self-reliant in providing for their own social, health, employment and housing needs.

Free market economic theories and images of the independent farmer and sturdy frontier folk conditioned American mythologies. But early pioneers could be cooperative and provided collective support and protection, as did many

PLATE 11.1 The Ronald Reagan Institute of Emergency Medicine, George Washington University, Washington, DC was established (1991) in response to the global growth of and need for emergency medicine. It also recognized the Emergency Department's role in saving the life of President Reagan after the 1981 attempted assassination. The university is involved in disaster medicine, emergency care, education, training, systems, planning and response.
© GFC Collection/Alamy

Native American communities. Such contrasting images illustrate the tension in US life between individualism and communalism. They also affect how Americans respond to debates about provision of social services today.

Industrialization and urbanization increased in the late-eighteenth and nineteenth centuries, bringing wealth to many people but misery to others. Social assistance was still largely private and individualistic or sometimes provided by voluntary charities, such as the aid given by ethnic and religious groups to their members. However, a small amount of help was also supplied by state and local governments. This mixture of services was conditioned by the tradition of self-reliance. There was (and still is) a distinction made in the US between the "deserving" poor who could be helped to better themselves through aid and the "undeserving" poor who were allegedly unwilling to work and improve their own conditions.

Most Americans did not approve of central government organizing too many of society's affairs and jealously protected their independence. Politicians avoided intervention in, and government spending on, social help. Consequently, no adequate national system of public social services developed in the late-nineteenth and early-twentieth centuries.

This system of self-reliance, fragmented aid and laissez-faire social philosophy (letting things take their own course) could not cope with the economic collapse and large-scale unemployment of the 1930s Great Depression, which followed the 1929 stock market crash caused by an over-supply of money and institutional weakness in the financial system. The resources of private, public and voluntary organizations proved insufficient in the 1930s when an estimated 40 percent of the population lived in relative poverty.

The situation improved with Democrat President Franklin D. Roosevelt's New Deal in the mid-1930s. He wanted to rectify faults in the free enterprise economy and to provide social protection. Contemporary government aid programs stem from his policies, which recognized federal responsibility for the poor and needy. Agencies were created to regulate the economy. Social security legislation in 1935 established pension and unemployment benefits for workers, which depended on the contributions paid by employees during their working lives. The Wagner Act protected labor rights for collective wage bargaining and the Fair Labor Standards Act introduced a minimum wage and restricted working hours. The Works Progress Administration provided jobs in public sector programs for the unemployed and tried to improve the social and economic problems of African and Native Americans.

However, these programs were not comprehensive and were directed toward people who were willing to work. Publicly financed non-contributory welfare was unpopular in 1930s America, and there was antagonism toward those who would not help themselves. But new federal welfare programs, Aid to Families with Dependent Children (AFDC) and General Assistance (GA), did help the needy families, children and people with disabilities.

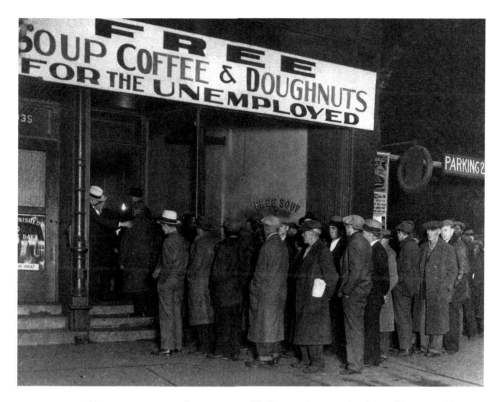

PLATE 11.2 Men waiting outside gangster Al Capone's soup kitchen, Chicago, November 13, 1930, which distributed free food to the unemployed and needy during the Great Depression.
© *Bettmann/Getty*

After the 1930s, reformers argued for increased services. Federal and state governments became more involved in planning social policies. Government thinking changed as publicly funded programs expanded after the Second World War. War veterans, for example, were given federal medical, educational and housing benefits ("GI Bill of Rights"). A new culture of "entitlement" or "rights" to public services became apparent and it was felt in some quarters that the US should be able to care for more of its citizens in need.

Although the federal government gradually became more concerned with providing public social services, this expansion was piecemeal and a response to need and popular pressure, rather than a commitment to a consistent national policy. Nevertheless, social programs were developing and covered greater numbers of people.

From the 1960s to the 1980s, more federal and state money was spent on public social services. Medicare (1965) provided health care for the those over 65-years-old based on subscription charges during their working lives; Medicaid

(1965) organized health services for the poor under 65-years-old without subscription; and a food-stamp program gave coupons (electronic debit cards since 2004) to the needy for the purchase of food in specified shops. Government departments, such as the US Department of Housing and Urban Development, Department of Transportation and Corporation for Public Broadcasting supervised social developments.

President Lyndon Johnson (Democrat 1963–8) introduced important programs in his "War on Poverty" and "Great Society" campaigns, which were intended to alleviate need and suffering. He introduced initiatives (such as preschool "Head Start" classes for children of low-income families, funding for school districts and grants to enable poor students to enter college) that attacked poverty and unemployment through education, job training and regional development. These policies were intended as opportunities for people who were prepared to work and better themselves.

Nevertheless, the reforms formed a basis for future public social services, and more agencies and departments were established to implement the new programs. In this expansive climate, some of the poor and needy increasingly came to regard non-contributory "welfare" and healthcare as a right and the number of claimants grew.

Spending on public social services increased through the 1970s and 1980s, and there was a move away from having huge defense and military expenditures. But presidents after Johnson differed in their attitudes to social service and welfare schemes. It also became more difficult to persuade Congress to allocate public money to these developments. Economic problems by 1980, such as rising inflation, curtailed new social legislation.

President Ronald Reagan (Republican 1980–8) tried to reduce the cost of public programs. He wanted Americans to be more responsible for their own lives through self-help and to depend less on government aid. However, the cost of social security and welfare schemes to the federal budget increased. Public social programs grew relatively quickly, but Republican administrations have not been keen to raise income taxes to pay for them.

President George W. Bush (Republican 1988–92) also wanted to reduce public spending but had to meet increased demand by tax increases. The Clinton administration (Democrat 1992–2000) tried to introduce universal health care in 1993, financed by individual and corporate contributions, that would improve the delivery of health services by controlling costs. The reform collapsed due to public and business opposition. Instead, there were demands from a Republican Congress for greater curbs on social-services spending.

In 1996, Clinton changed US welfare policy by cutting public spending on AFDC. Some saw this as an unraveling of New Deal programs, returning the US to semi-privatized social services and negatively affecting large numbers of people, such as families and children. Others argued that the welfare reforms moved the US positively from a system of debilitating non-contributory benefit entitlement to one of personal responsibility.

Welfare aid was devolved from federal authorities to the individual states in 1996–7. There are now different programs [Temporary Assistance for Needy Families (TANF)] and scales of help. Federal grants have been directed by the states to training schemes and many people have moved from welfare into jobs, education and training. But economic downturns and rising unemployment can create problems for individuals, families and welfare programs.

Opinion polls during the George W. Bush (Republican 2000–08) administrations suggested conflicting attitudes to social services. For example, while some of the public seemed to favor universal healthcare financed out of increased taxation, others (including the corporate sector) did not. A partial privatization of social-security and welfare programs to offset the costs of the system was initially welcomed but later opposed.

There was also opposition when the Obama administration (Democratic 2008–16) passed the Affordable Care Act (ACA) through Congress in 2010. The Act was meant to extend health insurance coverage to 50 million uninsured Americans by 2014. It was a landmark healthcare reform, like Medicare and Medicaid; its provisions were upheld by the Supreme Court in 2012; but it may be curbed by a Republican Administration in 2017.

The organization of contemporary social services

Americans rely for their social protection on contributory and non-contributory federal and state programs (public sector); insurance-based services paid for by individuals or work place groups (private sector); and help given by publicly supported voluntary bodies to the needy. These sectors overlap, and people may receive help from several of them at various times in their lives as they privately insure themselves by paying for healthcare and pension plans in addition to contributing to federal Social Security and employer benefit packages. They also benefit from subsidies in education, housing, tax breaks, food help and Medicaid.

Social services in the public sector are large budget items for government, but the quality of some public services varies from state to state. This is partly because of "matching-funds" policies (whereby states have to equal federal grants or groups compete in matching programs and finance within a state); the wealth of individual states; their prioritization of programs; states' cost of living conditions; and their need to produce balanced budgets.

Budget responsibilities for the main public-sector organization are allocated between Washington, DC and the states. At the federal level, public services are administered through government programs and different Departments, such as the Department of Health and Human Services. The creation as the Department of Health, Education and Welfare (HEW) in 1953 acknowledged national responsibility for and the importance of social services.

The state and local levels deliver their own and federal public social services. These are also often divided between separate bodies, although, in some states, there are umbrella agencies that combine health, welfare and other related programs.

Public social services

Public social services form a patchwork of provisions but are divided into two main parts. The first is the Social Security system, to which workers contribute during their working lives and through which benefits are earned for them and their dependents. The second includes people who receive assistance based on need. This is given according to means or income ("means-testing"), but it is not tied to contributions and is generally known as "welfare."

Some citizens depend on a welfare safety net based on public funds. Others debate its bureaucratic complexity, inefficiency, incompleteness, effects on the morals and initiative of welfare clients, abuse and cost. Public sector services (particularly in healthcare, Social Security and welfare) continue to be controversial issues in American politics.

Social Security benefits

Social Security is the largest social services program in the US and directly affects most people. It is administered from Washington, and in 2016, its total annual payments to beneficiaries amounted to $929 billion. But critics argue that it does not keep all people over 65 out of economic difficulties.

Social Security originated in the 1935 Social Security Act. It is a social insurance program and covers one main area: the Old Age, Survivors, Disability and Health Insurance program (OASDHI). This is concerned with benefits, such as retirement pensions, healthcare, disability, survivorship and death payments. Employees, employers and the self-employed contribute to Social Security, and 59 million people (including survivors/dependents and families) received benefits in 2013. For example, pensions on retirement at the age of 65 amounted to a monthly maximum of $2,431 in 2014 for a single worker.

Medical care for the elderly over 65 (Medicare) is usually grouped under Social Security. It was established in 1965, covered much of the costs for the hospital medical treatment of elderly and disabled people and in 2016 cost $595 billion. However, because of the incomplete coverage of Medicare, many elderly people cannot afford the full cost of some long-term treatments. They usually need additional private insurance or savings for the balance of medical fees. The 2010 Affordable Care Act (ACA) created a panel to study Medicare spending and attempts to find ways to reduce waste and fraud in the system.

Unemployment payments are also included under Social Security. The US Treasury holds a trust fund for unemployment compensation, which is directed by the Department of Labor to individual states that administer their

PLATE 11.3 Campaigners in favor of protecting and maintaining Social Security protest at the US Capitol, Washington, DC against a Republican tax plan that would cut Social Security benefits, September 24, 1998.
© *Richard Ellis/Alamy*

own program. Most workers are covered; unemployment benefits last for up to 26 weeks; and the compensation is between 50 and 70 percent of an average weekly pretax wage. In 2013, the average weekly benefit was $310.

Social Security is problematic because more workers are needed to support a growing elderly population and the cost of the system increases. It has been estimated that the fund will be exhausted by 2041 and that pensions will be progressively reduced and eventually abolished if taxes are not raised and other alternatives such as privatization and reduced benefits are not accepted. The future of Medicare is more precarious, and the program may be exhausted by 2020. Alternatives to collapse are higher taxes, capital injections, privatization and fewer benefits. As part of the ACA 2010 healthcare reforms, Medicare benefits for the old and disabled were increased in 2011, and drug companies were obliged to pay annual fees.

Since Social Security may not cover all the bills payable for old age, illness and unemployment, many Americans have to call upon additional private resources, such as savings, investments and insurance. Some employers and unions may also provide further retirement, unemployment, health and life insurance services for employees, sometimes based on employer, union and worker contributions.

Welfare programs

Public debate about poverty in the US led to federal legislation in the 1960s. This provided financial help, work, training and rehabilitation for the needy and poor, resources to house and feed the homeless and healthcare for the sick. Aid was dependent on means-testing of individuals to prove lack of financial provision. The total government spending on welfare in federal, state and local programs in 2016 was $1,084 billion, including $610 billion on Medicaid and $474 billion on other welfare programs or some 6 percent of the federal budget.

Until 1996, the main federal welfare programs, or non-contributory aid to the needy, consisted of Medicaid, AFDC and food stamps. There are other programs under the GA scheme that provide income support, cash grants, housing aid, Supplemental Security Income (SSI) for the elderly and poor, school meals and help with other basic necessities.

Medicaid is a direct federal health program that started in 1965. It provides health coverage to Americans, such as eligible adults, children, pregnant women, elderly adults and people with disabilities, who lack the money or insurance to pay for services. It is administered by states according to federal requirements. The scope of Medicaid is still variable among states, with some providing more aid than others.

Under the ACA (2010), the poorest Americans without insurance will be potentially included in an improved Medicaid program. Medicaid is intended to be a partnership between federal and state governments, and each state has their own Medicaid eligibility standards based on a percentage of federal poverty levels. A number of states are expanding Medicaid to allow more people to qualify, reaching 72.5 million in 2014. However, not all states have chosen to expand their eligibility standards for increased federal funding (27 states in 2014 or 10 million low-income citizens). Without increased state Medicaid, residents who would otherwise be eligible remain uninsured, unless supported by federal subsidies.

AFDC was, until 1996, a program of federal aid to the poor. Aid to families (including single parents) with children was based on need. Payments varied between states, with southern states generally paying less than northern ones. By 1996, AFDC supported 15 million persons, of whom two-thirds were children.

AFDC was abolished in 1996. Welfare responsibility passed to the states, which receive federal grants to run programs, called TANF. The states determine eligibility and benefit levels. There is a five-year lifetime limit on welfare benefits, which are not automatic, and most fit adults are required to work after two years on welfare. In 2012, TANF payments covered 28.9 million recipients annually. The states with greatest TANF expenditure were California, Florida, Texas, Illinois, Massachusetts, Michigan, New York, New Jersey, Pennsylvania, Ohio, Wisconsin and Washington.

As part of TANF schemes, "Workfare" (work + welfare) programs require that welfare recipients, such as single parents, should be prepared to work (often in public service jobs), take part in job training schemes or attend educational courses. Care facilities are sometimes provided for families with small children, but these are often inadequate. Such programs were intended to encourage recipients to move off welfare and into secure jobs.

The "food stamp" federal program derives from the 1964 Food Stamp Act, but it is now called the Supplemental Nutrition Assistance Program (SNAP). It provides food aid for low- or no-income people and their families, who lack an adequate diet. Recipients received coupons or stamps, which were used to buy food in approved shops at reduced prices. Food stamps were a symbol of poverty, but they were changed to electronic benefit transfer (EBT) cards in 2004 and are limited to three months, unless the recipients are working. The Department of Agriculture annually defines an adequate low-cost diet and administers the federally financed program through state governments.

In 2014, experiencing job losses, rising prices and a credit squeeze, 46.5 million Americans relied on the food program to feed themselves and their families, an increase from 40.2 million in 2010 at an annual cost of $74.1 billion, or an average of $125.35 for each person per month in food assistance. But price increases have reduced the value of the benefits, which have not increased relative to costs, although it is an essential part of the federal social safety net for low-income Americans.

This welfare system provides some assistance for the needy, but people who are unemployed for long periods (and who have no resources) may receive little help from the government. Employment is therefore a crucial factor for most Americans and determines their ability to provide for themselves. The restructuring of AFDC means that after two years on welfare, an individual must find a job. Hardship exemptions are available for the very poor who cannot find work when the benefit ends. But most people will be dependent on gaining jobs, which tend to be poorly paid and difficult to obtain for welfare recipients in hard times.

According to the US Census Bureau, 52.2 million people (21.3 percent of the population) were enrolled in means-tested government assistance programs ("welfare") in 2012. People entered or left the programs at different times during the course of a year and from year to year. But participation rates in 2012 were highest for Medicaid (15.3 percent) and SNAP (13.4 percent) and lowest for TANF and GA.

The needy and the poverty line

Welfare payments in the US have historically been made to people who do not have the resources to live at an appropriate minimum standard. Eligibility for many welfare programs is based on the "official poverty level," which is calculated annually by the Federal Social Security Administration. It determines earned income levels below which a household is classified as "poor," exclusive of non-cash benefits such as food cards. The annual average poverty threshold for a family of four in 2013 was $23,834 and $11,888 for single people.

The number of people living in poverty fluctuates because of unemployment and the state of the economy. The US Bureau of the Census has reported that the percentage of those of all races below the poverty line was 13.5 percent in 1990, which then declined to 11.3 percent in 2000 before rising again with the subprime crisis of 2008 to 14.5 percent in 2013. This figure amounted to 45.3 million Americans, of whom 27.1 percent were Black, 10.4 percent were Asian, 12.3 percent were White and 23.5 percent were Latino.

Poverty remains a reality for a sizeable minority of Americans who have low or no incomes. The poorest and most deprived people are concentrated in inner-city areas, but poverty is also a feature of rural regions. Poor households may consist of single mothers or fathers with children, or people who may be pensioners, disabled or unemployed.

A tax aid designed to lift the working poor (with or without dependent children) above the poverty line is the earned-income tax credit (EITC) established in 1975. Instead of facing higher taxes as their incomes increase, low-earning individuals can claim EITC and qualify for a tax credit up to a maximum amount from the Internal Revenue Service (IRS). More people would be in poverty without this aid, but the working poor are still a vulnerable group. EITC has been part of political debates in the US as to whether raising the minimum wage or increasing EITC is a better idea to help eradicate poverty. Majorities in surveys suggest that the EITC program should be expanded.

Fewer Americans are poor today than in the past, and the official poverty rate for 2015 decreased to 13.5 percent or 43.1 million people. But the gap between rich and poor is considerable. Critics maintain that the federal government should provide funds to eradicate poverty. Others feel that welfare programs are expensive and inefficient and do not give incentives to the poor to help themselves. It is argued that an "under-class" has developed that is dependent on welfare ("the dependency culture") and includes disaffected people who have opted out of national life. The 1996 restriction of federal welfare may break the cycle of dependency, but its success assumes growth in the national economy and the creation of jobs.

Single-parent families

US Census Bureau figures showed that in 2013 there were 116.3 million households of varying sizes and composition in the US. Of these, some 20.8 million were single parent families, including 15.2 million that were headed by single mothers with no husband present (13.1 percent of US households) and 5.6 million were headed by a single father with no wife present (4.8 percent). Around half of these parents never married, and the other half were divorced, separated or bereaved. Some 55 percent of Black children and 31 percent of Latino children live with one parent, compared to 20 percent of White children and 13 percent of Asian children. These proportions have remained relatively constant.

Single parent families are associated with the poverty line, welfare programs and minorities. The 2013 Census reported that, of those children being raised without a father present, 45 percent lived below the poverty line. For those living with a father only, about a quarter lived below the poverty line. Many more Black and Latino children are raised in poverty and often have a harder time financially than White children. By comparison, some 13 percent of children with both parents present in the household live below the poverty line.

Two-thirds of single mothers were working outside the home in 2013, although only half were employed full-time all year long for variable wages. In single father families, employment was more frequent, although still not highly paid for many. However, some one-parent families have incomes above the official poverty level, and their children receive only a minimum of welfare payments, such as free school meals. The overall picture reflects a diverse situation, with gradations between forms of poverty. But children raised in single-parent households in the US are far more likely to live in conditions of relative poverty and hardship than households where both parents are present.

Voluntary services

Given the inability of federal and state governments to meet all the social requirements of the population, the existence of voluntary organizations that help those in need continues to be important. They are a complementary third sector to the private and public sectors.

A range of social services are organized by local and national bodies, which help the disadvantaged and campaign on their behalf. Historically, contributions (with tax breaks or relief) by Americans to such bodies are generous, and 75 percent of households give money to them. Nationally, institutions like the Rockefeller and Ford foundations and other smaller bodies perform important roles in funding care research and health and welfare programs.

On a grassroots level, voluntary organizations (such as charities and churches) and unpaid volunteers are crucial for people in local communities. They provide professional and non-professional aid; organize help for sick or elderly people; run hospitals, care centers, clinics, retirement homes and shelters for the homeless; and visit old, disabled and needy people. They give what is often much-needed assistance and comfort. An estimated 50 percent of Americans over 18 (particularly retired persons) do volunteer work.

Healthcare

According to Centers for Disease Control and Prevention (CDC) in 2014, the US allocated 17.5 percent of its GDP ($3.0 trillion) to healthcare, which was among the highest global figures. But another 2014 study by The Commonwealth Fund found that the US system did not achieve better outcomes for the money spent than Australia, Canada, France, Norway, Germany, the Netherlands, New Zealand, Sweden, Switzerland or the United Kingdom, and it was in last place for access, efficiency and equity. It is argued that many people are still excluded from US healthcare, and there is insufficient preventive care.

However, the US carries out more diagnostic and preventive procedures on people such as cancer screenings and scans than other developed countries. More people who are diagnosed with diseases receive successful treatment, and there are high survival rates.

Yet a study by the National Institutes of Health Committee on Population 2013 found that the US was behind other comparable nations on some medical conditions such as obesity, car accidents, infant mortality, heart and lung disease, sexually transmitted infections, adolescent pregnancies, injuries and homicides. The World Health Organization (WHO) in 2014 reported that US life expectancy for both sexes was a relatively low 78.8 years, with males at 76.4 and females at 81.2, globally ranking the US in 34th place.

US healthcare is divided into private, public and voluntary sectors. Hospitals and clinics are largely operated as private businesses, although some are community- and volunteer-run and owned by the local government. The quality and availability of medical provision is variable. Adequate care may depend upon the wealth, gender, ethnicity, location, age and insurance coverage of patients. Healthcare has been traditionally driven by the private sector, with workers, families and employers benefiting from health insurance policies that allow them to access treatment. Many of the population under 65 had this insurance, while those over 65 subscribed to the federal Medicare program during their working lives. Medical treatment and insurance are expensive; some people buy additional insurance, but others remain uninsured. It is estimated that 25 percent of senior citizens declare bankruptcy due to medical expenses and 43 percent are forced to mortgage or sell their property to cover costs.

In 2010, it was estimated that about 84 percent of Americans (and their families) had private health insurance or Social Security Medicare. But the US Census Bureau reported that 51 million people, or 16.6 percent of the population, had no health coverage because they could not afford it, did not sign up for Medicaid or saw no need for coverage. Many people were without coverage for shorter periods. Others received public sector healthcare (often emergency) from state hospitals, Medicaid facilities, voluntary nonprofit hospitals and TRICARE, the Children's Health Insurance Program and the Veterans' Health Administration.

The state of the healthcare system led to debates about how it might be reformed in terms of insurance, the right to healthcare, access, fairness and efficiency. Organizations, like the OECD, argued that the US was among the few industrialized nations that did not guarantee universal access to healthcare for its population. It was claimed that lack of health insurance causes 45,000 to 48,000 US deaths every year.

In 2010, the ACA made changes in health insurance. New procedures were introduced, and hospitals and doctors had to achieve better healthcare results, lower costs, and accessibility. ACA was intended to reduce the uninsured rate by compulsory insurance coverage. It introduced mandates (individual and company insurance), federal subsidies for the poor to buy insurance, and insurance exchanges (where insurance could be bought). These had to cover all applicants, offer the same rates regardless of pre-existing conditions or gender, give coverage to children under 26 on their parents' policies; and encourage people to choose cheaper health care plans.

ACA is intended to restructure healthcare coverage and give an improved system. It should reduce the number of uninsured people and provide health insurance for most Americans by 2019. Some 32 million citizens had taken out insurance from 2014 when the system became active. Subsidies will decrease as incomes increase, and those earning a certain percentage of the poverty level will receive no subsidy.

ACA also expands Medicaid coverage to the poorest individuals under the age of 65 whose annual income is within federal poverty levels. For example, a family of four earning less than $29,326 would be eligible for Medicaid. But expansion of Medicaid depends on state approval, and states are not obliged to join the program. Some uninsured poor adults may not gain access to Medicaid if states reject expansion nor would they qualify for exchange subsidies. But if states decline to cover their poorest adults, they would not lose federal aid for groups such as pregnant women and families with children.

Those who do not comply with the ACA will be fined, and the Supreme Court ruled in 2012 that the "individual mandate" should be treated as a tax and is therefore constitutional. Companies with more than 50 employees will be fined ("the employer mandate") if full-time employees lack company coverage and require a government subsidy to purchase health insurance. The exchanges are intended to control the ACA and give advice to people about health plans. The Congressional Budget Office estimated that the ACA would cost $940 billion over 10 years but would lower budget deficits and healthcare costs.

The implementation of ACA, and its success or failure, will take time. There was no Republican support for the ACA, and Democrats argued that insurers were given too many benefits. Other critics estimated that there would still be 23 million people without insurance in 2019 and that costs to taxpayers will increase. Since Medicaid and Medicare will continue, the ACA should strengthen these programs and curb costs and fraud. But it has faced challenges from Congress, federal courts, state governments, labor unions, and small business organizations. However, the CDC reported in 2015 that the average number of uninsured had declined by 11.9 percent. In April 2016, Gallup found that the percentage of uninsured adults had dropped by 11 percent.

People's anxieties about illness are still conditioned by high insurance premiums and the cost of treatment, which can be very expensive for serious or chronic illness. There is often criticism of the medical profession and drug companies, whom the public suspect of pushing up medical and drug costs. Doctors and insurance companies constitute influential professional interest and lobbying groups, many of whom are traditionally opposed to "socialized" medicine in the US.

Private hospitals and clinics are generally well-equipped, efficient and run by a variety of commercial organizations. Many of those in the public sector, financed by state and federal funds, tend to lack resources and adequate funding. The US therefore has a range of high-quality medical facilities, but gaining access to them is a problem for many people.

The percentage of GDP derived from private, public and voluntary health care services constitutes a major business sector and is larger than health spending in other countries. Much of it is derived from incomes of the medical profession (with primary care doctors having a median annual salary in 2010 of $202,392 and specialists earning $356,885), management or administrative costs and the expense of equipment and drugs.

Pharmaceutical companies spend billions of dollars on research and development of new drugs, medicines can be expensive and the profits on successful new drugs are consequently high. Hospitals and medical schools also spend substantial amounts on research, because new techniques and discoveries will bring them prestige, patients and money, while also benefiting many people. The result for many consumers is improving quality and effectiveness of medical care but more expensive treatment.

It is argued that, since medical services can vary, Americans are not receiving the full benefit of such expenditure. Compared with other countries, the US spends more on health care but helps fewer people. It is argued that the top 10 percent of Americans are the healthiest people in the world, the middle group has a mediocre health deal, while the bottom 5–10 percent receive bad service. The main reasons for poor quality US healthcare are inadequate access to healthcare and the variable facilities on offer. It is alleged that overall, the US still does not receive good value for its healthcare investment.

Healthcare costs grow steadily. In an expanding compensation culture, there have been more lawsuits by patients against doctors and hospitals because of alleged inadequate or wrong treatment. Trial lawyers can profit considerably by fighting personal injury lawsuits on a contingency fee basis (no win, no fee), and the rise in such cases forces doctors to insure themselves against the risks of being sued. Medical care and vital decisions can be adversely influenced by these considerations. Drug companies also have to pay high compensation when medicines harm patients. Medicaid spending has had to cope with the high healthcare costs involved in treating AIDS (acquired immune deficiency syndrome), HIV (human immunodeficiency virus) patients and others with acute and chronic illnesses. Lawyers' fees, insurance policies and higher drug prices increase the overall cost of treatment, which passes to the patient or insurer, while both the public and private sectors have to spend more to alleviate serious illness. Despite the ACA, healthcare coverage and cost, for some critics, remains the single biggest domestic crisis facing the US.

Housing

Homes have traditionally been important for many Americans and their families and give a sense of material satisfaction and personal identification. But the ideal of the home-owning nuclear family unit has faded because of high divorce rates, single-parent households and single-occupier properties.

Americans may move their home many times, and homeownership is associated with socioeconomic mobility. A family will move frequently in the early years from apartments to houses and up the rungs of the housing market. There may be further transfers from urban locations to the suburbs in the same city; to new areas of the same state; or to different states.

Most Americans want to own their own homes, after renting in early adult years, and two-thirds seem to prefer living in suburban areas. Ownership and mobility are affected by income fluctuations, poverty and unemployment. The housing market is consequently divided between the private sector for those who are able to buy or rent and the public sector that is mainly for those who require assistance in obtaining low-rent property.

According to the 2013 American Housing Survey, there were 132.8 million total housing units in the US. Of these, 75.7 million (57.0 percent) were occupied by homeowners and 40.2 million (30.3 percent) were occupied by renters. The units include houses and apartments and fixed trailers or caravans in trailer parks. Of the first type of housing units, a large percentage were single-family houses, often of a detached type, usually having front and back yards. The second type illustrates the traditional place of renting properties in the American market, whether by choice or necessity. The housing industry grew strongly in the 1970s and 1980s when 35.8 million units were built, and later in the 1990s and early 2000s. But house prices rose faster than incomes in the 1980s and prevented many people from buying homes. The housing market suffered from an economic recession in the early 1990s, after which prices and house-building increased again.

Most private houses and apartments were reasonably priced historically, but they are also subject to price movements and market problems. They are often

PLATE 11.4 Up-market, colonial-style housing in Georgetown, Washington, DC.
© *Jordan Oakland*

of a good standard, with many amenities. Owners generally buy their properties by borrowing money (a mortgage or loan), which is secured by the value of their house and income. In 2014, the median price of a home was $212,000 (a price reduction from 2009) bought with an average mortgage of some 15.6 percent of the monthly average family income.

However, in 2007–08, the private housing market suffered seriously from the subprime or credit crisis and the Great Recession. Owner-occupied home rates declined to 67.4 percent in 2009 after the housing market crash in 2008. Individuals over-borrowed on loans and mortgages, and lenders over-extended themselves. The market collapsed when borrowers could not repay their mortgages and there was insufficient credit available to maintain the system or to provide loans. People lost their properties to foreclosures (3.9 million in 2009) and house prices halved. In 2013, although the market was recovering from recession, 12.9 million units (9.7 percent) were vacant and 4.1 million (3.1 percent) were seasonal.

US public-sector housing is administered and subsidized by federal, state, voluntary and local agencies. It provides for low-income Americans who are

PLATE 11.5 Harlem is historically a deprived, mainly Puerto Rican/African American area of New York with its own diverse identity. The "Spirit of East Harlem" on Lexington Avenue, commissioned by Hope Community Inc in 1978, was created by Hank Prussing and others. The four-story mural features local residents engaging in everyday activities.
© *Soltan Frédéric/Getty*

unable to buy property or afford private rented accommodation. The supply of social housing has historically been conditioned by the bias toward private provision. Individuals were expected to make their own arrangements, rather than assuming that housing was a public responsibility, despite economic and social conditions that caused poverty and homelessness.

The growth of urban slums and substandard housing in the nineteenth century resulted in social misery and threats to public health and led to the creation in 1934 of the Federal Housing Administration. This body (now the Department of Housing and Urban Development) provided loans to organizations that built low-rent accommodation for low-income and needy people. Local and state governments also constructed public housing and implemented stricter building and planning codes, health protection and public-sanitation regulations to deal with slum conditions. It was argued that public housing should be priced below current market rates and would allow people to live in locations that provided jobs and stop the drift from cities to find lower rents. Public housing originally consisted primarily of one or more concentrated blocks of low-rise and/or high-rise apartment buildings

Subsidized apartment buildings, often referred to as housing "projects," have a complicated and difficult history in the US. While the first decades of projects were built with higher construction standards, public housing increasingly became the last resort for the poor. In many, cities, housing projects suffered from mismanagement and high vacancy rates. They have also arguably increased concentrated poverty in communities, resulting in high crime rates, drug usage, and educational underperformance. Attempts to create more low-cost public housing with federal funds in the cities and other areas in the 1960s and 1970s were often opposed by property owners and sometimes by state and local governments for political, economic, racial and religious reasons. Although racial and religious discrimination in renting such housing has been curtailed, it still exists. While many states and cities have imposed fair housing laws, some low-income people and minority groups in urban centers live in barely habitable housing, and entry to low-cost housing for those who are unemployed or on welfare can be restricted. Recently, there have been moves to exploit inner-city land and to replace inferior buildings with low-cost housing. Bad housing conditions are also experienced by people living in small towns and rural areas.

Despite economic growth in the late 1990s and early 2000s, housing problems for the poor worsened. There was a shortage of affordable apartments, and four million families paid more than half their income in rent. Those spending more than 30 percent of their income on rent also increased between 2000 and 2005 due to stagnating wages for the unskilled, high property values and government's failure to supply enough subsidized housing. However, in 2008, President George W. Bush's National Housing Trust Fund provided some communities with funds to build, rehabilitate and preserve housing for people on the lowest incomes.

It is estimated that some 15 million households qualify for federal housing assistance, but only about 4.5 million receive it. About one third of these live in public housing projects, while the rest receive subsidies that allow them to live in private housing. The tenants often contribute 30 percent of their income toward the rent and the government provides the rest. The public housing sector also suffered because of the 2010 Great Recession.

As a result of various problems, many housing projects constructed in the 1950s and 1960s have been demolished. In recent decades, public housing has increasingly taken on different formats. Since the 1970s, subsidized housing was funded through rent vouchers rather than the construction of subsidized units. From the 1990s, rather than constructing large subsidized complexes, the federal government has used funds under the HOPE VI Program to tear down distressed public housing projects and replace them with mixed communities constructed in cooperation with private partners.

The homeless

Homelessness in the US is of concern for social service providers, government officials, and society generally. Although this may be a temporary situation, homeless people are visible in many American communities. However, it is difficult to define who the homeless are and what can or should be done to help them. Action is restricted by a lack of reliable information on the causes of homelessness and the actual number of people living on the streets, in transitional housing or emergency shelters. Local, state and federal governments in the US have failed to provide sufficient low-cost rented accommodation for low-income groups, and the federal government reduced subsidies for such housing from the 1980s.

The number of poor Americans fluctuated in the 1980s and 1990s and resulted in homeless people throughout the country, particularly African Americans, men, families with children and armed services veterans. Estimates of their current numbers vary widely, with official figures from the Department of Housing and Urban Development in 2012 of 633,782 across the country. The National Law Center on Homelessness and Poverty in 2015 reported that an estimated 2.5 to 3.5 million men, women and children (1.35 million) experienced variable homelessness on an annual basis and the housing crisis was deepening.

Determining the number of homeless people is difficult, particularly of those under the age of 21. Many adolescents, teens and runaways are uncounted, because young people living on the streets do not want to be counted for various reasons. One out of 50 children in the US will be homeless each year. In 2013, this number jumped to one out of 30 children, or 2.5 million. There were an estimated 57,849 homeless veterans during January 2013; or 12 percent of all homeless adults, and some 8 percent of homeless veterans are female. Texas,

California and Florida have the highest numbers of unaccompanied homeless youth under the age of 18. The turnover in the homeless population means that the number of people who experience homelessness for a few nights during a year is thought to be higher than counts taken over a period. Amnesty International USA suggests that vacant houses outnumber homeless people by five-fold.

Voluntary organizations, funded by private donations, attempt to help the homeless by providing shelter and food for limited periods. There are a large number of federal assistance schemes for the homeless controlled by a range of departments. Despite this federal funding, known as the McKinney program, states and cities finance most of the care for the homeless. They have recently successfully developed an initiative ("housing first") that places homeless persons in apartments of their own and has cut chronic homelessness.

Attitudes to social services

A Gallup poll in August 3–7, 2016 reported that the most important non-economic problems facing the country were healthcare (including Medicare, Medicaid and Social Security) in the eighth position and poverty, hunger and homelessness in nineteenth place.

People's concerns about social services reflect traditional US attitudes. While most Americans support contributing to social services such as Medicare and paying for medical insurance, they are ambivalent about the role that government should play in helping the poor obtain non-contributory aid, such as Medicaid and insurance subsidies under ACA. Seventy-one percent of respondents (85 percent in 1994) to a Pew Research Center survey in April 2012 thought that many poor people are too dependent on government assistance/ welfare programs and that the government cannot afford to do more for the poor than it does already. But 59 percent agreed that the government has a responsibility to care for those in need and provide all citizens with the basic necessities of life (39 percent disagreed). An ABC News/*Washington Post* poll in June 2008 found that 66 percent of respondents felt that providing healthcare for all Americans (with raised taxes to pay for it) was more important than keeping taxes down (31 percent). But views on government assistance varied between Republicans and Democrats, with relatively few Republicans supporting government responsibility to aid the poor.

Many people thought that the ACA in 2010 was controversial, complex and inadequately explained by the government. According to a Pew Research Center poll in March 2010, 48 percent of respondents opposed the legislation, while 38 percent favored it. A Gallup poll in February 2012 found that 66 percent of respondents felt that the requirement for every American to buy health insurance (individual mandate) was unconstitutional (87 percent of Republicans, 65 percent of Independents and 38 percent of Democrats), and 20 percent thought that it was constitutional. Other polls have reflected the perceived strengths and weaknesses of ACA. They suggest uncertainty as to whether or not it will improve healthcare, increase access and restrict costs. Healthy Americans have seen large increases in their insurance premiums to arguably support the individual mandate, and middle-income Americans do not receive the subsidies for which the poor are eligible.

An April 27, 2016 Pew Research Center poll found that 54 percent of respondents disapproved of the ACA and 44 percent approved. The poll found that 78 percent of Democrats approved of the Act (19 percent disapproved), 89 percent of Republicans disapproved (9 percent approved) and Independents' support had declined from 45 to 39 percent. Lower-income families, younger people and minorities approved of the legislation with large majorities. However, a CBS News/New York Times poll in June 2015 reported that 47 percent of Americans approved of the ACA; this was the first positive majority result. ACA is still in its early days and once the complexities of its provisions are understood, American divisions over healthcare may be resolved. It also appears that there is a public desire for the ACA to be improved rather than repealed.

Social Security and Medicare are other aspects of social services that are also regarded as problematic. Majorities of respondents in recent opinion polls have consistently supported these programs and would not vote for politicians who want to cut their budgets.

A poll conducted by the University of New Hampshire Survey Center for the National Committee to Preserve Social Security and Medicare (NCPSSM) in 2016 reported that 64 percent of respondents thought that Social Security provides security and stability to the US economy; 20 percent saw the program as a drain on the economy; and 70 percent believed that the 2008–10 recession emphasized the crucial role that Social Security plays for families in need. The poll revealed that 98 percent believed that Social Security funds belong to the contributors and their beneficiaries; and 71 percent said that Social Security is a promise to all generations that should not be broken. Only 2 percent of respondents believed that Social Security was a major cause of the federal deficit; and 77 percent did not think that policymakers should change or cut Social Security in order to reduce the deficit. Seventy percent of Americans expect to need Social Security on retirement. Substantial majorities of all demographic groups, including two-thirds of younger Americans and Republicans, thought that Social Security should be left alone.

There is concern about the Social Security system, and many people are worried about its condition. A Gallup poll in July–August 2015 reported that 45 percent of respondents thought that the Social Security would be able to pay them a benefit when they retired and 51 percent did not think so. Forty-nine percent of retired respondents thought that they would continue to get full benefits, but 43 percent believed that there would be cuts in their amounts. Such responses led 21 percent to think that Social Security was in crisis; 45 percent think it has major problems; and 28 percent think it has minor problems. Suggestions for ensuring the long-term future of the system were raising taxes (51 percent) or curbing benefits (37 percent). Other suggestions include raising the retirement age or supporting privatization of the program by allowing investments of Social Security taxes in the financial markets. Most people are opposed to raising the retirement age to preserve Social Security.

Exercises

Explain and examine the significance of the following names and terms:

welfare	AFDC/TANF	one-parent families
Medicaid	ACA	War on Poverty
medical lawsuits	poverty level	unemployment compensation
OASDI	debit stamps	GI Bill of Rights
Medicare	self-reliance	non-contributory benefits
New Deal	mortgage	Social Security
homeless	HEW	EITC
trailers	subsidies	"individual mandate"

Write short essays on the following questions.

1. Critically discuss the provision for healthcare in the US and the effects of the ACA. In your view, will the ACA improve healthcare provision for Americans?

2. Examine the division between public, private and voluntary provision for social services.

3. Explain what is meant by Social Security and discuss its present state and possible future.

4. Assess the varied attitudes of Americans to US social services.

Further reading

Alcock, P. and Craig, G. (2001) *International Social Policy: Welfare Systems in The Developed World*, London: Macmillan/Palgrave.

DeNavas-Walt, C., Proctor, B. and Mills, R. (2004) *Income, Poverty, and Health Insurance Coverage in the United Sates, 2003*, Washington DC: US Census Bureau.

Fields, J. (2004) "*America's Families and Living Arrangements: 2003*," US Census Bureau Reports, November.

Gilens, M. (1999) *Why Americans Hate Welfare*, Chicago, IL: University of Chicago Press.

Patterson, J. T. (1981) *America's Struggle Against Poverty, 1900–1980*, Cambridge, MA: Harvard University Press.

Peterson, P. (1999) *Gray Dawn: how the Coming Age Wave Will Transform America – And The World*, New York: Random House.

Putnam, R. (2000) *Bowling Alone: The Collapse and Revival of American Community*, New York: Simon and Schuster.

Skocpol, T. (1995) *Social Policy in the United States*, NJ: Princeton University Press.

Stiglitz, J. (2003) *The Roaring Nineties: Seeds of Destruction*, New York: Norton.

Websites

Homelessness and links: womenshousing.org
Health: www.hhs.gov
Medicine: www.medicare.gov
Social Security: www.socialsecurity.gov
Social services: usinfo.state.gov/usa/infousa

Chapter 12

Education

American attitudes to education: high expectations

Since the colonial period, Americans have expected a great deal from their educational institutions. Just teaching the usual subjects rarely satisfied demands on the schools. Americans wanted learning to serve other social institutions, ideals and goals. Such expectations invite disappointment and controversy. Combined with the circumstances of the country's history, they have also led to a distinctive educational system.

The founding fathers on the east coast hoped schooling would discover natural merit in citizens and nurture an elite to defend the republic from tyranny. People on the frontier dreamed that education would be the "great leveler," a compensator for their alleged inferiority to coastal society and a guarantee of democratic equality. Well into the twentieth century, schoolbooks fairly glowed with faith in the possibility of endless self-improvement for boys dedicated to American ideals. The schools taught girls to play a supportive role, African Americans to know their place, Native Americans to be civilized and immigrants to be American workers. Until recently, only a few private institutions and schools outside the mainstream provided correctives to this hierarchy.

American educational history

Local control over education developed early and remains characteristic of educational institutions in the US. During the colonial period, British authorities did not provide money for education, so the first schools varied according to the interest local settlers had in education. Reading, writing and arithmetic (the so-called "three Rs") were the core subjects and, through them, pupils prepared for local religious, economic and political life.

Higher education began with the founding Harvard College in 1636. By the Revolutionary War, nine colleges prepared a male elite for the ministry and leadership in public life. Although these colleges encouraged religious toleration, rivalry among them was evident, in part because all but two (Columbia and the University of Pennsylvania) represented one of the major Protestant denominations. At this point, Americans did not separate church and state, and private church-based higher education received public funding.

Building a society along the frontier also motivated the early development of schools. Because they were few and the wilderness vast, the settlers discovered that law, order and social tradition broke down unless people established basic social institutions. Thus, "school-raisings" became as much a standard part of community building as house- or barn-raisings.

Before the Civil War

Nonetheless, only five of the 13 original states included provisions for public schools in the constitutions they wrote during the War for Independence. In 1830, none offered statewide, free public education. Support for common schools was strong, however. Thomas Jefferson, Benjamin Franklin and other founding fathers insisted that universal public education was essential to produce the informed citizenry on which a democracy depended. In the 1780s, the federal government passed laws providing land for schools in the states of the Great Lakes.

Jefferson envisioned replacing Europe's aristocracy of birth with a school-bred *meritocracy* of talent. In the 1830s, President Andrew Jackson's Democratic Party opposed that ideal as elitist and supported public schools as an equalizer that would give every man a chance to rise in society. Around the same time, reformers in the Northeast, such as Horace Mann, publicized the notion that public schools could reduce the growing crime, poverty and vice of the cities by helping to assimilate their growing immigrant population. Toward those ends, Mann led a movement to lengthen the school year, add "practical" subjects, raise teachers' salaries and provide professional teacher training. By the Civil War, all states accepted the principle of tax-supported, free elementary schools. Every state had such schools in some places, but teacher training remained poor, and the quality of the schools was considerably lower in the South and West. Most children went to school sporadically or not at all. In the North, only one out of six white children attended public school in 1860. In the South, the figure was one in seven, and it was illegal to provide slaves with schooling.

At the time, public opinion rejected mandatory school attendance, mainly because people believed parents, rather than governments, should provide education. Most parents needed their children's work or wages to make ends meet. Secondary education was available at some 300 "free academies" across the nation, for those who could spare their children's economic contributions.

As the states abolished established religions in the half century after the revolution, church and state became separate. Only gradually, however, did Protestant instruction disappear from public schools. In the North and Midwest, immigrant groups began to establish parochial (private, church-related) elementary and secondary schools in the 1840s to preserve their ethnic heritage and avoid pressures to assimilate in public schools.

The pattern of higher education transformed before 1865. The Supreme Court distinguished between public and private colleges in 1819 and freed private institutions of higher learning from state control. Thereafter hundreds of private experiments in higher education appeared, even though public funding dropped to very low levels. During the Civil War, the Morrill Act (or Land-Grant College Act) set a revolutionary precedent by laying the foundation for the state university. The beginning of the federal government's involvement in public higher education, the Act gave each state huge land areas for higher education. The result was dozens of land-grant colleges, which developed into state universities. Equally important, it promoted the higher education of larger numbers of students and called for courses in agriculture and technical and industrial subjects, to attract students from the working class. Colleges for African Americans and women also opened before the Civil War.

Immigration, assimilation and segregation, 1865–1945

The rapid pace of urbanization, industrialization and immigration brought a turning point in American education after 1865. The immigrant slum child became the symbol of the dangers of these processes, and governments asked the public schools to remedy the situation.

Assimilation through the schools seemed increasingly necessary as immigrants from Southern and Eastern Europe and several Asian nations arrived in large numbers. The schools strove to Americanize these exotic newcomers by teaching English, the principles of American democracy and the skills needed for the workplace. Just as importantly, the schools also got immigrant children out of unhealthy tenement housing, off the streets, out of factories and away from gangs. To reach these goals, states enacted compulsory school attendance laws. By 1880, almost three-quarters of school-age children were in school.

These laws also applied to racial minorities. After the Civil War, the federal Freedmen's Bureau and other Northern organizations founded many schools in the South for the former slaves. However, whether African, Asian or Native American, minority students everywhere attended separate schools. In 1896, the Supreme Court's *Plessy* v. *Ferguson* ruling gave legal backing to the segregation that already existed.

Politicians quickly put children in school, but they did not as quickly appropriate money to hire more teachers and erect new buildings. Overcrowded, poorly maintained schools and staff shortages were typical of American public schools between the 1880s and 1920s. Opening teaching to women (often the daughters of immigrants) provided the new teachers, and "normal schools" to train them grew rapidly in number. Around 1900, Americans did not consider public school teaching a profession. The average annual salary for teachers was lower than that of an unskilled worker, and many teachers had no more than a high school education themselves. Yet real progress appeared in teacher preparation after the passage of compulsory attendance laws. States set standards for teaching licenses, which increasingly included a college degree with courses in pedagogy. After the 1920s, "school marms" and "schoolkeepers" were members of a profession called "educators." Salaries, however, remained low, and the profession was one of the least prestigious.

In the same period, reformers assigned the schools new priorities and duties. John Dewey and others held that curricula and teaching methods had to be changed. Instead of moralistic piety and rote memorization, the schools had to give pupils practical skills suited to their environment and the habit of discovering knowledge for themselves. "Learning by doing," personal growth, and child-centered rather than subject-centered teaching became the goals.

Public schools were to become community centers and the means of social progress. About this time, progressive education introduced physical education, music, fine arts, and vocational subjects (training in skilled occupations) as electives (optional courses). These educators also developed the after-school extracurricular activities, such as team sports, that became a typical aspect of American education. In 1917, the federal government offered financial support to any public secondary school that emphasized vocational education. Some immigrant parents criticized progressive education because they felt electives took time away from academic subjects. They also objected to the frequent assumption that immigrant children did not need academic studies, since they would not go on to higher education.

After 1865, private church-related colleges, often founded by European immigrant groups, rapidly increased in number, especially in the Midwest. Coeducational higher education (colleges open to both men and women) became the norm there during the Civil War, when fee-paying women were necessary to replace the men who joined the Union armies. Coeducation continued to spread, and by the 1920s, almost half of American college students were women. Further east, however, the so-called Ivy League universities (Harvard and other prestigious schools from the colonial period) remained men's institutions and, as a result, benefactors established separate women's colleges in that region. Racial segregation extended to higher education during this period, when colleges founded by Blacks for African Americans, such as Howard University and the Hampton Institute, appeared in the South. In 1890, a new Morrill Act provided land for African American public colleges that emphasized manual and industrial education.

After 1900, graduate and professional schools became more common. Advanced degree programs began to transform some well-established universities into research institutions. States and private groups founded engineering schools, business colleges, law and medical schools in growing numbers. For all but a small elite, however, a college degree seemed a luxury. Even in 1940, less than two out of ten college-age people attended institutions of higher learning. Instead, as parents less often had farms, handicrafts or family businesses to pass on, they secured their children's future through further education at vocational, office, secretarial or management schools.

PLATE 12.1 The prominent, historically African American institution of higher learning, Howard University; Frederick Douglass Memorial Hall, Washington DC.
© *Mira/Alamy*

The Second World War and the Cold War

The Second World War was a watershed in American higher education. To ease the return of veterans to civilian life, Congress passed the Servicemen's Readjustment Act (the so-called "GI Bill") in 1944. Under the Act, the federal government paid tuition and living costs for veterans in higher education and directly funded the expansion of study programs for the first time. Within two years, half the people in college were veterans, many of them from working-class families with little education. More students graduated than ever before, and the typical student ceased to be a member of the upper-middle or upper classes. By 1971, when the program ended, nearly 2.5 million veterans had benefited from it. Higher education had become mass education, which Americans saw as a right rather than a privilege.

The launching of the Soviet satellite *Sputnik* in 1957 spurred another increase in the federal government's role in public education. Now the US enlisted schools in the Cold War to meet the challenge of Soviet technology. The National Defense Education Act (1958) provided federal money for research and university programs in science and technology, as well as loans to college students. The legislation also allotted federal funds for teaching science, mathematics and foreign languages in high schools. After 1958, the federal government provided funds for college-level foreign language instruction, the equipping of language laboratories, and eventually for the humanities in general.

In the 1950s, state after state required teachers to sign "loyalty oaths," and Senator Joseph McCarthy (among others) attacked the universities as hotbeds of communism. Education became a patriotic obligation as well as a right.

Race and school desegregation

The Supreme Court's *Brown* v. *Board of Education* decision struck down the principle of separate-but-equal educational facilities for the races in 1954. One year later, the court ruled that public school districts all over the nation had to present plans for achieving "racial balance" in their schools. Federal school policy showed a profound change in priorities.

From 1955 to 1974, the court tried to desegregate America's public schools. It settled on bussing as the most effective way to integrate them. Until very recently, one universal rule in America had been that pupils attended the school closest to their homes. Since African Americans and Whites lived in different residential sections of US cities, they attended different school districts. Residential segregation produced segregated schools. Therefore, the Supreme Court decided to "bus" students until "racial balance" in all city schools resulted.

In city after city across the nation, parents, school authorities and politicians of both races protested and resisted, but the court held firm, with the result that Whites fled to the suburbs in greater numbers and the small percentage who

PLATE 12.2 Federal paratroopers, sent by President Eisenhower, escort black students to Central High School in Little Rock, Arkansas. This gave notice that the executive-in-chief stood behind the Supreme Court's *Brown v. the Board of Education* ruling that called for the integration of public education across the nation.
© *Rolls Press/Popperfoto/Getty*

could afford it sent their children to private schools. Federal authorities decided that bussing plans could produce integrated schools only if they included the "lily-white" suburban schools around major cities. After such plans transported white pupils into city schools, the public outcry grew louder. By 1974, the nation's mood had become strongly anti-bussing, and when asked to decide whether a city-and-suburbs bussing plan was constitutional, the Supreme Court backed down, saying no tradition in American public education was more deeply rooted than the local control of schools. Thus, bussing stopped being effective for school desegregation.

The trend toward increasing integration of the races in the schools slowed, and by the late 1980s, the trend had reversed. Resegregation of the schools began. By 2016, more than 40 percent of the schools were mostly or entirely African American. An even larger percentage were "racially segregated" if the definition includes schools that were predominantly Latino, Asian and African American. Most of these schools were located in the North, West, or Southwest, because the court integrated Southern schools first and did not support bussing between the suburbs and inner cities of the North after 1974. Not only the end of bussing, but the continued "white flight" to the suburbs and decades of high immigration of non-white, poor Latinos and Asian Americans contributed to the growing school resegregation. As the portion of these minorities who were middle class grew in the first decade of the twenty-first century, however, the diversity of the student body increased in many regions of the country, even in suburban areas.

Affirmative action and the schools

Starting in the 1960s, the federal authorities fought the effects of prejudice and the related problems of poverty through involvement in educational programs. In 1963, Congress began providing money for college and university buildings. In 1964, it decided that federal funding was available only to educational institutions that proved they did not discriminate based on race, religion or national origin. The Higher Education Act of 1965 helped minority and "disadvantaged" students get college loans. State and federal grants to poorer public schools generally came in two ways. First, laws made the income levels in local districts the basis for distributing public funds. "Low income" areas qualified for extra grants and special programs to attract good teachers. Second, governments more than tripled their contribution to the general budgets of cities with social and educational problems.

In general, federal government policy aimed to implement the principle of affirmative action that President Lyndon Johnson expressed in his commencement speech at Howard University in 1965:

> You do not take a person who for years has been hobbled by chains and liberate him, bring him up to the starting line of a race, and then say, "You are free to compete with all the others," and still justly believe that you have been completely fair.

Affirmative action programs to improve women's and minority groups' access to education proliferated during the early 1970s. On the primary and secondary levels of public education, affirmative action first led to a redesigning of teaching programs and textbooks. Schools and publishers replaced discriminatory references to women and minorities with evenhanded treatments or, more often, with "positive role models" and examples of how women and minorities contributed to American history and culture. History and literature books, especially, changed because of this effort.

Governments required educational institutions to become equal opportunity employers, which affected the hiring of staff on all levels. That meant hiring more teachers from minority groups at elementary and secondary schools and more women professors at universities and colleges. By law, educational institutions must encourage minority group members to apply for teaching positions.

A school might lose government funding if it does not seek out and interview staff from these groups. Finding qualified women and minority group members for positions became somewhat easier after the 1970s because of affirmative action plans for teacher training programs and the increased number of students from these groups who completed university degrees.

Educators designed two affirmative action programs to help "disadvantaged" pupils succeed in primary and secondary schools. Head Start provides preschool tutoring to children in educationally deprived families to help them begin formal schooling at the same level as those families that are more fortunate. Upward Bound supplies remedial teaching, private tutoring and work – study programs for older children. Upward Bound has suffered repeated funding reductions. Head Start, a political and educational success, has continued to receive additional congressional appropriations. It benefits close to a million children today.

Affirmative action programs in education provoked a number of US Supreme Court decisions. These did not call for the end of affirmative action, but they changed the methods used to put it into effect. The best-known court cases in this area involved complaints from white males denied admission to university programs, in their opinion, because female and minority group applicants received preferential treatment. In the *Bakke* decision (1978) the Supreme Court ruled that it is unconstitutional to increase the number of female and minority students in university programs by setting numerical quotas. In the 1990s and early 2000s, voters ended affirmative action programs in several states by supporting referenda to eliminate them. Supreme Court ruling in cases involving the University of Michigan in this period more strictly limited admissions policies that favored minorities in the interest of recruiting a diverse student body.

Perhaps understandably, a mood of disappointment with educational institutions has been evident in the US because most of the social dilemmas the schools were supposed to solve remain serious problems. Bussing ended, racial separation grew and the controversial effects of affirmative action led to its curtailing. In 2017, the public asked for better funding, national standards, religious values, testing, charter schools and vouchers to improve the schools.

Elementary and secondary schools

Local control over schools is traditional in the US. The Constitution makes no mention of education, which reserves power over education to the states or people, according to the Tenth Amendment. State constitutions have quite specific provisions about education. Generally, these clauses (and state education laws) define the state's role and delegate primary responsibility for schools to local governments. Because the states create local authorities, they can also change their powers over education.

Local authorities set up independent school districts, whose elected local boards of education make most decisions regarding public elementary and secondary schools. Generally, the districts organize their schools into kindergarten for five-year-olds, elementary schools for six- to 12-year-olds, middle schools (or junior highs) for pupils from 13 to 15 and high schools for students between 16 and 18 years old. The overall structure of education has several variants progressing from kindergarten through to doctoral degrees. See Figure 12.1 for a diagram of the most common of these.

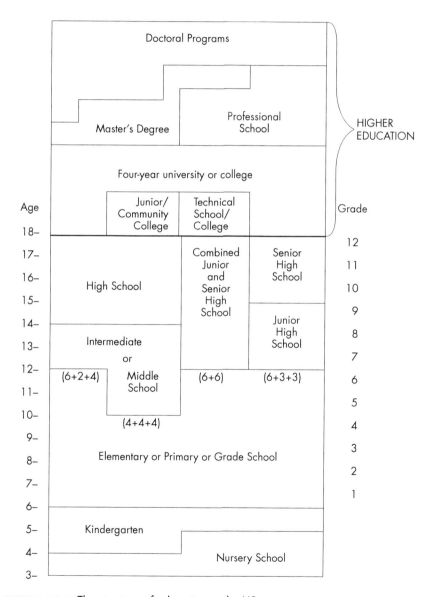

FIGURE 12.1 The structure of education in the US.

Only when specific powers given to the federal government in the Constitution are involved, such as the protection of rights guaranteed in the Bill of Rights, do the federal authorities get *directly* involved in educational issues. The federal government seldom interfered with local schools to protect civil rights until the 1950s. Mostly, it influences local school policy *indirectly* through the conditions attached to granting federal grants for special educational projects and the requirement that funds must go to nondiscriminatory practices.

The federal government's involvement in education remains quite limited. Its administrative agency for overseeing and formulating educational policies developed late and still has a small staff compared to those in other developed countries. Congress did not set up a federal Office of Education in the Department of Health, Education and Welfare until the 1950s. It did not establish a separate Department of Education until 1979. Ronald Reagan received considerable support when he promised to eliminate the department if elected. Even today, the federal government provides on average only a little over 7 percent of the funding for public primary and secondary schools.

Until the 1950s, almost all state governments limited their involvement in education to two areas: establishing public state universities and setting general

PLATE 12.3 Kindergarten children working with laptops.
© *Tetra Images/Erik Isakson/Getty*

guidelines for public primary and secondary education. A state board of education, appointed by the governor, formulated the guidelines, and the state's agency or Department of Education was to implement them in local districts.

The state Board of Education commonly sets only general minimum standards. It determines the number of days in the school year, the procedures for licensing teachers and administrators, the school-leaving age (usually 16), the "core curriculum" that pupils must complete at each level of school and minimum requirements for academic progress at different grade levels. To graduate from secondary school, for example, students must pass a core curriculum that usually includes four years of courses in English, three in social studies and two in mathematics and science.

These common requirements serve several purposes. By establishing a degree of uniformity among diverse school districts, they allow educational leaders to keep the schools in line with standards in other states and developments in pedagogy. Hence, the core curriculum also facilitates the evaluation of individual schools and makes it easier for pupils to move from one district or state to another and gain admission to colleges and universities around the nation.

Current trends in public school reform

In recent decades, state boards have increasingly implemented testing programs to make individual districts more accountable for reaching a certain level of academic achievement at specified points in pupils' schooling. Many states use the same tests, and the results for districts and states are publicly available. The state board and parents are therefore better able to judge the relative success of the local schools in meeting educational goals. Between the 1980s and 2017, many state boards won approval for statewide tests to measure *teachers'* mastery of core subjects and educational methods.

Under the second Bush and Obama administrations, the No Child Left Behind (NCLB) Act increased federal funding for public education. The act involves an unprecedented degree of federal intrusion into state and local control over the schools. It required the formulation of national and state standards of achievement in core curriculum subjects, greatly increased use of standardized testing of pupils and teachers to hold individual schools accountable to these standards, and a system of sanctions against public schools that do not meet annual targets for improvement. These include vouchers for sending pupils to other schools, including private religious institutions, and the establishment of charter schools at a much quickened pace.

Between 2009 and 2012, opposition to NCLB from teachers' core subject organizations, their unions and from state boards of education grew considerably. The Obama administration used executive action rather than new or revised legislation to deal with the mounting dissatisfaction. By mid-2012 Obama and his secretary of education, Arne Duncan, gave 26 states waivers from partici-pating in NCLB. They became free to use a combination of other measures to judge and report the progress of their schools. Many state educational leaders felt relieved that they no longer needed to struggle toward unrealistic goals measured through the inadequate means of centrally made quantitative tests. In 2015, both parties and Obama agreed on a much more flexible federal regime for the schools, the Every Student Succeeds Act (ESSA), which strengthened local and state options within national guidelines and testing.

Localism and public education

Three important kinds of localism result from the delegation of state authority to local education districts (LEDs). All these forms of localism remain very important, despite the greater state and federal intrusion brought by the NCLB. Financial localism generally refers to the delegation of responsibility for funding schools to local districts. In recent decades, state and federal spending on edu-cation increased significantly. Yet, on average, local real-estate taxes still raise around half of LED budgets. In other words, local money still makes a very significant difference for public schools.

In a rich LED with valuable homes and businesses, local funding represents the resources for better teaching salaries, buildings and equipment than those in most other districts. In the smaller school budget of a poor LED, the local half from taxes represents less money, and that has a proportional effect on resources for its schools. Each district is free to decide how high it wants to set property taxes for education. Even when poor LEDs approve higher tax rates than those of wealthy districts, they raise less money for schools because local property has so little value. Financial localism (in combination with the causes of the great economic differences between school districts) causes wide variations in Amer-ican public schools.

The aim of state plans to redistribute local property tax money is to reduce the educational inequality resulting from financial localism. Redistribution plans collect the real-estate taxes in the state and place them in a fund for public education. State authorities then distribute these funds to even out the differ-ences in school budgets across the state. Such plans can bring drastic changes in the school budgets of both rich and poor LEDs. Usually they take money from the suburbs and give it to inner-city areas. Hence, there has been less money for mostly white schools and more for schools with many minority students.

As expected, redistribution plans have met opposition. Some suburban groups have tried to preserve the advantages of their schools through private donations or special local taxes. One state (New Jersey) responded by ruling that any increase in the school budgets of richer LEDs would result in an auto-matic equal increase in the budgets of poorer LEDs. State courts in several parts of the nation have demanded redistribution programs. Increased state contributions to local school budgets and redistribution plans have given state boards of education greater leverage in enforcing statewide standards.

State authorities often show a reluctance to use their power. Like the public they serve, they often believe that in a democracy, central authorities should not impart education policy, but allow the people in the governments closest to the schools design local education. Such thinking and the opposition of suburban voters have limited the effects of redistribution plans. The result is that the money spent per pupil in predominantly white suburban schools is commonly two to three times that spent in racially mixed city schools. American traditions of financial localism in education remain strong.

The members of the LED's board of education exercise political localism. They have more power over the schools than members of the state board, and local residents elect them. Anyone who lives in the district can be a candidate for the board. The majority of those elected are parents, teachers and local business people. It is also common to elect a student to the board. The school system's chief administrator is usually an ex officio member of the board with no vote but great informal influence over decisions. While some boards have difficulty reaching agreement because members represent opposing political views, often the board as a whole reflects the district's predominant conservative or liberal political attitudes.

The local board is powerful because it makes a range of important decisions. It determines the size and content of the school budget and controls the hiring and firing of teachers and administrators. The choice of subjects, programs and educational goals beyond the state minimums is the board's, as is the definition of school disciplinary rules and routines. It must approve the selection of textbooks and library books, as well as plans for designing, constructing and maintaining educational facilities. Local boards make decisions on whether the LED should apply to the state or federal government for aid under specific programs. The boards that are most resourceful in applying for these funds get more help. In practice, that means districts with well-educated populations (and usually higher incomes) often succeed in getting more money from the state and federal governments.

Another important source of political localism is the Parent–Teacher–Student Association (PTSA). The PTSA is a voluntary organization that elects its own officers. It has no legal authority to make school policy, but its discussions often frame the issues debated and decided by the school board. Moreover, local residents often elect people who have been active in the PTSA to the school board.

The third kind of localism in American education, social localism, refers to the distinctiveness of LEDs' educational priorities and goals that result from differences in their populations' social attitudes. These attitudes generally reflect the local population's dominant socioeconomic class and mix of occupations, religions, races and ethnic groups. It can be argued that social localism produces differences in the public schools that are quite as significant as those caused by differences in districts' ability to pay for schooling. School board members and PTSA leaders, who may not be representative of the local population, cannot afford to ignore these attitudes and the social characteristics from which they spring.

Social localism is significant because local boards make important policy decisions. It has led to public schools emphasizing agricultural methods, industrial arts, commercial studies or college-level "advanced placement" courses. It has inspired religious, white supremacist and assimilationist policies in some LEDs and opposing policies in others. Extreme examples of social localism have resulted in replacing evolutionary theory with the biblical story of creation in science courses, removing literary classics from school libraries, sex-education lessons and the presentation of alternative lifestyles and sexual orientations in elementary schools. District boards have decided to teach that American society is the world's greatest or to refuse the children of illegal immigrants public schooling. Judicial rulings and public reactions frequently strike down or change such extreme social policies.

PLATE 12.4 Members of the Readington Township Board of Education listen to a parent during a school board meeting in Readington Township, New Jersey, April 23, 2013. A New Jersey principal's ban on strapless dresses at a junior high school dance because they would be "distracting" to boys enraged parents, who called for its reversal on the grounds it violated their daughters' constitutional rights.
© *REUTERS/Alamy*

The schools discarded the goal of Americanizing immigrant children. Today, after the civil rights movements of the 1960s and 1970s, support for equal educational opportunity and pluralism (the belief in allowing several alternatives) is standard in the rhetoric (although not as often in the practice) of American school districts. Equal opportunity today means that state and federal governments sometimes deem it necessary to intervene in the affairs of local school districts to ensure that minority students are given an education fitted to their special circumstances. See the section on increasing limits to local control.

Pluralism produces even more various public schools, as some local districts tailor their curricula to suit Native American or African American as well as Latino and Asian immigrant children and add ethnic studies courses and bilingual education programs. It has also increased debate over the core curriculum. Led by scholars in college education departments who question the traditional content of required subjects, districts, states and even the federal government have tried to redefine common standards and the canon (accepted principle content) of subjects in recent decades. Committees of recognized experts in many fields have met (sometimes for years) to develop national standards for subjects and a national curriculum. In the US, however, that can only consist of

PLATE 12.5 Students in a Catholic high school enjoying a lesson. The teacher and religious, scientific, and patriotic symbols are in the rear of classroom.
© *Yakoniva/Alamy*

suggested guidelines. NCLB, for example, offers national models for appropriate standards in core subjects at different grade levels, but it bows to the states' constitutional authority over education by leaving it to them to define each state's legal variant of the Act's rules. States still control educational programs. The standards adopted in many LEDs and states to meet the national guidelines of the law caused publishers to redesign textbooks in core subjects.

Private elementary and secondary schools

Pluralism means not only permitting great variety in the public schools but also allowing a wide variety of private schools. During the 2014–2015 academic year, 10 percent of the school-age population attended one of the nation's 33,619 private elementary and secondary schools. Private educational institutions show even more variety than the public schools. Four out of five are parochial schools (run by religious groups). By far the largest number of these are Catholic institutions, but fundamentalist sects, a range of other Protestant denominations, orthodox Jews and Islamic and Asian religious groups also run parochial schools.

Non-sectarian private schools have a weak religious allegiance or are entirely secular. They are quite diverse but frequently promise a high standard of academic excellence, adherence to a particular theory of education, the ability to instill discipline and maturity, or some combination of these qualities. The Montessori schools offer a specific method of learning. Elite college-preparatory boarding schools (so-called "prep schools") have exceptionally well-qualified faculties whose goal is to help the children of the wealthy gain admission to prestigious universities such as those in the Ivy League and to eventually take their place in the country's upper class. Varieties of military academies specialize in dealing with "problem children" whose parents can afford to reform their habits by subjecting them to the rigors of a regimented life away from home.

Private schools depend heavily on endowments (private donations), investments and income from fee-paying students to meet their expenses. Public funding amounts to less than 10 percent of their budgets. Until very recently, the courts limited the public funding available to parochial schools to programs that benefit school pupils in general, rather than particular institutions. Thus, all children can receive government aid for some medical services, nutrition supplements and transportation to school.

A recent development is that in some areas parents can receive grants (or government vouchers) to pay for tuition at private schools. Especially in the inner cities, where private schools have a better record than nearby public schools, states operate voucher plans. The NCLB makes this possible when a local school repeatedly fails to meet improvement goals.

Some private educational institutions offer financial aid to attract students from different social backgrounds, while others follow a restrictive admissions policy to maintain a homogeneous student body. Exclusivity has always been an important attraction of many private schools. Bussing programs to end segregation contributed to increased enrollment at all-white private schools. The Supreme Court's ban on prayers and religious instruction in public schools caused others to turn to private education. Dissatisfaction with the public schools' academic standards, lax discipline, drug abuse or crime convinced yet more parents to pay for private education. These problems are certainly more avoidable in private schools, since the expulsion of pupils who cause them is much simpler for private institutions.

Higher education

High school graduates enter higher education through a process of mutual selection in a system that is decentralized, diverse and competitive. Colleges and universities select a student body according to criteria set by the individual institution rather than by a central authority. The federal government has only an indirect influence on these standards through equal educational opportunity programs, civil rights laws and constitutional rights. State approval is necessary for institutions of higher learning to operate and grant degrees, but otherwise, state involvement is usually minimal.

This large degree of institutional independence has encouraged grassroots experiments and innovations in higher education. The resulting diversity is enormous. The public sector includes the national military academies, 50 state university systems and thousands of local technical or "specialty" schools, community colleges and city universities. In the private sector, there are also many thousands of institutions, ranging from specialty schools to small church-related colleges to major universities with separate undergraduate, graduate and professional schools.

Entrance criteria reflect the character of the institution and the competition it faces from institutions of a similar sort. High school graduates try to gain admission to a school that suits their individual needs. Students' requirements also vary greatly because the population is so heterogeneous and secondary schools so different in type and quality. Such a system requires devices to help institutions and students make informed choices in the selection process. No battery of public national examinations determines who can receive higher education. That fact and the great variation in the programs and quality of US secondary schools make evaluating applicants' academic achievement difficult for colleges. To provide a basis for comparing pupils' skills, private firms have developed competitive college entrance examinations that pupils all over the country take on the same day. Almost all colleges and universities require applicants to take the best known of these, the Scholastic Achievement Test (SAT), and many prestigious schools require pupils to submit their scores on other national tests.

In addition, institutions have admissions departments that visit and evaluate secondary schools, interview applicants and review pupils' application forms. Secondary school guidance departments evaluate colleges and universities and recommend programs suited to their abilities and test scores. Regional organizations called accrediting bodies monitor the quality of secondary schools and institutions of higher education.

A closer look at some of these institutions of higher learning illustrates the choices students have. Post-secondary technical or "specialty" schools offer training for specific occupations, such as accounting, computer programming, laboratory work or business management. These institutions have become particularly numerous because of rapid technological change. Today, a few specialty schools are as prestigious as well-known universities. Community colleges give courses for the first two years of college, at little or no cost to local residents. After that, students may graduate with an associate in arts (AA degree) or transfer into the third year of a full college or university program and continue toward a Bachelor of Arts or Science (BA or BSc degree). Community colleges run by local authorities offer many shorter certificate programs suited to the occupational needs of a local area. Many of their students are mature adults who study part-time.

Although a clear majority of colleges and universities in the US are private, three-quarters of high-school graduates chose public institutions in 2012. One important reason for this situation is that the tuition (the cost of instruction) at city and state universities is often a small fraction of the fee charged at a private institution. Location also reduces the cost. City or state residents pay much lower tuition rates than students who come from other places. Public systems have purposely built campuses in many parts of the city or state so that students can live at home while they study.

Public systems also attract more students because some have open admissions policies and many have minimal acceptance requirements for area residents. The majority of secondary school graduates who have average grades can thus avoid rejection in the intense competition for acceptance at more selective schools. Most of those are private, but city and state systems also have an enormous range of standards and programs. Most states operate two university systems, one of them usually more oriented to applied studies and the other to academic work leading to research and the more prestigious professions. Many outlying "branch" campuses of public universities are much like community colleges, but some concentrate on excellence through advanced courses in a limited number of fields. State university systems usually have a main campus that maintains higher overall standards. The best of these, the Berkeley campus of the University of California and the Madison campus of the University of Wisconsin, for example, have reputations that equal those of such elite private universities as Harvard, Yale, Princeton and Stanford.

Private higher education in the US is typical of American pluralism. The private sector that educates a quarter of university-level students in the US is large compared to that in other western nations. Yet private institutions could expand their size greatly if they wished. On average, private colleges and universities accept only one in ten applicants.

There is no single or simple cause for this restrictive admissions policy. Inability to pay school costs is rarely the main reason for turning down an applicant. Good private institutions have little difficulty finding enough fee-paying students. Stipends, scholarships, low-interest loans, part-time work–study programs or a combination of these are available to people the institution wants. Private colleges and universities recruit as much as a third of their students among well-qualified poor, minority and foreign groups. Even the most prestigious institutions offer some of these recruits extra help (so-called remedial courses) as a form of affirmative action, because they believe in helping promising students in economic difficulty and think that studying with people of varied backgrounds is a vital part of a good education. As noted in Chapter 4, however, in the last two decades such affirmative action has faced rising opposition in public opinion.

The reasons most private institutions have for remaining relatively small arise from their concept of a quality education. A few concentrate on high academic standards as their single definition of quality. Many more combine that goal with the ideal of a special community of learning. The institution often builds a community by requiring students to live on campus and by having small class sizes to encourage the close contacts between students and faculty. A sense of community can also result from bringing together staff and students who share a religious or ethnic background or socio-political orientation. Most American racial, nationality and religious groups have founded at least one private college or university.

Some institutions are common to both public and private higher education. The four-year liberal arts college, which about two-thirds of American students attend, is the most important of these. One of several units in a university or an independent organization, its purpose is to provide basic courses in a broad range of humanities and sciences. Liberal arts students usually do not specialize until their third year. That "major," the capstone of their undergraduate education, is a requirement for the BA or BSc degree.

A primary goal of the liberal arts college is producing "well-rounded" individuals (generally well-informed and cultured people). By requiring a core curriculum, these colleges help maintain a common culture in the US. Until around 1980, few questioned this canon of study, which aimed to expose students to fundamental values of American and western culture. Since then, however, having a canon has conflicted with the ideal of pluralism.

Debate over the canon became so intense in the academy and educated public that Americans speak of the "culture wars." Nothing less than a redefinition of American identity or realizing cultural equality has been attempted. By 2000s, scholars successfully argued that the canon of many subjects must include the work of women and the non-western cultures of many Americans. Debate continues, but the core curriculum is already much changed.

A bachelor's degree is required before students can enter graduate schools. These may be professional schools, such as law or medical schools, or advanced schools that offer masters degrees (the MA or MSc) and doctorates (the PhD). For entrance to graduate schools, students must normally take a competitive examination, either an entrance test for the professional school or graduate record exams (GREs) in liberal arts subjects. A hallmark of the best universities, America's high-quality graduate schools are internationally famous centers of research and magnets for well-qualified students from abroad.

Higher education in the US is a competitive struggle. Between 2001 and 2011, when around 20 million people enrolled at colleges or universities each year, the central problem seemed to be that only half of these students completed a degree. City and state universities normally "weed out" one-third to one-half of the freshman class through tough introductory courses and exams. Half of those enrolled in a first degree program do not graduate. All American institutions of higher education use the system called continuous evaluation. It requires students to take mid-term and end-of-term examinations, write essays and term papers and complete additional tasks the instructor chooses.

PLATE 12.6 Harvard University, founded in 1636 and the oldest of the universities in the "Ivy League."
© *CHARLES SYKES/REX/Shutterstock*

Course grades result from a weighted average of the student's marks on these assignments. A minimum overall grade average is necessary to continue one's studies.

Recent problems and policy debates

Many recent educational controversies in the US revolve around so-called "failing" local schools and the growing intervention of state and federal governments to remedy the situation. "State of the nation" evaluations have become a regular part of debate about American education. Presidential candidates, federal commissions and the US secretary of education, associations of the states, organizations of educators and private foundations regularly identify problems and suggest policy changes.

In the 1950s, civil rights movements made school reform the center of debate over how to offer equal opportunity, high quality public education for a multiethnic, multiracial nation. These efforts culminated in the Elementary and Secondary Education Act (ESEA) in 1965, which emphasized providing services and funding for low-income school districts with large number of minority students. The government has periodically reauthorized the ESEA, and new versions of the law brought turning points in American school policy.

The Reagan administration released its highly critical evaluation of the schools, *A Nation at Risk* in 1983. In the 1980s and 1990s, the most common initiatives combined a focus on setting higher standards for core subjects, such as reading, math and science, with measuring progress through a rigorous system of standardized testing, not only of pupils but also of teachers and schools. In the early 2000s, such "outcomes-based reform" in cities and states became *federal* policy through the setting of national standards in core subjects and President George W. Bush's NCLB Act. As critiques of that law mounted, President Obama let over half of the states opt out of it. At the end of 2015, he won bipartisan support for another revision of education policy, the ESSA. To better aid weak schools and pupils in the nation's diverse districts, the new law returns to more local flexibility and funding.

Around the same time, other movements merged into a new, contested pattern of reform. Growing numbers of states intervened in failing local schools to create "charter schools," which taxpayers' money funds but private businesses run independently. This privatization takes the control of schools out of local residents' hands. It also adds commercial motives to the goal of providing high quality public schools. Since 2003 growing numbers of states, including Louisiana, Tennessee, Michigan, Nevada and Georgia, have established state-run schools without local voter approval. Usually state authorities define a category of "weak" schools by law, take them out of local control, and turn their operation over to university education departments, or more frequently, to private

PLATE 12.7 Canton Charter Academy, Canton, Michigan, one of 75 charter schools in nine states operated by National Heritage Academies (NHA), a for-profit corporation based in Grand Rapids, Michigan. In 2011–2012, NHA was the third largest for-profit charter school company in the United States, based on its number of schools. Its 50,000 students made it the nation's second largest charter school company, judged by the size of its combined student body. Opponents charge that NHA is a major force in the privatization of the public schools though its agreements with local school boards to run problem schools. Most of its schools and students are in Michigan. In 2012, the Michigan Department of Education identified NHA as the operator of more than half of the charter schools that the state labels as "focus schools" because of poor student performance. © *Dwight Burdette*

charter school companies that promise to raise standards for profit. To date, nearly all the state takeovers occur in schools with mostly African American and Latino pupils. Opposition has grown intense in communities that claim this process amounts to systematic disenfranchisement in their children's education. In 2017, President Trump's newly appointed Secretary of Education, Betsy DeVos, a leader of the charter school movement in Michigan, promised to explore its benefits nationwide.

Efforts at reform have stabilized falling test scores on national public school tests and college entrance examinations but have not raised them significantly. Average achievement levels in language skills, mathematics and science have remained lower in the US than in many other developed nations, according to comparative studies of secondary pupils, which also show that American students spent less time doing homework.

In 2015, institutions of higher education in the US found that a large portion of college-age youth were not among the "college ready" (high-school graduates who had completed a minimum of secondary-level courses and scored at least up to a basic level on a national test). In the high school "class of 2014," for example, only 33 percent were college-ready, 30 percent had dropped out earlier and 37 percent who graduated did not have the academic achievements for acceptance at a college. In the fall of that year, 36 percent of the class began their college careers. About two-thirds did not go on to higher education because they had not reached the necessary academic level. Whites and Asian Americans had the highest rates of readiness and attendance, while Latinos, Native Americans and blacks had lower rates.

The causes of unsatisfactory quality in public education provoke much debate. Some commentators on elementary and secondary schools claim that only the achievement levels of inner-city districts are a problem and that their poor results skew the national averages. There is agreement, however, that continued "white flight" to the suburbs and private schools produced increased racial segregation and inadequate funding in urban areas. Others thought the problem of quality was nearly universal in the public schools.

In the wake of school shootings from Columbine to Sandy Hook, the schools continue to strive to improve security. They prioritize dealing with the causes of violence, such as problems at home, the availability of guns, violence and the attention given school shootings in the media, teasing and bullying, and the loss of a sense of community that results from how often American families move.

Expert analyses of the causes of decline of school quality focus on curriculum changes. Some critics assert that students neglect basic skills because they can to choose too many vocational or undemanding electives. Such criticisms provoke heated responses, especially when linked with allegations that pluralism, the introduction of women's or non-western "multicultural" components, has weakened the core curriculum. Revision of the academic canon is ongoing, as many institutions adjust their sense of the essential, and learn to function according to newly required state and federal standards under the NCLB and ESSA.

Proposals for policy changes in public elementary and secondary schools show the conflicting opinions about decreasing school localism. In Gallup polls, large majorities support requiring local schools to follow a central standardized national curriculum and to conform to national achievement standards. The same polls, however, reveal strong support for school choice programs, which often involve further decentralization. School choice allows families, rather than school authorities, to select the schools their children attend. Choice programs began with the decentralizing of school districts by giving individual schools the autonomy to design their own curricula. The first autonomous public schools were so-called magnet schools in inner cities. These institutions could specialize in particular subject areas (such as the fine arts or science) and received the funds and staff that, one hoped, would bring voluntary desegregation by attracting students from other districts.

By 2000, magnet schools were commonplace, especially in large urban school systems. School choice programs now center on charter schools as much as magnet schools. Both aim to maintain high standards by putting schools in competition with each other. In increasingly large areas, universal choice completely breaks the connection between a place of residence and the public school a pupil attends.

School choice advocates say the increased number of high-quality programs made available through choice gives students more chances to develop their abilities and point to reductions in racial segregation. Opponents argue that school choice relegates most staff and pupils to institutions that are weaker than ever before because they lack leadership and positive role models. They also criticize the concentration of the best faculty and pupils in magnet schools as an elitist approach that contradicts the ideals of American democracy. In 2014, over 2 million children in the US received schooling at home, because their parents decided to opt out of institutional schooling altogether. The number of children in home schooling has increased by around 10 percent per year since 2000.

Exercises

Explain and examine the significance of the following names and terms:

Meritocracy	Horace Mann	No Child Left Behind Act (NCLB)
Morrill Act	John Dewey	compulsory school attendance laws
GI Bill	Sputnik	coeducational education
bussing	affirmative action	progressive education programs
financial localism	decreases in localism	state redistribution plans
Local Education	state board of education	parochial schools
Districts (LEDs)	pluralism	private higher education
social localism	state university	continuous evaluation
community college	graduate school	school choice programs
liberal arts	college admissions policy	school vouchers
magnet schools	school choice charter schools	

Write short essays on the following questions.

1. What do you view as major developments in the historical evolution of American education? Defend your views.

2. Debate the advantages and disadvantages of localism in public elementary and secondary education, keeping in mind the recent limits put on local control.

3. Describe the private sector in American education. Is it good public policy for the US to support alternatives to public schooling?

4. Discuss the issues of current debate in American education. Why are these questions important or difficult in the US?

5. In what ways is entering American higher education a process of mutual selection in a system that is decentralized, diverse and competitive? Discuss the pros and cons of such a system.

Further reading

Cohen, D.K. and Moffitt, S.L. (2009) *The Ordeal of Equality: Did Federal Regulation Fix the Schools?* Cambridge, MA: Harvard University Press.

Department of Education (2016, annual) *Digest of Education Statistics*, Washington, DC: DOE.

Gitlin, T. (1995) *The Twilight of Common Dreams: Why America is Wracked by Culture Wars*, New York: Holt.

Kozol, J. (2012, reprint) *Savage Inequalities: Children in America's Schools*, New York: HarperCollins.

Meier, D. and Wood, G. (2004) *Many Children Left Behind: How the No Child Left Behind Act is Damaging Our Children and Our Schools*, Boston, MA: Beacon.

Ravitch, D. (2010) *The Death and Life of the Great American School System: How Testing and Choice Are Undermining Education*, New York: Basic Books.

Sowell, T. (1993) *Inside American Education: The Decline, the Deception, the Dogmas*, New York: Macmillan.

Websites

The National Center for Education Statistics (NCES): www.nces.ed.gov

nces.ed.gov/fastfacts

The National Education Association (NEA): www.nea.org

www.gallup.com/poll/indicators/education.asp

www.ed.gov

www.dese.mo.gov

www.nytimes.com/2012/07/06/education/no-child-left-behind-whittled-down-underobama. html?pagewanted=all&_r=0

www.capenet.org/facts.html

exchanges.state.gov

www.washingtonpost.com/local/education

The media

The term "media" includes channels of communication through which people are informed, instructed and entertained. In the US, it refers to the print media (newspapers, books and magazines); the broadcasting media (television and radio); new media sources, such as the Internet, e-Books, smartphones and social media like Facebook and Twitter. The information industries are a large and controversial business sector; are profitable parts of film, video, publishing, telecommunications, multimedia and advertising; and are growing strongly.

The media have evolved from basic methods of production and distribution to their present sophisticated technologies. Communications systems convey words, images and messages to a mass audience; offer diverse consumer choices; cover homes, educational institutions and businesses; and are a powerful and influential part of daily life.

Americans are conditioned by a variety of media types; technology has developed rapidly in recent years; and audience participation styles have changed markedly in response. According to Nielsen's Total Audience Report, US adults spent 10 hours, 39 minutes per day in the first quarter of 2016 consuming different types of media, an hour more than in 2015. This was due to an increase in smartphone and tablet usage at a time when live TV audiences had declined. In early 2016, US adults spent an average of four hours, 31 minutes watching live TV each day, amounting to some 42 percent of their overall media consumption.

According to the Institute for Communication Technology Management in 2015, US traditional media continued to dominate daily media consumption, with television and radio contributing 60 percent of total usage. However new digital sources are having major effects on most forms of media consumption with over half of media bytes now being received by computers and mobile phones. Earlier media consumption was mainly passive (sitting, watching and listening). New media consumption is more interactive, with time-delayed, multi-tasking, streamed and interrupted viewing becoming typical consumer behavior.

Polls suggest that Americans are losing interest in lengthy news programs and general current affairs and instead are concentrating on shorter bite-sized specific media. In 2013, Pew Research reported that television remained the dominant way that Americans received news items at home each month from network TV (65 percent), public and local television (71 percent) and cable TV news (38 percent). Since then, local and national newspapers, commercial and public radio have declined and, increasingly, the Internet and social media provide alternative, more frequent and shorter news and political items or flashes for Americans and for different demographics, such as millennials.

In its news programs, the media may influence public opinion and shape attitudes by deciding what is newsworthy and therefore publishable, although there is resistance to their dominant role. Historically, government has tried to license and muzzle the media (to little real effect after independence in 1776 and with the First Amendment guaranteeing freedom of the press in 1791). The press or media (sometimes called the "Fourth Estate"), claim to be guardians of US democracy and argue for equal status with the political and judicial branches of government. However, the media today is subject to considerable criticism and pressure as groups with different views attempt to promote reform of media outlets.

Radio and television historically minimized cultural and regional differences in the US, and reflected social diversity as they sought new markets and profits. Access to power could be gained through media sources, which politicians use to influence voters, particularly at election times. Political life and national and international events became more immediate for Americans with increased technology available. But the mass of information and images may also confuse and desensitize audiences, leading to distrust and rejection of the media and their methods of persuasion.

There are non-commercial media in the US, but most newspapers, magazines, publishing houses, radio and television stations, and electronic companies are privately owned. They are businesses operating for profit and are tied to commerce and sponsorship. Companies use the media to encourage consumers to buy their products through nationwide advertising, but critics increasingly oppose the alleged manipulative and negative influence of media advertising. Traditional media (like newspapers) have declined from being the largest source of advertising revenue. According to Statista research in 2015, television revenue in the US by 2020 was forecast to be $81.7 billion. Digital expenditure in 2015 was $72.09 billon, radio was $17.68 billon, newspapers were $23.57 billion and magazine were $15.1 billion. There is now greater diversification and competition among advertisers, with the Internet becoming more attractive to commercial companies.

Consumer opinion also influences the media and their agendas. They must respond to the public's wishes for a wide range of available entertainment, information and news if they are to be profitable. A ratings system for radio and television (statistics on audience approval) and print media circulation figures are still important determinants of success or failure.

Developments in mass communications and entertainment technology, such as interactive formats, the Internet and smartphones have expanded the scope of the media society and helped to shape the country's cultural life. The growth of media outlets has increased markets, reduced the dominance of traditional formats (such as newspapers, network television, videos, CDs and DVDs), appealed to more diverse groups in the population and increased participation by viewers, readers and listeners. The availability of American television programs, books, periodicals, satellite and cable news programs (such as CNN) and online newspapers has also internationalized the US media's influence.

Media history

Books and newspapers were the first media to emerge in early American history due to a public need for news, education and information. Book production increased when a printing press was set up in 1638 in Cambridge, Massachusetts. But presses and the print media were controlled politically by the British colonial authorities through a licensing system. Although the first basic newspaper, Benjamin Harris' *Publick Occurrences Both Forreign and Domestick*, was published in Boston in 1690, it was banned because it did not have a license.

The eighteenth century

Newspapers developed quickly in the eighteenth century. They gained influence and readership as they fought against licensing control and responded to political events and the demands of a growing population for information and communication. The first relatively comprehensive newspaper, James Franklin's *New England Courant*, was published in Boston in 1721. Papers were a unifying force in the fight for independence from the British and communicated news of east-coast revolt to western settlers.

Magazines were the last journalistic print media to emerge, expanded more slowly than newspapers and were partly influenced by middle-class wishes for entertainment and education. Andrew Bradford's *American Magazine* was the first magazine, appearing shortly before Benjamin Franklin's *General Magazine* (January 1741).

As the population grew and expanded westwards, the social role of the print media was emphasized. Presses and print shops were established by settlers, who published books of local laws, newspapers and magazines. After the War for Independence, newspapers declined in quality. They became abusive and biased propaganda tools of political parties and vested interests with vehement editorials in support of special causes and political programs. Nevertheless, by 1800 there were some 20 daily papers and about a thousand weeklies in local areas, which made greater attempts at objectivity in order to gain and retain readers.

Newspapers gained the protection of the First Amendment of the Bill of Rights in 1791, which guaranteed freedom of speech and the press and was bolstered by later court decisions. Americans knew that some papers had supported

THE
New-England Courant.

MONDAY Auguſt 7. 1721.

Homo non unius Negotii: Or, *Jack of all Trades.*

Mr. John Checkley

IT'S an hard Caſe, that a Man can't appear in Print now a Days, unleſs he'll undergo the Mortification of Anſwering to ten thouſand ſenſeleſs and Impertinent Queſtions like theſe, Pray Sir, from whence came you? And what Age may you be of, may I be ſo bold? Was you bred at Colledge Sir? And can you (like ſome of them) ſquare the Circle, and cypher as far as the Black Art? &c. Now, tho' I muſt confeſs it's ſomething irkſome to a Man in haſt, thus to be ſtop'd at his firſt ſetting-out, yet in Compliance to the Cuſtom of the Country where I now ſet up for an Author, I'll immediately ſtop ſhort, and give my gentle Reader ſome Account of my Perſon and my rare Endowments.

As for my Age, I'm ſome odd Years and a few Days under twice twenty and three, therefore I hope no One will hereafter object againſt my ſoaring now and then with the grave Wits of the Age, ſince I have dropt my callow Feathers, and am pretty well fledg'd: but if they ſhould tell me that I am not yet fit nor worthy to keep Company with ſuch Illuſtrious Sages, for my Beard do's n't yet reach down to my Girdle, I ſhall make them no other Anſwer than this, Barba non facit Philoſophum.

I make no Queſtion but, my gentle Readers, but that you're very Impatient to ſee me intirely diſſected, and to have a full View of my outward as well as inward Man, but as I ſtopt ſhort juſt now, meerly to oblige you, ſo I ſhall ſtop as ſhort here, and give no farther Account of my ſelf until this Day fortnight, when you ſhall have a farther Account of this uſeful Deſign, and of my great Endowments of Body and Mind.

And to engage the World to converſe farther with I, they'l find me in the good Company of a certain Set of Men, of whom I hope to give a very good Account,

Who like faithful Shepherds take care of their *Flocks*,
By teaching and practiſing what's Orthodox,
Pray hard againſt *Sickneſs*, yet preach up the *POX*!

N. B. This Paper will be publiſhed once a Fortnight, and out of meer Kindneſs to my Brother-Writers, I intend now and then to be (like them) very, very dull; for I have a ſtrong Fancy, that unleſs I am ſometimes flat and low, this Paper will not be very grateful to ſome.

Dr Douglaſs

abnormis ſapiens. —— Hor.

At the Requeſt of ſeveral Gentlemen in Town: A Continuation of the Hiſtory of Inoculation in *Boſton*, by a Society of the Practitioners in Phyſick.

THe bold undertaker of the Practice of the Greek old Women, notwithſtanding the Terror and Confuſion from his Son's Inoculation-Fever, proceeds to inoculate Perſons from Seventy Years of Age and downwards.

The Select Men (or Managers of the Town Affairs) in duty bound to take Cognizance of the Matter, deſire a Meeting of all the Practitioners in Town, to have their Opinion whether the Practice ought to be allowed or not; they unanimouſly agreed that is was raſh and dubious, being entirely new, not in the leaſt vouched or recommended (being meerly publiſhed, in the Philoſophick Tranſactions by way of Amuſement) from Britain, tho' it came to us *via* London from the Turks, and by a ſtrong *viva voce* Evidence, was proved to be of fatal & dangerous Conſequence. B——n is deſired by the Select Men to deſiſt.

Notwithſtanding the general Averſion of the Town, in Contradiction to the declared Opinion of the Practitioners, in Oppoſition to the Selectmen, and in Spite of the diſcouraging Evidences relating to this Practice, Six Gentlemen of Piety and Learning, profoundly ignorant of the Matter, after ſerious Conſideration of a Diſeaſe one of the moſt intricate practical Caſes in Phyſick, do on the Merits of their Characters, and for no other reaſon, with a *Vox praterieg*; nihil, aſſert, &c. If this Argument, viz. their Character, ſhould prevail with the Populace (tho' here I think they have miſſed of their Aim) who knows but it may oblige ſome profhane Perſon to canvas that ſort of Argument. I think their Character ought to be ſacred, and that they themſelves ought not to give the leaſt Occaſion to have it called in queſtion. They ſet up for Judges of a Man's Qualifications in the Practice of Phyſick, and very laviſhly beſtow all the fulſome common Place of *Quack Advertiſements*. One would think they meant ſome *Romantick Character*, ſomething beyond that of candid *Sydenham*, the ſagacious *Radcliff*, or the celebrated *Mead*: They might indeed in reſpect of his moral and religious Qualifications, which lay properly under their Cognizance, have ſaid, That he was a modeſt, humble Man, a Man of Continency, Probity, &c.

At firſt reading of this Compoſure, many were perſwaded, that it was only a Piece of Humour, Banter, Burleſque,

MVSEVM
BRITAN
NICVM

PLATE 13.1 Front page facsimile of an early US newspaper, *New England Courant*, Boston, 1721, published by James Franklin, older brother of Benjamin Franklin. This was a relatively successful attempt at newspaper publishing in the new nation, after earlier failures due to British censorship and licensing of the media.

them against the British before and during the War for Independence. They were determined that Congress and government should not have the power to infringe press freedom. This development formed the basis of "prior restraint" (the doctrine that the authorities cannot muzzle the press before publication).

The nineteenth century

By the mid-nineteenth century, the print media became more influential as social and cultural forces. Literacy rates increased and an expansion of schools and libraries created a mass market of readers. High-speed presses were manufactured to satisfy the demand for news, entertainment, education and information. New magazines and mass newspapers emerged after 1825 (such as the *New York Sun* in 1833) and the market for novels, textbooks and general books increased as publishers organized the book industry into its modern structure.

There was a strong demand for novels, which sold in large numbers, and many were written by women. Novelists were aided by the introduction of paperback books in 1842, which began as supplements to newspapers and were later printed by conventional booksellers. Paperbacks are still an important part of publishing firms' structure and are relatively inexpensive purchases for consumers.

Newspapers became a cheap and genuine mass medium and rapidly increased. They were mostly owned and edited by powerful and influential individuals who were personally involved in their papers. They introduced new publishing methods and forms of communication. James Gordon Bennett founded the first modern American newspaper, the New York *Herald*, in 1835. He employed reporters to gather news, appointed the first foreign correspondents, developed a Washington press corps and delivered the news before his competitors by using the telegraph and fast transportation methods.

Bennett was followed by Horace Greeley with his New York *Tribune* (1841), whose editorial page was very influential nationwide, and by Henry Raymond, who published *The New York Times* (1851). These and other owners improved news-gathering methods and developed innovative newspaper structures.

By the end of the nineteenth century, Joseph Pulitzer and William Randolph Hearst, with the *World* (1887) and the *Journal* (1895) respectively, dominated US newspapers. They were fierce rivals in a struggle for bigger circulation figures, produced papers which mixed sensational news reporting ("yellow journalism") with social crusading and introduced Sunday papers and the classic American comic strip. A significant development occurred when E. W. Scripps founded the first newspaper chain (a collectivist structure under one owner) from 1889. This trend became important in the twentieth century.

Newspapers (about 2,326 dailies by 1900) and other print media were established as the primary means of communication for the population and had very large readerships. But journalism also became big business for some news organizations, which focused less on social crusading and accurate reporting and more on profitable populist material.

The twentieth century

Personal newspaper ownership continued in the early twentieth century, although the total number of daily newspapers declined from their nineteenth-century high point. Joseph Patterson printed the New York *Daily News* in 1919 (the first modern tabloid) and Robert R. McCormick published the *Chicago Tribune* from 1910.

Owners and editors also realized that objective reporting rather than bias attracted more readers. Newspapers became more conservative because advertising, on which they now depended financially, replaced circulation figures as the main source of income. Advertisers initially aimed at a middle-class market but later divided the population into all the class and income groups. Different types of newspapers appeared, which reflected varied lifestyles, social status, education, political ideologies and consumption levels. Most newspapers were

PLATE 13.2 One of President Franklin D. Roosevelt's radio broadcasts to the nation in the 1930s.

Courtesy of Franklin D. Roosevelt Library Public Domain Photographs, 1882–1962, National Archives.

still concentrated in local areas and cities and were owned by individuals or companies. But economic pressures by the middle of the twentieth century forced many owners to sell their papers or join large chains that then dominated the media business.

Magazines and newspapers were similar in form and content and often embarked on crusading investigative journalism, which President Theodore Roosevelt called "muckraking" (exposing scandal and corruption). Investigative reporting had previously been largely political. But it now also included criticisms of the general social system and attempted to gain public support for specific campaigns. Such investigative journalism became a feature of the print industries and spread to radio and television later in the twentieth century.

The print media were challenged first by Hollywood's silent films and later by sound motion pictures, which became the dominant entertainment sources of the 1920s and 1930s and an alternative attraction for audiences. These media forms also had to compete with radio broadcasting in the 1920s. Radio provided a new national and world perspective for many Americans. It unified country and city, minimized rural isolation, contributed greatly to cultural standardization and continues to be significant for news and entertainment formats. Commercial television was introduced at the New York World's Fair in 1939, but the Second World War and conflicts between competing television production companies hindered its progress. After the war, television began to dominate the other broadcast and print media. Its information service threatened the news and comment functions of newspapers, and its entertainment role challenged magazines, books and films. The other media had to cope with this and later competition (such as the Internet).

The twenty-first century

Today, the US has the most varied mass media in the world. They are relatively decentralized and are comprised of newspapers, magazines, radio and television stations, publishers and Internet websites, and most are owned by multimedia or specialist concerns. US books, dramas, comedies, television soap operas and series, films and music attract a global following. The early twenty-first century also saw great advances for the Internet and other electronic/digital media, such as broadband, cell phones, social networking sites like Facebook and Twitter, smartphones, tablets, and a large increase in blogs (independently written websites). The print media have lost circulation as their functions were transferred online either by subscriptions to existing newspapers and magazines or by independent writers on the Internet and social media networks. These developments were characterized by instant communication, vast audiences, interactive websites and alternative advertising and revenue sources. But there is concern that the creation of huge media conglomerates, such as a proposed merger in 2016

PLATE 13.3 Advertising poster for the New York World's Fair 1939, which introduced television to the US, together with fiercely competing television companies.
© *Everett Collection Historical/Alamy*

between AT&T and Time Warner, has led to a concentration of ownership and power.

It is also argued that largely unregulated new media can lead to irresponsibility, abuse and inaccuracy. The United Nations Human Rights Council passed a resolution in July 2012 supporting freedom of expression on the Internet. According to Pew Internet Center, the question is whether Internet companies in the interests of profit and their financial backers will support governments that restrict their citizens from freely using the Internet. The domestic US media debate is also concerned with whether regulation of the First Amendment beyond existing legal and governmental restrictions is necessary, desirable or possible.

Freedom of the media

The First Amendment to the Constitution states that Congress shall not make any law that abridges "freedom of speech, or of the press." However, a July 2013 State of the First Amendment survey reported that 47 percent of respondents found that freedom of speech is the most important right for Americans, followed by freedom of religion (10 percent) and choice (7 percent), the rights to bear arms (5 percent), to vote (5 percent), to life, liberty and the pursuit of happiness (3 percent), and freedom of the press (one percent). The list suggests a distinction between freedom of speech and the press, although the Supreme Court has not given the press any greater rights than those of ordinary citizens.

The media today (not only the press) claim equal treatment under the First Amendment and there is no overt government censorship of content or form. This protection from government control has enabled the press to serve as a watchdog over official actions, executive abuses and violations of individual rights.

But freedom from prior restraint is not absolute. The Supreme Court has indicated that injunctions preventing publication may be granted if material clearly jeopardizes national security, and other exceptions have occurred in areas such as school newspapers. There are also licensing and anti-monopolistic regulations by the Federal Communications Commission (FCC), which arguably makes the broadcasting media less free than the print media. While the media appear to be constitutionally free, they are arguably subject to and conditioned by advertising, concentrated ownership patterns, economic pressures and consumer opinion.

US attitudes to the constitutional freedoms are divided. Respondents to a State of the First Amendment Survey in July 2009 found that the press has too much freedom to do what it wants (39 percent); the right amount (48 percent); and too little (7 percent). But while a survey in 2012 reported that 75 percent of respondents agreed that the media should act as a watchdog over government action, 20 percent disagreed. Only 33 percent of respondents believed the news media attempt to report news without bias; 81 percent said that the First Amendment does not go too far in the rights it guarantees, while 13 percent said it does. A First Amendment report in July 2016 by the Newseum Institute found that 40 percent of respondents were unable to name any freedom protected by the First Amendment and only 54 percent were able to identify that the Amendment protects freedom of speech.

Respondents to an ABC News Nightline poll in January 2003 felt that the right to a free press is essential/very important (38/49 percent) and 59 percent thought that the government should not have the right to control what information the news media can report. But, in a war situation, 60 percent argued that the priority was the government's need to keep military secrets, rather than preserving a free press (34 percent); 56 percent thought that the media should support the government (rather than questioning it); and 66 percent felt that the government has a right to prohibit the media from reporting sensitive military information.

According to the Worldwide Press Freedom Index 2016 compiled by Reporters Without Borders, the US was in forty-first place in a list of 180 countries evaluated for their degree of press freedom. This decline from twentieth position in 2010–11 was reportedly attributed to alleged police actions against journalists and photographers who had covered protests in the US, such as the "Occupy" movements. It was argued that press freedoms were being eroded.

The media, in pursuing their constitutional rights, have often pursued an adversarial or confrontational line toward public authorities and individuals. They have published official secrets, revealed classified documents and exposed corrupt practices, unethical behavior and injustices in American life. This has led to tension between the media and public authorities.

For example, *The Washington Post* and *The New York Times* published the "Pentagon Papers" in 1971. These classified US defense papers contained details of the American role in the Vietnam War. After government appeals, the Supreme Court ruled that the newspapers had a constitutional right to publish the information. *The Washington Post* also disclosed the Watergate scandal (resulting in the resignation of President Richard Nixon). The media revealed the 1968 My Lai massacre by US troops in Vietnam and the 1986 Iran–Contra affair involving secret and illegal dealings by US government officials. Contemporary investigations continue into the activities of politicians, institutions and public figures (such as the Clintons' Whitewater business dealings in the 1980s–1990s). In 2001 the White House did not want television networks to broadcast videotaped statements by Osama bin Laden and his associates, although they had shown another bin Laden tape. The networks agreed not to broadcast such statements again without reviewing them. It was argued that the decision meant that the media was not fulfilling its responsibility to report all the news.

The question of the media's role, influence and power is controversial and debatable. Critics argue that the media have become too powerful and influential, that their freedom should be curtailed and that they should show more responsibility. The news media are accused of bias, distorted journalism, invasion of privacy, manipulation of events, and actively trying to shape public opinion by setting particular agendas. Legal actions for libel, obscenity, contempt of court (to force the identification of journalists' sources) and injunctions may be used against the media. These can protect individuals, the authorities and organizations and prevent absolute free expression by the media.

There is a close (arguably unhealthy) bond between authorities and the media. Each needs and uses the other to mutual advantage and gains access to sources and policymakers. One example was "embedding" reporters with military units in the 2003 Iraq war. This connection may be thought inappropriate for the media and limits their independent role.

The mainstream press has historically tended to ignore the private lives of its political leaders. But this relationship has changed as tabloid newspapers, 24-hour TV news channels, talk radio stations, social media, websites and independent blogs probe the private and official lives of public figures. It is argued that such people have chosen their roles and may be investigated, particularly if their private actions affect their public duties. The Internet, social media and interactive talk radio in particular have expanded opportunities for extreme commentary, abuse, scandal-mongering and disclosure of classified information. Increasingly, it has been argued that these media are as accountable as more traditional media. Nevertheless, other commentators feel that a wide dissemination of information is healthier and more democratic than suppression and censorship.

The contemporary print media

The press (newspapers)

In 2013, some 1,395 daily newspapers (mornings and evenings during the week) were published in the US, with a circulation of 40.7 million. This was a decrease from 2010 and continues a pattern of print decline. Sunday papers had increased to 934 from 2010, but their circulation dropped to 43.3 million. Traditional weekly, semi-weekly and monthly local newspapers have seen declines in numbers and circulation. In 2013, there was also a decrease in total advertising revenue income from newspapers of 7.1 percent.

Newspapers cater to different readerships. Some are characterized as "quality" or "serious" papers, which tend to be located in the big cities, and have in-depth international and national news and feature coverage. Others are "popular" or "tabloid" publications, which emphasize crime, sports, comic pages, sex and scandal. However, some US papers have pretensions to quality and seriousness rather than ferocious and sensational presentation.

It is often argued that the US does not have a national press or newspapers that are available in all parts of the country on the same morning. This is due partly to the nation's size and different time zones, but also because of a concern with local issues and identity. One newspaper, which is aimed at a national readership and regional distribution through satellite technology and Internet production, is the top-selling *USA Today*, which first appeared in 1984. It has brief articles rather than longer stories and a popular tabloid style.

However, most US papers are now also available in online and updated format (often by subscription charge) on the Internet across the country. The national and international influence of some large quality metropolitan newspapers, such as *The New York Times*, *The Washington Post*, the *Los Angeles Times* and *The Wall Street Journal* is considerable.

TABLE 13.1 Average circulation of main daily newspapers, 2014

Newspaper	Description	Circulation
USA Today	popular	2,676,586
The Wall Street Journal	quality	2,273,767
The New York Times	quality	1,897,890
Los Angeles Times	quality	671,797
New York Post	popular	576,711
(San Jose) Mercury News	quality	571,804
(New York) Daily News	popular	467,110
Chicago Tribune	quality	453,568
(Long Island) Newsday	quality	437,457
The Washington Post	quality	431,521
Chicago Sun-Times	quality	419,364
Dallas Morning News	quality	411,929
Los Angeles Daily News	quality	410,068
Denver Post	quality	403,039
Houston Chronicle	quality	356,347
Orange County Register	quality	330,246
Philadelphia Inquirer	quality	310,002
Minneapolis StarTribune	quality	300,495
Newark Star-Ledger	quality	285,249
Honolulu Star-Advertiser	popular	265,099
The Boston Globe	quality	253,373

Source: Alliance for Audited Media, 2014

Newspapers have experienced fundamental changes and developments in recent decades and have been forced to adapt to new markets, structures and policies in order to survive. There has been a continuous decline in the sales of most papers since the mass circulation years of the early twentieth century due to news and advertising competition from television, radio, the Internet and social media. The number of newspapers has also decreased because of mergers, conversions and closures. Readers have embraced new media habits (such as using the Internet rather than paper newspapers for their news) and circulation battles between different print formats (like magazine supplements) have increased. But some small local dailies and weeklies have nevertheless increased in number, circulation and quality by reflecting specific news stories and geographical interests.

Newspaper decline and amalgamation have been accompanied by a reduction in competition in many urban centers and a lack of variety in publications. The number of cities and towns with competing newspapers has been reduced, and many have only one remaining daily paper. Ownership is held by a few publishers or corporations (media conglomerates) and 75 percent of daily papers are now owned by newspaper chains. But there are still papers with clear powerful identities such as *The New York Times* and *The Washington Post*.

Concentrated ownership of newspapers by large groups supposedly results in economies of size, efficiency and rationalization and gives greater profitability. But it also causes monopolistic conditions, a similarity in content and format and raises questions about objectivity and accuracy. While some quality papers are local monopolies, it is argued that a greater diversity of newspapers would result in the reduction of potential error and bias.

Newspapers have experienced technological changes in recent years, such as automated composing rooms and the use of computer and electronic technology to process news. Some news is still gathered by individual reporters, but most newspapers and radio and television networks worldwide now obtain their news directly from US-based news agencies, such as the Associated Press (AP), Bloomberg LP and United Press International (UPI). They are independently owned and collect national and international news items that are sold to newspapers and other media. A few news sources therefore dominate the US market, resulting in comparatively homogeneous international and national news.

However, the big American papers still provide some of their own news stories and sell copyrighted news and features to international and national papers. This allows the wide dissemination of news throughout the US and contributes to the influence of the larger papers. Similarly, the articles of independent syndicated columnists appear simultaneously in many newspapers. The stories in the big papers often influence local newspapers and television news programs in their choice and presentation of newsworthy items.

It is argued that, following competition from television, newspapers generally have become more responsible, make their news columns as fair and accurate as possible, attempt to be objective in their reports and try to separate news from opinion (which is usually confined to politically influenced editorial pages).

Investigative journalism is still a part of the newspaper trade, although costs have reduced its use. Small newspapers concentrate largely on local news, but they may also cover issues of concern such as pollution, nuclear leaks and climate change, and they have revealed cases of local political and social corruption and cover-ups, which have wider national ramifications. Some large city papers are the most active in investigative journalism and have the resources for in-depth coverage. However, the amount of investigative reporting carried out by the US media should not be exaggerated. Few journalists engage in such work, and many rely on common sources rather than their own independent investigations.

Investigative (and other) journalists may argue that they uphold press freedom; promote important social change with their news presentations; maintain that they perform a necessary democratic service; and see themselves as servants of the public rather than officialdom. However, some critics oppose vigorous reporting and argue that it constitutes a serious invasion of privacy in many cases, gives newspapers too much social and political influence, and encourages irresponsibility.

Magazines and periodicals

Some 11,000 magazines and periodicals are published in the US at varying times from weekly and monthly to quarterly and biyearly. About four out of five adults read magazines, which cater to most tastes and interests. Some have small and others large circulations, with the top 93 selling over one million copies each. Some of these have international editions or are translated into other languages. Six magazine companies account for half the total magazine revenue, indicating a high conglomerate concentration and influence. The best-selling (specialist) magazines deal with retirement (*AARP The Magazine* and *AARP The Bulletin*) and have sales over 22 million. The list in Table 13.2 refers to generalist and specialist popular magazines covering television news, reading, travel, women's interests, news and video gaming. The main income revenue of magazines comes from advertising and digital subscriptions, but paper circulation continues to fall.

Mass-circulation magazines declined from the 1950s because they had to compete for advertising and sales with television, newspapers and online. Rising costs of production and paper led to smaller formats and fewer magazines. Classic publications such as *Life*, *The Saturday Evening Post* and *Look* did not survive as weeklies. A shift to specialization in specific areas has occurred, as magazines try to establish market positions and profitability.

However, general magazines (such as *Reader's Digest* with its international market) are an important element of American cultural life. They were originally designed for entertainment, but they could also be influential in social and political areas. Today, general magazines are mainly informational and are concerned with very varied aspects of social life. They are aimed at readers in specific age, interest or economic groups.

The more specialist magazines are targeted at people with particular professional occupations and interests and serve as an important means of communication among them. In fact, the majority of all magazines and periodicals are "trade" or specialist publications. They cover business, professional, technical, industrial, scientific and scholarly areas.

US news magazines were more successful than those of other countries in this field, but sales and the number of publications have declined significantly since 1999. *Time* (sales per issue of 3,286,467 in 2014) is a paper and online news magazine and has international editions. *Newsweek* was launched in 1933 and, after recent problems, returned to print and global online editions in 2014 with sales of 100,000 in 2015.

Some influential periodicals specialize in coverage of educational, political and cultural topics, such as *The Atlantic Monthly, Harvard Educational Review, The New Republic, National Review, Scientific American, Foreign Affairs, Smithsonian* and *The New Yorker*. These, together with other specialist professional journals, supply the more serious end of the magazine market, and some of their material is reprinted internationally.

The leisure or hobby end of the market is catered to by magazines that deal with sports, popular pastimes, motoring, fashion and leisure activities.

TABLE 13.2 Main general magazines: average circulation, 2014

Magazine	Paid circulation
AARP The Magazine (special interest)	22,837,736
AARP The Bulletin (specialist)	22,183,316
Better Homes and Gardens (specialist)	7,639,661
Game Informer Magazine (specialist gaming)	7,099,452
Good Housekeeping (women's interest)	4,325,330
Family Circle (women's interest)	4,015,728
National Geographic (specialist)	3,572,348
People (celebrity life)	3,510,533
Reader's Digest (general interest)	3,393,573
Woman's Day (women's interest)	3,288,335
Time (specialist-news)	3,286,467
Ladies Home Journal (women's interest)	3,226,731

Source: Audit Bureau of Circulations (ABC), 2014

Some, such as *Cosmopolitan* (sales per issue of 3,019,778 in 2014) also sell well internationally.

Book publishing

There was concern in the twentieth century that radio, film and television might reduce the appeal of buying and reading books. But book purchases increased, and the US led the world in the number of books read per person. However, book sales have fluctuated.

Although computers, tablets and e-Books were supposed to eradicate the print book genre, publishers have continued to produce new books, particularly business, economic, medical, law, scientific and technical books and journals. The Association of American Publishers (AAP) reported that conventional trade paper sales were slightly up by 2.2 percent in 2015, but e-book sales declined in the children's, young adult and adult categories. Downloaded audio books grew in popularity, particularly among adults, and it is estimated that sales figures for print-on-demand or self-published titles have also increased. The future of the printed book continues to be debated, but paperback books are the most popular format of units sold, and hardback book sales have grown (with a total sale of 2.71 billion book units, or $28 billion revenue). Online sales are strong, but purchases from physical stores are increasing.

Historically, US schools have generally encouraged reading and a love of books, public libraries have actively sponsored reading in local communities nationwide and there are no restrictive laws that control bookselling and prices. There is an open market in new and used books, which are sold in a variety of sales outlets, such as supermarkets, in addition to standard book shops.

American books cover a comprehensive range from fiction to technical works. They are an important leisure, as well as an educational and professional, activity. There are some 1,800 major book publishers in the US, with about six conglomerates accounting for more than half of total book revenues, which differ in size and variety of publications. A large export trade has contributed to the worldwide influence of American books, especially in the scientific and technological fields. About a quarter of the publishing structure deals with books intended for a general audience, such as fiction, bestsellers, biography, art books and children's books. Three-quarters of the publishing business is divided among textbooks, reference works, subscription book clubs and scientific and technical publications.

The contemporary broadcasting media

The broadcasting system (radio and television stations) is characterized by its diversity and division into commercial and non-commercial sectors. The commercial sector is largely financed by businesses that pay to advertise goods or services before, during and after programs, or by subscriptions from cable and satellite users. Advertising's connection to the media is increasingly controversial because of its alleged influence and methods.

The non-commercial radio and television sectors, such as the Public Broadcasting Service (PBS), do not carry advertising, are largely nonprofit, educational or cultural in nature and are run by bodies such as colleges and universities. They are funded by individual subscriptions, sponsorship, grants from foundations, private bodies, educational sources and the government, but they have to survive on relatively limited budgets.

All radio and television stations must be licensed to broadcast by the FCC. This is an independent federal agency, financed by Congress, whose members are appointed by the president. It controls stations by granting limited licenses to applicants and has a supervisory and regulatory role. The FCC does not control the reception of broadcast programs through the air. This means that there are no license fees in the US for owning equipment, such as television sets. Broadcast reception is freely available in most cases, except for cable and decoded satellite services, and underwent a switchover from analog to digital reception in June 2009.

There is no direct government censorship of broadcasting content, but the FCC, with its licensing power, does regulate media ownership by trying to ensure that there are no monopolies and that a variety of services, programs and frequencies are provided throughout the country. Its "fairness doctrine" also requires stations to give equal time to opposing views, and commercial stations must show free "public-service" announcements, such as Red Cross blood drives and Alcoholics Anonymous programs.

Television

In 2014, according to Nielsen Media Research, 115.8 million (99 percent of) US households owned at least one television set and 84 percent had two or more; 80.9 percent had a DVD player; and 48.5 percent had a DVR. The majority of TV sets were color, and viewing time for all viewers was 33.46 hours per week. Surveys suggest that television is still an important source of news for Americans, although the network share is declining in competition with online and cable news. It can be influential in forming opinions and may be potentially capable of affecting the outcome of political elections.

The Federal Communications Act of 1934 established local television stations that are legally responsible for their output, no matter where their programs originated. In 2011, there were about 1,774 television stations in the US, which vary in size, have separate identities and characteristics, and have different transmission strengths. Some 350 were non-commercial or educational.

Most commercial television stations are affiliated with and receive many programs from the current Big Four private television networks, which buy much of their material from independent production companies. The current Big Four are the American Broadcasting Company (ABC, established in 1943), the National Broadcasting Company (NBC, 1926), the Columbia Broadcasting Service (CBS, 1928) and Fox Broadcasting Company (1986). The Fox network broke the dominance of the original Big Three networks, ABC, CBS and NBC.

The networks compete against each other to attract the highest audience ratings and advertising revenue, which are crucial for the survival of individual shows. Most TV programs follow the same formats and offerings nationwide (see Table 13.3), and they are shown at the same time during "prime time" (8 p.m. to 11 p.m.). This structure traditionally gave the three older networks (ABC, NBC and CBS) great influence. Until the 1980s, they dominated American television, having a combined share of 90 percent of the total television audience.

In addition to an entertainment role, the networks have news-gathering organizations in the US and worldwide. They broadcast nationwide news and current-affairs programs throughout the week and have developed classics such as CBS's *Sixty Minutes* and NBC's *Meet the Press*. Local commercial television stations also have news teams, reporters and film crews to provide local news programs, but they may be parochial and limited in their scope.

However, a large television network, and an alternative to commercial television, is the advertising-free PBS. This system was created in 1969 by the Public Broadcasting Act, has some 350 stations sharing programs, reaches about 73 million people each week and delivers quality and educational programs. The growth of PBS has been considerable, although it has a smaller total audience than commercial television. The high standard of its news, entertainment and educational programs (such as children's programs, imported drama series and films) has attracted selective audiences.

Americans' television viewing habits changed significantly in June 2009 when the FCC stipulated that all US-based TV signals must be transmitted digitally. Some 97.5 percent of homes complied with the switchover from analog reception. Americans are also changing the way that they watch television. From 2008–09 more people have watched recorded or "time-shifted television" (DVR), and the major networks attract viewers by providing free episodes of popular shows streamed from their website. Other sites offer episodes of traditional television shows and specially made Internet programs that are supported by advertising.

Independent, cable and satellite television

Since the 1980s, the power of the original Big Three networks has declined because of competition, such as the Fox network, and cable systems. Challenges have also come from other independent television stations that were originally unaffiliated with the networks and broadcast syndicated programming, comprising mostly of repeats of earlier network series. They have built larger audiences nationwide by expanding the quality and range of their services and by using broadcast technology and cable and satellite facilities.

Cable stations originally provided television programs to subscribers in communities that could not receive good reception from air broadcasts because of geographical and physical limitations. In the past 30 years, cable has changed television broadcasting by attracting audiences from existing channels to watch cable programs for varying periods of time. This has split the total television audience, which is now shared by more competitors.

According to Nielsen Media Research, the number of household subscribers to basic cable was 103.7 million in 2014 or 89.6 percent of households with TV sets. The general pattern is for consumers to watch cable during a week while sharing their viewing with other media. Cable subscribers may also pay for enhanced digital and premium cable systems. The top basic cable networks in 2013 were The Weather Channel (with 99.7 million subscribers), C-SPAN (99.4 million subscribers), TBS (99.1 million subscribers), Food Network (99.1 million subscribers), Discovery Channel (98.7 million subscribers), and Nickelodeon/Nick at Nite (98.7 million subscribers). Fox News is the leading US cable news network.

There are now many different types of cable systems and programs. Companies transmit cable-produced and network affiliated independent and public television services. They are financed by advertising and a fee from subscribers for the cable service. Viewers may also pay additional sums for specialist

TABLE 13.3 Top ten favorite prime-time commercial TV programs, 2013–14

Rank	Title	Genre
1	NCIS (CBS)	naval crime investigation
2	The Big Bang Theory (CBS)	sitcom
3	Dancing with the Stars (ABC)	dance competition
4	Blacklist (NBC)	crime drama
5	NCIS: Los Angeles (CBS)	naval crime investigation
6	The Voice (NBC)	singing competition
7	The Voice (Tuesday; NBC)	singing competition
8	Grey's Anatomy (ABC)	hospital drama series
9	Castle (ABC)	crime-comedy series
10	Scandal (ABC)	political thriller series

Source: adapted from Nielsen Media Research, 2013–14

channels and live broadcasts. There has been a big increase in religious and ethnic cable stations and channels nationwide for African, Spanish, Latino, Jewish, Chinese, Japanese, Portuguese, Greek, Hindi and Korean interests.

Satellite television also undercut the dominance of the original Big Three networks. It initially offered programs to rural populations who could not receive cable systems. It gives people who have a satellite dish and pay subscriptions a wide range of television channels. After a period when there was a variety of satellite providers, many of which went out of business, there are now two main servers that compete against each other. DirecTV (1994) has national coverage and offers digital and multi-channel TV programming. DISH Network (1996) operates globally and delivers direct broadcast satellite products. While satellite programming has attracted ethnic and minority interests in the US and abroad, it has had technological, monitoring and regulation issues, and political conflicts on viability.

A historical threat to Big Three supremacy was the home video market, with videos for sale or rent. Although this has declined steeply, in 2006 there was at least one videocassette recorder (VCR) in 85 percent of American homes that had television sets. VCR was then challenged by huge sales of digital versatile disks (DVDs) and 80.9 percent of television households had a DVD player in 2014. These forms have now also been partly replaced by videos by made-for-Internet programs streamed from network and company websites, such as Netflix and Amazon, to televisions, smartphones and computer screens. Monthly time spent watching video online (including both user-generated content and recorded programs) has grown rapidly (particularly music streaming).

Traditional network television has thus faced severe competition to retain its audience as viewers have changed to other services and historic shares of viewing habits have changed. Cable, satellite and independent television stations and Internet providers offer many different channels and a range of alternative choices. There has also been a shift away from live television to time-shifted television, through DVRs and by viewing Internet video sharing websites and streaming of television shows.

Radio

Radio had a dramatic impact after its commercial introduction to the US in 1920, when it broke the print media monopoly. Its immediate news function helped to unify the population of the cities and the countryside, increased the national and world awareness of Americans, informed them about the events of the Second World War and allowed political leaders (such as President Franklin D. Roosevelt) to reach a mass audience. Radio was overtaken by television in the 1940s and has had to develop new markets and emphases to survive. It has become divided into formats that are directed at specific consumer markets, and this has increased the diversity of radio offerings. Some 98 percent of American households have at least one set, and radio is still popular and important, particularly on the local level, for its news, participatory (talk radio) and entertainment roles. According to US State Department publications, radio reaches 80 percent of the population at varying times of the day.

The US does not have one national radio station. Instead, cities and local areas have commercial stations regulated by the FCC, which grants them operating licenses. Town stations carry local interest items and news, and national and international news is derived from larger stations. Big cities have a large number of stations and different formats and services to satisfy varied tastes. News, sports and talk stations predominate on medium wave (AM), with music on FM. Subscription satellite and cable radio offer hundreds of stations that attract millions of customers. Freedom of expression is guaranteed by the constitution, and some broadcast outlets give airtime to radical political and religious views. There were some 4,793 AM and 5,662 FM commercial radio stations in 2010. They obtain their funding mainly by advertising on their programs, which is purchased from many different sources, although they do also make their own programs. Commercial radio ownership was earlier concentrated in the hands of relatively few conglomerates, but *Streema* reported an expansion to 31,236 stations (including Internet sites) in 2016, often with individual ownership.

The National Public Radio (NPR) network is an organization of some 1,460 public or non-commercial radio stations and provides quality news, debate and music without advertising. In a 2005 Harris poll, NPR was voted the most trusted news source in the US, and this reputation continues. The public radio stations are generally owned and operated by educational institutions and religious groups, with a similar high reputation as PBS for their debates, documentaries and arts programs.

Diversity of choice is the key element of radio in the US, and many stations provide 24-hour services to satisfy their customers. Most commercial radio stations are organized around and follow a specific format or genre, which is designed to attract particular audiences. Permission from the FCC is required if a station wishes to change its format.

Some stations consequently only provide music programs (mixed or specialist) such as country, popular music, rock and roll, light classics, classical music and jazz. Others concentrate on news, studio interviews and discussions, talk shows and interviews, phone-ins (audience participation by telephone) and religious programs. Stations with a talk format account for 10 percent of stations, and the number of listeners and active participants has increased considerably. Some stations broadcast only news for 24 hours a day, while most provide five-minute summaries hourly or half-hourly. Others offer a variety or mixture of these. According to *Inside Radio* in 2014, the primary format of the top commercial AM and FM radio stations were Country, News/Talk, Spanish, Sports, Classic Hits, Adult Contemporary, Top 40, Classic Rock, Hot Adult Contemporary, Religion, and Rock.

Online radio began in 1993 and had a simple structure until traditional radio stations began to broadcast online from 1994. Today online radio enjoys great popularity, and most major radio stations offer to stream some programs online, free of cost. Internet radio has grown to include thousands of music stations, listening hours have greatly increased and advertising revenue has expanded.

The Internet and new media sources

The original Internet was used by the US Defense Department in 1969 to provide better information, exchange and communication between government agencies. In the 1980s, the development of hardware and software enabled other computer networks to use the government system. Commercial servers, such as America Online, later expanded these communications systems and provided information for more computer users.

In the 1990s, the World Wide Web (WWW) became commercially available; new software increased Internet usage; and the Netscape browser allowed users to navigate the Net. E-mail broke the monopoly of letter and postal delivery until it was later challenged by mobile phone texting (SMS). SMS declined in 2012 and gave way to smartphones and social networking sites such as Facebook, Twitter and Instagram. The Internet has influenced individual and professional lives, is decentralized and largely unregulated.

In 2013 *Company Industry Almanac* found that the US had the most personal computers at 340.6 million, or 17.8 percent of the world total. *Digital Future* in 2015 reported that 91 percent of Americans were Internet users; 89 percent of households had a broadband connection; 78 percent of users made purchases online; with 64 percent admitting that this reduced their buying in traditional retail stores. Users were online for an average of 21.5 hours per week; with an average 16.1 percent hours at home and 12 percent at work (10 percent actively). Barriers of gender, age, income, education and race among online users have broken. Individuals and organizations have built their own websites and cyber expansion created new search engines such as Google, Yahoo, AOL and Bing.

The twenty-first century has seen great advances for the Internet and other forms of electronic/digital media in the US. *Consumer Electronics Association* reported that while desktop computer sales declined steeply to 2013, those of tablets, mobile PCs, DVRs, digital cameras, digital camcorders and portable media/MP3 players had increased. But the biggest growth since 2010 was sales of smartphones, which increasingly use a variety of other media platforms (such as fax, apps and the Internet). Americans also use social networking sites [such as Facebook, Twitter (declining), LinkedIn, Pinterest and Tumblr and a range of blogs].

Technological growth has made the Internet an important part of a sales market for producers of goods and services and a platform for online shopping. Much e-commerce is conducted between retail businesses, and the Internet has increased efficiencies of scale, cut costs, and established comparison websites for goods and services. But while online shopping by consumers is increasing, malls and physical shops are losing business. According to *Digital Future* the main online purchases in 2012 were books, clothes and travel (66 percent); gifts (60 percent); electronic goods/appliances (51 percent); videos/DVDs (42 percent); computers/peripherals (40 percent); software/games (37 percent); CDs (35 percent); and hobby products (34 percent). But many online sales are still completed by retailers, such as Amazon, and mail order and motor companies. The Internet from a low base in the 1990s developed into a major source of US commercial advertising and according to the *Interactive Advertising Bureau* advertising revenue in early 2016 grew strongly.

However, the Internet and social media have also been seen by some critics as a growing threat to personal privacy and property rights. Databases are hacked for information about usage habits, financial history and contact information, and US agencies have tried to protect privacy and combat identity theft

PLATE 13.4 Front page facsimile of weekend edition of newspaper *USA Today* on a New York newsstand. This is a popular best-selling newspaper that has a readily accessible structure and takes advantage of the latest technology to publish nationwide.
© *Richard Levine/Alamy*

and fraud online. But the United Nations (2012) and campaign groups support freedom of expression and information on the Internet. Despite some success in combating swap sites and downloading of popular music, users continue to pirate digital songs, music, games and books through online file-sharing systems, and copyright protection and intellectual property rights on the Internet are serious issues.

The increase in blogging and social media illustrates the positive and negative sides of the Internet. Blogs usually contain the personal thoughts or views of the site's owner as well as links to other sites of interest and can be a democratic method of spreading ideas and opinions, as well as serving as a campaigning source. But social media can be abusive with extreme views and personal attacks. It is also seriously alleged that digital addiction is weakening people's memories and attention spans. An ongoing debate about the Internet is concerned with whether and how it should be supervised and regulated and that digital overload should be reduced before populations are affected negatively.

A significant development involving the media and the Internet came in 2016 when AT&T (second-largest wireless-telecoms firm in the US) made an offer for Time Warner (the film and video conglomerate), in a purported effort to establish a business model that would combine distribution with content. If competition authorities approve, the acquisition could give AT&T possession of HBO and other premier cable channels (delivery), as well as collections of films produced by Warner Bros (content). With its collective assets, AT&T could rival Netflix and Amazon, which have challenged cable TV with cheaper services that stream content over the Internet. Traditional broadcast television is being replaced by streaming and manufactured packaging purchased for viewing on demand through subscription. Future television sets will probably have only a few channels with vertical libraries of material on integrated platforms that will dominate the future of viewing.

Attitudes to the media

Critics argue that the US media provide television, radio, books, newspapers and digital platforms that vary in quality and performance as they try to serve the needs of a diverse society. Most need to make a profit by satisfying advertisers and consumers that want news, entertainment, information or education. They may succeed or fail in the media markets.

However, the news function of television and the press attract the most critical attitudes from poll respondents, possibly because they are seen as involving the most serious, political, constitutional and important issues in society. News producers often argue that their decisions to focus on specific newsworthy items are based on editorial policy and individual journalists' opinions. They insist that they try to be objective, present all sides of a case and use self-censorship to avoid overt bias or partiality. But although a BBC World Service poll in 2007 found that 66 percent of US respondents thought that freedom of the press was very important to ensure a fair and stable society, they were critical of the media's honesty and accuracy, and only some 29 percent thought that the media did a good job in reporting news accurately. Twenty-four percent felt that media controls were lacking, and 74 percent believed that the concentration of media ownership in a few hands resulted in owners' political views emerging in reports.

According to AP–NORC Center for Public Affairs Research on Confidence in Institutions in 2014, Americans' confidence in press and television was low and had declined over the past 40 years. Seven percent of Americans expressed a great deal of confidence in the press, 47 percent express only some, and 44 percent have hardly any confidence. Similarly, 10 percent of Americans express a great deal of confidence in television, 49 percent express only some, and 41 percent say hardly any confidence. Historically, Republicans have less confidence in the press than Democrats or Independents, and Americans are turning to other sources (such as smartphones and digital news) for reliable information and to avoid trivialization of events and bias in news coverage.

Despite reactions to television's news functions, US television historically has had considerable entertainment value, and its impact on American society and culture still has a presence. It has aided the visibility and roles of racial minorities on TV by breaking through the color barrier and cable TV has attracted minority viewers. But the gradually expanding appearance and portrayal of women, gay and lesbian characters on TV has had a mixed record. The central TV image for many years was the American family, which from the 1970s increasingly dealt with images of social change and class. Religious broadcasting on TV emerged in the 1970s with the growth of discussion programs and religious services, often associated with evangelical churches. Despite criticism, television has historically served as the main source of political news and information, has shaped US politics and government and has examined official political candidates, campaigns and voting patterns.

But critics claim that television has also encouraged superficial political information and sound bites rather than using in-depth views on important issues. The high cost of political advertising on television has made running for office very expensive, negative campaigning is criticized and media regulation is weak. The content and quality of commercial television programs and products have a mixed reputation in the US. Television has been attacked for its bias toward mass-entertainment programs ("reality" shows with huge audiences, talk shows, soap operas and quiz games), which advertise goods and services. Some consumers criticize programming, which is aimed at the lower end of the television market, and argue that companies should develop more quality programs.

Television is also criticized for its portrayal of gratuitous violence and for the alleged impact of violence, explicit sex, immorality and bad language on both children and adults. The debate over possible links between violence on television and its imitation in society continues, although such programs are not now shown in the early evening and "v-chip" technology allows parents to censor children's viewing. There is a considerable amount of citizen involvement in other television-related issues, such as groups campaigning for better quality children's television. Minorities and women are also concerned with television programs and object to the representation of ethnic and gender stereotypes.

Commercial television networks and advertising companies are sometimes sensitive to such criticisms, since they can affect their profits. Some people argue that objections have made commercial television into a more conservative institution, but there are positive indications that advertisers and companies may be paying attention to the public's views.

Attitudes to American commercial television are not solely a list of complaints and negative comments. Some situation-comedy and drama series are excellent and very popular worldwide. Television can also perform essential educational and information functions, with high-quality documentaries and in-depth news presentations. It provides live coverage of important events from both domestic and worldwide sources. It has the capacity to closely examine politicians and their policies, so that viewers may make up their own minds about a range of issues.

Exercises

Explain and examine the significance of the following names and terms:

"yellow journalism"	William Randolph Hearst	ratings
soap operas	circulation	AM/FM
"muck-raking"	newspaper chains	networks
New England Courant	advertising	formats
broadband	F D Roosevelt	NPR
conglomerates	*The Washington Post*	Watergate
syndication	cable television	PBS
FCC	bias	UPI
blog	streaming	injunction
"Fourth Estate"	First Amendment	talk-shows

Write short essays on the following questions.

1. Should the freedom of the American news media be curtailed?

2. Analyze the contemporary significance of American newspapers in terms of their historical development and the influence of alternative media.

3. Discuss the structure and influence of US television.

4. Critically examine the American media in terms of the public opinion polls in this chapter.

Further reading

Abramson, J. et al. (1988) *The Electronic Commonwealth: The Impact of New Media Technologies on Democratic Politics*, New York: Basic Books.

Alterman, E. (2003) *What Liberal Media? The Truth About Bias and the News*, New York: Basic Books.

Bagdikian, B. H. (2004) *The New Media Monopoly*, Boston, MA: Beacon Press.

Dautrich, K. and Hartley, T. H. (1999) *How the News Media Fail American Voters: Causes, Consequences and Remedies*, New York: Columbia University Press.

Fallows, J. (1996) *Breaking the News: How the Media Undermine American Democracy*, New York: Pantheon Books.

Fuller, J. (1996) *News Values: Ideas for an Information Age*, Chicago, IL: University of Chicago Press.

Garry, P. M. (1994) *Scrambling for Protection: The New Media and the First Amendment*, Pittsburgh, PA: Pittsburgh Press.

Kovach, B. and Rosenstiel, T. (1999) *Warp Speed: America in the Age of Mixed Media*, New York: The Century Foundation.

Krimsky, G. A. and Hamilton, J. M. (1996) *Hold the Press: The Inside Story on Newspapers*, Baton Rouge, LA: Louisiana State University Press.

Kurtz, H. (1998) *Spin Cycle: How the White House and the Media Manipulate the News*, New York: Simon and Schuster.

McChesney, R. W. (2004) *The Problem of the Media: US Communication Politics in the Twenty-First Century*, New York: Monthly Review Press.

Teeter, D. and Le Duc, D. R. (1995) *Law of Mass Communications: Freedom and Control of Print and Broadcast Media*, Westbury, NY: Foundation Press.

The World Almanac and Book of Facts (annual), New York: World Almanac Books.

Wu, T. (2016) *The Attention Merchants: The Epic Scramble to Get Inside Our Heads*, New York: Knopf Publishing Group.

Wu, T. (2012) *The Master Switch: The Rise and Fall of Information Empires*, London: Atlantic Books.

Woodward, J. (2005) (ed.) *Popular Culture: Opposing Viewpoints*, Farmington Hills, MI: Greenhaven Press.

Websites

First Amendment: www.knightfoundation.org/publications/future-first amendment-2011
First Amendment: www.firstamendmentcenter.org/sofa
usinfo.state.gov/usa/infousa
usinfo.state.gov/usa/infousa/media/media.htm
usinfo.state.gov/usa/infousa/media/mediaovr.htm
www.gallup.com/poll/155585)
www.gallup.com/poll/indicators/indmedia.asp
usinfo.state.gov/usa/infousa/media/broadcast.htm
FCC: www.fcc.gov

Nielsen Media Research: mashable.com/category/nielsen

PBS: www.pbs.org/insidepbs

The Washington Post: www.washingtonpost.com

The New York Times: www.nytimes.com

CNN: www.cnn.com

Television's Impact on American Society and Culture, 2007: http://www.encyclopedia.com/arts/news-wires-white-papers-and-books/televisions-impact-american-society-and-culture

Television's Impact on Popular Leisure, 2004: http://www.encyclopedia.com/arts/news-wires-white-papers-and-books/televisions-impact-american-society-and-culture

Time: pathfinder.com/time/magazine/magazine.html

USA Today: www.usatoday.com

Chapter 14

Arts, sports and leisure cultures

- The arts
- Sports
- Leisure
- *Exercises*
- *Further reading*
- *Websites*

The diversity of US society is reflected in Americans' artistic, sporting and leisure lives. These reveal different cultural habits at all social levels; may be professional or amateur; and include participatory and spectator pastimes. They have varied in popularity over time, have been influenced by new cultural developments and many are based on traditional forms.

There are still differences between popular and elite cultures in the US. Popular culture includes mass-interest sports such as baseball, football and basketball; movies; and music such as jazz, rock, pop and country. Most early elite cultures were based on European visual art, symphony orchestras, opera, art galleries and museums. But the elitist has become more inclusive; music has been popularized and commercialized; and sports and the arts generally have been democratized. Cultural activities depend on funding from private and public donations, sponsorship and advertising, attendance fees and an economic system that responds to profit and demand. There is also some state and federal funding from the National Endowment for the Arts (NEA), the National Endowment for the Humanities (NEH) and congressional appropriations.

There are American aspects in arts and sports, which have developed internally over time and today convey distinctive national identities, but some have been influenced by European and other global influences. Baseball, country and folk music, some art forms and the musical arguably derive from non-American sources. "Ethnic" and folklorist artistic expression, such as slave and settler traditions, Latino music and dance, Jewish and Chinese theater, Native American art and Asian cinema reflect their culture of origin rather than a purely American identification.

All have created a distinctive collection of US cultural identities and an American-oriented internationalized culture. The latter is resented in some countries that seek to preserve their own artistic integrity and inheritance. Critics (including Americans) also criticize what they see as a US mass market and media that is allegedly directed to the lowest common denominator of taste and quality. But Americans have produced models in the arts, sports and leisure fields to which many people respond positively worldwide, both for their initial inventiveness and strangeness and their later incorporation into a global culture.

A general US work ethic, competitive ethos, ambition and drive for success and achievement has also influenced sporting, leisure and artistic pursuits. These are often taken very seriously on both professional and amateur levels. Americans who play professional sports do so because they want to win, as well as to achieve the large amounts of money available in many professional games. Amateur sports may be similarly driven, beyond a wish for fitness. The arts are part of a competitive business structure, and leisure activities for some may have a deliberately planned and goal-oriented context.

American values, such as self-improvement, are echoed by those people who go to concerts and the theater or who pursue other artistic activities. They indulge in these not only for fashionable reasons, but often because they feel that the arts are self-improving and admirable and positive things in themselves. Many Americans also exercise, take part in fitness classes and diet to improve themselves by becoming healthier and fitter in body and mind, although these pursuits can sometimes be short-lived fads. But many people are spectators rather than active participants, whether of sports, television and concerts or as visitors to museums and art galleries. Such activities may nevertheless have informational, recreational and entertainment value.

Sports, leisure and the arts are important for many people and central to their lives. This is reflected in the large amounts of money spent by Americans on attendance fees, sports equipment, training, musical instruments, electronic equipment, sports stadiums, concert halls, museums and art galleries. A huge advertising expenditure is normally devoted to them, through newspapers, television and the Internet. "Entertainment" (broadly defined) regularly comes near the top of total advertising fees, after automobiles and retailing services. However, personal and institutional spending on the performing arts, movie theaters, spectator sports and leisure activities declined in the recessionary economic climate of 2007–10 and continues to condition recreation expenditure. But the purchase of computers, electronic games and software is still a significant share of personal spending, which suggests that more people are following arts, sport and leisure activities through technology at home.

American sporting and artistic history have had their darker sides. Discrimination has been widespread, and African Americans, Native Americans, Jews and women have experienced considerable racism and exclusion. This applied not only to performers, but also to spectators who were segregated and to sports that were institutionally divided on color and ethnic lines. In the early twentieth century, there was a gulf between America's divided society and its democratic ideals, which forced civil rights onto the political agenda and encouraged attempts to widen equal access to cultural activity.

While racism and discrimination have been reduced, they still influence contemporary pursuits. Racial, gender and class stereotyping exists so that, for example, African Americans may find it difficult to advance in professional tennis and golf. Those individuals who do succeed, such as Althea Gibson, Arthur Ashe, Tiger Woods and the Williams sisters are seen as role models. The impact of women in some sports, such as soccer and athletics, has also increased considerably in recent years and breakthroughs by minorities into the wider US society have often come partly through sports and the arts.

The arts

The development of elite and popular arts in the US has been influenced by European traditions (sometimes brought to America by European immigrants) and distinctive domestic cultures. Historically, there has been a tension between the two traditions, and European sophistication was contrasted with American originality. Gradually, suspicion decreased and the two coexisted and intermixed. American painters, sculptors, musicians, dancers and filmmakers have developed their own (often controversial) artistic styles as a distinctive, diverse US culture has evolved through a process of innovation, experiment, variety and reaction to earlier art forms. Nevertheless, the US is still often stereotypically perceived as a society in which television, sports, film and other forms of popular or mass entertainment are more accessible than the "highbrow" arts and "high culture."

There are in fact hundreds of opera companies, symphony orchestras, youth orchestras and ballet and dance companies, divided between amateurs and professionals, attracting varying degrees of support and covering all age groups and abilities. Many of the top organizations have world reputations and international conductors, directors and soloists, and cultural buildings have been built throughout the US with lavish styles and facilities.

In 2013–14, the most performed composers by symphony orchestras were Beethoven, Mozart, Brahms, Tchaikovsky, Dvorak, Mendelssohn and Ravel. The most performed works by opera companies were Bizet's *Carmen*, Rossini's *The Barber of Seville* and Puccini's *La Bohème* (Sources: League of American Orchestras and OPERA America).

Surveys suggest that Americans of all ages and social groups visit classical and symphonic concerts, dance performances, music recitals and opera, as well as a varied range of museums and art galleries. These activities indicate a wider and more acceptable cultural profile for the "elite" arts than in the past. Artistic activity had developed from the 1960s, and there has been increased participation by amateur and professional individuals and groups in the visual arts, music, modern dance, theater, ballet and film. The media, such as newspapers, television networks and PBS, have helped to establish an interest in and support for the arts through their promotion, sponsorship and coverage of cultural events. However, the arts, sports and leisure, as well as participants were affected by the economic downturn in 2007–10, and recovery has been slow.

Visual arts

American painters and artists in the nineteenth and early twentieth century followed European styles. They continued established naturalist and realist traditions but gradually adapted these to specific American themes, locations, subject matter and techniques as they responded more to America's physical nature in the westward expansion of the population.

After the Second World War, new American painters arrived on the traditional scene with revolutionary and distinctively American concepts, such as cityscapes and gritty urban lifestyles. Modernist, cubist and abstract influences then arrived from Europe, from which developed an American abstract expressionism. This was initially begun by New York artists such as Jackson Pollock, Willem de Kooning and Mark Rothko in the 1940s, who rejected established painting styles and subject matter and organized their work around a fluid use of color, space and texture. These painters attracted international attention, and New York increasingly became the center of the art world.

Later generations reacted to abstract expressionism and moved to new styles. Painters in the late 1950s and 1960s, such as Robert Rauschenberg and Jasper Johns, concentrated on collage-type painting and used a variety of ordinary objects to produce works of mixed media. Other innovators, such as Andy Warhol and Roy Lichtenstein, introduced "pop art." This genre used everyday items of the consumer society and popular culture to reflect and comment on what the artist saw as distinctive features of modern America. In this process, the ordinary became iconic, and established concepts of culture and "reality" were challenged.

American painters and sculptors continue to experiment with a wide range of styles and materials and have created a number of exotically named artistic movements, such as "op," graffiti and performance art. Their distinguishing features have been change, reaction, variety, new techniques and a refusal to be restricted to specific philosophies, styles, schools or media. They gather their inspiration from many sources and influences. The very definition and existence of visual art is often ironically challenged in "postmodernist" work.

Music

Interesting as some of these styles have been, a more influential expression of US artistic distinctiveness has been in music (classical and popular). In previous centuries, American classical music was influenced by European traditions and standards. The breakthrough to a distinctive American voice came with George Gershwin and Aaron Copland in the early twentieth century, who allied domestic elements (such as African American influences, jazz, folk songs and country) with European idioms. This mixture of old and new styles continued through the century. There was also a movement to make classical music less elitist and more accessible to more people, as symphony orchestra directors and conductors introduced combined programs of mainstream and new music.

The more immediate and commercial forms of American music have historically been mainstream popular, ragtime, blues, jazz, the musical, country and

PLATE 14.1 Boston Symphony Orchestra (BSO), one of five major American symphony orchestras, was a resident at the Old Boston Music Hall from 1861 and now at Symphony Hall, Boston. They present 250 concerts a year, in addition to world travels and festivals. They are shown here performing at the Tanglewood Music Festival, Massachusetts, which is a regular performing base.
© *Albert Knapp/Alamy*

rock and roll, which have often mixed with and influenced each other over time. They became domestic American successes, but many have also been exported and greatly affected world cultures.

Mainstream popular music with a distinctive American voice was largely initiated by Stephen Foster in the early nineteenth century. He combined European styles with African American rhythms and themes to produce classic American songs. There was also a growth of light operetta shows and popular traveling stage reviews (vaudeville or Variety Theater) that provided songs, dance and comedy. By the end of the nineteenth century, popular music became more commercially successful. Writing and production were centered on New York City and its Tin Pan Alley. Songwriters like Irving Berlin and Cole Porter created American standards, which have survived to the present day.

A wide range of singers and performers have been associated with popular music, each having their own appeal and fan base. There are many lists from which respondents may choose their favorites. For example, a Saga Equity Release of June 16, 2014 found that respondents thought that Bob Dylan was the best US male singer of the 20th century. He also won the 2016 Nobel Prize for Literature, acknowledging a fusion of genres and styles within an American tradition. A B93 net selection of December 18, 2013 placed Ella Fitzgerald in first place as the best female singer of the 20th century out of 250 names. Other lists have selected a range of favorite artists who have appealed to different tastes.

African American composers also wrote and performed popular works in the late nineteenth and early twentieth century. Ragtime was an African American music that was popularized by Scott Joplin and derived partly from the rural blues tradition of often melancholic and fatalistic folk songs and church music that reflected the lives of poor African Americans. Bessie Smith was an early and popular exponent of the blues style and mixed the rural tradition with urban themes.

The blues also inspired jazz at the end of the nineteenth century. It is argued that this is America's most original and native music form. It was first played by African American musicians in the South, derives mainly from African influences and Southern slave culture, combines elements of ragtime, slave songs and brass bands and is a fluid, improvised and rhythmic form of music. Traditionally, New Orleans has been the city of jazz, but it later spread to other parts of the country. Jazz reached the height of its popularity in the 1930s and 1940s. It was then incorporated into big band music and popularized by artists and band leaders like Louis Armstrong and Duke Ellington.

Reflecting an American capacity for experiment, jazz developed alternative sounds and rhythms from the 1950s by individualistic artists such as Dave Brubeck. It also influenced music such as pop, rock and roll and American musicals. Today, jazz is popular in the US and overseas, although it has lost its mass audience appeal, and the best jazz is supposedly provided in New York, Chicago and Los Angeles, rather than in the South.

American country music has become very popular in the US and worldwide. It was based on the folk song traditions of Scottish, Irish and English immigrants. It developed into modern country music in the 1920s and was often played on the string guitar, banjo or fiddle. Its typically mournful or melancholic lyrics dealt with love, relationships, loss and poverty and reflected the disadvantaged rural life of poor Whites in the South, the Southeast and Appalachia. Country now tends to deal with more contemporary concerns and has expanded beyond its origins, but Nashville, Tennessee, is still regarded as its home. According to the Radio Book, country was the top-placed commercial radio primary format with 2,006 AM and FM radio stations in 2014, and it regularly scores highly in recorded music sales.

American folk music also has a worldwide audience. Originally, it had a working-class, underprivileged and rural emphasis, originating in the mountain regions of North Carolina and West Virginia, and was mainly based on immigrant Scottish, Irish and English folk ballads. It later took on American themes through figures such as Woody Guthrie. In the 1960s, it developed a wider and more commercial appeal with singers such as Judy Collins, Bob Dylan and Joan Baez, who often introduced social and political comment into their texts. Dylan later moved from acoustic to electric guitar and blended folk with rock, and other folk music became more commercialized.

Rock and roll developed in the 1950s as distinctively American popular entertainment when jazz was losing its mass audience. Many of its practitioners, such as Elvis Presley and later Jimi Hendrix, Janis Joplin and Bruce Springsteen, combined the traditions of African American rhythm and blues and country, with strong rhythms. It became a popular form of music with young Americans and others worldwide and was associated with a succession of rock icons. Its sounds, rhythm and style dominated the popular music scene and have influenced other forms of pop music, whether in imitation or reaction.

Rock has become very commercialized in recent decades. It was initially centered on live concert performances in huge stadiums or open venues, but these have decreased and rock and its derivatives generally became studio productions based on videos, compact discs (CDs) and DVDs. In 2015, rock was the best-selling genre in US recorded music with a 30 percent share of all music sold (Nielsen Music) and alternated with country in the lead place on commercial AM and FM radio stations. However, according to Pollstar, touring and live rock-based shows were increasingly played (1985–2013) by top-grossing foreign bands such as the Rolling Stones, U2 and the Police. Yet US rock in its many fashions has managed to re-energize itself, challenged established bands and retained its popularity.

Elvis Presley was long considered the greatest rock star of all time, but fashions change, and he has been replaced by a succession of other singers in the polls. However, large majorities in historical polls have felt that Presley had a lasting and positive impact on American culture. Nevertheless, rock has had a turbulent history and been widely criticized. An NBC News/*Wall Street Journal* poll in April 2002 reported that 41 percent of respondents thought that rock music has had a positive influence on American society, culture and values, while 34 percent thought that its effects have been negative.

Popular offshoots of these musical traditions, whether in reaction or modification, are found in a wide range of contemporary music such as rap and hip-hop; urban-influenced styles that can include R&B, blues, street, dance, disco, funk, fusion, Motown and soul; reggae with its Caribbean origins; gospel, hymn, Christian, inspirational, spiritual and religious songs; ethnic music; standards; big band; swing; Latin; mood and easy listening genres; electronic; and instrumental.

The modern stage musical originates in America (although some trace the genre to earlier Italian models and the English music hall/pantomime tradition) and developed in the early twentieth century. Its combination of acting, music and dancing was often allied to escapist plots and exotic shows in glossy theaters, typified by Broadway in New York City. Some later musicals became more serious and socially aware, but the entertainment emphasis continued. The US musical has recently fallen on hard times and had to compete with successful foreign imports, particularly from Britain that are indebted to the original American format. The longest-running Broadway musical as of September 2014 was Andrew Lloyd-Webber's *The Phantom of the Opera* with 10,951 performances, followed by his closed *Cats* with 7,485 performances. But American musicals, such as *Chicago* (revival), *The Lion King* and *Les Misérables* have been popular and successful.

Americans spend billions of dollars on music. According to Nielsen Music in 2015, sales figures derived from CDs, vinyl records, digital downloads and streaming the popularity of types or genres of music was calculated as rock at 30 percent; R&B/Hip-Hop at 22 percent; pop at 16 percent; country at 10 percent; Latin at 5 percent; dance music (EDM) at 4 percent; Christian/gospel at 3 percent; seasonal at 2 percent; jazz at 2 percent; classical at 2 percent; and children at 1 percent. These results can vary from year to year depending on changing tastes, new forms of music, new ethnic and age demographics; new publishing counting methods and new technology such as streaming. The joint top-selling individual albums of all time as of 24 August 2014 are *Thriller*, by Michael Jackson and *Eagles/Their Greatest Hits 1971/75*, by The Eagles both with 29 million unit sales, followed by *Led Zeppelin*, by Led Zeppelin, *The Wall*, by Pink Floyd and *Greatest Hits, Vols 1 & 11*, by Billy Joel (all 23 million).

These statistics illustrate varied musical tastes with significant regional differences in popularity but also declines since 2007 in rock, rap/hip-hop, R&B urban, jazz and classical, with increases in country, some pop and religious/gospel. They include traditional but also popular, urban-based, "ethnic" and constantly evolving and mixed music, which appeal to an important youth culture in the US. The music business is lucrative and profitable for record companies, although they have to cope with illegal downloading, pirated copies, site sharing, competition from other formats and declining sales of videos, CDs and DVDs. The consumer culture has commercialized native forms, and US music has capitalized on its global attraction. Americans also attend live music shows and concerts, and each form of music has its own musicians, clubs and followers, although some attendance figures have declined.

Dance and ballet

Modern dance developed as a new distinctively American art form in the early twentieth century. Isadora Duncan, one of its first exponents, based her dance styles on Greek classical art and was more successful in Europe than America. Her followers, such as Martha Graham in New York, combined modern dance with developments in American music and ethnic life. They rejected the formal restrictions of classical ballet and improvised expressive, random, and dramatic dance movements. Modern (and contemporary) dance in America has developed very successfully and has incorporated different elements like African American music, video, back projection, films and African dance movements into many different styles of dance practiced by professional and amateur dance companies.

US ballet was influenced by visiting European classical ballet companies in the early twentieth century and then by US-based foreign dancers, choreographers and administrators. These created a vibrant ballet presence, more companies were established throughout the country and ballet tried to minimize its elitist tradition by combining classic revivals, original offerings and experimental programs. An NEA survey in 2012 reported that 2.8 percent of adults (6.5 million adults) attended ballet performances (down from 2.9 percent in 2008) while 5.6 percent (13.2 million adults) attended forms of dance other than ballet (up from 5.2 percent in 2008) at least once a year. Some 31.6 percent of adults participated in social dancing.

Film

The film industry and Hollywood have been important influences on domestic American culture and have been very successful internationally. The film industry started on the east coast, but later moved to Los Angeles, and Hollywood became the center of American filmmaking. In the early twentieth century, the motion picture (first silent, then with sound) was the most popular and dominant art form. In the 1940s, Hollywood production studios were releasing some 400 films annually, seen by an estimated 90 million people each week.

Hollywood has always been an entertainment business concerned with selling a product. Its films were originally designed for American audiences, and it has reflected American culture in its handling of themes such as the family, romance, individualism, war, heroism, female roles, children and patriotism. These have been used in different film genres in different periods and have reflected changing social conditions and attitudes in the US. Filmmakers also strove for financial profits by making films with mass appeal and repeated successful formulas, such as westerns, gangster films, comedies, animation and musicals. But the system also produced classic films, whose appeal has endured, and quality products.

During the decades of Hollywood's golden age in the early to mid-twentieth century, films, movie stars and movie theaters were glittering and grandiose. The film industry sold a package in which the moviegoer was a consumer and the star was a commodity with a lifestyle and image specifically created for public consumption and approval. Associated merchandise and fan clubs were part of this package and sold to a mass audience.

Although the celebrity cult continues, the film industry and the star system have changed over the years. They have had to adapt to changing moral, social, economic and industrial climates. The original studio structure altered as a result of a series of mergers. The major companies were effectively taken over by financiers in the 1930s, and eight companies (Paramount, MGM, Warner Brothers, RKO, Twentieth Century Fox, Universal, Columbia and United Artists) were formed. After a prosperous period during the Second World War, the industry was split up by anti-monopoly legislation. In 2005, Hollywood's last major independent studio, Metro-Goldwyn-Mayer (MGM) negotiated a sale with Japan's Sony Corporation. MGM was formed in 1924 after a merger with other studios and produced classics such as *Ben Hur* 1959, *Gone with the Wind* and *The Wizard of* Oz. The production of movies has declined over the years, but the budgets of big blockbuster films have greatly increased. However, quality films are still made by independent producers and directors.

Table 14.1 represents a partial list of classic and contemporary films by respondents who were asked to suggest a list of the best movies ever made. The list was published in 1998 and updated in 2007, reflected shifting perspectives, and it showed a mixture of early and later favorites, reflecting historical, cultural and artistic worth.

It is interesting to compare Table 14.1 with a partial list of the all-time top-grossing American movies at the box office in the US and Canada (see Table 14.2). The latter suggests changing themes such as science fiction, fantasy, action and animation. The films have very large budgets, often corresponding to large profits for the production companies.

TABLE 14.1 Selection (1–13) from 100 best American movies of all time, 2007

Rank	Title	First released
1	Citizen Kane	1941
2	The Godfather	1972
3	Casablanca	1942
4	Raging Bull	1980
5	Singin' in the Rain	1952
6	Gone with the Wind	1939
7	Lawrence of Arabia	1962
8	Schindler's List	1993
9	Vertigo	1958
10	The Wizard of Oz	1939
11	City Lights	1931
12	The Searchers	1956
13	Star Wars	1977

Source: adapted from American Film Institute, 2007

TABLE 14.2 Selection (1–20) from all-time top-grossing American movies, 2014

Rank	Title (original release)	Gross ($ millions)
1	Avatar (2009)	760.5
2	The Avengers (2012)	623.4
3	Titanic (1997)	600.8
4	The Dark Knight (2008)	533.3
5	Star Wars: The Phantom Menace (1999)	474.5
6	Star Wars (1977)	461.0
7	The Dark Knight Rises (2012)	448.1
8	Shrek 2 (2004)	436.7
9	E.T. The Extra-Terrestrial (1982)	435.0
10	The Hunger Games: Catching Fire (2013)	424.7
11	Pirates of the Caribbean: Dead Man's Chest (2006)	423.3
12	Toy Story 3 (2010)	415.0
13	Iron Man (2013)	409.0
14	The Hunger Games (2012)	408.0
15	Spider-Man (2002)	403.7
16	Transformers: Revenge of the Fallen (2009)	402.1
17	Frozen (2013)	400.7
18	Harry Potter and the Deathly Hallows (2011)	381.0
19	Star Wars (2003)	380.3
20	The Lord of the Rings (2002)	341.7

Source: adapted from Rentrak Corporation, 2014

By the mid-twentieth century, the earlier classical Hollywood, with its powerful studios and business tycoons, had declined. Fewer expensive films were made, and independent production companies increased. Hollywood was moving away from the studio system and its large-scale productions to a culture of cost considerations and audience satisfaction. The post-war period saw the making of increasingly different varieties and genres of film, and Disney, for example, became an important source of full-length animated films. Disney is now a very large entertainment group after its 1995 merger with the ABC television network, and it has continued to develop its theme parks worldwide.

The increasing influence of television forced the film industry to redefine itself in order to keep its market share of leisure activities. The number of television sets in the US grew hugely from the early 1950s. Cinema audiences declined and were halved by 1953. Hollywood responded by making films for teenagers (a rapidly increasing consumer market) and western television series such as *Gunsmoke* and *Cheyenne*. It also introduced some innovations like Cinerama (wide-screen projection) and 3-D (three-dimensional) films.

Gradually from the 1970s and 1980s Hollywood studios were taken over by conglomerates with diverse business interests, such as Gulf and Western, and there was increased competition from independent film production companies. New technologies such as video developed, and media companies and film studios were increasingly owned by multimedia businesses such as Time Warner Inc. Time Warner merged with the Turner Broadcasting System (which owns the CNN cable-television news channel) in 1995 and with America Online in 2000 to become the world's largest media and entertainment group. AT&T made a bid for Time Warner in 2016, which would create a giant production/content mixed-media conglomerate and increase streaming platforms if successful.

Hollywood has therefore changed considerably as the film, media and entertainment industries developed. It is now a multimedia corporate business system, as well as a film industry, with many commercial tie-ins. Production costs and profits have become crucial, and it is difficult to find funding for new film ideas. While 59.4 percent of all adults in 2012 went out to a movie, the audience has changed. Young people watch television but still also go to the cinema for interest and social reasons. Older people tend to watch television films and series, videos or DVDs in the home. In 2012, 99 percent of American

PLATE 14.2 Annual Academy Award winners, 2016 (Leonardo Di Caprio for *The Revenant*, Brie Larson for *Room*, Mark Rylance for *Bridge of Spies*, and Alicia Vikander for *The Danish Girl*).

© *ZUMA Press, Inc./Alamy*

households had at least one television set, 91 percent had a VCR, 43 percent had a CD player, 84 percent had a DVD player and 86 percent received basic cable services (48 percent premium cable). But the sales and rental of videos, CDs and DVDs have declined as television networks, the Internet and smartphones replace them by streaming films and shows. Original television series, drama, soap operas and comedy sitcoms have been adopted by the film production industry, and studios rent films to television networks or Internet providers.

Blockbuster action films with huge budgets and expensive stars are still being made and new fantasy, futuristic and space genres have niche audiences. More are being filmed on locations outside Hollywood and California, such as New York and Texas as well as abroad, in an effort to cut rising costs as cinema audiences declined from the 1960s and to search for new markets and ideas. However, the US remains the largest producer of films for a world audience, some of which succeed, while others fail. American themes are still examined in films, but Hollywood is now both an American institution and part of international popular culture. The top grossing US movie in 2012 was *The Avengers* with $623.4 million, while the all-time top grossing US movie (as of 2014) is *Avatar* with $749.8 million. According to the NEA survey in 2012, 59 percent of all categories of adults, or 139 million persons, went to the movies at least once in the year, an increase from 2008. Although the golden age is past, film is still an entertainment medium with huge domestic and international appeal.

Instructional and motivational films are also being made by the film industry and can be used in business, industry, advertising and training programs. Hollywood and the film industry have consequently had to adapt to new ownership structures, different social tastes and audiences and technological changes to remain profitable and develop new markets. In the search for entertainment profits based on established themes and successful formulas, the quality of many of Hollywood's commercial films and blockbusters is criticized within the US; the price of ticket admissions is regarded as too high; and an alleged concentration on gratuitous violence and sexual explicitness is opposed.

The arts: performance and participation

The number of US arts-related companies or organizations has increased since the 1960s, although many suffered in the adverse economic conditions from 2007–10. Some arts activities are still associated with traditional ideas of "high culture", but many people follow other more popular art forms, such as film, dance and theater. Increasing numbers (particularly the young) are returning to these and other cultural pursuits (including electronic forms) in preference to television, which, although still enjoyed by the young, has arguably become the province of older viewers, although films and television productions are now streamed through computers and digital equipment.

The NEA Arts Profile and the US Census Bureau reported that 66.2 percent of all US adults in 2015 attended at least one visual or performing arts event or went to see a movie. These could involve visiting museums and art galleries: a live music, theater, or dance performance; a live book of poetry reading; an art exhibit; or going to a movie. Further, 43.1 percent read literature for pleasure, such as novels, short stories, poems or plays; 8.5 percent took arts classes or lessons, such as music, acting, theater, dance, painting or photography; and 45.1 percent in 2014 had personally performed (acting, singing) or created artwork (painting, creative writing or textile arts).

However, the NEA 2012 Survey of Public Participation in the Arts had suggested that there have been continuing declines since 2002 in most artistic activities, except for movie going, and that disparities were conditioned by gender, race/ethnicity and level of general educational attainment. Fewer adults had attended or participated in arts events. Museum and art gallery attendance had fallen, as had the proportion of adults visiting parks, historical buildings, craft fairs and visual arts festivals. Fewer adults attended performance arts, such as classical music, jazz, ballet or other dance, Latin or salsa music and opera.

PLATE 14.3 Broadway theaters, collectively known as Broadway, refers to 41 professional theaters with 500 seats (or more), located in the Theater District and Lincoln Center along Broadway in Midtown Manhattan, New York City. The theaters produce high quality commercial theater, mainly musicals in the tradition of Rodgers and Hammerstein, which are an established form of American popular culture.

© *David R. Frazier Photolibrary, Inc./Alamy*

Adults were not creating or performing as much, and only photography, classical music, choir/chorus and painting/drawing showed increased participation. Jazz remained stable, while opera, musical plays, non-musical plays, dance, pottery/ceramics, weaving/sewing and creative writing had seen reduced numbers.

Educated Americans were participating at lower levels, and college-educated adults had lower attendance rates at most arts events. Less educated adults significantly reduced their already low levels of attendance at art performances and museums and art galleries.

It is argued that the reasons for these declines were the bad economic situation from 2007–10, high gas and travel costs and weak consumer spending. This may be temporary, and general economic improvement might boost the arts scene, as suggested by 2015 figures.

However, the number of adults reading literature for pleasure rose. Significant numbers of American adults in 2008 enjoyed viewing and listening to the arts on the Internet; downloading music, theater or dance performances;

PLATE 14.4 The Smithsonian Campus, with constituent museums, photographed from the top of the Washington Monument and grouped along the National Mall, Washington, DC. The original Smithsonian Institution (redbrick building at center left of photo) was founded in 1846 and now consists of 19 museums and galleries, the latest of which is the National Museum of African American History and Culture, 2016.
© *Jordan Oakland*

viewing paintings, sculpture or photography; and posting their own art or performances. These results show an increased role for the electronic and online media in the accessibility and enjoyment of the arts.

The 2016 NEA survey found that more adults viewed or listened to broadcasts and recordings of arts events than attended live performances, except for live theater. The most popular were classical music broadcasts or recordings, followed by programs about the visual arts; programs about books/writers; Latin or salsa music; jazz; dance; musical plays; non-musical plays; and opera.

It also reported that attendees at arts events are becoming older than the average US adult, and that young adult (18–24 years-old) attendance rates have declined significantly for jazz, classical music, ballet and non-musical plays. This suggests that young people and young adults are finding alternative self-made, group or online entertainment. However, 45–54 year-olds, who are historically a large component of arts audiences, showed the steepest declines in attendance at most arts events.

This varied cultural experience is being carried out with some direct financial support for the arts from federal or state governments. Although their role in supporting, financing and sponsoring the arts increased significantly from 1970, funding and involvement decreased in the 1990s. The NEA was created in 1965 as an independent federal agency. It encourages and develops artistic activities by bringing them to Americans throughout the country and helping with arts education. It distributes federal funding to the arts at state and local levels. In its support role, the NEA is the country's largest annual federal funder of the arts. The NEH also provides funding, and the states collectively provide legislative appropriations. Although much of the money goes to administrative costs, activities such as music, museums, theater, arts in education, dance, opera, visual arts and literature benefit from this aid. However, orchestras, opera companies and other arts organizations have not historically received much public support.

The arts in the US have traditionally depended on private sources, commercial activities and admission fees for their survival and promotion. The private financial contributions of individuals, philanthropic foundations (such as Ford and Rockefeller) and corporate bodies are also important for artistic funding, particularly when federal money is declining. There is tax relief or deductions (tax breaks) on donations to the arts from individuals and companies.

Sports

Sport in the US was relatively isolated from national and international events and competition until the mid-twentieth century. It had a provincial and minority image, except for the traditional major sports of football, baseball, basketball and hockey, which provided many Americans with team identification and recreation. Sport now reflects the national condition. Issues such as international competition, prestige, drug abuse (particularly in cycling, track and field athletics and baseball), sex discrimination, labor–management relations, the power of television sports broadcasting and sales, sponsorship and advertising, racism, gambling and corruption have all been associated at various times with both amateur and professional sport. The billions of dollars spent on contemporary sports and their buildings can lead to an exaggerated image of sport's worth and also reflect adversely on local communities that might have prioritized their spending on other areas of social life. For example, the US Census Bureau reported that sales of sporting goods in 2012 were $1.26 trillion.

US sports are taken very seriously by many people and are large commercial businesses for others. Some Americans are obsessively involved with winning and money, but others may see sport as a positive means of enriching their lives, are involved in their sports as participants and spectators and are dedicated to the success of their particular teams.

American sports divide into the professional and amateur ranks. Professionally, the most popular and favorite spectator-oriented sports have historically been National Football League (NFL) games (with their Super Bowl finals), major league (National and American) baseball (with its World Series), basketball, National (Ice) Hockey League, horse racing and greyhound racing. The football season begins in early fall, basketball is an indoor winter sport and baseball is played in spring and summer, although there is now some overlap. The strong tradition of American football is reflected in its television and commercial figures. The 2016 Super Bowl, broadcast by NBC, was watched by 114.4 million viewers in the US and was the third most watched game in US television history. NFL television broadcasting rights are the most lucrative and expensive of any American sport, and four networks paid $39.6 billion a year for the period 2014–22.

Some sports have fluctuated in popularity. A Harris poll in 2015 reported that despite image problems with baseball, the favorite sports were professional football (33 percent), professional baseball (15 percent), men's college football (10 percent), automobile racing (6 percent), men's professional basketball (5 percent), ice hockey (5 percent), men's soccer (4 percent), men's college basketball (4 percent), men's golf (3 percent), men's tennis (2 percent), boxing (2 percent), track and field (2 percent), horse racing (1 percent), swimming (2 percent), track and field (2 percent), bowling (1 percent), and women's soccer (1 percent).

In terms of national representative quality and popularity, it is argued that baseball, football and basketball are uniquely American in their varying combinations of individualism and a teamwork ethos. For some, baseball is said to be the nation's premier sport, since most Americans have supposedly played it from childhood onwards, whether as the full game, Little League baseball or the softball variant (mainly for women). Baseball arguably originated in the US before the Civil War as "rounders." This is an English children's game played for centuries on the street, or in any open space, where the ball is thrown

PLATE 14.5 College football game at Peden Stadium, Ohio University, Athens, Ohio with Ohio's Donte Foster (3) in action against Norfolk State University, Sept 2012. Cheerleaders appear on the sideline. Ohio University's team (the Bobcats) has substantial support in the town and has had periods of success in regional and national championships.
© *Andrew Hancock/Getty*

underarm to the hitter, who then runs the rounds. It is also argued that baseball is more democratic and representative than football and basketball since it can be played by most people. But it has faced accusations of corruption and fraud in recent years that have tarnished the sport.

A 2012 Harris Poll found that different demographic groups have their own favorite sports. Respondents who indicated that professional football was their favorite sport were African Americans (48 percent), those aged 30–39 years (46 percent), and those with some college education (42 percent). In terms of baseball, respondents aged 50 to 64 (21 percent), Latinos (19 percent), and Easterners (17 percent) indicated that it was their favorite game. Respondents with a post-graduate degree (22 percent), college graduates (19 percent) and Midwesterners (18 percent) indicated that college football was their favorite sport. Many children have been attracted to American football, baseball and basketball. But it seems that they are now finding alternative sports, because football is declining due to expensive equipment, insurance costs, and the risk of injury; baseball is apparently too hard; and basketball players need to have above-average height.

A central feature of the American sports scene is that since few other countries play baseball, basketball and American football on a professional and large-scale level, competition in them is largely restricted to the US, and there is no international opposition as such in these sports. However, although seen as distinctively American sports, they are now more popular, are played in other countries and are viewed globally on television.

In other sports, the inaugural match in Major League Soccer (MLS) was held in April 1996 in an attempt to introduce a professional soccer league. Earlier ventures had failed, although soccer had been played at various levels in the US since the nineteenth century. Despite growing familiarity, until recently most Americans did not see soccer as a spectator option, even if they had played it themselves. It was hoped that the 1994 World Cup held in the US would generate new enthusiasm. Although MLS is not as organized and well-attended as the major leagues of football and baseball, it seems that attendance and television viewing figures are rising. There are some 20 million registered soccer players in the country, and surveys indicate that more than 50 million Americans are "soccer literate."

Although soccer has long been played in schools and on college and university campuses, it is now popular with corporate sponsors, schools (with equal number of girls and boys), Latinos and affluent households. Women are about 40 percent of all registered players; the US women's soccer team won the World Cup in 1999 and the soccer gold medal at the London Olympics in 2012 with a 2–1 win over Japan. There were 967 women's soccer teams and 23,650 women players in the National Collegiate Athletic Association (NCAA) in 2010 (more representation than males). The growth and success of women's soccer at the national and international levels has increased general interest in soccer in the US. It also rivals the traditional place of Little League baseball as the sport of young suburban families, although it will probably not overtake American football and baseball in spectator popularity.

Youth sports clubs have welcomed soccer as a supplement to or a replacement for American football because of high costs of the latter. The senior professional soccer game has yet to attract significant consistent support and organization, and soccer divides American opinion between those who find it tedious and slow and those who seriously support it. Increased interest may come as more US television networks buy the rights to screen European soccer leagues, such as the English Premiership and help to establish soccer as a major sport in the US. But the fortunes of the game continue to fluctuate.

Although professional and college sports such as football, ice hockey and boxing are tough action games, US sport does not suffer the same amount of spectator violence as some other countries. Events such as baseball and football can still be family outings. They have a carnival atmosphere and elements of show business, such as cheerleaders who orchestrate the crowds, marching bands that provide additional entertainment and musical breaks.

There is extensive media coverage of sports by newspapers and television, which reflects the popularity and commercial standing of sports in the US. Sports programs are an integral part of television and radio programming and attract large audience figures as the networks and other stations fight for a market share. Some cable stations, such as the Entertainment and Sports Programming Network (ESPN) are devoted exclusively to sports events, report for 24 hours a day and attract very large audiences. The various media, particularly television, have created a profitable, audience-based industry and also made sport accessible to many more people, who are either unable to attend or afford live events.

The media popularization of sports has led to increasing commercialization. Television networks and cable stations compete to obtain financially rewarding rights from the professional sports bodies that allow the stations to televise sports events. Advertisers are attracted by the mass audiences and pay television stations to advertise mainly male-oriented products on their programs. Advertisers benefit from the resulting sales of products, and the sports bodies receive fees and funding from their broadcasting rights contracts. Some, such as the NFL, receive much of their revenue from the networks and cable companies.

Professional baseball, basketball and football are big business in which team owners virtually control the players and realize their assets, investments and profits as players are bought and sold. In the case of baseball, the previous restrictive rules have been changed to allow players greater freedom and they (and other professionals) now earn huge salaries. Disputes between the players' union and owners have sometimes interrupted baseball seasons, and fans have become more dissatisfied with baseball and other professional sports because of strikes, high ticket prices, players' huge financial rewards and the big business ethos.

The commercialization of American professional sports can affect an athlete's career. Success and financial rewards are connected not only to the person's ability and competitive skills, but also to the marketability of the athlete, who must have agents to act on his or her behalf, take part in publicity campaigns, endorse and promote products such as sportswear and attract sponsorship by corporate advertisers.

American sports are very competitive. As they have become more profit-oriented, success has become paramount, and the importance of winning for participants and owners at all levels is considerable. Critics feel that this attitude has detracted from the traditional spirit of teamwork and the pleasure of playing sport, and fans can react negatively.

Increased commercialization of college (and even school) sports has also occurred. High schools and colleges provide a wide variety of sports activities as well as practice and match facilities for both male and female students. These are highly organized and competitive and generally receive substantial local publicity and support. The sports include American football, basketball,

PLATE 14.6 College basketball players in action in match between Boise State and San Diego State in Taco Bell Arena, Boise, Idaho, Feb 2017.
© *Steve Bly/Alamy*

baseball, tennis, wrestling, gymnastics, athletics (track and field), cross country running, soccer, swimming, volleyball, fencing, softball and golf.

Outstanding high school athletes receive scholarships to enable them to go to college or university, where sports are an essential part of the educational program. College sports are supposed to be amateur, but they have become very competitive and commercialized. College sports teams contribute financially (through television rights and ticket sales) and generate publicity for their institutions and are given considerable local community support. Football and basketball are the most financially rewarding college sports, and the top college teams can attract large amounts of money. The emphasis on recruiting top high school athletes can affect the college's overall reputation, because college sports stars have traditionally been recruited to play their sport, earn profits for the college and possibly to move on to the higher professional ranks, rather than to gain an academic education.

The apparent popularity of professional and amateur sports suggests that a large majority of Americans are avid and committed sports fans with a tribal affection for certain games and teams. A Marist poll in March 2012 asked respondents whether they would describe themselves as sports fans. A majority of 58 percent said they would, and 42 percent said they would not. A Gallup poll in December 2011 asked respondents whether they were fans of professional football. Forty-eight percent said they were; 6 percent said they were somewhat; and 46 percent said they were not. Such replies do not seem to represent overwhelming interest in or support for sport in the US.

These figures suggest that changes (possibly temporary) have occurred in Americans' attitudes to organized sport, particularly at the professional level. Fans have experienced a period of disillusionment resulting from strikes, high ticket prices, drug abuse, gambling scandals, excessive salaries of players, the behavior of club owners and an apparent disrespect for fans by both owners and players. Many have indicated that they prefer to watch college games rather than the professional games.

In addition to the large organized sports, the US Census Bureau reported that 270 million Americans in 2009 participated in sports more than once a year. The most popular activities were, in descending order: walking, exercising with equipment, camping, swimming, bowling, bicycle riding, weightlifting, hiking, aerobic exercises, fishing, running/jogging. The Outdoor Foundation reported that 143 million Americans, or 49.2 percent of the US population, participated in an outdoor activity at least once in 2013, and walking for fitness remained the most popular outdoor activity at 53 percent.

Leisure

According to a Gallup poll in August 2014, fully employed US adults (aged 18 and over) said that they worked 47 hours per week, which was above the standard of 40 hours. At a time of continuing economic difficulties, pressure from employers and sporadic unemployment, 50 percent worked more than 40 hours and 40 percent at least 50 hours to preserve their jobs. However, a Gallup poll in December 2015 reported that 52 percent of respondents had enough hours for leisure per week (20 hours), while 48 percent did not. Americans enjoy a variety of leisure activities, which include individual and collective physical and sporting pursuits, passive spectator pastimes, and other forms of entertainment, with the US leisure market being valued at $2.5 trillion in 2013.

After a period when participation in physical exercise was in decline, interest again increased from the 1960s and coincided with the new popularity of health fads, diet and exercise. In part, this was a reaction to research studies that showed that Americans smoked too many cigarettes and were overweight with sedentary lifestyles. Fitness was promoted by doctors and the government for health reasons, but it was also encouraged to national prestige and vitality. Running (jogging), aerobic exercises, dancing, racquetball (an American form of squash played in a four-walled court by two or four people using a short-handed racket), swimming, bicycling, tennis, golf, skiing, basketball and walking were encouraged and became popular. It was fashionable for people of all ages and both genders to exercise, to take part in sport, to be physically fit and to emphasize nutrition and diet.

But research on Americans' exercise habits suggest that sedentary habits continue, that participation in exercise has not greatly improved in recent years, and in some cases has declined. In 2012, the US Census Bureau Statistical Abstract reported that, in terms of passive/sedentary leisure by the adult population of 224.8 million, 53.3 million attended the movies and 30.6 million attended sports events. However, 52.9 million said they exercised, 26.3 million played sports, 28.2 million enjoyed physical outdoor activities and 41.2 million engaged in gardening.

Some Americans can be obsessive about fitness and health. Although spending on sports/exercise products and services fluctuates with economic conditions, significant numbers of individuals buy the latest training equipment, clothes, books and videos and feel that fitness is glamorous and connected to an ideal of healthy youth. Joggers and runners are very visible, aerobic exercises and weight training are popular with men and women, health clubs have increased gradually and there are public and private organizations that provide facilities for those who want to keep fit or play sports. Some of these are provided free by local communities or by commercial businesses for their employees. Others are private clubs for those who can afford to pay for their services.

Commercial businesses take advantage of these developments and supply stylish sporting clothes and equipment, reaping large profits. Book publishers, magazines and television programs dealing with health and fitness concerns also feed the market. Health companies produce supposedly beneficial products, as do food and beverage businesses. Affluent Americans spend substantial sums of money to achieve a desired result. Even those who cannot afford high prices for equipment and clothes might indulge in some exercise.

However, in spite of the facilities, good intentions and television debates about diets and exercise, 2011–14 data from US Centers for Disease Control and Prevention (CDC) showed that 36.5 percent of US adults were obese, an increase from 2009–10, and a relatively stable 17 percent of children and adolescents aged 2–19 were obese (12.7 million). Female adults were more likely to be obese than male adults. The figures contrast with the 1970s, when a quarter of the US adult population was recorded as overweight. These medical conditions can lead to serious health complications and rising medical costs for US society.

CDC surveys in 2007 reported that between 80 and 90 percent of Americans considered themselves to be unfit and lacking in exercise; one in four admitted to being completely sedentary; 40 percent rarely exercised; 23 percent smoked; 20 percent suffered from high cholesterol; and 80 percent said that their efforts to improve fitness and diet did not last long. Their condition was worsened by a fast food culture, lack of homemade food, employment stress and fatty foods.

Americans have a wide range of leisure pursuits, which vary between strenuous exercise and passivity. A Harris poll in 2013 (Table 14.3) reported that the top activities were watching TV, reading, computer/Internet use and spending time with family and friends. Thirty-five percent cited reading in Harris 2007, but in 2008 this decreased to 30 percent cent. TV watching increased from 18 percent in 2007 to 24 percent in 2008. Spending time with friends and family increased from 14 percent in 2007 to 17 percent in 2008. Exercise (aerobics and weights) moved from 5 percent in 2007 to 8 percent in 2008.

Most interests had increased in popularity in 2013. For example, watching TV held first place, computer/Internet activities had risen from 7 (in 2008) to 19 percent and going to the movies climbed from 6 to 11 percent.

TABLE 14.3 Selected Top 23 favorite leisure activities, 2013

Rank	Activity	% Total	% Female	% Male
1	Watching TV	42	42	43
2	Reading	37	48	24
3	Computer/Internet	19	18	20
4	Time with family/friends	18	23	13
5	Watching/going to movies	11	11	11
6	Exercise/working out	10	10	10
7	Video/computer games	10	8	13
8	Walking/running/jogging	8	10	7
9	Gardening	7	9	5
10	Concerts/listening to/playing music	7	5	10
11	Hobby-related activities	5	4	5
12	Eating/going to restaurants	4	4	4
13	Cooking/baking	4	5	3
14	Sewing/needlework/quilting	4	7	1
15	Attending/watching sports events	4	2	6
16	Shopping	4	6	2
17	Sleeping/napping	3	4	3
18	Relaxing/resting	3	2	3
19	Fishing	3	2	5
20	Crafts	3	5	1
21	Swimming	3	3	3
22	Golf	3	1	7
23	Playing with pets	3	3	2

Source: adapted from Harris Interactive, 2013

Note: Some respondents took part in more than one activity.

Exercise-related activities were not numerous, exercise/working out was 10 percent, walking, running and jogging were 8 percent, and swimming was 3 percent. Attending/watching sports events remained at 4 percent.

Reading fell to second place in this leisure list. Although there was a decrease from 2008, the *American Library Directory* 2015–16, reported an estimated 119,487 libraries in the US, which include 9,082 public libraries, 3,793 academic libraries, 99,460 school libraries, 6,966 special libraries, 252 armed forces libraries and 934 government libraries. Books and libraries have traditionally had a strong hold on the American public. Sixty-eight percent of Americans had a library card in 2008; 76 percent of card-holders visited libraries; and 41 percent visited online. Over 35 percent used a library between 1–5 times in a year, and 15 percent used it more than 25 times. Most people use libraries for borrowing books, CDs, videos and computer software; connection to the Internet; or to access reference material.

Ninety-two percent viewed the library as an important education resource; 72 percent agreed that it is a pillar of the community; 71 percent saw it as a community center; 70 percent saw it as a family destination; and 69 percent viewed it as a cultural center. People were satisfied with their libraries, and among those with a library card, 68 percent said that they are extremely or very satisfied. Despite competing with electronic sources, online services and computers, nine out of ten respondents expected libraries and books to exist in the future.

The state of reading in the US as a leisure and formal activity has been recently examined in the light of NEA surveys (see Further Reading) about its decline at all age levels. In 2004, it was reported that there had been a decline of 10 percent in literary readers from 1982 to 2002, particularly in the 18–24 age groups. The term "literary" included print fiction, such as novels, short stories or plays but excluded biography and history.

A later NEA report in 2007 examined all varieties of reading, such as fiction and non-fiction genres in books, magazines, newspapers and online reading. It found that teenagers and young adults read less often and for shorter periods of time compared with other age groups. Reading scores had worsened, especially among teenagers and young males. By contrast, the average reading score of 9-year-olds had improved.

An NEA survey in January 2008 reported that for the first time in more than 25 years, American adults were reading more literature, with an overall increase of 7 percent. Since 2002, the biggest increases (nine percent) and most rapid rate increases (21 percent) were among young adults, aged 18–24. Reading increased among Latinos (20 percent), African Americans (15 percent) and Whites (eight percent). The survey examined "literary reading" and noted that fiction (novels and short stories) accounted most for the new growth in adult literary readers; poetry and drama continued to decline; and 15 percent of all

US adults read literature online in 2008 or as downloads. The survey reported that a majority of adults (50.2 percent) read books (119 million) in any format and argued that the improvement was due to the growth of public and private reading programs.

However, the improvement in literary reading rates between 2002 and 2008 was reversed according to a 2012 NEA survey. Forty-seven percent of adults read a novel, short story, poem or play. But the share of adults who read any kind of book remained constant. Poetry reading demonstrates a long-term decline, non-Whites and Latinos maintained their 2008 reading rates and older Americans are reading more books of any type. Nevertheless, the results from the NEA's Annual Arts Basic Survey 2015 reported that only 43.1 percent of all US adults had read literature (novels, short stories, or plays not required for work or school).

Other critics argue that surveys should consider all forms of reading; that younger children should also be represented; that young readers should be examined on both leisure and formal (school and homework) criteria; and that the diverse examples of contemporary youth behavior should be fully explored to gauge the extent of reading proficiency, such as the use of the Internet, computer games, varieties of books, magazines, newspapers and comic books. More people also pursue several activities simultaneously. Although the electronic media are a dominant influence in young people's worlds, they arguably read in the widest sense, whether it is a print or online novel, an e-book, a non-literary book, a technical manual, game instructions, a newspaper, magazines or school homework.

Exercises

Explain and examine the significance of the following terms:

NFL	NCAA	vaudeville
Hollywood	modern dance	tax breaks
baseball	ragtime	soccer
"pop art"	banjo	college football
aerobics	racquetball	bowling
softball	elitist	abstract expressionism
NEA	the musical	rounders
ESPN	country	studio system
paperbacks	Super Bowl	jogger
fads	sedentary	obese

Write short essays on the following questions.

1. To what extent are some sports and films uniquely American?

2. Discuss the role of advertising and television in American sports, arts and leisure.

3. Critically examine the opinion polls on the arts, sports and leisure. What do these indicate about the diversity of American society?

Further reading

Balio, T. (1990) *Hollywood in the Age of Television*, Cambridge, MA: Unwin Hyman.

Cullen, J. (2001) (ed.) *Popular Culture in American History*, Oxford: Blackwell.

Davies, R. O. (1994) *America's Obsession: Sport and Society Since 1945*, New York, NY: Harcourt Brace.

Gabler, N. (1988) *An Empire of Their Own: How the Jews Invented Hollywood*, New York, NY: Crown.

Gabler, N. (1998) *Life the Movie: How Entertainment Conquered Reality*, New York, NY: Vintage.

Higgs, R. (1995) *God in the Stadium: Sports and Religion in America*, Lexington, KY: University of Kentucky Press.

Hills, P. (2000) *Modern Art in the USA: Issues and Controversies of the 20th Century*, NJ: Prentice Hall.

Mandelbaum, M. (2005) *The Meaning of Sports,* New York, NY: PublicAffairs.

Morgan, W. (1994) *Leftist Theories of Sport: A Critique and Reconstruction*, Urbana: University of Illinois Press.

National Endowment for the Arts, (2012) *Arts Participation 2012: Highlights from a National Survey*, Washington, DC.

National Endowment for the Arts (2004) *Reading at Risk: A Survey of Literary Reading in America*, Washington, DC: Research Division Report no. 46.

National Endowment for the Arts (2007) *To Read or Not to Read,* Washington D.C.: Research Report no. 47.

National Endowment for the Arts (2008) *Reading on the Rise: A New Chapter in American Literacy*, Washington DC.

NEA Annual Arts Basic Survey (2016) (AABS) *Arts Data Profile.*

Petracca, M. and Sorapure, M. (1995) (eds.) *Reading and Writing about American Popular Culture*, Englewood Cliffs, NJ: Prentice Hall.

Schatz, T. (1981) *Hollywood Genres: Formulas, Filmmaking and the Studio System*, New York, NY: Random House.

Schlosser, E. (2002) *Fast Food Nation*, New York, NY: Perennial.

The World Almanac and Book of Facts (annual), New York, NY: World Almanac Books.

Websites

usinfo.state.gov/usa/infousa/arts/arts.htm
usinfo.state.gov/journals/itsv/0698/ijse/ijse0698.htm
The National Gallery of Art: www.nga.gov
The National Football League: www.nfl.com
The National Archives: www.nara.gov/education
The National Endowment for the Arts: www.arts.gov and arts.endow.gov
Library of Congress: www.loc.gov
Harvard Library: www.lib.harvard.edu
Sport and recreation: www.outdoorfoundation.org

Appendices

Declaration of Independence in Congress, July 4, 1776

The unanimous declaration of the thirteen United States of America

When, in the course of human events, it becomes necessary for one people to dissolve the political bonds which have connected them with another, and to assume, among the powers of the earth, the separate and equal station to which the laws of nature and of nature's God entitle them, a decent respect to the Opinions of mankind requires that they should declare the causes which impel them to the separation.

We hold these truths to be self-evident: That all men are created equal; that they are endowed by their Creator with certain unalienable rights; that among these are life, liberty and the pursuit of happiness; that, to secure these rights, governments are instituted among men, deriving their just powers from the consent of the governed; that whenever any form of government becomes destructive of these ends, it is the right of the people to alter or to abolish it, and to institute new government, laying its foundation on such principles, and organize its powers in such form, as to them shall seem most likely to effect their safety and happiness. Prudence, indeed, will dictate that government long established should not be changed for light and transient causes; and accordingly all experience hath shown that mankind are more disposed to suffer, while evils are sufferable, than to right themselves by abolishing the forms to which they are accustomed. But when a long train of abuses and usurpation, pursuing invariably the same object, evinces a design to reduce them under absolute despotism, it is their right, it is their duty, to throw off such government, and to provide new guards for their future security. Such has been the patient sufferage of these colonies; and such is now the necessity which constrains them to alter their former systems of government. The history of the present King of Great Britain is history of repeated injuries and usurpations, all having in direct object the establishment of an absolute tyranny over these states. To prove this, let facts be submitted to a candid world.

He has refused his assent to laws, the most wholesome and necessary for the public good.

He has forbidden his governors to pass laws of immediate and pressing importance, unless suspended in their operation till his assent should be obtained; and, when so suspended, he has utterly neglected to attend to them.

He has refused to pass other laws for the accommodation of large districts of people, unless those people would relinquish the right of representation in the legislature, a right inestimable to them, and formidable to tyrants only.

He has called together legislative bodies at places unusual, uncomfortable, and distant from the depository of their public records, for the sole purpose of fatiguing them into compliance with his measures.

He has dissolved representative houses repeatedly, for opposing, with manly firmness, his invasions on the rights of the people.

He has refused for a long time, after such dissolutions, to cause others to be elected; whereby the legislative powers, incapable of annihilation, have returned to the people at large for their exercise; the state remaining, in the meantime, exposed to all the dangers of invasions from without and convulsions within.

He has endeavoured to prevent the population of these states; for that purpose obstructing the laws for naturalization of foreigners; refusing to pass others to encourage their migration hither, and raising the conditions of new appropriations of lands.

He has obstructed the administration of justice, by refusing his assent to laws for establishing judiciary powers.

He has made judges dependent on his will alone, for the tenure of their offices, and the amount and payment of their salaries.

He has erected a multitude of new offices, and sent hither swarms of officers to harass our people and eat out their substance.

He has kept among us, in times of peace, standing armies without the consent of our legislatures.

He has affected to render the military independent of, and superior to, the civil power.

He has combined with others to subject us to a jurisdiction foreign to our constitution, and unacknowledged by our laws, giving his assent to their acts of pretended legislation:

For quartering large bodies of armed troops among us;

For protecting them, by a mock trial, from punishment for any murders which they should commit on the inhabitants of these states;

For cutting off our trade with all parts of the world;

For imposing taxes on us without our consent;

For depriving us, in many cases, of the benefits of trial by jury;

For transporting us beyond seas, to be tried for pretended offences;

For abolishing the free system of English laws in a neighbouring province, establishing therein an arbitrary government, and enlarging its boundaries, so as to render it at once an example and fit instrument for introducing the same absolute rule into these colonies;

For taking away our charters, abolishing our most valuable laws, and altering fundamentally the forms of our governments;

For suspending our legislatures, and declaring themselves invested with power to legislate for us in all cases whatsoever.

He has abdicated government here, by declaring us out of his protection and waging war against us.

He has plundered our seas, ravaged our coasts, burned our towns, and destroyed the lives of our people.

He is at this time transporting large armies of foreign mercenaries to complete the works of death, desolation, and tyranny already begun with the circumstances of cruelty and perfidy scarcely paralleled in the most barbarous ages, and totally unworthy the head of a civilized nation.

He has constrained our fellow-citizens, taken captive on the high seas, to bear arms against their country, to become the executioners of their friends and brethren, or to fall themselves by their hands.

He has excited domestic insurrection among us; and has endeavoured to bring on the inhabitants of our frontiers the merciless Indian savages, whose known rule of warfare is an undistinguished destruction of all ages, sexes, and conditions.

In every stage of these oppressions we have petitioned for redress in the most humble terms; our repeated petitions have been answered only by repeated injury. A prince, whose character is thus marked by every act which may define a tyrant, is unfit to be the ruler of a free people.

Nor have we been wanting in our attentions to our British brethren. We have warned them, from time to time, of attempts by their legislature to extend a unwarrantable jurisdiction over us. We have reminded them of the circumstances of our emigration and settlement here. We have appealed to their native justice and magnanimity; and we have conjured them, by the ties of our common kindred, to disavow these usurpations, which would inevitably interrupt our connections and correspondence. They, too, have been deaf to the voice of justice and of consanguinity. We must, therefore, acquiesce in the necessity which denounces our separation, and hold them, as we hold the rest of mankind, enemies in war, in peace friends.

We, therefore, the representatives of the United States of America, in General Congress assembled, appealing to the Supreme Judge of the world for the rectitude of our intentions, do, in the name and by the authority of the good people of these colonies, solemnly publish and declare, that these United Colonies are, and of right ought to be, FREE AND INDEPENDENT STATES; that they are absolved from all allegiance to the British Crown, and that all political connection between them and the state of Great Britain is, and ought to be, totally dissolved; and that, as free and independent states, they have full power to levy war, conclude peace, contract alliances, establish commerce, and do all other acts and things which independent states may of right do. And for the support of this declaration, with a firm reliance on the protection of Divine Providence, we mutually pledge to each other our lives, our fortunes, and our sacred honour.

John Hancock and fifty-five others

Constitution of the United States of America and amendments

(Passages no longer in effect are printed in italic type.) Brief identifications of the content of provisions are underlined in parentheses.

PREAMBLE (the people establish the constitution)

We, the people of the United States, in order to form a more perfect union, establish justice, insure domestic tranquillity, provide for the common defense, promote the general welfare, and secure the blessings of liberty to ourselves and our posterity, do ordain and establish this Constitution for the United States of America.

ARTICLE I (Congress, the legislative branch)

Section 1 All legislative powers herein granted shall be vested in a Congress of the United States, which shall consist of a Senate and a House of Representatives. *(Bicameralism)*

Section 2 The House of Representatives shall be composed of members chosen every second year by the people of the several States, and the electors in each State shall have the qualifications requisite for electors of the most numerous branch of the State Legislature. *(Qualifications for voters)*

No person shall be a Representative who shall not have attained to the age of twenty-five years, and been seven years a citizen of the United States, and who shall not, when elected, be an inhabitant of that State in which he shall be chosen. *(Qualifications for members)*

Representative and direct taxes shall be apportioned among the several States which may be included within this Union, according to their respective numbers, *which shall be determined by adding to the whole number of free persons, including those bound to service for a term of years and excluding Indians not taxed, three-fifths of all other persons.* The actual enumeration shall be within three years after the first meeting of the Congress of the United States, and within every subsequent term of ten years, in such manners as they shall by law direct. The number of Representatives shall not exceed one for every thirty thousand, but each State shall have at least one Representative; *and until such enumeration shall be made, the State of New Hampshire shall be entitled to choose three, Massachusetts eight, Rhode Island and Providence Plantations one, Connecticut five, New York six, New Jersey four, Pennsylvania eight, Delaware one, Maryland six, Virginia ten, North Carolina five, South Carolina five, and Georgia three. (Apportionment according to the census)*

When vacancies happen in the representation from any State, the Executive authority thereof shall issue writs of election to fill such vacancies.

The House of Representatives shall choose their Speaker and other officers; and shall have the sole power of impeachment. *(Impeachment)*

Section 3 The Senate of the United States shall be composed of two Senators from each State, *chosen by the legislature thereof,* for six years; each Senator shall have one vote.

Immediately after they shall be assembled in consequence of the first election, they shall be divided as equally as may be into three classes. The seats of the Senators of the first class shall be vacated at the expiration of the second year, of the second class at the expiration of the fourth year, and of the third class at the expiration of the sixth year, so that one-third may be chosen every second year; and if vacancies happen by resignation or otherwise, during the recess of the legislature of any State, the Executive thereof may make temporary appointments until the next meeting of the legislature, which shall then fill such vacancies. *(Staggered Senate elections)*

No person shall be a Senator who shall not have attained to the age thirty years, and been nine years a citizen of the United States, and who shall not, when elected, be an inhabitant of that State for which he shall be chosen. *(Qualifications)*

The Vice President of the United States shall be President of the Senate, but shall have no vote, unless they be equally divided.

The Senate shall choose their other officers, and also a President *pro tempore,* in the absence of the Vice President or when he shall exercise the office of President of the United States. *(President pro tempore)*

The Senate shall have the sole power to try all impeachments. When sitting for that purpose, they shall be on oath or affirmation. When the President of the United States is tried, the Chief Justice shall preside; and no person shall be convicted without the concurrence of two-thirds of the members present. *(Impeachment)*

Judgement in cases of impeachment shall not extend further than to removal from the office, and disqualification to hold and enjoy any office of honour, trust or profit under the United States; but the party convicted shall nevertheless be liable to indictment, trial, judgement and punishment, according to law. *(Judgement regulations in cases of impeachment)*

Section 4 The times, places and manner of holding elections for Senators and Representatives shall be prescribed in each State by the legislature thereof; but the Congress may at any time by law make or alter such regulations, except as to the places of choosing Senators. *(Rules for congressional elections)*

The Congress shall assemble at least once in every year, and such meeting shall be on the first Monday in December, unless they shall by law appoint a different day.

Section 5 Each house shall be the judge of the elections, returns and qualifications of its own members, and a majority of each shall constitute a quorum to do business; but a smaller number may adjourn from day to day, and may be authorized to compel attendance of absent members, in such manner, and under such penalties, as each house may provide. *(Qualifications)*

Each house may determine the rules of its proceedings, punish its members for disorderly behavior, and with the concurrence of two-thirds, expel a member. *(Expulsion)*

Each house shall keep a journal of its proceedings, and from time to time publish the same, excepting such parts as may in their judgement require secrecy; and the yeas and nays of the members of either house on any question shall, at the desire of one-fifth of those present, be entered on the journal. *(Required congressional record)*

Neither house, during the session of Congress, shall, without the consent of the other, adjourn for more than three days, nor to any other place than that in which the two houses shall be sitting. *(Adjournment regulations)*

Section 6 The Senators and Representatives shall receive a compensation for their services, to be ascertained by law and paid out of the treasury of the United States. They shall in all cases except treason, felony and breach of the peace, be privileged from arrest during their attendance at the session of their respective houses, and in going to and returning from the same; and for any speech or debate in either house, they shall not be questioned in any other place. *(Pay and immunity)*

No Senator or Representative shall, during the time for which he was elected, be appointed to any civil office under the authority of the United States, which shall have been created, or emoluments whereof shall have been increased, during such time; and no person holding any office under the United States shall be a member of either house during his continuance in office. *(Limitation related to civil officers)*

Section 7 All bills for raising revenue shall originate in the House of Representatives; but the Senate may propose or concur with amendments as on other bills. *(The right to tax)*

Every bill which shall have passed the House of Representatives and the Senate, shall, before it becomes a law, be presented to the President of the United States; if he approve he shall sign it, but if not he shall return it with objections to that house in which it originated, who shall enter the objections at large on their journal, and proceed to reconsider it. If after such reconsideration two-thirds of that house shall agree to pass the bill, it shall be sent, together with the objections, to the other house, by which it shall likewise be reconsidered, and, if approved by two-thirds of that house, it shall become a law. But in all such cases the vote of both houses shall be determined by yeas and nays, and the names of the persons voting for and against the bill shall be entered on the journal of each house respectively. If any bill shall not be returned by the President within ten days (Sundays excepted) after it shall have been presented to him, the same shall be a law, in like manner as if he had signed it, unless Congress by their adjournment prevent its return, in which case it shall not be a law. *(Procedure of bills, veto power of the President)*

Every order, resolution, or vote to which the concurrence of the Senate and House of Representatives may be necessary (except on a question of adjournment) shall be presented to the President of the United States; and before the same shall take effect, shall be approved by him, or being disapproved by him, shall be repassed by two-thirds of the Senate and House of Representatives, according to the rules and limitations prescribed in the case of a bill. *(Presidential approval)*

Section 8 (Enumerated [specified] powers of Congress)

The Congress shall have power

To lay and collect taxes, duties, imposts, and excises, to pay the debts and provide for the common defense and general welfare of the United States; but all duties, imposts and excises shall be uniform throughout the United States;

To borrow money on the credit of the United States;

To regulate commerce with foreign nations, and among the several States, and with the Indian tribes;

To establish an uniform rule of naturalization, and uniform laws on the subject of bankruptcies throughout the United States;

To coin money, regulate the value thereof, and of foreign coin, and fix the standard of weights and measures;

To provide for the punishment of counterfeiting the securities and current coin of the United States;

To establish post offices and post roads;

To promote the progress of science and useful arts by securing for limited times to authors and inventors the exclusive right to their respective writings and discoveries;

To constitute tribunals inferior to the Supreme Court;

To define and punish piracies and felonies committed on the high seas and offences against the law of nations;

To declare war, grant letters of marque and reprisal, and make rules concerning captures on land and water;

To raise and support armies, but no appropriation of money to that shall be for a longer term than two years;

To provide and maintain a navy;

To make rules for the government and regulation of the land and naval forces; To provide for calling forth the militia to execute the laws of the Union, suppress insurrections, and repel invasions;

To provide for organizing, arming, and disciplining the militia, and for governing such part of them as may be employed in the service of the United States, reserving to the States respectively the appointment of the officers, and the authority of training the militia according to the discipline prescribed by Congress;

To exercise exclusive legislation in all cases whatsoever, over such district (not exceeding ten miles square) as may, by cession of particular States, and the acceptance of Congress, become the seat of government of the United States, and to exercise like authority over all places purchased by the consent of the legislature of the State, in which the same shall be, for erection of forts, magazines, arsenals, dock-yards, and other needful buildings; and

To make all laws which shall be necessary and proper for carrying into execution the foregoing powers, and all other powers vested by this Constitution in the government of the United States, or in any department or officer thereof. *(The "necessary and proper" clause, implied powers of Congress)*

Section 9 The migration or importation of such persons as any of the States now existing shall think proper to admit shall not be prohibited by the Congress prior to the year 1808; but a tax or duty may be imposed on such importation, not exceeding 10 dollars for each person. (Slave import and limited powers)

The privilege of the writ of habeas corpus shall not be suspended, unless when in cases of rebellion or invasion the public safety may require it. *(Habeas corpus)*

No bill of attainder or *ex post facto* shall be passed.

No capitation, or other direct, tax shall be laid, unless in proportion to the census or enumeration herein before directed to be taken.

No tax or duty shall be laid on articles exported from any State.

No preference shall be given by any regulation of commerce or revenue to the ports of one State over those of another; nor shall vessels bound to, or from, one State, be obliged to enter, clear, or pay duties in another.

No money shall be drawn from the treasury, but in consequence of appropriations made by law; and a regular statement and account of the receipts and expenditures of all public money shall be published from time to time.

No title or nobility shall be granted by the United States; and no person holding any office of profit or trust under them, shall, without consent of the Congress, accept of any present, emolument, office, or title, of any kind whatever, from any king, prince, or foreign state.

Section 10 No State shall enter into any treaty, alliance, or confederation; grant letters of marque and reprisal; coin money; emit bills of credit; make anything but gold and silver coin a tender in payment of debts; pass any bill of attainder, *ex post facto* law, or law impairing the obligation of contracts, or grant any title of nobility. *(Restrictions on powers of the states)*

No State shall, without the consent of Congress, lay any imposts or duties on imports or exports, except what may be absolutely necessary for executing its inspection laws; and the net produce of all duties and imposts, laid by any State on imports and exports, shall be for the use of the treasury of the United States; and all such laws shall be subject to the revision and control of the Congress.

No State shall, without the consent of Congress, lay any duty of tonnage, keep troops or ships of war in time of peace, enter into any agreement or compact with another State, or with a foreign power, or engage in war, unless actually invaded, or in such imminent danger as will not admit of delay.

ARTICLE II (the president, the executive branch)

Section 1 The executive power shall be vested in a President of the United States. He shall hold his office during the term of four years, and, together with the Vice President, chosen for the same term, be elected as follows:

Each State shall appoint, in such manner as the legislature thereof may direct, a number of electors, equal to the whole number of Senators and Representatives to which the State may be entitled in the Congress; but no Senator or Representative, or person holding an office of trust or profit under the United States, shall be appointed an elector.

The electors shall meet in their respective States, and vote by ballot for two persons, of whom one at least shall not be an inhabitant of the same State with themselves. And they shall make a list of all the persons voted for, and of the number of votes for each; which list they shall sign and certify, and transmit sealed to the seat of government of the United States, directed to the President of the Senate. The President of the Senate shall, in the presence of the Senate and House of Representatives, open all the certificates, and the votes shall be counted. The person having the greatest number of votes shall be President, if such number be a majority of the whole number of electors appointed; and if there be more than one who have such majority, and have an equal number of votes, then the House of Representatives shall immediately choose by ballot one of them for President; and if no person have a majority, then from the five highest on the list said house shall in like manner choose the President. But in choosing the President the votes shall be taken by States, the representation from each State having one vote; a quorum for this purpose shall consist of member or members from two-thirds of the States, and a majority of all the States shall be necessary to a choice. In every case, after the choice of the President, the person having the greatest number of votes of the electors shall be the Vice President. But if there should remain two or more who have equal votes, the Senate shall choose from them by ballot the Vice President. *(Electors)*

The Congress may determine the time of choosing the electors and the day on which they shall give their votes; which day shall be the same throughout the United States.

No person except a natural-born citizen, *or a citizen of the United States at the time of the adoption of this Constitution,* shall be eligible to the office of President, neither shall any person be eligible to that office who shall not have attained to the age of thirty-five years, and been fourteen years a resident within the United States. *(Qualifications for President)*

In case of the removal of the President from office or of his death, resignation, or inability to discharge the powers and duties of the said office, the same shall devolve on the Vice President, and the Congress may by law provide for the case of removal, death, resignation, or inability, both of the President and Vice President, declaring what officer shall then act as President, and such officer shall act accordingly, until the disability be removed, or a President shall be elected. *(Presidential succession)*

The President shall, at stated times, receive for his services a compensation, which shall neither be increased nor diminished during the period for which he shall have been elected, and he shall not receive within that period any other emolument from the United States, or any of them. *(Presidential compensation)*

Before he enter on the execution of his office, he shall take the following oath or affirmation – 'I do solemnly swear (or affirm) that I will faithfully execute the office of the President for the United States, and will to the best of my ability preserve, protect and defend the Constitution of the United States.' *(Presidential oath of office)*

Section 2 The President shall be commander-in-chief of the army and navy of the United States, and of the militia of the several States, when called into the actual service of the United States; he may require the opinion, in writing, of the principal officer in each of the executive departments, upon any subject relating to the duties of their respective offices, and he shall have power to grant reprieves and pardons for offences against the United States, except in cases of impeachment. *(Powers of President)*

He shall have power, by and with the advice and consent of the Senate, to make treaties, provided two-thirds of the Senators present concur; and he shall nominate, and by and with the advice and consent of the Senate, shall appoint ambassadors, other public ministers and consuls, judges of the Supreme Court, and all other officers of the United States, whose appointments are not herein otherwise provided for, and which shall be established by law; but Congress may by law vest the appointment of such inferior officers, as they think proper, in the President alone, in the courts of law, or in the heads of departments.

The President shall have the power to fill up all vacancies that may happen during the recess of the Senate, by granting commissions which shall expire at the end of their next session.

Section 3 The President shall from time to time give to the Congress information of the state of the Union, and recommend to their consideration such measures as he shall judge necessary and expedient; he may, on extraordinary occasions, convene both houses, or either of them, and in case of disagreement between them, with respect to the time of adjournment, he may adjourn them to such time as he shall think proper; he shall receive ambassadors and other public ministers; he shall take care that the laws be faithfully executed, and shall commission all the officers of the United States. *(State of the Union message)*

Section 4 The President, the Vice President and the civil officers of the United States shall be removed from office on impeachment for, and or convictions of, treason, bribery, or other high crimes and misdemeanors. *(Impeachment)*

ARTICLE III (the supreme court, the judiciary branch)

Section 1 The judicial power of the United States shall be vested in one Supreme Court, and in such inferior courts as the Congress may from time to time ordain and establish. The judges, both of the Supreme and inferior courts, shall hold their offices during good behavior, and shall, at stated times, receive for their services a compensation which shall not be diminished during their continuance in office.

Section 2 The judicial power shall extend to all cases, in law and equity, arising under this Constitution, the laws of the United States, and treaties made, or which shall be made, under their authority; to all cases affecting ambassadors, other public ministers and consuls; to all cases of admiralty and maritime jurisdiction; to controversies to which the United States shall be a party; to controversies between two or more States; *between a State and citizen of another State*; between citizens of different States; between citizens of the same State claiming land under grants of different States, and between a State, or the citizens thereof, and foreign states, citizens or subjects. *(Jurisdiction)*

In all cases affecting ambassadors, other public ministers and consuls, and those in which a State shall be party, the Supreme Court shall have original jurisdiction. In all the other cases before mentioned, the Supreme Court shall have appellate jurisdiction, both as to law and fact, with such exceptions, and under such regulations, as the Congress shall make.

The trial of all crimes, except in cases of impeachment, shall be by jury; and such trial shall be held in the State where said crimes shall have been committed; but when not committed within any State, the trial shall be at such place or places as the Congress may by law have directed. *(Jury trial)*

Section 3 Treason against the United States shall consist only in levying war against them, or in adhering to their enemies, giving them aid and comfort. No person shall be convicted of treason unless on the testimony of two witnesses to the same overt act, or on confession in open court.

The Congress shall have power to declare the punishment of treason, but no attainder of treason shall work corruption of blood, or forfeiture except during the life of the person attainted.

ARTICLE IV (the states)

Section 1 Full faith and credit shall be given in each State to the public acts, records, and judicial proceedings of every other State. And the Congress may by general laws prescribe the manner in which such acts, records, and proceedings shall be proved, and the effect thereof.

Section 2 The citizens of each State shall be entitled to all privileges and immunities of citizens in the several States.

A person charged in any State with treason, felony, or other crime, who shall flee from justice, and be found in another State, shall on demand of the executive authority of the State from which he fled, be delivered up, to be removed to the State having jurisdiction of the crime. *(Privileges)*

No person held to serve or labor in one State, under the laws thereof, escaping into another, shall, in consequence of any law or regulation therein, be discharged from such service or labor, but shall be delivered up on claim of the party to whom such service or labor may be due. (Fugitive slaves)

Section 3 New States may be admitted by the Congress into this Union; but no new State shall be formed or erected within the jurisdiction of any other State; nor any State be formed by the junction of two or more States, or parts of States, without the consent of the legislatures of the States concerned as well as of the Congress. *(New states)*

The Congress shall have power to dispose of and make all needful rules and regulations respecting the territory or other property belonging to the United States; and nothing in this Constitution shall be so construed as to prejudice any claims of the United States, or of any particular State.

Section 4 The United States shall guarantee to every State in this Union a republican form of government, and shall protect each of them against invasion;

and on application of the legislature, or of the executive (when the legislature cannot be convened), against domestic violence. *(Promises to states)*

ARTICLE V (amendments)

The Congress, whenever two-thirds of both houses shall deem it necessary, shall propose amendments to this Constitution, or, on the application of the legislatures of two-thirds of the several States, shall call a convention for proposing amendments, which, in either case, shall be valid to all intents and purposes, as part of this Constitution, when ratified by the legislatures of three-fourths of the several States, or by conventions in three-fourths thereof, as the one or the other mode of ratification may be proposed by the Congress; provided *that no amendments which may be made prior to the year one thousand eight hundred and eight shall in any manner affect the first and fourth clauses in the ninth section of the first article*; and that no State, without its consent, shall be deprived of its equal suffrage in the Senate. *(Ratification)*

ARTICLE VI (effects of constitution)

All debts contracted and engagements entered into, before the adoption of this Constitution, shall be as valid against the United States under this Constitution, as under the Confederation.

This Constitution, and the laws of the United States which shall be made in pursuance thereof; and all treaties made, or which shall be made, under the authority of the United States, shall be the supreme law of the land; and the judges in every State shall be bound thereby, anything in the Constitution or laws of any State to the contrary notwithstanding. *(Supremacy clause)*

The Senators and Representatives before mentioned, and the members of the several State legislatures, and all executive and judicial officers, both of the United States and of the several States, shall be bound by oath or affirmation to support this Constitution; but no religious test shall ever be required as a qualification to any office or public trust under the United States. *(No religious test)*

ARTICLE VII (ratification)

The ratification of the conventions of nine States shall be sufficient for the establishment of this Constitution between the States so ratifying the same.

Done in Convention by the unanimous consent of the States present, the seventeenth day of September in the year of our Lord one thousand seven hundred and eighty-seven and of the Independence of the United States of America the twelfth. In witness whereof we have hereunto subscribed our names.

George Washington and thirty-seven others

The Bill of Rights (the first ten amendments)

Amendment I (1791) (basic freedoms; separation of church and state)

Congress shall make no law respecting an establishment of religion, or prohibiting the free exercise thereof; or abridging the freedom of speech, or of the press; or the right of the people peaceably to assemble, and to petition the government for a redress of grievances.

AMENDMENT II (1791) (the right to bear arms)

A well regulated militia being necessary to the security of a free State, the right of the people to keep and bear arms shall not be infringed.

AMENDMENT III (1791) (quartering of soldiers)

No soldier shall, in time of peace, be quartered in any house without the consent of the owner, nor in time of war, but in a manner to be prescribed by law.

AMENDMENT IV (1791) (search and seizure)

The right of the people to be secure in their persons, houses, papers, and effects, against unreasonable searches and seizures, shall not be violated, and no warrants shall issue but upon probable cause, supported by oath or affirmation, and particularly described, the place to be searched, and the persons or things to be seized.

AMENDMENT V (1791) (rights in court cases)

No person shall be held to answer for a capital, or otherwise infamous crime, unless on a presentment or indictment of a grand jury, except in cases arising in the land or naval forces, or in the militia, when in actual service in time of war or public danger; nor shall any person be subject for the same offence to be twice put in jeopardy of life or limb; nor shall be compelled in any criminal case to be a witness against himself, nor be deprived of life, liberty, or property, without due process of law; nor shall private property be taken for public use without just compensation.

Amendment VI (1791) (rights of the accused)

In all criminal prosecutions, the accused shall enjoy the right to a speedy and public trial, by an impartial jury of the State and district wherein the crime shall have been committed, which district shall have been previously ascertained by law, and to be informed of the nature and cause of the accusation; to be confronted with the witnesses against him; to have compulsory process for obtaining witnesses in his favor, and to have the assistance of counsel for his defense.

Amendment VII (1791) (the right to a trial by jury)

In suits at common law, where the value in controversy shall exceed twenty dollars, the right of trial by jury shall be preserved, and no fact tried by a jury shall be otherwise re-examined in any court of the United States, than according to the rules of the common law.

Amendment VIII (1791) (bail; cruel and unusual punishment)

Excessive bail shall not be required, nor excessive fines imposed, nor cruel and unusual punishment inflicted.

Amendment IX (1791) (rights retained by the people)

The enumeration in the Constitution, of certain rights, shall not be construed to deny or disparage others retained by the people.

Amendment X (1791) (reserved powers)

The powers not delegated to the United States by the Constitution, nor prohibited by it to the States, are reserved to the States respectively, or to the people.

Later amendments

Amendment XI (1798) (lawsuits against states)

The judicial power of the United States shall not be construed to extend to any suit in law or equity, commenced or prosecuted against one of the United States by a citizen of another State, or by citizens or subjects of any foreign state.

Amendment XII (1804) (electoral votes)

The electors shall meet in their respective States, and vote by ballot for President and Vice-President, one of whom, at least, shall not be an inhabitant of the same State with themselves; they shall name in their ballots the person voted for as President, and in distinct ballots the person voted for as Vice President, and they shall make distinct lists of all persons voted for as President, and of all persons voted for as Vice President, and of the number of votes for each, which lists they shall sign and certify, and transmit sealed to the seat of government of the United States, directed to the President of the Senate.

The President of the Senate shall, in the presence of the Senate and House of Representatives, open all the certificates and the votes shall then be counted.

The person having the greatest number of votes for President shall be the President if such number be a majority of the whole number of electors appointed, and if no person have a majority, then from the persons having the highest numbers not exceeding three on the list of those voted for as President, the House of Representatives shall choose immediately, by ballot, the President. But in choosing the President, the votes shall be taken by States, the representation from each State having one vote; a quorum for this purpose shall consist of a member or members from two-thirds of the States, and a majority of all the States shall be necessary to a choice. And if the House of Representatives shall not choose a President whenever the right of choice shall devolve upon them, before *the fourth day of March* next following, then the Vice President shall act as President, as in the case of death or other constitutional disability of the President.

The person having the greatest number of votes as Vice President shall be the Vice President, if such number be a majority of the whole number of electors appointed; and if no person have a majority, then from the two highest numbers on the list the Senate shall choose the Vice President; a quorum for the purpose shall consist of two-thirds of the whole number of Senators, and a majority of the whole number shall be necessary to a choice. But no person constitutionally ineligible to the office of President shall be eligible to that of Vice President of the United States.

Amendment XIII (1865) (abolition of slavery)

Section 1 Neither slavery nor involuntary servitude, except as a punishment for crime whereof the party shall have been duly convicted, shall exist within the United States, or any place subject to their jurisdiction.

Section 2 Congress shall have the power to enforce this article by appropriate legislation.

Amendment XIV (1868) (citizenship for former slaves; due process and equal protection clauses)

Section 1 All persons born or naturalized in the United States, and subject to the jurisdiction thereof, are citizens of the United States and of the State wherein they reside. No State shall make or enforce any law which shall abridge the privileges or immunities of citizens of the United States; nor shall any State deprive any person of life, liberty, or property, without due process of law; nor deny to any person within its jurisdiction the equal protection of the laws.

Section 2 Representatives shall be appointed among the several States according to their respective numbers, counting the whole number of persons in each State, excluding Indians not taxed. But when the right to vote at any election for the choice of Electors for President and Vice President of the United States, Representatives in Congress, the executive and judicial officers of a State, or the members of the legislature thereof, is denied to any of the male inhabitants of such State, being twenty-one years of age and citizens of the United States, or in any way abridged, except for participation in rebellion, or other crime, the basis of representation therein shall be reduced in the proportion which the number of such male citizens shall bear to the whole number of male citizens twenty-one years of age in such State. *(Apportionment)*

Section 3 No person shall be a Senator or Representative in Congress, or Elector of President and Vice President, or hold any office, civil or military, under the United States, or under any State, who, having previously taken an oath, as a member of Congress, or as an officer of the United States, or as a member of any State legislature, or as an executive or judicial officer of any State, to support the Constitution of the United States, shall have engaged in insurrection or rebellion against the same, or given aid or comfort to the enemies thereof. Congress may, by a vote of two-thirds of each house, remove such disability.

Section 4 The validity of the public debt of the United States, authorized by law, including debts incurred for payment of pensions and bounties for services in suppressing insurrection or rebellion, shall not be questioned. But neither the United States nor any State shall assume or pay any debt or obligation incurred in aid of insurrection or rebellion against the United States, or any claim for the loss of emancipation of any slave; but all such debts, obligations, and claims shall be held illegal and void.

Section 5 The Congress shall have power to enforce, by appropriate legislature, the provisions of this article.

Amendment XV (1870) (voting rights for freed male slaves)

Section 1 The right of citizens of the United States to vote shall not be denied or abridged by the United States or by any State on account of race, color, or previous condition of servitude.

Section 2 The Congress shall have power to enforce this article by appropriate legislature.

Amendment XVI (1913) (federal income tax)

The Congress shall have power to lay and collect taxes on incomes, from whatever source derived, without apportionment among the several States, and without regard to any census or enumeration.

Amendment XVII (1913) (the direct election of Senators)

Section 1 The Senate of the United States shall be composed of two Senators from each State, elected by the people thereof, for six years; and each Senator shall have one vote. The electors in each State shall have the qualifications requisite for electors of (voters for) the most numerous branch of the State legislatures.

Section 2 When vacancies happen in the representation of any State in the Senate, the executive authority of such State shall issue writs of election to fill such vacancies: Provided, that the legislature of any State may empower the executive thereof to make temporary appointments until the people fill vacancies by election as the legislature may direct.

Section 3 This amendment shall not be so construed as to affect the election or term of any Senator chosen before it becomes valid as part of the Constitution.

Amendment XVIII (prohibition, 1919, repealed 1933)

Section 1 After one year from the ratification of this article the manufacture, sale, or transportation of intoxicating liquors within, the importation thereof into, or the exportation thereof from the United States, and all territory subject to the jurisdiction thereof, for beverage purposes, is hereby prohibited.

Section 2 The Congress and the several States shall have concurrent power to enforce this article by appropriate legislation.

Section 3 This article shall be inoperative unless it shall have been ratified as an amendment to the Constitution by the legislatures of the several States, as provided by the Constitution, within seven years from the date of the submission thereof to the States by the Congress.

Amendment XIX (1920) (voting rights for women)

Section 1 The right of citizens of the United States to vote shall not be denied or abridged by the United States or by any State on account of sex.

Section 2 The Congress shall have the power to enforce this article by appropriate legislation.

Amendment XX (1933) (the president's term of office)

Section 1 The terms of the President and the Vice President shall end at noon on the 20th day of January, and the terms of Senators and Representatives at noon on the 3rd day of January, of the year in which such terms would have ended if this article had not been ratified; and the terms of their successors shall then begin.
(The start of sessions of Congress)

Section 2 The Congress shall assemble at least once in every year, and such meeting shall begin at noon on the 3rd day of January, unless they shall by law appoint a different day.
(Presidential succession)

Section 3 If, at the time fixed for the beginning of the term of the President, the President-elect shall have died, the Vice President-elect shall become President. If a President shall not have been chosen before the time fixed for the beginning of his term, or if the President-elect shall have failed to qualify, then the Vice President-elect shall act as President until a President shall have qualified; and the Congress may by law provide for the case wherein neither a President-elect nor a Vice President-elect shall have qualified, declaring who shall then act as President, or the manner in which one who is to act shall be selected, and such persons shall act accordingly until a President or Vice President shall have qualified.

Section 4 The Congress may by law provide for the case of the death of any of the persons from whom the House of Representatives may choose a President whenever the right of choice shall have devolved upon them, and for the case of the death of any of the persons from whom the Senate may choose a Vice President whenever the right of choice shall have devolved upon them.

Section 5 Sections 1 and 2 shall take effect on the 15th day of October following the ratification of this article.

Section 6 This article shall be inoperative unless it shall have been ratified as an amendment to the Constitution by the legislatures of three-quarters of the several States within seven years from the date of its submission.

Amendment XXI (1933) (repeal of prohibition)

Section 1 The eighteenth article of amendment to the Constitution of the United States is hereby repealed.

Section 2 The transportation or importation into any State, Territory, or Possession of the United States for delivery or use therein of intoxicating liquors, in violation of the laws thereof, is hereby prohibited.

Section 3 This article shall be inoperative unless it shall have been ratified as an amendment to the Constitution by conventions in the several States, as provided in the Constitution, within seven years from the date of submission thereof to the States by the Congress.

Amendment XXII (1951) (term limits for the president, 2 terms or 10 years)

Section 1 No person shall be elected to the office of President more than twice, and no person who has held the office of President, or acted as President, for more than two years of a term to which some other person was elected President shall be elected to the office of President more than once. But this article shall not apply to any person holding the office of President when this article was proposed by the Congress, and shall not prevent any person who may be holding the office of President, or acting as President, during the term within which this article becomes operative from holding the office of President or acting as President during the remainder of such term.

Section 2 This article shall be inoperative unless it shall have been ratified as an amendment to the Constitution by the legislatures of three-quarters of the several States within seven years from the date of its submission to the States by the Congress.

Amendment XXIII (1961) (Electoral College votes for the District of Columbia)

Section 1 The District constituting the seat of Government of the United States shall appoint in such manner as the Congress may direct:

A number of electors of President and Vice President equal to the whole number of Senators and Representatives in Congress to which the District would be entitled if it were a State, but in no event more than the least populous State; they shall be in addition to those appointed by the States, but they shall be considered for the purposes of the election of President and Vice President, to be electors appointed by a State; and they shall meet in the District and perform such duties as provided by the twelfth article of amendment.

Section 2 The Congress shall have the power to enforce this article by appropriate legislation.

Amendment XXIV (1964) (prohibition of poll taxes)

Section 1 The right of citizens of the United States to vote in any primary or other election for President or Vice President, for electors for President or Vice President, or for Senator or Representative in Congress, shall not be denied or abridged by the United States or any State by reason of failure to pay any poll tax or other tax.

Section 2 The Congress shall have the power to enforce this article by appropriate legislation.

Amendment XXV (1967) (presidential succession)

Section 1 In the case of the removal of the President from office or of his death or resignation, the Vice President shall become President.

Section 2 Whenever there is a vacancy in the office of the Vice President, the President shall nominate a Vice President who shall take office upon confirmation by a majority vote of both Houses of Congress.

Section 3 Whenever the President transmits to the President *pro tempore* of the Senate and the Speaker of the House of Representatives his written declaration that he is unable to discharge the powers and duties of this office, and until he transmits to them a written declaration to the contrary, such powers and duties shall be discharged by the Vice President as Acting President.

Section 4 Whenever the Vice President and a majority of either the principal officers of the executive departments or of such other body as Congress may by law provide, transmit to the President *pro tempore* of the Senate and the Speaker of the House of Representatives their written declaration that the President is unable to discharge the powers and duties of his office, the Vice President shall immediately assume the powers and duties of the office as Acting President.

Thereafter, when the President transmits to the President *pro tempore* of the Senate and the Speaker of the House of Representatives his written declaration that no inability exists, he shall resume the powers and duties of his office unless the Vice President and a majority of either the principal officers of the executive department(s) or of such other body as Congress may by law provide, transmit within four days to the President *pro tempore* of the Senate and the Speaker of the House of Representatives their written declaration that the President is unable to discharge the powers and duties of his office. Thereupon Congress shall decide the issue, assembling within forty-eight hours for that purpose if not in session. If the Congress, within twenty-one days after receipt of the latter written declaration, or, if Congress is not in session, within twenty-one days after Congress is required to assemble, determines by two-thirds vote of both Houses that the President is unable to discharge the powers and duties of his office, the Vice President shall continue to discharge the same as Acting President; otherwise, the President shall resume the powers and duties of his office.

Amendment XXVI (1971) (voting rights for young people)

Section 1 The right of citizens of the United States, who are eighteen years of age or older, to vote shall not be denied or abridged by the United States or by any State on account of age.

Section 2 The Congress shall have the power to enforce this article by appropriate legislation.

Amendment XXVII (1992) (timing of congressional pay raises)

No law varying the compensation for the service of Senators and Representatives shall take effect until an election of Representatives shall have intervened.

Index